Luigi Einaudi

Luigi Einaudi

Selected Economic Essays

Edited by

Luca Einaudi

Riccardo Faucci

and

Roberto Marchionatti

on behalf of the
Ente per gli Studi Monetari, Bancari e Finanziari Luigi Einaudi

palgrave
macmillan

First published 2006 by
PALGRAVE MACMILLAN
Houndmills, Basingstoke, Hampshire RG21 6XS and
175 Fifth Avenue, New York, N.Y. 10010
Companies and representatives throughout the world

PALGRAVE MACMILLAN is the global academic imprint of the Palgrave Macmillan division of St. Martin's Press, LLC and of Palgrave Macmillan Ltd. Macmillan® is a registered trademark in the United States, United Kingdom and other countries. Palgrave is a registered trademark in the European Union and other countries.

ISBN 13: 978–1–4039–4777–2
ISBN 10: 1–4039–4777–5

This book is printed on paper suitable for recycling and made from fully managed and sustained forest sources.

A catalogue record for this book is available from the British Library.

Library of Congress Cataloging-in-Publication Data
Einaudi, Luigi, 1874–1961.
[Selections. English]
Luigi Einaudi : selected economic essays / edited by Luca Einaudi, Riccardo Faucci and Roberto Marchionatti.
p. cm.
Includes bibliographical references and index.
ISBN 1–4039–4777–5
1. Economics. I. Einaudi, Luca. II. Faucci, Riccardo. III. Marchionatti, Roberto, 1950– IV. Title.
HB177.E43 2005
330–dc22 2005050864

10 9 8 7 6 5 4 3 2 1
15 14 13 12 11 10 09 08 07 06

Printed and bound in Great Britain by
Antony Rowe Ltd, Chippenham and Eastbourne

Contents

Acknowledgements

We wish to thank the Einaudi family for permission to reproduce Luigi Einaudi's writings and in particular Roberto Einaudi, who provided enthusiastic support at every stage and revised the translations. The *Ente per gli Studi Monetari, Bancari e Finanziari Luigi Einaudi* in Rome organized and coordinated the whole project. We are most grateful to Ignazio Musu (President), Pierluigi Ciocca and Antonio Pedone (members of the Board of Directors) and Marcello De Cecco (Chairman of the Scientific Committee). Our special thanks go to the Director of the *Ente Einaudi*, Flora Pierelli, for her unstinting assistance. We also wish to thank Giorgio Brosio, Francesco Forte, Massimo L. Salvadori and Terenzio Cozzi (Chairman of the Scientific Committee of the Fondazione Einaudi in Turin) for their helpful comments and suggestions. The team led by John Smith had the difficult task of translating Luigi Einaudi's colourful and complex idiom into English and succeeded brilliantly. The *Bank of Italy* has provided support for the publication of the volume, while the *Fondazione Luigi Einaudi* of Turin met part of the costs and made its collection of Einaudi's writings available for the choice of the texts. Lastly, we thank the *Bank of Italy* for permission to reproduce the English translation of the annual report for 1946.

June 2005
Rome, Italy

LUCA EINAUDI
RICCARDO FAUCCI
ROBERTO MARCHIONATTI

Editors' Introduction

Luca Einaudi, Riccardo Faucci and Roberto Marchionatti[1]

There are several reasons for publishing a selection of Luigi Einaudi's works in English. The first is the contemporary relevance of many of his ideas, from European federalism to fiscal policy. The second is the very limited availability of Einaudi's writings in languages other than Italian, which prevents his contribution to economics and economic history from being fully appreciated in the English-speaking world.

Luigi Einaudi, economist and political figure

Luigi Einaudi (1874–1961) was a leading liberal Italian economist, economic historian and political figure.[2] Professor at the University of Turin, where he taught public finance, he developed several concepts typical of the Italian tradition, among which the taxation of consumption rather than income features prominently. For a few years he also taught at the Bocconi University in Milan. Several generations of economists and politicians followed his lectures and had him as their thesis supervisor regardless of their ideological views, from Sraffa to Gramsci, Gobetti, Rosselli and Togliatti.[3] He edited *La Riforma Sociale*, an important academic journal, and through it conducted a continuous battle against monopolies, protectionism and the abuse of government power, especially by the liberal governments of Giovanni Giolitti.[4] *La Riforma Sociale* was closed by the Fascist regime in 1935. To avoid censorship, Einaudi decided to study the history of economic facts and policies; he founded the *Rivista di Storia Economica* the following year.

Einaudi also played a national role and reached wider audiences as an economic columnist for leading Italian newspapers, first *La Stampa* and then *Il Corriere della Sera*, interrupting his contributions only during fascism and during his time as President of the Republic. He also served more discreetly for *The Economist* from 1908 to 1946.[5] His academic research was always linked to the analysis of practical economic issues; it was often related to the national and international political and economic problems of his time, but always drew on his copious knowledge of the past. He was a member of the Italian Senate from 1919 onwards, remaining one of the isolated liberal anti-Fascist figures throughout the Mussolini regime. Together with Benedetto Croce he greatly influenced the development of Italian liberalism through a long-lasting debate on the content of political liberalism and free market economic liberalism. After the Second World War, he combined the intellectual effort of rethinking the basis of democratic institutions with active participation in the drafting of the Republican Constitution and the running of the country, serving as Governor of the Bank of Italy (1945–8) and Deputy Prime Minister and Minister of the Budget (1947–8). In that capacity he developed and implemented the *Einaudi Plan*, which was intended to stabilize the lira and halt inflation, creating the conditions for stable growth and political support for the centrist governments of the time. Luigi Einaudi became President of the Italian Republic (1948–55) in time to see the beginning of the economic boom.

At the end of the nineteenth century, when a prosperous future for the Italian economy was hard to foresee, Einaudi picked up the first signals of the economic take-off in the rise of a new entrepreneurial class and the emergence of a pugnacious, but collaborative working class. These market-oriented forces were supported by a wise monetary policy that combined growth with stability. After the First World War, Einaudi acknowledged that the golden age of laissez-faire, free trade and stable international money was over. He objected to the new features of the economy, such as increasing State interference, a managed currency and awkward international economic relations. His faith in the excellence of laissez-faire capitalism did not translate into a pure individualist credo, however. Between the State and the individual there was a network of intermediate economic entities, principally based on voluntary action, whose function he praised highly. Although he identified economic liberalism with political liberalism, his vision of the 'good society' was by no means restricted to an efficient market economy. Self-government, town planning, a genuinely free press, full competition between State and private education through the abolition of the legal effects of academic diplomas, and, last but not least, a political European federation (as he was rather sceptical about a merely economic one) are the building blocks of his legacy.

Luigi Einaudi was a prolific writer in all fields. He left dozens of books and his bibliography includes more than 3,800 titles, including 1,700 economic articles for the *Corriere della Sera* alone. Einaudi's crisp and colourful style made him a classic and greatly contributed to the popularity of his writings in Italy. His style is also extremely difficult to reproduce faithfully in English, especially in view of his frequent references to examples of material conditions of life and work that are very distant from those of today. The saving habits of a Piedmontese peasant are not something we can relate to very easily.

The choice of texts to publish was far from easy, given the encyclopaedic nature of Einaudi's interests and the sheer volume of his writings. The aim that guided the editors' choice was to present his main fields of interest (money, public finance, the role of government in the economy and European economic integration) and to select the most original and representative results of his research. The more political works, which testify so effectively to his continuous commitment to a democratic society of active citizens will be published in a separate volume. In order to introduce the reader to Einaudi's practical approach to the economic problems of government, his famous article 'Know before Legislating'[6] has been placed at the beginning of this collection.

Political and economic liberalism

The book is divided into four sections. The first is on political and economic liberalism and explores the link between the rules of the market and social and political rules. Luigi Einaudi's dynamic view of the free struggle between social forces was based on his anti-monopolistic and anti-*étatiste* approach in which conflict, together with competition, shape the best economic outcome. Such views had a strong moral and civic component in addition to the mere evaluation of their positive economic effects. An anti-socialist and anti-communist polemic was associated with an equally strong opposition to fascist and corporatist positions. Einaudi continuously challenged the 'hole-drillers' of the State budget, who prospered by calling for subsidies, asking for protection against the market and building monopolies. His decidedly free market stance was always tempered by a refusal to oppose or support any intervention of the State without looking at the specifics of the case:

> In the face of concrete problems, the economist can never be an absolute free market liberal or an interventionist or socialist at any cost. From time to time he opposes protective customs duties ... he supports laws limiting work by women and children ... he is against universal socialization ... but he wants the State to consider the railways a public industry.[7]

Not only must the State intervene to protect free competition, but it must also regulate economic activity, limit inequality through taxation and public spending and provide public goods.[8] Inequality could be reduced by making the maintenance of existing fortunes depend on the ability of the various generations of heirs to conserve and increase their capital despite substantial inheritance taxes. Einaudi also supported equality at the start of every individual's life. Opportunities, but not outcomes, had to be equitable, both in legal terms (non-discrimination) and in economic terms (grants for students and appropriate forms of social insurance). Einaudi did not want a society of equals, which he believed would be a dead society, but a society of free men and women.

A democratic system had to be engineered that would combine the rule of the majority with respect for the rights of minorities, as a fundamental component of a liberal democracy. Substantial limits to the will of the majority were needed to prevent the dictatorship of the majority and the oppression of economic, political, religious or ethnic minorities. Such limits on political majorities were the respect due by the current generation to the experience of previous generations, instructed by the mistakes preceding and accompanying the fascist period.

One of Einaudi's most effective descriptions of the working of a market economy is his 'Lectures on the Market'[9] (see Chapter 2 in this book), written in 1944 as an introductory course in economics for Italian political refugees in Swiss camps awaiting their return to a democratic Italy. The market described by Einaudi is frequently that of rural Piedmont in the early twentieth century, but it is in fact an ideal, used to give colour and life, flesh and blood, to a timeless theoretical model of the market economy. If the market is to succeed in its role of bringing about changes in the quantities produced according to the movements in prices, it has to be defended against distortions introduced by monopolies. Laws and institutions serve not only to prevent monopolistic power and unfair practices but also to temper inequalities (not eliminate them), in order to offer every individual the opportunity to fulfil his potential and advance his condition according to his talent and work.

'The Beauty of the Struggle'[10] (see Chapter 3 in this book), written at the request of Piero Gobetti,[11] is a description, at times almost lyrical, of the pleasure brought by results achieved through hard work and by the composition of labour conflicts after harsh but free confrontations. The article must be understood not just in terms of the Schumpeterian view of unstable and ever-changing market equilibria but also in the context of the political and social conflicts in Italy in the 1920s. After a period of socialist and catholic interference with the free market, the early stages of the fascist regime were marked by an opposite but somehow similar distortion of free economic mechanisms. First, in 1919–20, the so-called 'Two Red Years', in some parts of the country socialist trade unions had imposed levels of employment or wages, while northern factories had repeatedly been occupied and temporarily managed by workers' councils, guided by the myth of the Russian revolution. Agrarian and industrial interests turned to the newborn fascist bands of blackshirts in 1920 to undermine the communist and socialist unions, associations and local governments, by violent means. Having destroyed the organization of the left and of the catholics, and having captured national government in 1922, fascism imposed a corporatist policy through fascist unions. Theoretically this was done in order to overcome differences between employers and workers in the name of the superior interest of the nation, but in fact it served the special interests which financed and supported the rise of fascism. Einaudi was appalled by both these economic and political models: he felt

> an irreducible scepticism, almost physical repugnance, with regard to benefits provided from the outside, to the well-being that it is intended to procure for workers through laws, regulations, collectivism, paternalism, the intermediation of ill-employed politicians ready to settle disputes by arbitration, by the intervention of specialists, by cutting the loaf in half; and a heartfelt approval of the efforts of those who desire to elevate themselves on their own and in this struggle, fight, falter, and rise again, learning at their own expense how to win and to better themselves.

Einaudi's ideas on economic equilibrium depended entirely on the way it had been reached and not on the level arrived at: a truly stable equilibrium could be achieved only through free and open struggle and protracted discussions between economic agents, never through the intervention of a government, a judge or an arbitrator. Even if the intervention of the latter happened to impose an optimal solution to a labour conflict or to establish an optimal price, it would be suspected by the other parties.

> People must be left to bruise their heads if they are to realize they are up against a wall and that it is useless to try to butt it down. Through struggle and debate one learns how to measure the adversary's strength, to understand his reasons, to fathom the working of the system that allows both rivals to exist.

For such an equilibrium to last, it must be continuously open to new challenges and to change through confrontation between the employer, proud of the enterprise he has built, and the worker who feels the satisfaction of a job well done.

Einaudi rejected the partial view of laissez-faire liberalism held by Keynes. He showed that the classics and their followers had developed a more sophisticated view of the role of the State in a liberal society than the motto 'laissez-faire' suggested. It was the Marquis D'Argenson, Jeremy Bentham and some propagandists of the Manchester School who popularized the concept, but Adam Smith and the classics never questioned the need for a measure of State intervention in the economy. Even if the number of cases in which the State should intervene according to economic theory appeared to have increased since the *Wealth of Nations*, Einaudi doubted whether the economic role of the State had actually increased in importance. He reminded the reader of all those intermediate bodies dear to Montesquieu, such as semi-autonomous authorities, local boards and charitable institutions, which are so easily forgotten but which had represented an important form of public action before the industrial era. Today, it would probably be difficult to hold such a view, but in 1925 few of the institutions and forms of State intervention known today existed. The Great Depression and corporatist forms of government in the 1930s, wartime planning and the post-war construction of the welfare state radically changed and increased the part played by the State in the economy.

Despite his misgivings about laissez-faire as a scientific principle, Einaudi believed that it could none the less be employed pragmatically. In a discerning manner it was still possible to use it as an excellent practical rule of conduct when dealing with cases outside the limited agenda of State intervention.

A further aspect of Einaudi's views is to be found in his decades-long controversy with Benedetto Croce on the respective roles and meanings of the political and ethical aspect of liberalism and the free market economic component, known as economic liberalism.[12] Einaudi's liberalism was of the British type, related to the theories of Adam Smith and the practice of Gladstone rather than to the progressive American liberals of the twentieth century, the followers of Franklin Delano Roosevelt. Benedetto Croce[13] argued that political liberalism (*liberalismo*) was a more general concept than free market economic liberalism (*liberismo*) and that the former could flourish even without the latter. One of Einaudi's many responses was the article 'Economic Liberalism and Political Liberalism'[14] (see Chapter 4 in this book). Einaudi accepted that political liberalism had a wider meaning and role than free market economic liberalism,[15] but denied that the former could survive the absence of freedom of initiative and enterprise. He recognized that the laissez-faire principle did not always correspond to collective interests and was not a rational or moral rule, but insisted that freedom of thought could not be separated from the possibility to develop personal abilities through private property and the constant search for improved means of existence. The means of liberty cannot be separated from its idea. Even if a communist society happened to be more productive economically than a free market, an eventuality Einaudi firmly rejected, it would still have been impossible to reconcile it with a free political structure. In practice, although the concepts were separate, political liberalism could not exist without economic liberalism. The opposite was possible, and Einaudi cited the example of the French economy under Napoleon III, certainly oriented towards free trade and the free market, but ruled by an authoritarian government.

The dilemma concerning the possibility of a democracy without a market economy or of a market economy without a liberal democracy can be discussed in contemporary terms with reference to China. How long can a free market economy continue to develop without the liberalization of society and the political system, even when emerging from a communist system denying freedom of speech and association?

Money and banking

Luigi Einaudi's monetary and banking writings span a period of more than fifty years. They are scattered in newspapers, magazines (*The Economist*), economic journals (mainly *La Riforma Sociale*), official documents of the Bank of Italy and the proceedings of the Constituent Assembly in 1946–7. These writings analyse the most important national and international events and in large part represent a critical study of a dramatic phase in the history of the capitalistic economy, scarred by the crisis and depression between the two world wars.

Einaudi's theoretical background is that of the orthodox neoclassical economics of his time, when the doctrines of the great marginalist economists – Walras, Menger, Marshall, Pareto and Fisher – were modified, developed and enriched by the contributions of economists such as Pigou, Robertson, Hawtrey, Robbins, Mises, Hayek, Viner and Marget. Einaudi does not make any original theoretical contributions. However, his thorough analysis of facts is of great help in understanding complex economic events and in extrapolating proposals for economic policy. In his writings he can be seen as representative of the historical and factual work done in Italy, which, as Schumpeter wrote,[16] really fertilized the field of economics and did not conflict with theory.

The 'equation of exchange' is the key to Einaudi's monetary thought. He explains what an 'equation of exchange' is and defends it against its critics in several articles written in the 1930s.[17] He distinguishes the 'equation of exchange' from the 'quantity theory of money'. This is an important distinction, which the writers of that period often did not make. Einaudi maintains that the 'equation of exchange' is not a self-evident truth, or a truism. On the contrary, it is the result of the theoretical and empirical work of generations of economists who have made the meaning of the letters that represent the variables of the equation richer and more meaningful, such as the quantity of money in circulation (M), the velocity of circulation (V), the price level (P) and the physical volume of trade (T). In this story, according to Einaudi, David Hume made a fundamental breakthrough in the eighteenth century when he suggested the different variables were interdependent. From that time on, the equation of exchange has signified not only that prices vary as a function of the quantity of money, its velocity of circulation and the quantity of goods and services produced and exchanged, but also that the variation of each variable is a function of the contemporaneous variation of the other variables and their consequent reactions. Einaudi properly defines the equation of exchange as a 'clothes-hook' on which theoretical developments can be hung. The most complex relationships can be summarized and organized in this equation, he emphasizes. He thinks that the formulas employed in the exposition of the equation are merely devices to enable us to bring together the principal causes which determine the value of money in an orderly way. His approach was a common one in the Marshall–Pigou tradition, to which Einaudi substantially belongs, at least as regards monetary thought.

Whereas the equation of exchange simply states that the quantity of money is one of the factors influencing prices, the quantity theory of money is a doctrine that contains one or more propositions on the importance of the quantity of money as a factor causing price variations. When the quantity theoreticians seek to quantify the influence of the quantity of money on prices, they tend to consider the velocity of circulation and the quantity of goods and services as constants. From a theoretical point of view, Einaudi is sceptical of the general cogency of this relationship. He holds it more correct to consider all the factors as variables because there are no logical reasons for considering some variables as constant in any practical situation. Einaudi's methodological proposal is this: economists should conduct systematic studies of the forces acting on the relevant variables from the analytical and empirical-historical points of view so that they can come up with the real values of these variables in the different situations. If this is not done, he judges that such research is largely a meaningless exercise. At most, he adds, the quantity theory of money can be used to explain certain great historical instances of price increases and decreases: for example, the 1550–1650, 1898–1906 and 1914–20 price increases, and the 1815–30, 1873–98 and 1920–32 price decreases. In all these cases Einaudi thought that it might be temporarily useful to consider all other factors constant in order to focus on one influential event, such as the inflow of precious metals, the abundance of paper currency or the exhaustion of gold mines. Einaudi considered the years in which he lived a period in which the quantity theory of money appeared to be 'true', at least as a first approximation – the reason why he is often considered a quantity theory economist.

According to Einaudi, the main objective of monetary policy is price stability, which ensures that variations in the value of the circulating medium cannot disturb existing contracts and expectations.[18] When Einaudi was educated as an economist at the beginning of the twentieth century, the international gold standard operated smoothly to facilitate trade, payments and capital movements. Balances of payments were kept in equilibrium at fixed exchange rates by a highly automatic adjustment mechanism. Annual inflation and deflation rates were low and preserved the value of money over the long run. This state of affairs strongly influenced Einaudi's conception of an international monetary system. He considered a monetary rule such as the gold standard, which caused the money supply to vary automatically with the balance of payments, to be the best one to ensure a sound monetary system.

With inconvertible paper, on the other hand, price instability becomes a crucial problem, as historical experience showed. Einaudi faced the traumatic experience of the years 1914–20, when European society was shattered by a very high rate of inflation. On the basis of the lessons learned in that dramatic period, Einaudi came to the conclusion that inflation was an intolerable evil, a point he kept on making throughout his life. When he analyses the inflationary process and its effects on Italy during the First World War, he connects monetary devaluation to the increase in the note issue: 'The political and social scenario was dominated by the paper-money printing press', i.e., by an excessive money supply. It was 'the main fact' in the Italian social, political and economic history of those years. Einaudi speaks of the 'poison introduced into Italian society by the monetary devaluation ... a moral poison that consumed society'. In fact, inflation caused the social discontent and unrest that paved the way for dictatorship in the 1920s.[19] After the Second World War, first as Governor of the Bank of Italy and then as Minister of the Budget, Einaudi confronted and defeated the inflation that threatened to repeat the damage caused after the First World War.

In the Governor's 'Concluding Remarks' (see Chapter 11 in this book) in the Bank of Italy's Annual Report for 1946,[20] Einaudi summarizes the inflationary mechanism in a way that resembles other classical analyses of the phenomenon, such as Part I of Keynes's *Tract on Monetary Reform*. Einaudi first notes that inflation modifies the distribution of income and wealth. It initially helps profits but hurts workers, whose incomes adjust with a lag. It also permanently affects the creditors of fixed monetary amounts. The positive effects of the redistributive change on investments – a consequence of inflation reducing taxation, improving business's financial situations and profit receivers having a relatively higher propensity to save – gradually fade away as the negative effects prevail. Individuals' propensity to hold money increases and the propensity to save decreases. The crucial problem is that inflation destroys the propensity to save as time passes: 'Why save if the product of saving vanishes as far as purchasing power is concerned?'. At the same time, inflation causes currency depreciation, which produces negative effects in the balance of payments (as shown in a masterful analysis by Einaudi's colleague and friend, Attilio Cabiati[21]). If this contagious disease is not blocked, it leads to a flight from money. 'This is the beginning of the end', Einaudi emphasizes. A vicious circle is created: the decreasing purchasing power of money makes it necessary to issue new notes in order to prevent the public finances from collapsing; in turn, this reduces the purchasing power of money in an endless spiral.

The essential point to emphasize in Einaudi's analysis is the negative effect that inflation has on the propensity to save. In fact, Einaudi conceives saving classically as the pre-condition for investment and the key factor in economic development. Although he does not ignore the difference between saving and investment, he certainly underestimates it.

According to him, to the extent that inflation discourages saving, it compromises a country's long-term growth. Einaudi stresses that 'saving is a function of the confidence in the monetary unit', and as a consequence, the objective of monetary policy must be monetary stability in order to maintain a country's propensity to save. He considers monetary stability and free trade to be the conditions for steady growth. When they are lacking, the economic mechanism inevitably seizes up and comes to a standstill.

According to Einaudi, the inflation of credit during and immediately after the First World War was the cause of the subsequent crisis. The inflation-crisis link is at the core of his controversy with Keynes and Fisher on the nature of the crisis and the possible positive role of reflation in the 1930s.

In *The Means to Prosperity* (1933) Keynes maintained that the crisis and the widespread poverty in the world at the beginning of the 1930s were not due to famine or earthquake or war, or a lack of material things and the resources to produce them, but to reasons of another kind.[22] Crisis and poverty came 'from some failure in the immaterial devices of the mind, in the working of the motives which should lead to the decisions and acts of will, necessary to put in movement the resources and technical means we already have' (Keynes 1971 [1933], p.335).

According to Keynes the way out could not be found by 'hard work, endurance, frugality, improved business methods, more cautious banking and, above all, the avoidance of devices' (1971 [1933] p.336). Rather, only an active economic policy could be a remedy for the crisis. This meant public works and an internationally coordinated plan to supply central banks with more reserves of international money to increase loan-expenditure. This policy would cause world prices to increase. This would be a positive factor because prices, Keynes claimed, would have to be raised in order to prevent the structure of contracts and instruments of indebtedness from breaking down. Keynes's pamphlet caused an international debate. Some economists – including the Swedish economist Gustav Cassel – agreed with Keynes; others, who were the majority at the time, disagreed or expressed doubts.

Einaudi objected to Keynes's analysis in a long article entitled 'My Plan is not Keynes's'[23] (see Chapter 10 in this book). He addressed two questions: the causes of the crisis and how to overcome it. With regard to the causes, Einaudi argued that the crisis was not due 'to a failure in the immaterial devices of the mind', as Keynes suggested. On the contrary, it was due to the effects of the war and 'the diseases it implanted into the minds of men', particularly the post-war inflation of credit, as Einaudi had already written in 1931 in two earlier essays on the crisis.[24] He believed that the crisis of those years was not a novelty: writing in 1932, he stated that 'the present crisis is not a new fact, strange and paradoxical'.[25] His view is based on his analysis of periods of prosperity and depression in the history of the capitalistic economy.

In particular, Einaudi believed that the period 1914–19 and the 1920s had something in common with the post-Napoleonic crisis: in both cases the ultimate cause of the crisis was monetary. This, according to Einaudi, helped to explain the length of the latter crisis. The key factor was the cost–price disequilibrium: 'The crisis and the lack of profits stem from the imbalances in prices, from the fact that some prices did not fall or were not left to fall; and since prices are revenues for some and costs for others, many lose and especially entrepreneurs.'

The crisis could therefore be overcome by re-establishing equilibrium between costs and prices. He believed that this could be achieved if the stocks of unsold goods were rapidly liquidated and the costs of the factors of production pushed down. This would happen sooner if the rate of interest were kept high, an opinion at that time strongly held by the economists of the Austrian School, with whom Einaudi and his group in Turin were then largely in agreement.[26] In this interpretation the major obstacle to the resolution of the crisis was the existence of rigidities: that is, prices fixed by law (taxes) or under long-term contracts (interest on public and private debts) or under rigid conventions among social groups (wages and salaries).

As for overcoming the crisis, Einaudi agrees with Keynes on the importance of a policy of public works because he recognizes such a policy to be 'advantageous' in the trough of the economic cycle. In this he conforms to classical theory, but neglects Keynes's theoretical innovation of the income multiplier. However, Einaudi's dissent is expressed most clearly when he holds that Keynes's case for reflation is wrong. Keynes had written that 'in all likelihood' in the process a rise in prices would be followed by a rise in profits. Einaudi believed that this was not necessarily so. A rise in prices due to public works carried out through the inflation of credit, Einaudi wrote, would leave the imbalance between costs and revenues unchanged. Moreover, he argued that the sentence 'the rise in prices recreates profits' was true only 'on the assumption that the public works carried out using credit push up precisely those prices that must rise to restore equilibrium'. In general, however, Einaudi noted that when there was a cost–price disequilibrium, it did not serve to create new liquidity. Einaudi considered Keynes's proposal to raise prices artificially a hazardous method and stressed his deep disagreement and mistrust of the managed currency policy. As already emphasized in his *Riflessioni in disordine sulla crisi* (*Scattered reflections on the crisis*), Einaudi maintained that post-war monetary instability, particularly inflation, was the cause of social disorder and insisted that 'to repeat the experiment [with paper money] today could imply the collapse of Western civilization'. Of course, Einaudi recognized that reflationists – 'inflationists', as he preferred to call them – claimed that reflation would be prudent, but he warned that 'the monetary device is like trying one's luck at Monte Carlo': it might work but it might also revive the disorders of 1919–20.

Einaudi completed his criticism in several papers published late in 1933,[27] where he criticized the reflationist thesis that a rise in prices would induce savers to invest their hoarded money. Einaudi asked why people hoarded and answered that the reason was simply that savers, in *that* period, considered gold or paper money or non-interest-bearing bank deposits to be the best possible *investment*. Such behaviour was rational at times of falling prices, because the value of money rose if prices fell. Of course, if prices rise, savers may be induced to change their behaviour, but this device must not induce deposit holders to transform money into goods for fear of a monetary devaluation. As Einaudi warned, 'frightened people make mistakes, they do not overcome crises'. Einaudi stressed that in this case the choice of savers between money saving and saving in the form of real goods turned into a choice between saving and consumption, which was ultimately chosen because saving was becoming more and more disadvantageous. Certainly, Einaudi recognized, when the percentage of investment in money exceeded the level considered 'normal', alarm and anxiety would follow. In this case public works could 'break the spell'[28] and also be a psychological device to help the recovery.

The American economist, Irving Fisher, suggested reflation as a solution to the crisis in a famous article published in *Econometrica* in 1933. Fisher's proposal was based on his debt–deflation theory. If prices decline, he argues, the real value of *private* wealth increases. This implies that the liabilities of debtors and the assets of creditors increase in real terms. Debtors have a higher marginal propensity to consume than creditors. Consequently, there is a reallocation of real wealth from debtors to creditors and thus the aggregate marginal propensity to consume declines. The result of price flexibility in situations of unemployment is again a decline in consumption demand and thus a further reduction in aggregate demand and employment. Liquidation causes the price level to collapse progressively and this, Fisher believes, can shake the foundations of the economic edifice. Hence he deduces the need for reflation from his analysis.

In 'Debts'[29] (see Chapter 9 in this book), Einaudi agrees with Fisher that the essence of the crisis lies in the existence of debts. In his reconstruction of Fisher's analysis, Einaudi emphasizes the sequence of events preceding the deflation effect. First there are new opportunities for profitable investment that give rise to investment; then businessmen's over-indebtedness forces them to liquidate, and this causes a fall in prices; then the relative reduction of businessmen's assets due to the fall in prices and the consequent increase in the burden of debt aggravates the crisis. Einaudi recognizes that Fisher's factual analysis is correct, but he considers Fisher's remedy unacceptable. This judgement is based on an analysis of the nature of the crisis. The word 'crisis', Einaudi argues, 'must not only conjure up the idea of doing badly', but also means movement, 'passage from one equilibrium to another'. In this sense Einaudi can maintain that the economic world has always been in crisis: 'crisis is the eternal law of a world inhabited by men, that is beings ready to invent, to be fired with enthusiasm and to imitate'. Crises lead to ruin only when 'the majority of entrepreneurs unwisely contract too many debts'. Moreover, factual analysis, Einaudi emphasizes, must distinguish between two types of crisis. On the one hand, we have 'crisis as a change in the economic mechanism triggered by changes of taste and by inventions that can satisfy new tastes or better satisfy old ones', i.e., crisis as the generator of *creative movement* – a concept that recalls Schumpeter's 'creative destruction'. On the other hand, we have 'crisis as an impediment or brake on the movement that ought to occur', hence crisis as the generator of a *destructive movement*.

According to Einaudi, the debt factor can be a condition of the first type of crisis: that is, as a condition of movement and progress. However, if too many individuals contract debts during the crisis, then this brings on the second type of crisis: that caused by 'men's mania, their imitative spirit and voracious appetite for swift gains'. This is what happened during the war and in the years that immediately followed. In this situation reflation cannot be the correct remedy. In fact, Einaudi emphasizes that the dross of the preceding cycle is not eliminated with reflation. On the contrary, the equilibrium of the past period is perpetuated, retarding adjustment. For Einaudi this is 'worse than crisis': 'The longer the period of tranquillity, the less intense the elimination of mistakes, the more frightening the collapse that ... will necessarily come.'

In 'Debts' Einaudi emphasizes the role of the central bank in preventing and solving crises. The bank of issue is responsible for preventing a salutary crisis from turning into a disaster. It should therefore intervene in the traditional and classic way taught by experience. It should discount all the good paper immediately, in order to enable commercial and saving banks to meet any demand for repayment. It should not rediscount bad paper under any circumstances. The real remedy for the crisis, Einaudi continues, lies in withholding credit or increasing its cost for imprudent people before mistakes can become dangerous. In other words, the task is to apply the brakes of the world economic machine with good timing. 'This is the art of the wise, farseeing central banker', Einaudi maintained. To do this, a central bank governor must be independent from political power: non-economic forces must not deter him from doing his duty.

In the same way, the central banker has to translate the postulate of stable currency into reality. In the late 1920s and the post-Second World War period, the stabilization of currencies was a top economic priority in Europe. Einaudi believed a fixed exchange rate regime, currency convertibility and the free movement of capital to be crucial steps in the adjustment process. In the 1920s Einaudi was deeply convinced of the need to return to gold and thoroughly analysed the Italian experience of monetary reform in the period 1927–31. In two interesting articles[30] he reaffirms the importance of the stability of monetary relations and, above all, emphasizes the need for a central banker to be firm and uncompromising. The central banker 'has to look coolly at the development of a necessary crisis, which has to drive the country to the fixed aim: an established exchange rate'. The central banker must have 'strong nerves' and must not authorize bailouts, lest they slow down the process of crisis liquidation and induce businessmen to expect future help.

In this respect, Italian experience was negative, as Einaudi pointed out in many articles from the late 1890s onwards. However, there was the commendable behaviour of Bonaldo Stringher, Governor of the Bank of Italy, during the period of stabilization.

According to Einaudi, conduct such as Stringher's served to ensure sound money and a balanced budget. First, it allowed a virtuous economic mechanism to be re-established, one based on the two pillars of Einaudi's economic vision: work and saving. Second, it allowed the banking system to do its proper task: to direct savings towards profitable uses.

Einaudi wrote many articles on the banking system, including 'On other Pseudo-commercial and Pseudo-bank Containers', 'Banks with Adjectives' and 'Are there too many Banks in Italy?' (see Chapters 6, 7 and 8 in this book).[31] According to Einaudi, the rules of behaviour of a good private banker can be reduced to just two: that 'the banker has only one duty, to his depositors, and the banker takes money from everyone, even the bad, but he gives it only to the good' and that 'The really essential point is not to make mistakes ... The mistake of mistakes in banking, the worst and biggest mistake of all, is to impose a rigid rule on oneself, or to seek to regulate bankers' conduct rigidly'. The organizational rules follow from this, according to Einaudi. Functional specialization or geographical specialization, bigness or smallness, etc., are empty formulas in themselves. Above all, bankers require independence in order to do their duty. Starting in 1924, when he commented on the possible creation of a 'fascist bank' in 'Banks with Adjectives', Einaudi severely and wisely kept on warning that:

> Banking is a very difficult art, and the addition of whatever adjective to the name perhaps serves only to increase difficulties that are already exceptional in themselves ... In countries where politics and banking are less developed, even banks without adjectives may have to pay a tribute to politics ... A bank with an adjective must face another risk. The manager has to fight not only against men who are not able and not upright, but also against those who, being neither able nor upright, ask him for money on the strength of that adjective ... It is the duty of the manager of a bank with an adjective to repudiate the adjective.

'The Theory of Imaginary Money from Charlemagne to the French Revolution'[32] (see Chapter 12 in this book) is one of Einaudi's monetary essays best known outside Italy, partly because of an early translation into English. Luigi Einaudi identified what he called 'imaginary money' in pre-

Revolutionary France as a stable abstract unit of account capable of translating the differences between a multitude of real metallic currencies which circulated together, regardless of their tendency to be debased (and occasionally revalued after monetary reforms). The imaginary unit of account never existed as a real coin. Its function was that of a standard of value, an anchor of stability in a world of fluctuating values of the medium of exchange. In a different way imaginary money can be understood as a simple technical device which serves to establish the parity between gold coins and silver coins in bimetallic systems with an adjustable gold to silver ratio. Imaginary money is simply a tool to adjust the ratio through a *numéraire*, a bit like the European Currency Unit (ECU) between 1979 and 1999, whose value was based on a basket of real currencies. This solved the conundrum faced after the French Revolution by bimetallic countries which adopted the French Franc Germinal after 1803 with the 15.5:1 gold to silver ratio fixed and not adjustable. This had been the great obstacle to the orderly operation of the Latin Monetary Union (1865–1927) between France and its Italian, Swiss and Belgian neighbours, and it ultimately led to the adoption of gold monometallism instead. The abolition of all forms of imaginary money, in the name of a simple, homogeneous and rational monetary system, as embodied in France by the Franc Germinal of 1803–1927, paradoxically had created other problems, in the form of the bimetallic–monometallic quarrel and the excessive rigidity in real exchange rates and real prices. The interest of Einaudi's contribution on imaginary money was twofold: first, it clarified the obscurity surrounding such mechanisms and the confusion felt by modern readers faced with the complexity of pre-Revolutionary European monetary operations; second, it explained why the old system, despite its complexity, had real merits and could inspire new and different ideas for solving contemporary monetary problems. For instance, Einaudi's theory has recently been used to show how international basket currencies can be constructed.

In conclusion, money and banking was an important focus of his research, given that he was active in the years of the classical gold standard – seeing its collapse with the First World War – active in the Great Depression, in a new war and in another period of monetary and economic stabilization, in which he was a front-line practitioner. While attached to the classical quantitative theory of money, Luigi Einaudi paid a great deal of attention to the banking system and to central banking. He stressed the importance of the independence of the banking system from the political system, at a time when political expediency was moving in the opposite direction. The duty of the good banker is to maintain good management, responsibility towards shareholders and customers, away from ideologies and political influences. In 'Noise'[33] (see Chapter 13 in this book) Einaudi argues that central bankers must use discreet moral suasion rather than changes in the discount rate, to avoid the clamour which inflates financial crises.

Luigi Einaudi's contributions to the theory of public finance

Einaudi was a major representative of the so-called Italian tradition (rather than school) of public finance.[34] This tradition includes Francesco Ferrara, Maffeo Pantaleoni, Antonio de Viti de Marco, Enrico Barone and Vilfredo Pareto, and their followers: Gino Borgatta, Benvenuto Griziotti, Guido Sensini, Mauro Fasiani, and others. These scholars did much to elevate the '*scienza delle finanze*', transforming it from a descriptive branch of economic and fiscal policy, as it was before 1880, to an important sector of economic and even political theory. Many of these authors corresponded with leading British and American scholars and wrote in the main scientific journals, but the Keynesian inter-war revolution obscured their thought – ideologically linked to classical liberalism – and many of them still await a revaluation.

In his early works Einaudi did not express an unambiguous vocation towards public finance. He dealt with topics such as the British agrarian crisis, the trend of prices of agricultural products in Italy, the emigration of Italian 'human capital' to Argentina, and the rent of mines. Apart from the latter, all these writings addressed contemporary policy issues. Only one of these works concerned fiscal policy,[35] more specifically local taxation, which at that time (about 1902) was a very fashionable topic in Italy because several towns had socialist administrations engaged in fiscal reforms. The young Einaudi, then a left-wing Liberal with Fabian sympathies, advocated taxation of the unearned increments of urban land, not only for the sake of fiscal justice, but for economic reasons as well. Such a tax would force landowners to build houses, turning themselves from speculators into entrepreneurs. These ideas involved some considerations on the elasticity of demand for houses, which led Einaudi to reject the argument that, since the demand was inelastic,[36] the tax was shifted from owners to tenants.

The core of the essay consisted in the definition of the 'effects of tax'. Einaudi did not limit his research to the shifting and incidence of taxation, but also considered various kinds of markets for taxed goods (free competition and monopoly), carefully analysed from a Marshallian perspective, and he considered the divergence between the objective effects and the subjective motives which prompted policymakers to assess the tax.[37]

Only in his subsequent works did Einaudi acknowledge that the study of the effects of taxes on economic equilibrium needed a Walrasian general equilibrium approach, but he confessed that his poor mathematical training prevented him from performing such a task as well as he wished.[38]

In parallel with theoretical and applied fiscal studies, Einaudi produced historical studies in public finance. In 1907–8 he published two large volumes on the budget receipts of the Piedmontese monarchy during the Spanish War of Succession at the beginning of the eighteenth century and on Piedmontese finance during the same period. Thanks to very thorough archival research (carried out with the help of his wife, Ida), Einaudi was able to show that, despite the conservation of *ancien régime* institutions, Piedmont had successfully managed its budget to meet war needs. The relationship between theoretical schemes, history and the institutional framework was from that time onwards a constant feature of his research.

His framework was mainly a free competitive economy, with the State operating as a private agent. In 1911, in his *Lezioni di scienza delle finanze,* he started from a strictly theoretical issue: that of a pure theory of 'natural' taxation, considering a State in which the delegates of the citizens had to substitute the latter in their choice of public goods. This was a branch of public economics opened by Pantaleoni's work on the allocation of public expenditure,[39] and based on the assumption that public finance should be approached using the analytical tools familiar in the study of the working of the private sector.

Finally, in 1912, Einaudi issued his major study on the taxation of consumed income. The theoretical framework was provided by John Stuart Mill and Irving Fisher. The former (1848) had argued that taxing of saved income would result in double taxation if the new income produced by invested savings was taxed as well. The latter (1906) had maintained that only the income destined to final consumption is true income, while all income which is not actually consumed is 'capital' and ought not to be subject to income tax.

Both Mill and Fisher were concerned about the negative effects of progressive taxation, since it could discourage capital accumulation. Sharing the same concern, Einaudi conceded that only proportional taxation means 'equality' or equity (intuitively, but in a questionable way, defined as that principle according to which, if 'one lira is taxed with a 10 cent tax, every other lira, belonging to whatsoever income equal, higher or lower ... must be taxed with the same 10 cent tax'[40]). The theoretical implication is that the marginal utility of income is constant.

Although there were obvious difficulties in coordinating Mill's classical (objectivist) theory of double taxation and Fisher's neoclassical (psychological) definition of income, Einaudi was particularly brilliant in demonstrating that all existing fiscal systems exempted earned savings from taxation and mainly (or exclusively) hit income used for final consumption. They all respected the 'equality postulate', thanks to exemptions, deductions and other forms of qualitative discrimination. In this demonstration Einaudi's mastery of fiscal law was of great help.

The implication of his theory was that taxation should not be based on the *source* of revenue but on its final *use,* for consumption or for saving. Of course, Einaudi acknowledged that it was very difficult to ascertain how taxpayers actually allocated their incomes. But in most cases, he observed, we can fairly presume that some earned income will be allocated to consumption and therefore will be taxed, while some will be allocated to saving. For instance, households allocate a part of their income to the necessities of life, or to maintain the purchasing power of their capital unchanged. This kind of spending was not authentically 'consumption', but 'presumed saving', which improved the capacity to work and produce and therefore had to be exempted. The income of labour deserved such fiscal treatment.

This article gave rise to a lively debate. From the point of view of practical finance policy, Einaudi was accused of excessively narrowing the basis for taxation, well below the needs of a modern State (in fact, he advocated taxes on conspicuous consumption, including horses and luxury carriages). From a more theoretical perspective, Pigou (himself a follower of the double taxation of savings doctrine) observed that the 'postulate of equality' should have been more rigorously settled. Umberto Ricci and Benvenuto Griziotti objected that the returns on the saved–invested income should be considered as 'new' income and therefore that there was no ground for a tax exemption.[41]

Consumption tax was only one element in Einaudi's complete theory of taxation. He laid another cornerstone of it in an article on tax amortization.[42] As is well known, amortization takes place when capital value is diminished by a tax on its income returns. The traditional doctrine states that if a tax is general (i.e., if it is uniformly spread over all branches of production) then there cannot be amortization, because the rate of interest will also be uniformly lowered. In fact, if the tax is general, an income of 45 (after a 10 per cent tax) at the interest rate of 4.50 per cent will give a capital of 1,000, exactly as will an income of 50 at the interest rate of 5 per cent before the tax. On the contrary, if the tax is special (i.e., if it is imposed on some branches of production only, and not on the others), the rate of interest will not be lowered and amortization will reduce the capital value. In his comments on E. R. A. Seligman – the American economist whose *Shifting and Incidence of Taxation* (1898) was very well known in Italy, thanks to its translation in the *Biblioteca dell'economista* – Einaudi settled the problem in a new way. A general and uniform tax is one that does not alter the general equilibrium of the economy; in particular, it is one that does not modify taxpayers' consumption or investment habits or alter the trade-off between the different ways of employing the factors of production.[43] But the requisite of generality, uniformity and neutrality (used by Einaudi as synonyms) cannot depend only on the objective effects of taxation on prices and incomes. Generality is the requisite of 'a tax that weighs with equal force on incomes having equal value in the time span considered, such as to leave the *judgement* of every man unchanged with respect to every unit of income'.[44] The 'postulate of equality' is thus redefined in subjective terms.

Nevertheless, in his search for a 'neutral' tax Einaudi preferred to develop a historical–empirical approach. He therefore focused on the taxation of land, based on the cadastre, which was distinguished by being assessed not on realized incomes but on 'normal' or 'ordinary' incomes. He concluded that both the 1750 Lombardy cadastre and the 1886 Italian Kingdom cadastre were the best approximations to his 'ideal' scheme. In Einaudi's vision, a tax on land seemed to be the best model for a reform of personal taxes, since its goal was 'normal' income, based on clear-cut, objective 'economic categories': rent, profit and wages arising from its exploitation, independently of the condition of the taxpayers.[45] Einaudi's preference, therefore, was for a system of real proportional taxes even for mobile incomes.[46] He undoubtedly gave priority to efficiency over equality. In fact, entrepreneurs who gained more than the normal income were exempted from the excess part, while those who gained less were nevertheless taxed (and eventually discouraged from continuing their job). The fiscal system could therefore contribute to the formation of the economic ruling class (elite) of the country.

In order to formulate a definite verdict of 'neutrality', it is necessary for taxpayers to have some information about the effects of the public expenditure financed by the tax. It is therefore important to assess the impact of taxation on general welfare.[47] Indeed, there are some kinds of taxes whose effects are entirely negative, insofar as they either fail to give anything to taxpayers in terms of welfare (which Einaudi called 'hail-tax') or, still worse, end up financing welfare-reducing expenditure (which he called 'ransom-tax').[48] Only a tax which covers productive expenditure can properly be considered as 'economical'.

The rest of the 1919 essay was a eulogy on the benefits that State expenditure brought by promoting positive externalities (education, the environment and town planning, improved leisure, and so on). In fact, public expenditure contributes decisively to raising normal incomes and therefore to enlarging the basis for taxation. In separate essays Einaudi showed that in the past there had been authors who shared both a view of productive expenditure and the idea of the taxation of final consumption.[49]

Einaudi was proud to defend such a positive view of the functions of the State. It could be imagined as relating to his early sympathies for Fabian socialism, but in fact it derived mainly from his classical Liberal beliefs. In a 1930 controversy with the fascist ideologue, Ugo Spirito, who accused the 'Liberal' economists of having neglected the role of the State, Einaudi objected that all the great economists of the past, beginning with Adam Smith, were convinced supporters of '*buongoverno*' (good government) and, therefore, of an active presence of the State in the economy.[50] Of course, he had in mind the Liberal State, not fascist corporatism, which in a subsequent essay he called 'a monster', since it pretended to interpret the interests of the whole community while 'neglecting those of the living men that compose that community'.[51]

In his view of the Liberal-democratic State Einaudi was very close to Antonio de Viti de Marco, an economist who had to resign his university professorship in order to avoid a pledge of loyalty to fascism. In another long essay,[52] Einaudi began by quoting the statement made by Antonio de Viti, that 'every part of income reaches its recipient as if it were already loaded by its tax debt'.[53] This premise descended from de Viti's theory of the State as a productive factor, and was common to both authors. As regards the definition of income, however, Einaudi took a different position from de Viti. While de Viti considered income that was actually produced to be taxable, Einaudi stressed that a tax on produced income was not a 'neutral tax', since it could not resolve the complex problems due to the different duration of productive processes and neglected the dynamics of production, considering every moment as separate from the following ones. By contrast, a neutral tax would not discourage entrepreneurs engaged in production requiring a longer time, and therefore would not cause any distortion in the employment of factors. At the end of this essay Einaudi admitted that the difference between taxing produced or consumed income was not so great, provided that the tax was levied approximately at the time of consumption.[54]

After disputing the notion of produced income, Einaudi moved on to dispute that of earned income. In his 1938 book *Miti e paradossi della giustizia tributaria*[55] he exercised his wit as a pamphleteer to ridicule those he called 'tax avengers' for searching everywhere for surplus incomes to tax. The taxation of surpluses was in fact advocated by the school of Benvenuto Griziotti, a former socialist economist who Einaudi accused of being a doctrinaire since he did not consider the vagueness of the concept of earned income. If we studied the source of the surpluses, Einaudi argued, we would see that some were the result of human labour and not, strictly speaking, surpluses, while others would be found to have a non-monetary value, and the rest would be the result of State interference in the economy and would cease to exist when this interference ceased. The conclusion was that the very concept of earned income was useless.

Symmetrical to his demolition of traditional concepts of taxable income was the effort to cancel the notion of State coercion in taxation. This is a fundamental feature of Einaudi's most mature thought. For the majority of the representatives of the *scienza delle finanze*, beginning with Pantaleoni, State coercion was necessary to cover the cost of public goods. The concept of coercion was enriched by Amilcare Puviani in his theory of fiscal illusion: taxpayers fail to perceive the real need for public services and the modern State substitutes subtle deception[56] for traditional force. All these concepts looked (and really were) inspired by Machiavelli: in every historical age the lions/foxes of the ruling classes made bad use of their power by extorting the maximum amount of wealth from the community of taxpayers. Democracy, aristocracy and monarchy – or, if we prefer, democracy and dictatorship – did not differ greatly in this sense. Einaudi reacted sharply to this pessimistic presentation. According to him, in the history of humanity there had been moments marked by cooperation between rulers and ruled. For example, in classical Athens taxes for public works and public performances (*leithourgiai*) were paid voluntarily. In *Miti e paradossi* the name of Pericles recurs more frequently than that of de Viti de Marco.

The conclusion reached by Einaudi in his almost forty years of reflection on income and taxation may seem at first sight utopian. Yet, consumption has revealed itself to be an increasingly important item of taxation, though in a different macroeconomic context.[57] Moreover, his idea of cooperation between the State and taxpayers for a transparent control of public expenditure and fiscal decentralization is very modern. Thanks to a sort of repetition of historical phenomena – or historical nemeses! – ideas that seemed old-fashioned when Einaudi formulated them, have been revived in our day.

European economic integration

Einaudi was a very early proponent of European monetary and economic unification. His proposals anticipated all the developments of the following 60 years. European federalist ideas had developed in the nineteenth century, gaining some popularity in certain key historical phases, as in 1848 and the late 1860s, but they had reached a low point during the age of imperialism preceding the First World War. In 1918 Einaudi, under the pseudonym of Junius, launched attacks in the *Corriere della Sera* against the 'dogma of national sovereignty' and the 'myth of absolute independence and economic autarchy'. Not only had they fuelled the most destructive and absurd of all wars but such dogmas and myths were undermining the possibility of a lasting peaceful settlement. The League of Nations, still in the making, was already doomed because it only provided for a permanent alliance to defend a peaceful international order among fully sovereign states, but the latter ultimately maintained all the means to undertake new wars. Einaudi called for a much stronger federalist link because 'only free nations will be able to limit each other mutually, as components of a superior State organization, to guarantee each other true security against attempts at hegemony to which in the current international anarchy the strongest state is inevitably attracted by the deadly dogma of absolute sovereignty'.[58]

The long period of fascist dictatorship in Italy was not a time when such thoughts could be freely developed and expressed, but the Second World War only reinforced Einaudi's belief in the urgency of a federalist solution to European war. Federalist ideas had been developed further during the 1920s, thanks also to the Pan-European Movement of Coudenhove-Kalergi,[59] and culminated at the political level in the proposal made to the League of Nations in 1929–30 by the French Prime Minister, Aristide Briand. This sought to establish 'some kind of federal bond' between European states.[60] Despite further development of federalist ideas in the United Kingdom in the 1930s by Lionel Robbins, Lord Lothian and others,[61] the storm of the Great Depression, the fall of Briand and his German partner, Chancellor Gustav Stresemann, had pushed federalist proposals to the background again, and they only survived in the mocking Hitlerian version of the New European Order. As soon as the fascist censorship ended with the collapse of Mussolini's regime on 25 July 1943, Einaudi reopened the discussion.[62] As early as 1 September 1943 'Why we Need a European Economic Federation' (see Chapter 17 in this book) was published anonymously.[63] Only a few days later Hitler ordered the occupation of Italy, and the return to power of Mussolini. The blackshirts came to arrest Einaudi as a prominent anti-fascist and he was forced to seek asylum in Switzerland, crossing the Alps by foot at the age of 69. In Switzerland he found the example of a pragmatic confederation which helped him to develop his ideas further. 'The Economic Tasks of the European Federation'[64] (see Chapter 18 in this book) was written during the 15 months of Einaudi's Swiss exile. It was the most comprehensive study of the economic aspects of a European federation and developed the ideas of 1943 in greater detail. To provide a clear idea of Einaudi's views within the limited space available, different sections have been selected from the two texts. The arguments justifying the need for a European federation have been selected from the 1943 work, which is much more wide-ranging than the later one, while the economic tasks of the European federation are examined in greater depth in selections from the 1944 work.

Einaudi ridiculed the absolutist theories of subordinating economic phenomena to purely political ones, and the supposed need for breathing space in order to expand production and dump excess supplies on subordinate states through imperial constructions. In his view, such practices would only lead to further conflicts and the destruction of Europe. The recognition of interdependence and free, peaceful commercial competition on a cooperative footing were the only alternatives. He considered that the chief objective of a United Europe should be to prevent military conflict between fully sovereign states. However, the economic intercourse of post-Napoleonic Europe showed a strong tendency to reach global economic unification through ever-extending networks of transport and communication. A European Federation would represent the only political and economic solution accommodating such pressures without continuous national clashes in defence of anachronistic particularism.

Einaudi set out an ambitious economic agenda: free trade, free movement of people, the unification of infrastructures and a single monetary system, all of which have been primary goals of the European Economic Community and the European Union from 1957 to today and pursued through the Single Act of 1986 and the Maastricht Treaty of 1991. Einaudi also expected the federation to have its own forms of fiscal income, from duties on imported goods to taxes on production (such as Value Added Tax) but also through its own tax on citizens' net income. His programme did not focus, as was customary, on the political and diplomatic side of the issue, but was a far more comprehensive and detailed economic plan than anything else published before.

Drawing extensively on historical evidence, Einaudi argued for a federation endowed with substantial powers. Weak confederations had historically failed because they lacked three essential prerequisites:

(a) access to direct financial resources rather than dependence on uncertain contributions from member states;
(b) direct control over an army rather than having to ask national governments to send contingents according to the circumstances;
(c) a single executive and legislative body rather than dependency on the unanimous vote of the member states.

Einaudi wanted a clear delimitation of federal powers in the constitutive act. With an early perception of the subsidiarity principle, Einaudi wished to prevent member states from interfering with the proper use of federal powers; at the same time he sought to avoid giving the federal level the opportunity to extend its reach beyond its proper limits and impinge on the prerogatives of local levels of government. The federation was to be directly responsible for regulating transport, communication, emigration and foreign trade.

Einaudi was very straightforward and very optimistic about his preferences for a common currency and central bank. 'The devolution to the federation of the regulation of the currency does not appear to be controversial.'[65] Einaudi listed the most common advantages normally associated with monetary unions by later advocates, namely the reduction of transaction costs and the simplification of payments. His foremost priority, however, was to make it impossible for governments to finance budget deficits through an excessive note issue, so as to secure sound public finances. In that way new expenditures would have to be financed exclusively by taxes and government bonds, which could be issued only as long as the government maintained the confidence of the public. Confirming his adherence to a monetarist point of view, Einaudi believed that a powerful source of inflation would be taken out of the hands of unscrupulous politicians by the introduction of the single currency. The depreciation of purchasing power through monetary inflation caused by irresponsible government spending had impoverished Italy and most of Europe at the end of the First World War. A ruined middle class had been driven into the arms of fascism and Nazism and thus opened the way to dictatorship and further catastrophe. Einaudi added that:

> If the European Federation only managed to withdraw the rights of individual states to finance public works by cranking up the printing presses – and forced them to make do with taxes and voluntary loans – that alone would be a magnificent achievement. It would be an achievement of healthy and efficient democracy because the governments of the federated states would no longer be able to mislead the people with the illusion of works built without cost through the false miracle of bank notes. Instead, in order to obtain support for new taxes or credit for new loans, they would have to prove that they are providing real advantages to their citizens.[66]

In response to the Keynesian view of crises, Einaudi imagined, as an intervention of last resort, that a temporary de-synchronization of economic cycles within the federation could be countered by issuing non-federal banknotes in a limited geographical area if exceptionally critical circumstances justified it. This would amount to a local increase in the money supply with the possible introduction of an exchange rate between the federal currency and the temporary additional local currency.

In 1947 Einaudi had become Governor of the Bank of Italy and insisted on a single central bank to manage a single currency: 'Just as currently each city and province, and tomorrow each region, are not authorized to create their own banks of issue, so in the future Federal State only one issuing institution will exist'.[67]

Even if the need to have a single central bank in a monetary union appeared natural only to Einaudi, it was an innovative idea. None of the monetary unions of nineteenth-century Europe had seen such a bank, and the United States and the Helvetic Confederation only created theirs at the beginning of the twentieth century. A federal central bank was not included in the programme of the 1941 Ventotene Manifesto, or in the 1957 Treaty establishing the European Economic Community, or in the 1970 Werner Report (except for a Fund for European Monetary Cooperation). Only the 1989 Delors Report really introduced the prospect of a central bank system.[68]

The political engineering of the federation had to be based on the US and Swiss examples, rather than those of Germany, the Hanseatic League or the United Provinces of the Netherlands. Hamilton's *Federalist Papers* were clearly an important source of inspiration. To manage the federation Einaudi advocated the creation of a federal army, a supreme court presiding over a federal magistrature, a federal police, and a common diplomatic corps, all of which would be competent for federal issues only and not for purely national ones. At the political level the executive would have a technical character and would deal only with economic matters. It was not expected to be reformed too often, leaving contentious political concerns to national or local authorities. The legislative level would be divided between a Council of States and a Legislative Council. The former would preserve the interests of the smaller members through the principle of one vote per state, while the latter would be composed of elected members representing all European citizens and prepare an emerging conscience of a common federal citizenship.

1
Know before Legislating*

'The solution is too long in coming'; 'now that the problem has been raised, it must be solved'; 'the matter is urgent, it must be addressed without further delay'. Those who read these and similar comments might well think: why are the government, the parliament, the minister responsible, so slow to act? These hasty people don't stop to ask: is this really *the* problem and not just one of the many? How is it that every day there are so many different urgent problems, whose solution cannot be put off without harm, indeed without serious harm? Why is the list of urgent problems so long and the list of documents in which their substance is clearly explained so short? How can we legislate without knowing?

Nothing, however, is more repugnant than knowledge to many, perhaps too many, of those who are called upon to solve problems. Some months ago, it fell to me to read both a majority and a minority report on the question of the Institute for Industrial Reconstruction (IRI), and, caught between these two very different reports, I concluded that together they did not make the problem known to those who were supposed to decide. The majority report, based on what are commonly referred to as broad theoretical principles, was too marred by the usual social commonplaces, destined, because they overlook the antiquated needs of balanced budgets, to ensure the failure of public and private enterprises and increased unemployment. The minority report, on the other hand, though well constructed on the basis of past experience and economic good sense, did not sufficiently illustrate the historical precedents and the rich vicissitudes of the past. It was sufficient to express the hope, devoid of any judgement, that together with the majority and minority reports there should also be published an old report by Donato Menichella and another by Giovanni De Maria that was included in the preparatory volumes of the Constitutional Assembly, as

*First published as 'Conoscere per Deliberare' in Luigi Einaudi, *Le prediche inutili* (Turin: Giulio Einaudi Editore, 1956).

well as accounts and statistics capable of properly explaining the current condition of the grandiose industrial complex, for some immediately to exclaim that the mere request to make the problem known to the lawmaker and the public implied a desire for delay and inaction; as though premature solutions that have not been thought through did not inevitably give rise to a new muddle and the urgent need to find remedies for even worse ills.

Today there is renewed debate about the salaries of public employees, especially those of teachers, but I am not aware that the fundamental data concerning what is supposed to be the proposed solution have been made public in official documents, to inform those who will be called upon to pay the bill, or that any newspaper has asked the adepts to furnish the data. Apart from recognition of the inadequacy of the pay of every sort of public official, the most you find is: the issue is only how much of an increase the treasury can afford without being forced to push taxes beyond what is usually known today as the breaking point. It is not exactly clear what is meant by this 'breaking point': while many are sceptical and doubt the very existence of such a limit, since it has been talked about for so many years without anything ever happening, others predict dire prospects of ruin for the lira and consequent social and political disorders.

In reality, varying the compensation of civil servants is synonymous with varying the distribution of total national income among the social groups living in Italy. But in order to evaluate the desirability, or the possibility or the fairness of any particular variation, we would need to know the following.

The sum of the pay packets, including all the complements and supplements, received during the year, divided by twelve. For those interested in making precise calculations and comparisons, the invention of the year composed of thirteen months, now fourteen for some groups, only half of which are public, and even sixteen for others (bank employees and others, public in whole or in part), has been a veritable calamity. It serves only to disguise the real rate of compensation and, together with family and attendance allowances, fixed overtime and extra overtime, special allowances for the military, for the judiciary, for university teachers, for hardship zones, travel allowances (albeit reduced in accordance with the rules applied for the calculation of taxable income), as well as daily allowances, per diems, special premiums and bonuses, examiner's fees, etc., etc., makes the figure for an employee's salary worthless, so that the only valid figure for calculating the monthly income of public and semi-public employees is what is now called the total annual take-home pay divided by twelve.

I believe this figure is unknown. Years ago, when I was at the Budget Ministry, the state accounting office had released – and, exceptionally, the newspapers had published – a calculation that, though not taking into account all of the addenda, came tolerably close to it. Whereupon a tax assessor sent an insolent telegram to the Minister of Finance that read, roughly: 'I see that the state accounting office attributes to my level a compensation of [I don't remember the exact figure in the telegram, so I'll use a hypothetical figure] 100. Since I receive 70, please send me the difference.' The telegram was insolent because, upon examining the writer's case, it was found that in the last few months he had been paid not 100 – the average calculated by the accounting office for his level in the hierarchy – but 110. The wife of another employee, complaining to me about his pay, added that she had not included his thirteenth-month salary because, in her opinion, it covered extraordinary end-of-the-year expenses and therefore did not help to meet household needs. As though extraordinary expenses were not household expenses too.

To be sure, pay packets are more difficult to calculate than salaries and they vary from case to case. But it is not beyond human capacity to hypothesize the real amounts for the various levels of the hierarchy of public employment, for the various levels of seniority, for typical household compositions, and add up the totals. Unless these calculations are made and reported in the newspapers, throwing out the useless tables of absolute and percentage increases devoid of meaning and good only to confuse public opinion, debates will be held and decisions made in the dark, without knowing what is being debated and to be decided.

The calculation of pay packets is not conclusive, since it includes only income in money. Who has ever calculated the value of benefits received in the form of favourable rents, government-subsidized cooperative housing, consumer goods purchased at discounted prices in outlets to which the state grants rent-free premises, with or without free electricity and heating and the services of employees and sales staff paid from the budget of some ministry? In order to ascertain the real figure for the remuneration of state employees, the savings on their cut-rate railway tickets should also be added to the pay packets. Naturally, the calculation relative to public employees should also be accompanied by a calculation of the allowances and indemnities, benefits and free travel, subsidized housing, and personal automobiles charged to the state for Ministers, Undersecretaries, Commissioners, Senators, Deputies, etc.

Since not all employees enjoy the above-mentioned and other lesser known benefits, information regarding their relative importance would be extremely useful in clarifying the differences between groups of employees; between residents of the capital and the provinces; between the privileged and those subject to the ordinary conditions of the market.

When employee associations adduce data regarding those who do not enjoy certain special facilitations, which are nevertheless enjoyed by hundreds of thousands of people, they are simply following the age-old and accepted method of all those asking for something from the state. Has anyone ever seen a trade association, when asking for tariffs against the invasion of obnoxious foreign products, brandish the costs of the abler and better-equipped entrepreneurs, who could probably very well withstand the foreign competition on their own? No, never! The data always refer, if not necessarily to the most down-at-heel producers, to those not very far from the brink who, not knowing how to get on because they don't know how to apply themselves, blame their misadventures on the infamous foreigner. Public employee associations do the same. They don't cite the examples, numerous though they are, of those who manage by entirely legal means to round up their income, pointing instead to the simple employee who gets nothing but his official salary, or not much more. The method of the industrialists desirous of protection is mistaken and unreliable, but equally mistaken and unreliable are the reticent tables showing the salaries of public employees.

It is logical, in the debate on salaries, to talk about their adequacy with respect to the increased cost of living. There is a widespread impression that, expressed in terms of money having equal purchasing power, today's salaries are lower than those in the past, whether in 1938 or in 1913. Considering that since 1914 there has no longer existed, in any country in the world, the exact reference to a given weight of fine gold, by virtue of which comparisons were made that were at least roughly accurate, it seems to me preferable to talk in terms of the salaries of 1913 rather than those of 1938. The Italian statistical yearbook has calculated at around 252.4 the multiplier for the change in the cost of living from 1913 to 1954. Those paid a salary of L1 then should be paid L252.4 today. The multiplier, I hasten to add, does not take account of the increase in needs brought about by the increase in human productivity realized over the course of the last four decades. Italians have succeeded in achieving a higher standard of living through more work and greater technical and organizational ability. If we did not produce more, we could not consume more without taking the difference from some foreign nation, which not only do we not want to do but has not happened. By how much has Italy's productivity increased, in real – not monetary – terms, in the last 40 years? If in the meantime we had enjoyed uninterrupted peace, the increase would have been greater than 100 per cent and therefore, taking account of the increase in prices, the nominal increase in national income would be twice 252.4, or about 500. Owing to the destruction caused by the two world wars and the consequent monetary and social upheavals, the increase has certainly been less than that. The Italian statistical compendium calculates (on p.330 of the 1955 edition) the increase in net product per inhabitant at market prices over the same period from 1913 to 1954 as 1 to 351.1. In certain economic sectors the increase was much greater, but for all fields of employment, including agriculture, crafts, the professions and clerical work, an overall average of 351.1 seems close enough to reality. This means that the multiplier to be applied to 1913 salaries should not be the figure of 252 corresponding to the increase in the cost of living, but the larger figure of 351.1, with the average growth in Italian productivity taken into account. A multiplier greater than 351.1 would have to be considered incorrect. After all, where do the incomes of the various social classes come from, in every country of the world, if not from the common pie? Consider, however, the hypothesis, perhaps not easily accepted by other Italians, that the average productivity of public employees has increased more than the average, and so round up the multiplier from 351 to 400. A friend asks: suppose public employees were offered the full salary (that is the pay packet) of 1913 multiplied by 400 or, put another way, if they were offered a remuneration increased markedly more than the increase in the net product that all Italians are called upon to divide among themselves, what would happen? An interlocutor responds without hesitation: the great majority would not accept the proposal because their current pay packets are superior to the amount obtained by applying the multiplier. I dare not give an answer, for the usual reason: no one knows anything on this matter. First know, then debate, then legislate.

Another topic much debated since 1945, or since the start of international conferences, meetings and congresses, is that of comparisons with foreign countries. Diplomats, generals, directors general and officials of the treasury, foreign commerce, and all sorts of ministries, come and go, pocketing indemnities and per diem allowances calculated in part in the Italian fashion and in part according to the rules of that mixed nation that in the Middle Ages was known as Frankish, and later Geneva-based and now American. They make mortifying comparisons and conclude: we are the worst-paid public servants in the world. First come the Americans with five or six times as much, everything of course being reduced to dollars, then the English and the Belgians with two or three times our pay, then the French, then us. The problem has come to the fore with the Atlantic Pact, owing to the need not to treat generals, colonels and officials of the same rank differently when they work side by side and do work that is equally appreciated. Can we go on paying some five and others one? If the generals, colonels and officials assigned to the Atlantic units and offices are Italians, will we pay them, out of the same budget, differently from the foreigners? If those thus assigned were paid five or three while their peers at home were paid one, what would become of internal hierarchy, order and discipline? The problem is very serious; and I don't know how we're going to get out of this fix.

Meanwhile, the invidious comparisons between Italian pay and foreign pay require a decision. And a decision cannot be made without knowing the facts. Here too, we know almost nothing. It's not enough to say that the circumstances are different; that foreign salaries are higher than ours but the cost of living is higher too, so that the balance re-establishes itself spontaneously. It's not enough, because it isn't true, or at least we don't know to what extent it is true that 'real' salaries are in balance. In the United States, where salaries are the highest, it's not true that the cost of living is proportionately higher than in Italy, since ordinary consumer goods are generally cheaper and personal services more expensive. Bread, meat, fruit, milk, ready-made clothes, etc., etc., cost less; but if you have to replace a broken window, you must be patient and will have to pay a fortune, so that it's better to do it yourself. Everything that can be mass-produced or manufactured on a large scale is cheaper, while goods made by craftsmen and personal services are much more expensive. The increasingly few first-generation Italian-Americans do small home and furniture repair jobs themselves and probably spend less, given the same standard of living, than in Italy; the others perhaps more. In any event, such comparisons are difficult and uncertain.

Monetary comparisons are uncertain for another reason. Suppose American public-sector salaries expressed in dollars are four to five times analogous salaries in Italy. What about the average income of the citizens who pay those salaries? If it is true that Americans' average annual income is about $1,700, whereas ours is around $400, it would also be true that they are more or less on a par; that is, the American public employee who is paid a salary equal to four–five times the salary of an Italian public employee would be getting no more than what is reasonably due to him by virtue of America's higher productivity and higher average income. In which case, how could a request to receive more than Italians can afford to pay be justified? I use the conditional, because in truth, as noted above, we know little or nothing about Italian take-home pay, and even less – except through hearsay or by reading tables compiled by unknown authorities on the basis of equally unknown criteria – about foreign take-home pay. As regards knowing the amount, country by country, of the various kinds of salaries, not in absolute dollar figures but in relation to the national average income, which is to say in relation to the collective ability of tax-payers to pay taxes, we humbly confess that we know nothing and that we are unable to say anything on the merits of the controversy as to what would be a fair level of earnings for Italian public employees compared to other countries.

Anecdotal evidence provided by my university colleagues confirms the utility of exact comparisons. Let it be said, to the credit of our university teachers, that they ask nothing for themselves – and this, so I'm told, was also the prevailing and perhaps unanimous view in recent gatherings. They ask on behalf of their assistants. The best students, whom their professors would willingly hire as assistants and who would be happy to continue their academic careers, must forgo the opportunity. They are forced to choose between the L40,000 per month offered by the university and the L70,000–100,000 or L120,000 offered straightaway by large Italian industries to young engineers, physicists and chemists who graduate with good marks. The complaint is not unique to Italy; competition between universities and industry is also intense in England and the United States. In fact, the Anglo-Saxon universities, not compelled to offer equal salaries across the board, are now deciding to offer young technicians and physicians higher salaries than those paid to new faculty members in the humanities or theoretical disciplines. Italian university professors who have reached the third or fourth level of the hierarchy do themselves credit by worrying about those who are supposed to ensure the continued good quality of education in the future, but who are now forced, bowing sadly to family needs, to take industrial jobs that are spiritually less attractive but better paid.

Perhaps my colleagues also have a vague sensation of the difficulty of comparing their own financial situation to that of their foreign colleagues. Are foreign faculty salaries really so high? Isn't the normal salary of the teachers called *professors* in the great English universities (who are a minority compared with those in Italy with the title of *professore ordinario*; most English university teachers are *lecturers* or *readers*, respected in practice on a par with the others – indeed, Keynes was never a professor – but lower in the hierarchy and more modestly remunerated) approximately £2,000 per year, or about L3.5 million, reduced on average by the income tax all pay to around L3 million? Don't the average earnings of Italian university professors, taking into account all the add-ons, the thirteenth-month salary, a special appointment (which everybody has) as well as the various allowances, fees and taxes, come to around the same figure, as demonstrated by actual payslips recently shown to me?

I don't draw any inferences from this example, which could be unique. I won't go into the strange legends making the rounds with regard to the extraordinarily high salaries of English judges. These tales almost always fail to mention that the figures are subject to taxes that reduce them to from two-thirds to one-half the nominal amount. I say only this: we know nothing and our decisions lack the most fundamental basis: knowledge.

Is it useful to legislate without knowing? Legislation must be followed by action. One legislates when one knows one is able to implement; legislation is not enacted in order to show off fruitless ambitions. But premature legislation gives rise to nothing. Has anyone ever counted the laws that have remained dead letters because the first attempt to apply them met with difficulties that should have been foreseen, or that perhaps were foreseen but the criticisms were disregarded, as though the opponents of the law had spoken only out of prejudice? Hastily approved laws give rise to new laws meant to amend and perfect them, but the new ones, dictated by the urgent need to remedy the defects of the earlier, badly-formulated ones, are inapplicable, except at the cost of some subterfuge, and must be further improved. Very soon the whole thing becomes an inextricable tangle from which no one can escape and we are forced to follow the path of least resistance, which is to do nothing and in the meantime to hold meetings and write reports and draw salaries in offices wholly occupied with beating the air about urgent reforms.

Action also meets with failure because not infrequently knowledge compiled with zealous fervour is not organized around some guiding principle. It is not he who searches that knows, but he who knows how to search. Consequently, the commissions assigned the task of knowing must not be composed only of practitioners, adepts and functionaries. It is useful to include a small, or better a very small, dash of theoreticians. In saying the theoretician I don't mean the 'experts' – known in Italian as *periti* – who know everything about the problem down to the tiniest detail: precedents; comparable foreign experiences; past, present, and future debates; everything except the guiding principle that will reveal the real problem to be solved. The experts always have the perfect recipe for the solution; and there's no need to be an expert because the perfect recipes are in the public domain, readily available in letters to the editor from readers amazed that they haven't yet been adopted. Do we need to employ the unemployed? All we have to do is reduce the working week from 48 to 40 hours, from 40 to 36, from 36 to 30; or just fire the sons, the daughters and the wives of employees now working so that just as many jobs will open up and unemployment will disappear. With few exceptions, not related to the remedy but to various events occurring contemporaneously or independently provoked, the recipes are almost always as useful as a poultice on a wooden leg. A theoretician, or a man with common sense who knows how to reason and has a critical view of the past and of the infinite errors that have been committed, helps to fend off the most obviously mistaken proposals, the poorly conducted analyses, and serves above all to inspire a healthy scepticism about the possibility of reaching a logical solution in the complicated social and economic situations of this imperfect world; made even more complicated by the enormous difficulty of discarding politically popular analyses and solutions and adopting instead good ones that are necessarily unpopular. It is the special task of practitioners and politicians to make public opinion swallow solutions that are good and unpleasant by dressing them up to look bad and agreeable.

However, knowledge cannot be obtained if instead of the theoretician or man of common sense the search for truth is entrusted to a doctrinarian. The latter is someone who possesses a doctrine and places all his faith in it. He doesn't reason on the basis of the information known to him and the great or small capacity for ratiocination received at birth from Mother Nature and perfected by study and experience. No, the doctrinarian reasons from a 'point of view'. Before studying, he already knows what he has to say. Even if he is not a member of any party, even if he doesn't fear being expelled from his parliamentary group, even if he doesn't speak and vote in conformity with the platforms approved by the assemblies of his faction, he is generically liberal or socialist or communist or Christian democrat or social democrat or labourite or corporatist. He therefore knows, from 'the point of view' of his social and political faith, the solution is that one. It is not important to know the proper nature of the problem: its source, its cause, its precedents. The solution is ready-made. Sometimes, pressed by the persuasive observations of his opponents, he may even confess: yes, what you say is right and should be taken into account, but regretfully I must remain steadfast to the principles that inform my behaviour. In reality, those 'principles' are nothing, are anything but 'principles'. There are no 'principles' that are not founded on experience and reasoning and that cannot be contradicted by other arguments and other experiences. The 'point-of-view' men do not voice 'principles', but well-flogged clichés that, maybe, a century or half a century ago, in other circumstances, had some substance but are now shadows of their former selves. However, since the human mind – outside physics, chemistry, mathematical calculus and similar fields forbidden to dilettantes and chatterboxes – is lazy and at the same time enamoured of novelty, especially if popular and seductive, and hates new things that promise little after a lot of hard work, what once appeared to be new and became part of the cultural baggage of a certain ideological current continues, by inertia, to be magnified into the most excellent modern innovation produced by the most daring progress. Did liberals once adopt, for excellent reasons and within well-defined limits, both still quite valid, the principle of 'laissez-faire and laissez-passer'? Even today, some think of themselves as liberals only because, upon hearing any proposal for government intervention, they jump up like jacks-in-the-box and declare that going down this road will lead to communist tyranny, even when the measure in question is aimed at, and often succeeds in, promoting private enterprise and competition among producers. Did socialists, at one time, a century or more ago, adopt as their banner the nationalization of industry? Why, even today, those who profess to be socialists believe they must choose any solution whatever just because it nationalizes something. Meanwhile, experience has demonstrated that nationalization, in itself and applied on principle to every case, is a load of humbug, tiresome even for the Fabians who between 1880 and 1890 first theorized it and for the Labourites who later translated it partially into action. The Fabians and the Labourites have not abandoned the formula; they still hang it out in their annual party platforms, which contain lists of hundreds of such proposals, but then defend it in subdued tones as they anxiously search for some new principle, more promising for the good of the country. Until there is some change in the wind of words, nationalization will continue to be the 'principle' to whose 'point of view' socialists will have to subject themselves. Could it be that, where there exists a 'point of view', it behoves us to keep on searching and, by searching, to know?

Part I

Political and Economic Liberalism

2
Lectures on the Market*

1 What a market is

Have you ever been in a country town on the day of a fair? Amidst the clamour of the children, the elbowing of the peasants, men and women, who want to get close to the stalls where cloth, clothing, footwear, etc., are being sold, to see, to compare, to touch, and the cries of the vendors, who want to persuade you that their goods are the best, the only ones that you will tire of wearing before they wear out, the ones that are a real gift considering the little money you will have to spend to buy them? That fair is a market, that is to say a place where on a fixed day, known in the surrounding towns, hundreds of sellers' trucks, carts and pushcarts come together, laden with goods, with the most diverse things, from clothes to shoes, from kitchen casseroles to ploughshares, from sheets to pillowslips, from odds and ends for children to gifts for fiancées. Everything is offered at the fair, and there are always many who offer the same thing. And from every direction, from the circle of villages and farmhouses around the large town, where there are squares and inns that can put up and feed so many people, thousands, multitudes of buyers converge to acquire the things they lack. The crowd of buyers and sellers is especially large at the Easter and All Saints' Day fairs. The buyers come in swarms, knowing that where there is a large gathering it is always easier to find what one needs, and to find it at the best price. And the sellers arrive in great numbers, knowing that where there is a multitude of people desiring to buy, it is always easier to sell their goods, and to sell them well. The buyers desire to buy at a low price and the sellers to sell at a high price. Spurred by opposite motives, they hurry towards the same place, the fair, the market.

---

*First published as 'Che cos'è un mercato' (Locarno: Tip. F.lli Molè, 1944) and then became the initial chapter of the *Lezioni di politica sociale* (Turin: Giulio Einaudi Editore, 1949), under the title 'Lezioni sul mercato'.

A shop too is a market. In the same city neighbourhood, often on the same street, if it is a busy one, there are many shops where the same vegetables, the same meat, the same quality of bread or cloth or shoes are sold. People pass in front of the shop windows, look at the qualities and prices and compare. If the customer decides to enter, he may find himself alone, face to face, with the shopkeeper. In reality, however, neither of them is alone. The shopkeeper knows there are other shopkeepers nearby, sellers of the same goods who are ready to take his customer away if he demands too high a price. The customer has already observed and compared and knows there is little to be gained in trying to bargain down the price since he wouldn't find the goods cheaper elsewhere. The competitors – sellers and buyers – are not physically present, trying to snatch customers or goods from each other, but, though invisible, they are there.

It may have befallen you some morning, between eleven o'clock and noon, to pass in front of a building on which 'STOCK EXCHANGE' was written. If curiosity has spurred you to enter the central hall or approach the glass pavilion in the middle of the main courtyard, you will probably have seen a large crowd of gentlemen, rather well-dressed, who every now and then take a notebook and pencil from their pocket and jot something down. Some are seated and silently make a note following imperceptible signs that they catch on the lips of some colleague. Others, their faces flushed, shout words that you don't understand to persons far away, who also shout incomprehensible words. Errand-boys, messengers and clerks scurry incessantly between the group of silent or vociferous people and certain booths situated along the walls of the hall, which you discover are telephone booths, and carry messages back and forth, oral or hurriedly pencilled on pieces of paper. This too is a market. The goods being traded are not in sight, for it is not always necessary to see and to touch, as one does at fairs and in shops. In stock exchanges government securities, corporate shares, municipal or mortgage-bank bonds are sold, that is to say pieces of paper having a higher or a lower value, but all of those of the same kind identical. It is not necessary to see and to touch, because when it is time to execute the contract the seller cannot deliver anything except that precise piece of paper on which certain words are written and not others. There are stock exchanges where commodities are traded instead of pieces of paper: wheat, maize, silk, wool, cotton, silver, copper, tin, zinc, lead, iron, etc. In this case it would appear necessary to see and to touch; but it would be an enormous complication for hundreds and thousands of sellers to come to the stock exchange each with a large load, even if it were made up of tiny samples to be distributed to the buyers as a token of the quality of the goods to be delivered. Samples do exist, but they are *ideal* and are already fixed by the rules of the stock exchange. For example, when wheat is traded, buyers and sellers tacitly refer to one or another given type of wheat, winter wheat or spring wheat, durum or common wheat, of a given specific weight, for example 78 kilograms per hectolitre, with a given degree of impurity, or foreign matter, let us say 1 per cent. It is that specific wheat that is traded and must be delivered at the agreed price. Of course, it is not always possible to deliver wheat of exactly that quality. The specific weight might be 78.30 or 77.50 instead of the agreed 78 kilograms, or the impurities 2 or 0.50 instead of 1 per cent. But the rules of the stock market, which are known to all beforehand, have already established the percentage premiums and discounts to be applied to the agreed price if the actual quality is somewhat better or worse than the 'standard'.

Further examples could be given, but it is clear enough by now what a market is. It is a place where many buyers and many sellers come together, desiring to buy or sell one or more goods. Instead of goods, it is possible to trade what are called *services*. At the wheat harvest or grape harvest, everyone knows that the reapers and grape-pickers who intend to hire themselves out gather in certain squares of the town, as do the farmers who have the wheat to be reaped or the grapes to be picked. In cities the system is somewhat different, and there are public and private employment offices where employers come who need workers and workers come who wish to find work. The essential point to keep in mind is that the market is a place where *many* buyers and *many* sellers come together. Some other words need to be added immediately to the word *come*: it is a place buyers and sellers can *leave* when it is not worth their concluding the deal. If, for example, the wheat-reapers or grape-pickers who have come to the market were taken by the scruff of the neck, so to speak, by the *carabiniere* or forced to harvest wheat for L30 a day when the market price is L50, or to pick grapes for L10 instead of L20, that would no longer be a market but an instrument of *slavery*. What we want to explain here is what a market is and not what life imprisonment with hard labour was in the past and may still be in certain countries. Similarly, when we speak of goods, for there to be a true market the seller must be able to refuse to sell or the buyer refuse to buy without incurring too large a loss. Certainly, if it is worth it, it is always better to sell or buy immediately rather than to wait; but, within limits, it may be worth waiting. For there to be a true market, however, the two parties must be free *not* to reach agreement. If the seller has a bulky, heavy good that would cost a fortune to ship back to the warehouse, or fruits and vegetables that will rot if not sold at once, this does not mean that the market no longer exists; it still exists, but for one of the parties it involves risks that need to be considered beforehand to avoid being taken by the throat by the other party.

2 Why it is incorrect to speak of fair price and unfair price: the market price

Although each may have has his own idea of fairness, when buyers and sellers come to the market the former aspire to pay and the latter to receive the fair price. To begin with, one must get it into one's head that the adjective *fair* stuck in front of the noun *price* is a foreign body that actually has nothing to do with the *market* we are dealing with. What is fair and unfair is determined by the judge when two parties appear before him to dispute the ownership of a piece of land or the right to open a window overlooking the neighbour's vegetable-garden. The judge can hand down a ruling because he can base himself on the code, on statutes, on regulations, on written and oral contracts, on the testimony of witnesses, which instruct him on the point in dispute. He can say to one of the two parties: you are in the wrong and you do not have the right to open a window overlooking your neighbour's vegetable-garden; or he may rule that he is in the right and that the neighbour is wrong not to want to let him open it. But what could the judge say about two peasants, one demanding L2,000 for his cow and the other wanting to pay no more than L1,800? Both of them are wrong and both right. Unless a law or a regulation or a commission appointed under a law in exceptional circumstances, as happens in wartime, says that the cow is worth L1,900, the judge has nothing to say on the matter. Each of the two contracting parties has his ideas about the price of cows. The first has always sold cows of that breed, weight and capacity to produce milk and calves for L2,000 and he thinks he would be wronged if he got a penny less. Or he knows he bought it for L500 when it was a heifer and that it subsequently cost him so much hay, so much bran, so much meal to raise it and bring it to its present point, that he really cannot sell it for less than L2,000 without, as he says, incurring a loss. Or else he turned down L2,100 at the last fair, when everyone was paying L2,150 for cows of that kind, and now, if he decides to sell it for L2,000 it is out of a feeling of friendship for the buyer, whom he has known for such a long time. Deep down, when he thinks it over, the seller considers the fair price for him to be that price which would give him the largest heap of money compatible with the ideas he and the others have gained on the possibility of making a good profit. When he arrives at the market, the seller would like to see no other cows around or as few as possible. In his opinion, there are always too many cows for sale. His ideal is scarcity.

The buyer starts out from opposite ideas. When the seller tells him he cannot part with the cow for less than L2,000 because otherwise he would not make up his expenses, he thinks to himself, 'He says he would lose; but even if it were true, and it isn't, he would lose only because he doesn't know his animals and raises them badly. In my hands, with less bran and less meal, which are too expensive, and more hay and grass passed through the fodder-cutter, which are more digestible and less wasted, I would have raised a fine animal and spent less. It isn't right that he should ask so much simply because he doesn't know about cows. It could have been sold for L2,100 at the last fair? Is it my fault if he didn't seize the chance when there were few cows on the market and they were worth a lot? Now there are many and their price has come down.' The buyer, therefore, would always like to have abundance, in order to pay a low price for goods.

What does 'fair' or 'unfair' have to do with the two groups arrayed in the market: producers, the sellers, who want scarcity so that prices are high, and consumers, the buyers, who favour abundance so that prices are low?

Between the two, it is the market that decides. The market does not say that one price is fairer than the other. It simply says: that is the price. The real price, the price actually paid, not the abundance price desired by consumers, the buyers, and not the scarcity price that would be ideal for producers, the sellers.

3 How the market price is 'made' and what it means

The price that is made in the market, the price that, to use the shortest possible qualifying adjective, we can call the *market price*, is neither fair nor unfair. It is what it is; it is a '*made*' price, nothing more, nothing less. And what is the price *that is made* in the market? Let us suppose that for a given All Saints' Day fair (1 November) or Martinmas Fair (11 November) 10,000 cabbages have arrived, which peasants and non-peasants alike are used to buying at that time of year to put in a ditch in the vegetable garden, well-covered with earth and branches, and to consume little by little over the winter, until the family vegetable-garden has begun to produce fresh vegetables. The 10,000 cabbages have arrived early in the morning and some people are already in the square. Words begin to be exchanged, bids and offers. From 70 cents bid and 1.20 asked, quick as a wink all 10,000 cabbages are sold for around 90 cents apiece. Certainly, that appeared to be a 'made' price, a market price. But other buyers arrive just after the existing supply has been exhausted, a good many other buyers, and they begin to cry about things being rigged: it is unfair that the first to arrive bought up all the cabbages at 90 cents a head, and that they, the newcomers, now have to pay 1.20, buying them from those who cornered the market. A dirty scheme, because the sellers had reached an agreement for the few early forestallers to buy up the market and leave nothing to be found.

The disillusioned buyers go to the mayor or the appointed alderman to complain that things have not been done properly. Usually, however, in order to avert disputes and recriminations, the mayor or alderman has already provided for the case, and a rule prohibiting the start of trading *before a certain time of day* has already been approved. What does this mean? That for there to be a market it is necessary not only that there be many buyers and many sellers, and that each be free to buy or to sell or to leave without having made any deals, but also that all, or at least all those who habitually arrive at the market during reasonable hours, be able to have their say, so that there will be no favouritism for any of the participants.

If these conditions are met, and others which it would be too long and complicated to set out, we can say that goods, foodstuffs and services are traded and exchanged on the market at a price at which, on that day and in the hours established by rules or custom, the quantity demanded is equal to that supplied. If at the price of L1, after the bell or the auctioneer has declared the fair open, all 10,000 cabbages offered are sold, if at the rate of L50 per day all reapers willing to work at that wage have found work with farmers ready to pay that same wage, we say that the price of L1 apiece for cabbages and the wage of L50 per day for reaping are the price and the wage at which all the sellers willing to sell cabbages at L1 apiece or less and all the workers willing to reap for L50 or less found buyers or employers ready to pay that price or that wage.

The market price tells us nothing about the theoretical fairness of paying L1 apiece for cabbages or L50 for a day's work. It only tells us that at that price the market has cleared. The buyers who thought the cabbages too dear at L1 have gone home, the sellers who hoped to sell them later at L1.10 have stored them in some warehouse and no unsold merchandise has been left at the fair. The reapers who found L50 a day insufficient have gone home, probably because they thought it was not worth putting up with all that heat and sweat when they were assured a less tiring day's work for L30. The farmers who considered it excessive to pay L50 per day for harvesting have gone away, reckoning that all told they could resort to the alternative of sweating and harvesting themselves a bit longer, until far into the night. The moon is out, and it casts its light; and even if the work will take an extra day, the weather is turning good and the risk of hail on the crop does not seem large enough to warrant shelling out L50. Each one has made his own individual calculations and the result is that the cabbages sold have changed hands at L1 and the reapers hired have agreed to L50. The rest have gone, the square is empty. A different price would not have emptied the square. If, for example, the price of a day's work harvesting were initially only L45, then instead of a supply of 100 reapers hired at L50 there would be a supply of only 90 and a demand for 110. If it were L55, there would a supply of 110 reapers and a demand for only 90. The situation would be false, unstable; in disequilibrium, economists would say. The price of L1 for a cabbage or L50 for a day's reaping that renders demand equal to supply and clears the market is called the *market* or *'made'* price. In the books written by economists it is also called the *equilibrium price*. In common speech it is simpler to call it the *market price*.

4 In a competitive market prices tend toward costs

What is the meaning or, better, the content of the *market price* in a *competitive* market, that is to say a market in which many buyers and many sellers participate, all of whom can leave without buying or selling; in which no buyer or seller is so large and dominant as to dictate the law to the others, in which all can have their say in conformity with the rules known to the public in which it is certain that the contracts concluded will be fulfilled?

The substantial and essential meaning is that the price in question *tends* to be that price which compensates the expenses needed to produce the good in the case of goods; or which, in the opinion of the interested parties, based on their respective positions, compensates the effort of carrying out the work in the case of services, that is the performance of manual or intellectual labour. If cabbages cost only 80 cents apiece, taking into account the expense of rent of the land, cultivation, fertilizers, harvesting and transport, in the long run the price will be 80 cents and not L1. At a price of L1, farmers earn too much and some will plant more fields with cabbages, and a greater amount of these will arrive at the All Saints' Day fair. If all are to be sold, it will be necessary to reduce the price to 80 cents. If 50 cents for a day's harvesting is higher than the normal compensation requested for that kind of work, the good news will travel like lightning and new reapers will arrive from the mountains and from distant villages who at home earned only L20 a day and are willing to put up with the blazing July sun in the lowlands even for only L40. In this case, given the greater abundance of reapers, to clear the square it may be necessary to reduce the reaper's daily wage to L45, and that will be the new market price.

5 Why a price is paid even for gifts of God

The market does not only equalize prices and the wages paid for different kinds of work. We said above that it may cost only 80 cents apiece to produce cabbages, because that is what has to be spent for cultivation, fertilizer, harvesting, transport and for *rent of the land*.

What is the expenditure item called rent of the land? It is immediately clear why it is necessary to pay what is necessary for the work of the peasants who hoe the cabbage field, weed it and take care of harvesting and transporting the crop. It is clear why it is necessary to pay for the managerial and administrative work performed by the farmer, who runs the risk of paying the expenses in advance and does not know whether he will be able to sell the cabbages well or at a loss. But it is not clear why it is necessary to pay something for the use of the land where the cabbages are planted. Is not the land a gift of God, a gift of nature?

Just two thoughts on the matter. It is not true that land, at least the land we know in civilized countries and particularly in Italy, is a gift of nature. A great Italian, a great patriot from the time of the Risorgimento, Carlo Cattaneo, wrote that land is not a creation, it is a construction. Cultivatable land does not exist in nature; there are only swamps, forests, deserts, untilled and unproductive land. The land we know in Italy is the fruit of centuries, indeed millennia of toil, of applied intelligence, of sacrifices on the part of past generations of Italians. If people today insisted on not wanting to pay anything for its use, who would continue to want to set aside savings and use them in order to preserve and continually improve the land? In a few short years – a few years suffice to destroy the work of generations – the land would return to the unproductive, wild state.

Second, if nothing were paid for using land to grow cabbages, who would tell us whether *that land* was better for growing cabbages or potatoes?

6 The market registers demands, not needs, and guides production to correspond with demand

We come here to the heart of the discussion. The market is not only a means of establishing prices that simultaneously satisfy producers and consumers and give each of those who have contributed to production compensation proportionate to their costs and effort, neither more nor less than what is sufficient to that end; it is above all an instrument, a mechanism by means of which people orient and guide production so that precisely those things, those goods, and precisely of the quality and in the quantity corresponding to the effective demand for them, are produced. Note well that in saying that the market is the instrument that guides production to turn out goods and services precisely in the quantity and of the quality demanded by people, we are not saying that the market *also* guides production to turn out goods and services in the quantity and of the quality that people would *desire*. People express the demand they can, with the means and money they have available. If they had different or greater means, they would express a different demand – for the same goods in greater quantity or for other goods of different quality. Demands, not needs, are satisfied on the market. A woman who passes in front of a shop window feels an intense *need* for the elegant pair of shoes on display, but if she has no money in her purse, or not enough, she does not express any *demand*. The market is constructed to satisfy demands, not desires.

Are people demanding cabbages and potatoes? Cabbages in one quantity and potatoes in another? If they are willing to pay L1 apiece for cabbages and L100 per quintal for potatoes, the buyers are telling farmers who have suitable land: be sure to earmark for cabbages the most suitable land for growing cabbages and for potatoes the most suitable land for growing potatoes. If the farmers get it wrong and grow potatoes on arid hillside land rather than in the mountains and cabbages in the mountains rather than on the plain, the land put to poor use will leave no margin after the expenses are paid. The farmer, the tenant will not be able to pay the rent to the landowner and will go bankrupt. Bankruptcy is the sanction, the penalty, necessary and beneficial, for those tenant farmers, industrialists and shopkeepers who do not know their trade, who make poor use of land, capital, materials, machinery, clerks, workers. The rent paid for land is maximum when each field is used for the crop or the rotation (a sequence of different crops in successive years or seasons) that yields the best result on it. Accordingly, every landowner is interested in seeking and finding precisely the crop for which his land yields the best results. If one paid rent equally at zero or L100 or L1,000 a year for all kinds of land, what reason would there still be to seek the best use of the land?

In the same way, the consumer guides the best industrial output. Who is to decide whether more railway engines or more automobiles are to be produced? The purpose of industry is not to manufacture railway engines and automobiles, but to satisfy people's demand. It is not machines that must command people, but people who must say what must be built in order to satisfy their desires, desires that manifest themselves in effective demand. Are people travelling more by rail? Are they crowding the trains? Are the railways' receipts therefore increasing? If so, the railway company managers will order railway cars and engines, and people will then travel faster and more comfortably – exactly as they desired. Do people prefer cars instead? Do they aspire to own at least one car per family, as is already the case in some countries? If so, people will order cars and producers will turn out millions of them a year. With the offer of better wages, technicians, workers, engineers and accountants will move from other industries to the automobile industry; and the heads of the automobile companies will demand fresh savings in order to purchase machinery, expand factories, buy raw materials, and they will take those savings away from other companies by offering a higher interest rate. Just as the fields that can yield the highest rents are earmarked for the most suitable crops, for the foodstuffs most demanded by buyers, so the need to pay interest in order to obtain capital results in savings being employed in industries that are able to yield at least that rate of interest and not in others, which are unable to do so. This means that the need to pay interest and the desire of entrepreneurs (industrialists and farmers) to earn the highest possible profit for themselves beyond the interest to be paid to savers-capitalists spur entrepreneurs to engage in the production of those goods and services for which buyers are willing to pay the most alluring price, or, more precisely, those goods and services that are most demanded, with the greatest relative intensity of demand on the part of the buyer. Naturally, if some consumers (buyers) were better supplied with means of purchase (money) and others had less abundant means at their disposal, the demand of the two groups would be different from what it is: the former, with an increased demand, would better satisfy certain needs that today they must compress; the latter would have no choice but to demand less, leaving unsatisfied certain desires which they indulge today.

The market, which does not recognize needs but demands, is the obedient servant of existing demand. It satisfies demand that does not remain in the Platonic sphere of desires but is manifested effectively, backed by the possession of a corresponding purchasing power (money). It guides production to satisfy existing demand. If the type of demand changed, the market, which is a means and not an end, would adapt by itself, automatically, to satisfy the new demand. We cannot ask the market to give us more than it can give; for example, to give money (purchasing power) to those who have little or none, so that they are able to demand things that can satisfy desires they may feel intensely but have not been able to satisfy; or to take money from those who have it in abundance and are able to demand things that can satisfy certain needs of a kind which most people usually regard as mere whims.

If that function is deemed appropriate, it is entrusted not to the market but to other institutions or other mechanisms; for example, progressive taxation of high incomes on the one hand and compensation for industrial accidents on the other. The market registers that which exists. Is demand changing? Then we see the market registering the new demand, setting new and different prices, new and different wages, offering production new and different guidance.

7 Let us not confuse the mechanism of the market with the mechanism of the distribution of wealth

There are some writers, technicians and propagandists, who imagine they have made a great discovery when they say that in the future production should no longer be directed towards giving a profit to entrepreneurs but to serving people, to satisfying consumers' true needs. These people create a great muddle. They confuse two different mechanisms that satisfy two different needs. One mechanism is that which, *given existing demand*, seeks to satisfy it in the best possible way. This mechanism, this instrument has been known for centuries and is by no means waiting to be discovered: it is called *market*, and it is the mechanism that we have sought to describe above. It is also the only effective mechanism for the purpose, tried and proven by centuries-long, indeed millennial experience.

It is, in addition, the only effective mechanism if one adheres to the principle that the master of the decisions to be made is man himself, who, having desires, aspirations and needs, seeks to satisfy them *within the limits of the means at his disposal* and in the way he himself decides.

Is there some other mechanism – or do we wish there to be one – thanks to which people, to satisfy their desires, will in some cases have more means of purchase, means of transforming desires and needs into effective demand (and here the reference is above all to the poor), and in other cases less (and here the reference is to the rich and very rich)? It is widely held that something, indeed much can be done to this end. But in order to fulfil the intent it is not useful to destroy the existing market mechanism, built to achieve a given purpose, when one wants instead to achieve a different purpose, it too very important. It is useful instead to create a separate mechanism, one not easy to devise and probably composed of numerous different pieces, capable of achieving this new and different purpose – in essence, a more egalitarian distribution of the means of purchase, of what is commonly called wealth and would better be called income, with less want below and less abundance above.

To confuse different ideas means getting nowhere. To confuse, as so many do here, different mechanisms means breaking them both, to no advantage.

8 Can the decision about people's needs be entrusted to someone else?

There is a group of these muddlers who began to come up with a fine idea for better satisfying people's needs: that people did not know what they were doing, i.e., that what they demanded did not correspond to their *true* desires, their *true* needs; and that it was therefore necessary for *someone else* to take it upon himself to decide for them what they ought to buy and sell. Naturally, if we start out from the principle that individuals, each for his own account, should not decide what they want to acquire on the basis of the means they possess, but that the decision should be made by *someone else*, we can do without the market. In some cases it may be reasonable, even necessary and socially advantageous, for the decision on what the individual is to consume to be left not to the individual but to *someone else*. It can and indeed must be said that the field in which the decision is left to someone other than the interested party has been vast in some historical eras and some circumstances, and that it could once again become very important in the future.

Convents flourished in the Middle Ages and they still exist today. Who are monks and nuns if not persons who have relinquished to their superiors every right to express desires, to make free choices as to how these are to be satisfied? They eat, dress, sleep, keep vigil according to the rule and according to the orders of the guardian. Theirs is not a market economy, but one of obedience to orders from superiors. If they are happy to live this way, why not respect their will? Ordinarily, however, people like to live as they please and not as monks in a monastery.

In a besieged city, in a large or small country surrounded by enemies, the market cannot function because even if consumers demand a greater quantity of bread and not a single newspaper, producers cannot follow their indications. Between one harvest and the next, bread can be produced only within the limits of the existing supply of wheat, while newspapers can be produced up to the number allowed by the supply of newsprint. And so *someone else*, in this case the government, has to say: if the supply of bread is to last until the end of the siege or the war and no one is to die of hunger, it is necessary that each person consume no more than 100 or 150 or 200 grams of bread a day, to institute rationing, ration books, etc. Since *someone else*, again the government, has an interest in there being newspapers and these publishing the news and communiqués desired by that *someone else*, the paper-mills might be ordered to continue to turn out newsprint, with pulp from poplar trees or straw or other raw materials that could be put to what buyers consider more urgent uses, in order to print and sell many newspapers with different names but all of them the same, whereas a single daily bulletin on a small sheet would suffice to disseminate the news desired by the public. In the case of bread the *someone else* does what everybody desires, in the case of newspapers what everybody would probably be glad to do without if free to decide. While the necessity of siege or war *imposes* rationing and ration books, is it nevertheless not evident that as soon as it is possible everybody will breath a sigh of relief when the market can be restored.

Sometimes the *someone else*, for reasons that public opinion normally considers good, does not want consumers to be able to express their tastes freely in the market and thereby guide production. For example, almost all countries hinder the sale of alcoholic beverages with duties, prohibitions, limitations on hours and on sales to certain groups of persons (e.g., young people and women); all of them prohibit and punish the buying and selling of drugs. They limit and suppress the market on grounds of health, morality, salvation of the younger generations, prevention of the terrible diseases caused by the use of drugs and the abuse of alcohol.

For most items of consumption, however, the choices are innocuous and bring no harm either to those who make them or to others, and they can therefore be left freely to the interested parties. At most it may be useful that *someone else* – public entities, religious or charitable or educational institutions – engage in work aimed at teaching consumers to make good choices from the standpoint of substantial utility, evaluated according to objective scientific criteria, and at dissuading them from purchasing goods whose objective, nutritional or physiological utility is less than the loss incurred by forgoing other things that could have been purchased at the same price. The public not infrequently allows itself to be guided by interested publicity, and it is useful if a scientifically impartial and objective education attenuates the mistakes men make in distributing income among the various items of consumption, though leaving the final decision to them.

Possibly, that *someone else* is persuaded that many individuals spend their income badly, consuming too many beverages, for example, or indulging in useless extravagance with clothing accessories or wasting money on adornments or toiletries, and dedicating too small a part of their wages to their homes. If statesmen consider a good family life, the ownership of even a small house or a modest vegetable-garden to be the solid foundation of a healthy and prosperous society, it is admissible that the state, in order to encourage the access of the working classes to ownership of a home or vegetable-garden, build suitable roads by extending streetcar lines, install the necessary lighting and water and sewer facilities and thus favour the creation of agreeable and attractive working-class towns in the vicinity of the city. If need be, it will also provide public parks, schools, public services, recreation fields, churches and so on.

The state might also subsidize the construction of houses, so that these can be sold at lower prices on long-term instalments. Since these houses will probably be in great demand, in all likelihood in a number exceeding that supplied, it will be necessary to find some rule other than the market rule to select those who are to have a house; and preference will be given, for example, to the heads of large households, to old people, to the most diligent workers, to long-term residents of the place, etc., etc.

9 People do not intend to renounce their right to choose the things they want to acquire

It must be borne firmly in mind, however, that these are exceptions, which are acceptable and even useful as long as they are exceptions. There can even be major exceptions without abolishing the rule of the freedom of people to direct their demand in the direction each of them individually prefers. If they became the rule, it would mean we had accepted the principle that men can no longer decide by themselves what they want to acquire, and that *someone else* would always decide. It is probable that the great majority of individuals desire to spend the means they possess as they think best, without having the law laid down by anyone else; that they desire, that is, the continuation of the market, the sole means discovered until now of achieving the purpose.

10 Monopolists and monopoly prices

However, the market is not always like that described above. Usually, there are many buyers and they compete with each other in buying and driving up prices, but sellers are not always numerous and ready to compete with each other. On occasion, the maker of a good may be the only one and dominates the market. Or else the makers are many, but one or several are so big that it said that they 'make' prices. You may have heard about that manufacturer of bricks and tiles who in his own town, where he is the only one selling them, sells bricks at L150 per thousand and tiles at L200 (these are prices of several years ago, before the present war); and who instead in towns further away, where he has to reckon with the competition of other brick-makers, sells the *same bricks* and the *same tiles* at L120 and L150 respectively. 'Fine justice, fine respect for fellow townsmen', the local people say, 'to charge us dear for bricks and tiles and sell them cheap to outsiders!'

And yet, from the brick-maker's point of view, this is natural: in his town he is the only one selling, while outside there is competition. Competition, the safeguard of consumers, no longer exists in his town, and customers are taken by the throat. Producers who are alone or almost alone are called *monopolists* or *quasi-monopolists*. It can happen that there are a few or even quite a few of them, but they agree to act as one; in this case, as a group they are known as a *consortium, syndicate, trust* or *cartel*.

The result is always the same: the monopolist is no longer forced by competition to set a price equal to the cost of production; instead, he can set the quantity of goods he wants to produce or sell, *or* the price he wants to be paid, and the price will therefore naturally tend to be that which gives him the *maximum net profit*. His success in this will not always be complete, because there is always a little competition and he may fear that if he makes too much profit, as he could, others will be prompted to open a competing factory. But, in general, he aspires and tends to obtain the maximum net profit.

11 Under monopoly, less is produced and the reduced output is distributed worse

By doing so, the monopolist causes, together with other injuries, two major ills. In the first place, in order to gain more he has to raise prices, by a little or a lot, in comparison with competitive prices, and accordingly, at higher prices, sells and produces less. If one million kilograms of a given good are produced and sold at a price of 8, at a price of 10 demand and, consequently, production and sales will fall to, say, 800,000 kilograms. A good number of buyers, those who consumed the 200,000 kilograms, remain empty-handed and have to tighten their belts, while those who continue to consume the 800,000 kilograms left have to pay 10 instead of 8. Second, monopoly profits and earnings arise. Before, when the market was competitive, producers had to be content with earning what was *necessary* in order to induce them to risk their own savings and those borrowed from banks and to organize and manage firms, which is an indispensable and very productive species of work. Now, they pocket big additional profits due not to their *merit* of working, organizing and risking, but to their *demerit* of sweeping all competitors from the field or agreeing with their former competitors to overcharge consumers.

12 Two kinds of monopoly and two ways of fighting them

It can therefore be said that while the *competitive* market is a benefit and renders a service, the *monopoly* market is harmful and renders a disservice to the generality of the population. Since the aim in these pages is only to *describe* the market and broadly explain its working, this is not the place to dwell on means of eliminating or reducing the ills of monopoly. It will suffice to mention that the fight against monopolies must be considered one of the main objectives of the legislation of a state whose leaders are concerned with the welfare of the majority and do not intend to coddle the interests of the minority. The fight against monopolies can be waged in two directions. There are monopolies, the majority according to some, that owe their existence precisely to a law of the state. If the state has established customs duties, quotas, prohibitions on imports, prohibitions on building new factories, and so forth, the state, *with its own law*, has reduced or destroyed the competition that could come from abroad or from new manufacturers. In such cases it is clearly enough to abolish the law that *created* the monopoly and the monopoly will be destroyed. In other cases the monopoly is due to causes independent of the law, to technical causes. For example, competition between many bus companies, many water or gas or electricity companies in the same city or the same neighbourhood, and, within certain limits, between different railways connecting the same cities is not possible and will not last if it is attempted. Since in this case the monopoly can be said to be almost natural, it can no longer be abolished and must be regulated. The state intervenes to set the maximum tariffs, the kinds of services, or it can decide to run the monopoly industry itself, charging only enough to cover the cost. Provided it does not get to like this too much. Centuries ago, when the tobacco leaf was introduced in Europe, some states declared that they wanted to run that industry for the protection of consumers. Everyone knows how this ended, with tobacco being sold in certain countries at 3, 4 and even 10 times the cost of producing cigars and cigarettes.

It happened by accident that governments, taking advantage of the tobacco monopoly to make an enormous profit, did an irreproachable thing. The tax that governments collect by means of the tobacco monopoly is one of the best taxes imaginable. Since we cannot do without taxes, it is better that they be levied on a widely consumed good, one which for many is almost as necessary as bread, but which can, however, be considered as indicating an amount of disposable income voluntarily allocated to satisfying a need to which the lawmaker attributes less importance than public needs; an amount on which the state may therefore impose even a heavy levy without too many qualms. But the practice of creating a state monopoly of this or that product must not become generalized. 'State quinine', which for that matter was not a monopoly, had good effects, but harmful ones have come from the monopoly of *salt*, an essential food. And recently, when cars and trucks began to compete in earnest with the railways to the great advantage of the public, did we not see quite a few states that owned railways, instead of rejoicing for the general advantage, grow alarmed over the blow to their finances and put every sort of spoke in the wheels of the beneficial competition offered by the new motoring systems?

There is no remedy for these dangers, other than a vigilant, enlightened public opinion able to discover the truth amidst the tangle of pretexts and bromides serving to mislead it.

13 Market prices are neither arbitrary nor controlled by producers

Prices in a market dominated by competition, prices in a monopolistic market and prices in the many other kinds of markets, in which there is less than perfect competition but not yet a perfect monopoly, have a characteristic in common: they are *not arbitrary*.

One of the most widely held ideas is that prices are determined by those who sell, by those who produce, by those who bring the goods to market. Certainly, producers *desire* to sell at the highest possible price, but 'hell is paved with desires' too. We all desire something we do not have, but then we adapt and make do. The same goes for producers and sellers. Even a monopolist who would like to sell at L10 has to adapt and sell at 8 if too many buyers evaporate at L10 and he loses more by selling little than he gains by raising the price. If he took consumers by the throat and forced them to buy all the goods he wants to saddle them with at the price he sets, his bullying would know no limits. Luckily for them, consumers have a way out: to turn their back on him and his goods, or, if not that, to reduce their purchases or resort to substitutes. One fine day it occurred to an Italian government to encourage a Sicilian sulphur consortium, which raised the prices paid by the British and the Americans, large consumers of sulphur. After all, they are rich – it was said – and they can pay! Instead, they got angry and began first to extract sulphur from pyrite and then to search for sulphur by land and sea and, searching, searching finally found it in Texas, where, to boot, it was cheaper to mine than Sicilian sulphur. Another fine day the Brazilians had the idea to valorize coffee, that is to say to demand a semi-monopoly price for coffee. We are – they said – the world's leading coffee producer, and the North Americans, French, Italians, etc., great drinkers of coffee, will find they have to come to us! It turned out badly for them, because coffee-growing spread in other countries and, above all, owing to the attraction of the artificially high price, it spread in Brazil itself. At a certain point there was so much coffee on the market that it could no longer be sold at the so-called valorization prices; and there was the scandal, of which all the newspapers spoke, of coffee being thrown into the sea or used to fire railway engines. This was no scandal at all, but the logical consequence of the mistake of creating a monopoly and expecting to make consumers pay an exorbitant price. The scandal, it should be noted in passing, lay elsewhere: it was that at the same time the governments of some consumer countries made coffee inaccessible to their citizens by levying very high customs duties or even prohibiting its importation.

In a free market no one does what he wants, neither producers nor consumers. Has the government increased the tax on houses? Then everyone says, 'Landlords will feel no pain, since they only have to raise rents.' Incorrect. Landlords do wish to raise rents, but if they had been able to do so, they would have raised them without awaiting the stimulus of the tax increase. If they did not do so, it was because tenants cannot be taken by the throat. If rents rise, they crowd into flats with fewer rooms; they forgo certain conveniences; they go to live in the suburbs. Vacant flats emerge, and if the landlords want to rent them they have to make up their minds to lower the rent. The question of the influence of taxes on prices is certainly more complicated than this. Suffice it to observe that even in this case landlords cannot do what they want.

They must obey the market, which automatically, through the entry of sellers when rising prices leave an attractive profit margin and the exit of buyers when the rise in prices forces buyers not to translate their desires into effective demand, and through the corresponding exit of sellers and entry of buyers when prices fall, works to establish that price at which the quantity demanded is equal to the quantity supplied. Likewise, the prices of labour (wages and salaries), capital (interest) and land (rent) are established automatically. Did the owner of a building site in the centre of Milan or Rome act arbitrarily when he asked for and got – we are speaking about ten years ago or so, when lira prices meant something – a price of L20,000 per square metre, at a time when certain parcels of farmland in some Italian regions were worth perhaps 10 cents per square metre (L1,000 per hectare)? No, in the contest between buyers and sellers, the market automatically performed a process called *capitalization of income*. It is true that the building site in Milan or Rome yielded nothing, not even an ear of corn, whereas the farmland in Basilicata produced a little corn. But the prospective buyer of the building site did his sums on the income of the six- or eight- or ten-storey building he would be able to put up and on the net income he would obtain by renting it out as shops, offices and flats; and if the calculation showed that after taxes, operating expenses, insurance, maintenance, depreciation and interest on the capital invested in constructing he would have a net return of L100 per square metre per storey, or, multiplied by ten storeys, of L1,000 per square metre, he was willing to pay L20,000 per square metre for the site because his investment would give him a return of 5 per cent, which was the going return for that type of investment. By contrast, if the prospective buyer of the farmland in Basilicata, after figuring the conditions of the land, the capital to be invested in livestock and dead stock, the yield in wheat, the costs of cultivation, harvesting, transport, taxes, etc., etc., came up with the very plausible result of a net income of L50 per hectare, he was not willing to pay, capitalizing the income at the interest rate of let us suppose 5 per cent, a price higher than L1,000 per hectare, i.e., 10 cents per square metre. In forming these two very different prices of L20,000 and 10 cents for an identical area of one square metre (located in different places), the will of the landowner is neither here nor there. The market is sovereign and decides on the basis of a debate in which the relevant factors are gone over by those who have opposing interests and do not want to be bested: prospective output, costs and uncertainty of success, probability of future events. Everything is weighed and measured, and the give and take of the market brings forth the market price, sometimes very quickly, almost instantaneously (stock market prices), sometimes very slowly, painfully, with brokers going back and forth tens and hundreds of times, only after days, months or years (prices of farmland). It is at that price that the good, service, security, house or land is transferred. Nothing has been invented up to now to replace the market mechanism, apart from its abolition and replacement by a system governed from above through commands and decisions transmitted from the supreme to the intermediate authorities and from the latter on down to the lower authorities and finally to the population, as has always happened in barracks and prisons.

Anyone who does not want to transform the whole of society into an immense barracks or prison must acknowledge that the market, which arrives automatically at the result of guiding production and satisfying consumers' effective demand, is a mechanism that cannot be rashly smashed just to see what's inside, the way children do with toys. On the contrary, it deserves to be studied carefully, so that it can be perfected little by little.

Before the First World War it had reached a high degree of perfection; it would be great accomplishment if in a few years we managed to recoup the enormous ground we have lost in the last 30 years!

14 What lies round the fair and influences it

Up to now we have spoken of the *market*, both the beneficial competitive one and the harmful monopoly one, as if it were something that exists by itself. In explaining things, one is forced to proceed like this, in order to avoid creating confusion in the reader's mind. So complicated and varied and mutable is the real world that in order to get ideas straight and see clearly into it, the description has to proceed step by step This is what has been done so far with the market. But all those who go to fairs know that a fair could not take place if, besides the sellers crying out how good are their wares, and the crowd of buyers who admire the fine voice but who first want to handle the shoes to see if they are made of leather or cardboard, there were not something else: the two-pointed hats of the pair of *carabinieri* passing through the square, the uniform of the municipal constable quieting two people who have quarrelled, the town hall, with the secretary and the mayor, the magistrate's court and the office of the Justice of the Peace, the notary who draws up contracts, the lawyer you turn to when you think you have been tricked in a contract, the parish priest, who recalls the duties of a good Christian, duties that must not be forgotten even at the fair. And there are the squares and roads, the former hard, the latter muddy, leading from the farmhouses in the countryside to the centre, there are the schools where the children go to learn. And there are so many other things without which the fair could not be held or would be completely different from what it actually is.

15 The influence of habits on prices

A complete description of the influence of the surroundings on the market is impossible in a few pages. We must necessarily limit ourselves to a few cases.

Why does the peasant or the villager like to buy at the fair? Not only because there is a wider selection of goods than there usually is in the village; not only because there are many sellers competing with one another; but also because he *does not know the sellers personally* and is not afraid to offend them by walking away if he does not find the goods or the price advantageous and approaching someone else to see whether a better contract might not be made. In his own town he usually would not dare act like that. His father and mother have always bought from that shop. The shopkeeper and the customer are family friends. If he had his shoes resoled by another cobbler, the same day it would be the talk of the whole village and it would be trouble for him. 'What wrong have I done you for you to stop dealing with me?', his cobbler friend would ask or have others ask. 'Is it that the other man's work is better than mine?' How to answer him! That the resoling job cost L3 less? But the answer to that is ready: 'Your father, your mother, you and your wife have never had cause to complain about me. My work is done according to the dictates of conscience. If the three lire matter, it's a sign you don't respect a job well done.' How to tell him that the other cobbler also works conscientiously? There would be coldness, unpleasantness, enmity. Not infrequently, therefore, *habit* is a very important factor modifying the results in comparison with what would be obtained in a proper market, which is one in which the buyers and sellers do not know each other or behave as if they do not, and prices are determined exclusively by economic advantage. In a proper market, where one party does not know the other or, better, there are no motives of friendship, submission or dependence between them, prices, wages, rents, etc., move more rapidly and continuously; where habit, custom, neighbourly and family relations dominate instead, one pays for each thing or each service what one is used to paying for it, what is considered fair, what everyone thinks corresponds to what ought to be paid. We frequently hear the response: 'Pay what you will. You know more about it than I do. You know what you have always paid.' The response is embarrassing and often forces one to pay a bit more than what one knows is the market price. But one pays in order to preserve good neighbourly relations and to remain on greeting terms. It will be easier to find a good or procure a service the next time it is needed.

16 The law's influence on the market

Among the circumstances that influence the market, we must not forget *the law*. Even if you do not know the civil or commercial or penal code, you have probably gone to a lawyer or notary to draw up a legal instrument or settle some troublesome business. And you noticed then that you cannot do everything you want to do; you cannot even agree with another party to do what both of you would like to do. There are rules you must obey, systems you must adhere to. If you want to make a will, you cannot leave all your land to one child and none to the others; all to your sons and none to your daughters. Most peasants would find it only natural to leave everything to their sons, who have always worked alongside their parents. They do not believe they are wronging their daughters when on the day of their last journey they leave them to God with their simple blessing. Why shouldn't the daughters be satisfied with the dowry they received at their wedding? If their husbands were satisfied then, what reason have they today to put their nose into the business of the legacy and create problems for the sons, who already probably have trouble enough dividing up that little bit of land into equal parts? And yet they have to resign themselves: Italy's former civil code allowed them to dispose freely of only half of the estate; the other half, the legitime, necessarily had to be divided into equal parts among all the children, male and female. The new code further reduces the freely disposable part, to one-third or one-quarter. The notary may have explained to you that the civil code does this to prevent all the land from being left to the firstborn son, as was once the custom. The other sons had to roam the world looking for a living, and the eldest son stayed home, well provided for. For this and for other reasons it came to be that there were too many large estates, too many of what in Italy, from Rome south, are called latifundia, poorly farmed, because the owners had too much land. The division among the children imposed by the code had the consequence that large estates were broken up in quite a few regions of Italy, in France and in Switzerland; every landowner had less land to farm and farmed it better. The output of the land increased. Peasant labourers, in greater demand, received better wages and worked a greater number of days. In the market, everything changed: wages, rents and prices.

To be sure, they did not change only for the reason just mentioned, but the latter contributed in some degree to the change. It can therefore be seen that a provision of the law, such as that whereby a father may freely dispose of only part of his estate while the remainder, often the larger part, must be divided equally among his offspring, is able to influence the market.

17 The importance of inheritance taxes

You know, possibly because you or your parents have gone to pay some tax at the Registry, that legacies do not always pass entirely into the hands of children and relatives, but that the state takes a good cut of its own, a cut that increases the larger the legacy or the more distant the kinship of the beneficiary. This happens not only because the state has to survive and needs the population to pay taxes. It also happens because those who drafted the laws thought it would be best if children and distant relatives did not enjoy all of the fruit of the labour and saving of their elders and in order to prevent fortunes from remaining immobilized in the same family from generation to generation. The proverb says: the father sacrifices, renounces, saves and builds up an estate; the son preserves it and the grandson devours it. In general, this is probably close enough to the truth. But the lawmakers thought it best to give this natural process a push, not least so as to intervene in time to allow all of society, represented by the state, to enjoy at least part of the estates accumulated in the past before the grandchildren and great grandchildren devour them. If someone is to devour them, it was said, it might just as well be the state, in the name and on behalf of all. Here, again, the thesis should not be pushed too far. The ideal thing would be if no one devoured estates, neither the grandchildren nor the state. And there is the other reason, already mentioned in connection with the legitime, that levying a higher tax the larger the estate prevents the perpetuation of overly large estates and favours their division.

There are some who, bearing this last point in mind, would like inheritance tax to be modified further by having estates pay not only according to their size but also according to their age. For example, that field should pay 10 per cent when it passes from father to son; the *same* field should pay another 40 per cent when it passes from son to grandson and the remaining 50 per cent when it passes from grandson to great-grandson, so that in reality the great-grandson would no longer inherit any of it. But if to the old field the grandson has added a new one, then the great-grandson would pay only 10 per cent on the latter, and so forth. Naturally, the tax would be levied on the *value* of the field, not on the field itself. The gist of the idea is that legacies would be transferred only within certain limits from one generation to the next, in order to force the new generations to work instead of spending their time in idleness. In any case, it can be seen that laws on inheritance influence production and the distribution of wealth and, hence, markets, wages and prices. Good laws produce good results, bad laws bad results. The former encourage work, the latter encourage waste. Prices are always formed automatically in the market, but the prices that are formed differ depending on whether there are few or many owners, depending on whether people are encouraged to work, to invent, to go forward, or instead to languish in idleness. It is therefore very important to make good laws.

18 The influence on the market of good money and bad, good government and bad

Think of the harm suffered by the majority and the gains obtained by the minority owing to the bad money that governments have printed and put into circulation in different countries.

Recall what happened to the German mark, the Austro-Hungarian crown, and, to a lesser extent, the Italian lira, the French franc, the Belgian franc, etc., after the First World War. Governments, not collecting enough taxes and not finding sufficient credit, printed banknotes, some in enormous quantities, to cover public spending. The population, finding itself with all that paper in its hands – which it received as salaries, wages, payments, etc. – sought to buy goods and made prices rise. Governments therefore had to pay more for all they needed and printed even larger amounts of paper money than before. Those who received it and wanted to spend it had to pay even more for everything. It was a vicious circle without end. Nobody saves under such conditions. Why save, why put aside 100 marks or crowns or lire or francs that today can buy one litre of oil if tomorrow the same 100 units will buy only half a litre and then a quarter of a litre? But if no one saves, tomorrow how will industries find the capital they need; how will they be able to employ workers? Every month the latter must ask for a pay increase in order to compensate for the increasing rise in the cost of living; but the more wages rise, the more things cost to produce and the more their prices have to be raised. It is a race towards disorder and the ruin of everyone. Everyone is discouraged and angry. The only ones who gain are intermediaries, speculators, those who are quickly able to sell their goods at the higher price *before* their expenses in raw materials and wages increase. What is the luck of the few worth in comparison with the ruin of the country? Why did this happen? A lot could be said about the subject, but the essential thing to keep in mind is this: in Switzerland, the country was administered well by a Federal Council composed of good and honest people who wanted to act in the interest of the population that ultimately elected them. The Federal Council met the needs of the Confederation (and the cantonal governments those of the cantons and the municipal governments those of the municipalities) with ordinary means, *without resorting to the printing press*, that is to say without printing more new banknotes than necessary. In Italy, by contrast, things went the way we all know; while they said they wanted to defend the lira to the death, they continued to print banknotes, and by dint of the expansion of that paper – of which there was only 20 billion in circulation 20 years ago but maybe 200 billion now and the figure is growing every day – it has become nearly worthless. In Germany and Austria, marks and crowns ended up worthless. We hope that the slide stops short of that in Italy, that the lira's fall can be arrested at some point. But the comparison is obligatory.

And so we see the importance of a good government and of an honest administration that knows how to inspire confidence in the future and security in the present; and, on the contrary, of a government that only breeds lack of confidence, insecurity, disorder in prices, in values, in incomes, in everything that concerns daily life.

19 Freedom to form trade unions and to strike, and wages

One last example – but it would be possible to continue at length – of the influence of laws on market prices. Wages are the price paid for a worker's day of work. They vary, of course, depending on the kind of work, the ability and diligence of the worker and many other circumstances. But they also vary depending on the penal code and how it is interpreted. Before

1880 the day's work of an agricultural labourer in the Po Valley, the most fertile provinces of Italy, was paid a rate of about 1 lira for men and 50 cents for women. This was something the Honourable Giovanni Giolitti, the former prime minister, recalled more than once in Parliament. There were many causes, but one specifically deserves to be remembered: the penal code of the day considered strikes a crime, agreements among workers a crime and inciting a strike an even greater crime.

How could workers, one by one, state their case? In wage-bargaining, they were in a weaker condition than the owners, who, being few, could easily agree among themselves without letting anyone know and keep wages low. Workers went on strike all the same. There were famous trials, among them the one in Mantua, that drew Parliament's attention to the injustice of the code.

The new penal code of 1889, named after Luigi Zanardelli, the Minister of Justice who proposed it, abolished the crime of striking. Agreements became lawful; only acts of *physical or moral violence* intended to prevent those who did *not* want to strike from going to work were prohibited. And this is fair, since everyone must be free to work or not to work, as he pleases, if we do not want to see slavery reborn.

> The result was that workers began to strike freely and wages rose. The owners complained for a while, but in the end they had to admit that every cloud has a silver lining. Under the pressure of higher wages, they had to use improved machinery and adopt more modern production methods in their factories if they did not want to go to rack and ruin. In the countryside they began using chemical fertilizers, applied more rational crop rotations, introduced mowing machines, mechanical reapers, tractor ploughs; and by producing more they were able to pay higher wages. This is how a modification of the penal code helped to bring more corn and cattle to market, to lower prices, to raise wages.

The analysis of the phenomenon offered by the Honourable Giolitti, with his usual method of extreme simplification, was perhaps not entirely exact. It cannot be said that the legalization of trade unions and strikes and the action of trade unions and strikes were the decisive cause of the increase in wages, the adoption of agricultural machinery and the improvement of Italian agriculture after 1890. Here, again, it is necessary to avoid making the mistake of believing that it is sufficient for workers *to demand* something and to strike and to organize in order to obtain what they want. Just as industrialists and farmers cannot set the prices they want, so workers cannot obtain the wages they want. Ultimately, the market commands both sides. Nevertheless, the market must take account of the changes that have taken place in the world. Those peasants of the area around Mantua and the Lombard lowland who were paid a lira a day were wretchedly poor, unschooled, expected little and perhaps produced even less. The peasants of the next generation, able to understand each other and join together, to care for the common cause, to resist with their unions what they considered acts of arrogance, were people of a different sort, who had begun to appreciate schooling, even technical and agricultural education, and, knowing they were worth more, demanded to be paid more! It is natural that wages rose.

The workers arriving on the market were new and different. So too were the farmers who employed them: able to apply new farming methods, to obtain more output. With the givens of the problem changed, the results changed and there were higher wages, increased output, higher incomes from land and higher land prices.

Later, another government came and it took away the workers' right to strike and replaced it with corporations that claimed to reconcile the interests of all classes. In reality, that system represented the interest and will of a single person and of the group around him. Although I do not wish to get into politics here, I must at least express the doubt that the new system benefited the nation, or producers, or workers or consumers.

20 The influence of the access of all to apprenticeship and education

Since we are talking about wages, let us further discuss a fact that may have caught your attention. Bank office-boys, shop clerks (not the old, experienced, trusted ones who keep the shop but the young ones who run errands), hotel lift-boys and bicycle delivery boys are often badly paid. They receive plenty of cuffs on the head but precious little money. They spend the best years of their lives in this way and, after performing military service, if the barracks have not improved them, are no longer fit to run errands and have to adapt to every sort of trade. Trades of the sort that anyone can perform, that do not require much education, a long apprenticeship, and are the worst paid of all. And yet if they had not had to begin running errands at age 15, they too could have learned some good trade, with greater apprenticeship and educational requirements but also more secure and better paid.

The explanation given is always the same: the boy's parents were poor and had to put him to work immediately. And boys, as everyone knows, like to race about on a bicycle and to strut when they open the lift-door in their handsome uniform with shining buttons, all the more so if they also have some money in their pocket and receive tips. Then, when they are old, they pay for it. This explanation does not always hold; sometimes the boy's parents were not poor but drunkards or uncaring and unable to guide their children. Be that as it may, there is something wrong with the education of so many boys and girls and with the wages that are consequently formed in the market. Suppose that instead of being forced or lured into working too soon, those boys and girls had been able to continue to study, to attend a technical or vocational school or perhaps even a grammar school, according to their inclination. Suppose that all willing youngsters could study until their desire to learn was satisfied, without encouraging the lazybones who only want to warm a school bench; that a modest, sufficient scholarship were given to all those who desired one and showed, by hard study, that they deserved the aid offered; would they not have entered the labour market at the age of 18, 20, 25 as technicians able to design and run machines, industrial chemists, accountants able to keep the books, peasants able to prune fruit trees, experts in horticulture, floriculture, the cross-breeding of livestock and poultry, etc., etc.; in short, people capable of contributing to the growth of production and deserving much higher wages than those to which a poor devil can aspire who is no longer able to run errands and carry packages but can only do what anyone can? And note that there would be fewer of those who continued to carry packages and perform common chores, so that their jobs would be more secure and better paid. Can it be excluded that one or another of these young people, having the chance to study, will not make some great discovery? Even without exaggerating this possibility, and bearing in mind that those who truly have the spark of genius succeed not too infrequently in finding their path through the hardest experiences, it must be acknowledged that sometimes the difficulties the poor face are so large that no 'where there's a will there's a way' can surmount them. Here we see how a poor or a good educational system, how the possibility offered only to some or to all to follow the different stages of education, from primary school to middle school to higher, university education, can influence economic life, the formation of prices, wages, salaries and profits, and how it can slow or stimulate the production of wealth. Enormous strides were made in education during the last century and in the present one. Let us recall this, to avoid making the mistake of thinking that nothing was done in the past. From the day in which almost everyone in Italy was illiterate to today, when illiteracy is the exception, great progress has been made indeed. And it is precisely this progress that convinces us of the equally important steps forward that remain to be made. It is a serious mistake to think it is detrimental to have so many people study. There can never be too many, as long as some people between the ages of 20 and 25 have not had the opportunity to study as much as they wanted and could. The trouble does not lie in too much education, just as it does not lie in producing too many goods. There are never too many goods in the world. What is necessary is that there not be too many of one kind but not enough of another. By the same token, as regards education, the trouble does not lie in there being too many educated people, but in there being too many lawyers but not enough doctors, too many designers but not enough accountants, too many peasants growing cereals but not enough growing potatoes, and so on.

21 Conclusion: the market's task and how it can be guided

Offering appropriate indications; saying what must be done and what must not be done; guiding producers, industrialists, farmers, tradesmen towards branches of work where there is relative scarcity and turning them away from those in which there is relative abundance by comparison with the existing demand for the corresponding products; teaching young people or their parents what kind of education is most suitable at a given time: the market does all this. It does it by causing the prices of goods produced in overabundance to fall and those of which there is a scarcity to rise. It does this by raising the wages of workers for whom demand is greater and lowering those of overcrowded trades. It does it by giving profits to entrepreneurs who discover new goods or provide services demanded by the public and bankrupting those who produce bad products for which there is no demand or produce at too high a cost.

The market cannot be left to itself, however. Lawmakers, that is to say we who must elect those who make the laws, know that the market can be distorted by monopolies. The little trenches that each producer digs around himself to protect himself against competitors are harmless; we can tolerate, indeed we are not displeased, that a kind shopkeeper, with good words, courteous smiles and cordial thanks, may exercise a kind of monopoly of customers, to the detriment of a grumpy and rude one. But we can prevent the real monopolists from raising prices, diminishing production and making fat profits.

And we can and must make the market use its ability to regulate the production and distribution of wealth within certain limits, limits we consider fair and in conformity with our ideals of a society in which all men have a chance to develop their potential in the best way and in which excessive inequalities of wealth and income do not exist – without arriving at absolute equality, compatible only with the life of the ant colony and the beehive, which for humans are called tyrannies, dictatorships, totalitarian regimes. We must therefore give ourselves good laws and institutions, create a good educational system that is accessible and suited to the various human capacities, and instil sound customs. We must therefore seek to be conscious human beings, desirous of enlightenment and education, and we must, in a noble competition, set our sights high. The market, which is already an astonishing mechanism, giving its best results within the limits of existing institutions, customs and laws, can yield even more astonishing results if we succeed in perfecting and reforming the institutions, customs and laws within which it operates, in order to attain higher ideals.

We can if we want to.

3
The Beauty of the Struggle*

Rereading the articles on labour problems that the publisher Piero Gobetti[1] asked me to recover from the journals and newspapers in which I had published them from 1897 onwards, I realized that they all conformed to a set of fundamental notions, to which – despite the occasional nature of the articles, written in response to circumstances that changed from day to day – I see, with a certain forgivable satisfaction, that I have remained faithful: an irreducible scepticism, almost physical repugnance, with regard to benefits provided from the outside, to the well-being that it is intended to procure for workers through laws, regulations, collectivism, paternalism, the intermediation of ill-employed politicians ready to settle disputes by arbitration, by the intervention of specialists, by cutting the loaf in half; and a heartfelt approval of the efforts of those who desire to elevate themselves on their own and in this struggle, fight, falter, and rise again, learning at their own expense how to win and to better themselves. Scientific socialism and Russian collectivism, as schemes for the organization of society or attempts to apply them in practical terms, do not interest me. They amount to less than nothing. By contrast, the socialist sentiment, of the kind that permitted the workers in the Biella area and the port of Genoa to proudly raise their heads, and persuaded them to reach out to their fellow workers – to think, to debate, to read – was indeed something great, which left its mark on Italian history. Collectivism is an ideal good for drudges with sleevelets and serves only to make people die of hunger and boredom. They are pure socialists, of the boring kind, those who want to see labour issues resolved by impartial arbitrators charged with balancing the scales of justice fairly, and labour laws drawn up by higher councils, in which, alongside and above the two contending parties, the specialists, the

*First published as 'La bellezza della lotta', *Rivoluzione Liberale*, II, n.40 (18 December 1923), pp.161–2, then included in Luigi Einaudi, *Le lotte del lavoro* (Turin: Piero Gobetti Editore, 1924).

experts, the erudite and the uncommitted, teach the contestants the rules of impeccable etiquette.

Nowadays bureaucratic ideals are back in vogue. Under another name, the aspiration of the leaders of fascist corporations to identify a method, a principle, to force owners and workers to get along, is the same collectivist ideal of old. The battle waged to teach workers that Leninist internationalism was a destructive idea and that the nation was a condition of civil society, was sacrosanct; but the belief that the perfect idyll between industrialists and workers can be achieved on earth under the guidance of some interpreter authorized to act in the supreme national interest is a purely bureaucratic-communistic notion. Many are unwitting socialists; just as many of those who called themselves socialists or led workers' movements against industrialists were instead pure liberals. An industrialist is liberal when he has faith in his own spirit of initiative and joins with his colleagues to negotiate with workers or to buy and sell together; he is a pure socialist when he asks the State to impose protective duties. A worker believes in freedom and is liberal when he joins with his comrades to create a common instrument for cooperation or protection; he is socialist when he invokes an exclusive privilege from the State in favour of his own organization or calls for a law or court judgment to prohibit strikebreakers from working. Liberal is he who believes in material or moral improvement achieved through voluntary effort, sacrifice and willingness to work in harmony with others; socialist is he who desires to impose improvement through force, who will not allow it when obtained using any other methods than those he prefers, who does not know how to win without privileges and without orders excluding the reprobates. The names do not matter; the ideal remains intrinsically the same, however it is labelled.

Today the labour question in Italy has changed name: instead of red or white or yellow federations and local labour committees, we speak of fascist corporations. What substantial contribution have they made to the labour question? I mean the principles, not the details. It is unimportant that in many instances the corporations behave in the same way as the red antagonists, that they too at times resort to violence against opponents, strikebreakers, or the followers of other faiths, and that they declare anathemas or boycotts against others, or aspire to monopolies. These might be shortlived fortuities, that have no part in the doctrine. What this doctrine is I would attempt to clarify as follows:

> The principle of the struggle between the two classes of owners and workers is detrimental to production. Each of the two adversaries imagines it can achieve maximum benefit by destroying and expropriating its opponent. The owner attempts to reduce the worker's wage to a minimum; the worker wants to annul the return on capital. As a result of the struggle and the oppression of one party by the other, both are damaged in the long run, and above all the nation is damaged. Production falls and therefore society is made poorer; the State is weak-

> ened externally and crumbles internally. The Corporation comes into being to combat this suicidal conduct. Its very name asserts the idea of construction, of deference to the higher principle of the nation, to which class interests must sacrifice themselves. The Corporation does not sacrifice the worker to the industrialist; nor the industrialist to the worker; rather it aims to reconcile the two hitherto hostile groups in a higher synthesis. The workers' and employers' corporations must remain distinct and independent one from the other; but, while safeguarding its own interests, each must be aware of the need to avoid injuring the industry and weakening the nation. If the two corporations fail to reach a productive agreement, there must be someone who, at the critical moment, pronounces the last word, declares a fair solution which all must accept.
>
> The arbitrator must have the mentality neither of the employer nor of the worker. He must be someone who is guided by national needs, schooled in the doctrine of sacrificing today for tomorrow, able to produce a synthesis of the conflicting views and interests of the two parties whose sole aim is immediate gain.

The doctrine outlined here is a new formulation, using different terminology, of theories which from time to time have attempted to recover the unity lost as a result of conflicts between men and classes. Is it not perhaps true that the economic harmonies of Bastiat, the theory of economic equilibrium, are other attempts at synthesis, efforts to identify the point in the market at which, for an instant, the forces balance each other out and obtain the most felicitous result for the collectivity? Economists, as is their wont, speak of equilibrium, of prices, of the market, of maximum satisfaction. The theorists of corporations speak of the nation and the subjection of classes to the superior will that embodies the interest of the nation. The terminology differs, the content is substantially the same.

The problem is not to deny the possibility of an equilibrium between the opposing forces, which would be absurd. Rather, it is how to identify a method by which this equilibrium can be reached at the lowest cost, and with the least amount of friction. It is not even necessary for this purpose to choose one formula over another; direct negotiations, unions, corporations, arbitration, even the taking in hand of the situation by a person in a position of authority to extricate the parties from the dead-end they have reached can all be useful to arrive at equilibrium. The ideal of the nation or that of the collective interest, the dream of cooperative or shared ownership, are all formulas able to lead to equilibrium. But they are also instrumentalities that will only be effective and productive when adopted in favourable conditions.

These conditions cannot be specified once and for all. I list below some of the most frequent scenarios.

Equilibrium attained through debate and struggle is preferable to that imposed by an external force. The solution imposed by the owner, the government, the judge, the officially appointed arbitrator may be the best; but it is looked upon with suspicion precisely because it comes from others. Man desires to know the motives behind decisions and to have the illusion of deciding voluntarily. People must be left to bruise their heads if they are to realize they are up against a wall and that it is useless to try to butt it down. Through struggle and debate one learns how to measure the adversary's strength, to understand his reasons, to fathom the working of the system that allows both rivals to exist.

A stable equilibrium is more easily obtained by a technician than a politician. In other words, to entrust the resolution of labour issues to a minister, prefect, fascist fiduciary or enlightened conservative Member of Parliament is a sign of a limited knowledge of industry. The solution towards which the politician tends serves to promote political and not economic equilibrium. Factors linked to external tranquillity, electoral jockeying and the conciliation of political groups all come into play. Since the equilibrium based on purely economic factors would be different, one or other of the parties or both seek compensation for the loss they are saddled with by obtaining economic favours from the political authorities: 'fair' treatment is coupled with an increase in transport subsidies, the control of factories by workers is behind the customs tariff of July 1921, the small concessions wrung out of prefects preferring the quiet life are sweetened by the knightly honours that industrialists, who knows why, are so fond of. The damage caused to the economic equilibrium is always short-lived. Somebody always pays the bill.

The training of technicians capable of solving labour issues is achieved through conflict, the more open and fair the better.

Orator fit. The good arbitrator is not made through books, in electoral meetings, in prefectures, in political groups or in parliaments. Only the worker at the mine or in the factory knows the life of work; only the industrialist knows glory and takes pride in his undertaking. Too many lawyers, petty politicians, clever, accommodating, solution-driven men have ruined the Italian workers' movement. There have been too few plain-spoken men, ready to tear each other apart, but also ready to listen to what deep down in their souls they shared: love of a job well done, pride in a masterpiece, the desire to bring it perfect into the world. Only through face-to-face discussions can these two breeds of men acknowledge each other's sovereignty: the first with respect to the direction, organization and invention of the enterprise; the other with respect to its own capacity to work. Sovereignty over bricks, machines or goods does not count. It is an inanimate thing, that lives only because the organizer and the worker recognize and turn to account the contribution each makes to the common undertaking. It is right that each should jealously guard the exclusive dominion over his own task which is, for the industrialist, that of organizing the business, and for the worker, that of providing manual or intellectual labour. It is right that each should be highly resentful of the meddling of the other in its sphere. The tired industrialists who resign themselves to being controlled by their employees, the workers without pride who entrust the safeguarding of their work to fiduciaries from outside their own ranks, are half-men. You cannot build a future with insignificant men like these. Granted, they may make money, but industry will not be furthered, and neither will the value of human personality be enhanced.

For equilibrium to last, it must be under constant threat of not lasting. Those who wish to read the pages of this book will see for themselves how long-standing is my repugnance for owners' and workers' monopolies. At a certain point, the red unions, realizing that they had become powerful in a world of cowardly bourgeois, amidst magistrates who were only too willing to do favours rather than hand down sentences, wanted to be the only ruler of labour: they denied the white and yellow unions the right to exist, they claimed for themselves the exclusive right to elect representatives to the Supreme Labour Council and set out to deny the right of Parliament to modify the decisions of the Labour Council, which had fallen under their control. It presaged their ruin. Today the fascist corporations appear to be preparing to make the same error. They too deny the right of defeated rivals to exist and one by one expel them from cooperatives, local labour committees and councils and from Parliament. *Solitudinem faciunt et pacem appellant.** Today, especially today, it is necessary to rebut the claim that equilibrium exists in monopolies, in the *de jure* or *de facto*† suppression of adversaries. In the opening essays of this volume I described the struggles of some groups of Italian workers in 1897 and 1900. So long after the event, recalling those youthful years when I participated in the workers' rallies on the terraces of Via Milano in Genoa, or exchanged pleasantries in the evenings in humble *tavern* in Biellese villages with weavers, I am both elated and moved. They were the heroic years of the Italian workers' movement. Those who witnessed with horror, in 1919 and 1920, the looting bloodthirsty crowds in the streets of the major Italian cities no longer recognized the sons of those men, who from 1890 to 1900 were born into collective life, understood their intrinsic human dignity, and believed they had to make themselves worthy of the high humanistic goal to which they aspired. The diabolic spirit of domination introduced by petty politicians who emerged from the dregs of bourgeois society overwhelmed them and led them to their ruin. Those workers who earlier, through persecution and jail, had headed the movement of their own class, were replaced from 1919 to 1921 by the passionate youths who called on Italians to rebel against Bolshevism. Now that they have attained absolute power, the thrill of being in command threatens to destroy what they accomplished. If the

*They create a desert and call it peace [Tacitus, *Agricola* §30].

†In point of law or as a matter of fact.

equilibrium is to last, it must be constantly in doubt. No legal authority must intervene to crystallize the forces in play, or to prevent new forces from emerging against the old ones, against the blessed incumbents. If industrialists are to render real services to the collectivity, the State must not grant them the privilege of serving the collectivity, safeguard them with protective duties against foreign competition, or organize them into consortiums closed to newcomers. If workers are to elevate themselves both morally and materially, it is important that at any time the red organizers can challenge the white ones, and these both the communist and the fascist ones and the yellow ones as well, and that they all be in constant dread of the emergence of rival standard bearers. It has become fashionable nowadays to scoff at the aim of inculcating competition in the world of owners' and workers' organizations; and the fascist corporations are held up by way of example, so fervently opposed to monopoly so long as this was in communist hands, but who now that they have the power to do so, claim it for themselves. Attempts are made to demonstrate that this is not just the result of political arrogance, but of precise economic calculation, given that only through a single and monopolistic organization can workers obtain the maximum benefit. This last point requires no discussion, because it is not the issue.

Let workers and employers go ahead and establish, if they can, a monopoly of labour or of business. The only thing not permitted is that the State legally sanction the monopoly itself, forbidding others from fighting it and destroying it, if they are bold enough. This is the crucial point, not whether the monopoly is beneficial. So long as the monopoly, be it the employer's or the workers', is free, so long as anyone can criticize it and try to demolish it, there may be some harm; but it is likely to be limited and short-lived. The necessary condition for lasting equilibrium, of advantage to the collectivity, of advantage not only to organized employers and workers but also to those that are not organized, not only to those alive today but also to those who will live in the future, is not the actual existence of competition. The only thing that must be asked of the State is that it create the conditions for all people to enter the contest, that it allow everyone the possibility of nullifying the monopoly of others. The possibility accorded by law of nullifying the monopoly is what lends it strength, if indeed it is truly useful to the group and perhaps to the collectivity, since its survival, despite the freedom of each person to combat it, is the only convincing demonstration of its right to exist. Indeed, what merit or virtue can be ascribed to those who, in order to live, invoke the sword of the secular authority?

In practice, moreover, when they have not been made obligatory by the State, organizations do not maintain a monopoly for long. The history of industrial consortiums and trade unions is a kaleidoscope of rises and falls, of perpetual transformation. At every turn they must demonstrate that they deserve the support of their members. And it is impossible, without the help of the secular authority, that they demonstrate this for long. Finding themselves at the head of a powerful organization, men are too selfish or wicked or ignorant not to succumb to the temptation of personal gain at the expense of those they represent, or not to rest on their laurels, or not to tyrannize those excluded from the dominant group. To rejuvenate the organization, make it once more operational and beneficial to members and outsiders alike, it must be continuously assaulted and besieged by *de facto* rivals or by the fear of their arrival. The equilibrium, referred to in books on economics, the supremacy of the nation which is invoked today, are not fixed ideals. They are ideals precisely because they cannot be attained, because man struggles constantly to reach a goal, which, once it appears to have been reached, is found to be higher and further away. Equilibrium consists in a succession of continuous uninterrupted improvements, through fluctuations, which give victory now to one, now to the other, of the conflicting forces. The joy of labour for the worker and of victory for the employer consists also in the danger of losing the positions gained and in the pleasure of the effort that must be made first to defend them and then to win new ground. Take away the danger, end the combat and the joy of living, of possessing, of working becomes different from what men have considered to be real joy from the French Revolution onwards. Not that the 'quiet' of those who desire nothing more than to enjoy what they possess cannot also be an ideal and its achievement noble. In a chapter of this book I have described the happy life of the Neapolitan idler in the wonderful eighteenth century, which was truly the golden age of contented living, good taste, tolerance, and amiability. Unfortunately, human nature is such that it finds the quiet, tranquil life repugnant in the long run. If it lasts too long, it is the quiet of slavery, the mortification of the spirit. The struggle that is life is preferable to the quiet that is death.

4
Economic Liberalism and Political Liberalism*

Einaudi outlined his idea of liberalism in response to Benedetto Croce's views on the birth of the 'religion of freedom' in Europe between 1815 and 1848. While praising Croce's stimulating ideas and vast culture, Einaudi differed on the intrinsic meaning of economic liberalism and of the empirical concept of 'laissez faire'. In his view, Croce was too dismissive of these concepts, denying that they could lead to a refusal to accept, as a matter of principle, the occasional socialization of some means of production.

In current language, used above all in the writings of laymen, what is held to be 'economic liberalism' is instead a purely *abstract* manner of reasoning characteristic of economic science by virtue of its being science and hence abstraction. If the economist writes, '*Let us suppose* that the contracting parties act in a free market in which there is competition between many sellers and between many buyers', laymen believe that because the economist has adopted such a premise he is 'also' an economic liberal in practice. But the economist also adopts different premises, as when he writes, '*Let us suppose* that in the free market there is only one seller and there are many buyers'; or when he postulates '*Let us suppose* that in a market with a single buyer and many sellers the market is not free but regulated by the state according to the criterion, say, of the maximum collective utility.' In the first case, the reasoner starts out from the 'premise' of free competition; in the second, from that of pure private monopoly; in the third, from that of public monopoly. The reasoner may believe in economic liberalism

*First published as 'Dei diversi significati del concetto di liberismo economico e dei suoi rapporti con quello di liberalismo', in *Riforma Sociale*, XXXVIII, Vol. XLII, Nos 3–4 (March–April 1931), pp.186–94. It was later republished under the new title 'Liberismo e liberalismo' in various different collections of essays in 1933, 1954 and 1957. Einaudi was answering to what was going to be published as the first chapters of Benedetto Croce, *Storia d'Europa nel secolo XIX* (Bari: Laterza, 1932). See Croce and Einaudi, *Liberismo e liberalismo*, ed. by Paolo Solari (Milan and Naples: Ricciardi editore, 1957).

or communism or some other faith. We know nothing of this in the sphere of scientific reasoning, where the only thing that matters is to pose appropriate premises for rigorous, abstract reasoning and to draw all the inferences they contain. The premise of the free market or of self-seeking individual agents is not an 'economic' principle; it is a pure tool of reasoning and has an exclusively abstract value. All economic science is and can only be a pure abstraction. No one can dominate all the factors of reality, in their multiplicity and continuous variability, and so it is obligatory to construct abstract schemas, manipulating a very small number of factors. Successive generations of economists have flattered themselves that they can gradually increase the number of factors manipulated and manipulate them with ever more sophisticated constructs. Woe to them if they did not entertain this illusion! Woe to them if they were not propelled by enthusiasm into thinking that they had sometimes come close to reality thanks to their choice of significant factors! In the midst of their labours, discouragement would set in and clip the wings of insightful imagination. The hiatus between abstract construct and reality remains unbridgeable for science; it can only be bridged by the politician's instinct and the historian's vision.

The abstract liberalist hypothesis of the type 'Let us suppose that ...' can turn into a *preceptive formulation* when the economist is asked to solve a concrete problem on the basis of pure economic reasoning. A terrible demand, which the economist would be right to evade, knowing well that pure economic reasoning cannot solve concrete problems. However, his sense of duty to the public interest is often stronger, and morally should always be stronger, than his scientific scruples; and so he is led to make his contribution to the desired solution, alongside and at the same time as the physicist, the chemist, the jurist, the historian, the philosopher, and the politician, who encompasses, or should encompass, them all.

In the face of concrete problems, the economist can never be a liberalist or an interventionist or a socialist at any cost. From time to time he opposes protective customs duties, because he believes that economic activity is maximized when the path is open without limits to competition from foreign goods; he supports laws limiting work by women and children, the prohibition of night work, compensation for industrial accidents, old-age pensions, because he considers these legislative curbs and safeguards effective means of increasing labour productivity; he is against universal socialization, because he predicts it would diminish the interest in producing, but he wants the state to consider the railways a public industry, considering private monopoly of the means of transport detrimental to the collectivity. And so forth: each problem will give rise to a specific solution, dictated by an appropriate calculation of advantage. If the solution is liberalist, it wins out not because it is liberalist but because it is more advantageous than the others. The advantage of a solution, evident on the basis of given premises, vanishes if the premises change. It is well known that by pure economic reasoning protectionism is preferable to free trade in certain cases involving infant industries (Hamilton, J.S. Mill) or temporary price reductions due to the exploitation of new territories or new inventions. In theory, the question is settled in favour of temporary protection. Rare, however, is the economist who after expounding the theory does not immediately add that practical prudence advises against applying the abstract conclusion. For it is very difficult, if not impossible, to discover, among the host of applicants, which young industry, assisted in its first years by customs duties against foreign competition, will eventually stand on its own feet; even harder to discern which is to be protected temporarily, because the foreign competition that would kill it today is destined soon to disappear and it is better to spare the country the loss of the capital invested today in the national industry and then the cost of its reconstruction once the danger has passed; and well-nigh unthinkable, lastly, omitting all else, that an industry temporarily protected on these grounds will admit that it has grown up or that the cloud that threatened it has passed. We are still dealing with the case of economic liberalism based on the calculation of advantage, but the calculation is more complex and takes a greater number of factors into account.

The frequency of the cases in which economists, for contingent reasons, tend to recommend liberalist solutions has led to the maxim of economic liberalism taking on a third – I would call it a religious – meaning. In this interpretation, 'economic liberals' are those who accept the maxim of laissez-faire, laissez-passer almost as if it were a universal principle, those who contend that the free action of the individual, guided by self-interest, always coincides with the collective interest. Some phrases of Adam Smith:

> Every individual is continually exerting himself to find out the most advantageous employment for whatever capital he can command. It is his own advantage, indeed, and not that of the society, which he has in view. But the study of his own advantage naturally, or rather necessarily, leads him to prefer that employment which is most advantageous to the society ... By promoting his own interest he frequently promotes that of the society more effectually than when he really intends to promote it ... He intends only his own gain, and he is in this, as in many other cases, led by an invisible hand to promote an end which was no part of his intention.[1]

Have given rise to the belief that the identification of the individual's interest with the general interest was an inherent 'principle' of economic science. However, too many are the places in which Smith himself insists on the opposition of interests between class and class, between individuals and the collectivity; too many are those in which he lists the reasons for state intervention to achieve ends either unattainable by or conflicting with individual action, to warrant ascribing to Smith's phrases anything more than a value that is historical (the 'invisible hand' recalls the 'Divine

Providence' or 'Nature' of the various terminologies used in his day) or linked to specific problems of the times he is discussing. The whole subsequent history of the doctrine demonstrates that economic science, as clarified earlier, has nothing to do with the religious conception of economic liberalism.

Yet I would not say that the religious conception of economic liberalism has no practical value. On the contrary, this value can be very great indeed. Faced with the custom of asking everything from the state, of putting all trust in collective action, great benefit comes from the economic liberal rising proudly to accuse the interventionist of sloth and the protectionist of greed. With science ruled out, in practical and political life the moral figure of the economic liberal towers a thousand spans over his opponents. Without him, the state would not limit itself to performing its proper tasks and complementing individual action where this is advantageous, but, by intervening in economic affairs at the behest of the foxes and fools, would harm the collectivity.

There is a nexus between the abstract, the preceptive and the religious conceptions of economic liberalism. Normally, one arrives at the liberalist precept through abstract reasoning. The believer in economic liberalism embraces that faith after being persuaded, with much or little abstract reasoning, that for all the concrete problems known to him the solutions other than the liberalist ones have been harmful to the collectivity (there are some exceptions even for the believer, but, since their importance is minimal, he soon forgets them). Furthermore, all three conceptions have this in common: that they pertain to the sphere of the economy and are not necessarily linked with the liberal vision of the world.

The economic liberal can be an advocate of an absolutist government; the best-known example of this remains the free-trade policy inaugurated in France by Napoleon III on the advice of Chevalier and against the criticisms of Thiers and other political liberals, who then did away with it under the Third Republic. And the reverse can be true: a political liberal can also be an economic liberal, as was Count Cavour in Piedmont between 1850 and 1860, against the opposition of the reactionaries, who were also protectionists.

However, there is one last conception of economic liberalism, one that I would call *historical* and that is so closely coupled, almost united with political liberalism, that it is nearly impossible to separate the two. Croce almost suggests that if 'the course of historical events led to the crossroads between harming or reducing the production of wealth by preserving the capitalist system, that is to say private property, and guaranteeing and increasing production by abolishing private property, ... liberalism would have no choice but to approve and advocate that abolition' (p.33).[2] An admission that Croce immediately overturns in one of his finest pages by observing that even if it were true that communism enriched men materially, it would impoverish them spiritually, reducing them to what Leonardo da Vinci called 'passageways for food'. The admission, even if immediately negated, remains too frightening, however, not to raise some doubts. I would formulate these as follows: would a liberalism that accepted the abolition of private property and the establishment of communism on grounds of its hypothetically greater capacity to produce material goods still be liberalism? In other words, can the essence of liberalism, spiritual liberty, exist where private property does not exist and everything belongs to the state? I am well aware that it is very difficult to define where private property ends and state property begins. Indeed, it is possible to conceive of a communism in which the state owns nothing and does not directly manage any property; the current economic structure of Russia, is, for example, very far from the legal absorption of all property in the state. And, on the other hand, there can be a legal regime of private property in which the state is all-powerful and private owners are *de facto* officials of the state. I do not want to discuss words here but substance, the gist of which is that if communism really exists, then forces independent from the state cannot exist. There can only be a single will directing and determining the production and distribution of economic goods. The single will can, according to circumstances, act by means of bureaucratic organs of a single centralized administration or autonomous bodies or cooperatives or even limited liability company concession-holders. The chosen instrument of action does not matter. What is essential to the life of the system is that the instruments of action must not have a will of their own, different and independent from that of the state and of the political group embodying the state. If the will is single, the ideals of the communist state can be attained: maximization of material wealth or social welfare defined in the manner imposed by the dominant doctrine, distribution according to need or merit or a given combination of need and merit and still other criteria. By contrast, if the wills are plural and independent from each other; if, even with private property formally abolished, the 'cooperative' or the 'autonomous entity' (in Russia they call it a 'public trust') or the 'company holding a concession' has a power of its own deriving from the will of its members or workers, the collectivist organization is dead. In its place there are living organisms that intend to achieve their own ends, advantageous to the particular collectivity and not necessarily coinciding with the ends that the state deems beneficial for the general collectivity.

If the will is single and the collectivist society is perfect, there can be only one ideology, one spiritual creed. There can be no tolerance for competing ideologies, heresies which are as many independent forces that necessarily intend to destroy and supplant the dominant ideology, forces far more effective than material or formal ones because they are rooted in the spirit. Communism, then, cannot tolerate freedom of thought, which would rapidly undermine and transform it. Communism can admit technical criticism; and from what one reads in the writings of knowledgeable observers, technical criticism is widely admitted and, indeed, encouraged in Bolshevik Russia. In truth, technical criticism is inoffensive, because it starts out from the current Russian ideology's basic premise that the aim of life is to achieve the maximum total quantity of output in a given unit of time. Criticism at the level of principles, criticism that argues that the aim of life is not the one just mentioned, that there can be as many aims of life as there are social bodies, groups and units, is neither admitted nor admissible. It is heresy, and the leadership is well aware of this, knowing that if the legally recognized groups, 'autonomous entities', 'cooperatives', 'autonomous republics' of the USSR are given the freedom to determine their own aims, these will inevitably multiply; the groups will splinter and the multiplication of aims and groups will reach down to the level of the family and the individual. The will of each individual will rise again to oppose the collective will: each individual will once again conceive of life and its aims differently from the others and from the collectivity. Communist universality will end and liberty will bloom again.

Thus, liberalism cannot – not even as a figure of speech – assist conceptually at the advent of a communist economic order, as Croce appears to admit. It rejects it out of absolute incompatibility. Freedom of the spirit, freedom of thought, cannot exist where there is and must be but a single will, a single creed, a single ideology. If by freedom of thought one does not mean only the freedom to think and meditate – and even this freedom is mortified under these circumstances; if it implies the freedom to communicate one's thoughts to others, that freedom cannot exist under communism. Freedom of thought is therefore necessarily associated with a certain dose of economic liberalism, which does not signify – note well – linking it with just any one of the three technical meanings of economic liberalism given above. The historical conception of economic liberalism says that freedom cannot live in an economic society in which there does not exist a varied and rich efflorescence of human lives animated by their own vitality, independent from each other, not serfs of a single will. In other words, and to leave no opening to accusations of making the life of the spirit depend on the economy, the free spirit creates an economy consonant with itself and therefore cannot create a communist economy, which is an economy enslaved to an idea, whatever the idea, imposed by a will that by definition and *raison d'être* is intolerant of any other will. The spirit, if it is free, creates a varied economy in which there is coexistence of private property and the property of groups, bodies, state administrations; coexistence of classes of industrialists, tradesmen, farmers, professionals, artists, different from each other, all of them drawing the material means of life from their own sources, capable of living in poverty, if necessary, but without having to beg for alms from a single power, be it the state, a tyrant, a dominant class, or a priesthood intolerant of any but the orthodox faith.

In the free or liberal society, the individual, the family, the class, the group, the business concern, the charitable foundation, the school, the artisans' or workers' league must receive the consecration of legality from a supreme organ, called the state; but they must feel and believe they are living, and effectively live, their own lives, coordinated with the lives of others but not submerged in the life of the collectivity and not dependent on the tolerance of the organ representing the collectivity. How the multitude of vital, autonomous forces are to be made to coexist, how they are to contribute to the life of the collectivity and to the creation of the organ that embodies the universal interest is another question and would lead us far afield. Suffice it to have firmly fixed the point that without the coexistence of many forces animated by their own original spirit, a free society cannot exist, liberalism cannot exist. There can exist a communist society, the irreducible enemy of both economic liberalism and political liberalism.

5
The End of 'Laissez-faire'?*

The earliest written expression of the maxim of *laissez-nous faire*, attributed by tradition to the merchant Legendre in response to a question by Colbert, dates back to around 1751 in the *Journal Oeconomique* of the Marquis d'Argenson: '*Pour gouverner mieux, il faudrait gouverner moins ... La vraie cause de leur (de nos fabriques) declin, c'est la protection outrée qu'on leur accorde ... Laissez-faire, telle devrait être la devise de toute puissance publique, depuis que le monde est civilisé ... Laissez-faire, morbleu! Laissez-faire!!*'† After d'Argenson, the phrase became current in economic debates but it had a difficult time making its way into the economic literature. The tradition associating it with the Physiocrats, and especially with V. de Gournay and Quesnay, finds little support in their writings. The phrase 'laissez-faire' is not to be found in the works of Adam Smith, or Ricardo, or Malthus. Even the idea contained in the phrase is not present in a dogmatic form in any of these authors.

The phrase was first made popular in England by a well-known passage of Franklin's, and it was not until the later works of Bentham, 'who was not an economist at all', that one sees it adapted to the ends of Utilitarian philosophy. From then on, it was put to use in the propaganda tracts of the so-called Manchester school and the Benthamite Utilitarians, in the educational stories of Miss H. Martineau and Mrs Marcet, in the catechistic lessons of Archbishop Whately and in the religious *Credo*, entitled *Harmonies Économiques*, by Frédéric Bastiat.

Economists, starting with John Stuart Mill, were all resolutely opposed to the idea implicit in the phrase 'laissez-faire'. 'Scarcely a single English eco-

---

*First published as 'La fine del "Laissez-faire"?', *La Riforma Sociale*, XXXIII, Vol. XXXVII, Nos 11–12 (November–December 1926), pp.570–3. It was a review of John Maynard Keynes: *The End of Laissez-Faire* (London: The Hogarth Press, 1926).

†To govern better, one should govern less ... The real cause of their (of our factories') decline is the excessive protection they are granted ... Laissez-faire, that should be the motto of every public authority, since the beginnings of the civilised world ... Laissez-faire, for heaven's sake! Laissez-faire!!

nomist of repute', observes Professor Cannan, 'will join in a frontal attack upon Socialism in general', though, as he immediately adds, 'nearly every economist, of repute or not, is always ready to pick holes in most socialistic proposals'. Cairnes, in his introductory lecture on *Economic Policy and Laissez-faire*, delivered at University College London in 1870, was perhaps the first orthodox economist to unleash a frontal attack against laissez-faire in general: 'The maxim of *laissez-faire* has no scientific basis whatever, but is at most a handy rule of practice.' This has been, for 50 years, the opinion of all leading economists. One of the best-known labours of Alfred Marshall – to cite just one instance – had as its object the elucidation of the leading cases in which private interest and social interest are *not* in harmony.

Keynes recalls, with the words of Burke, 'one of the finest problems in legislation, namely, to determine what the State ought to take upon itself to direct by the public wisdom, and what it ought to leave, with as little interference as possible, to individual exertion'. For the State, the Benthamian distinction between *agenda* and *non-agenda*, must be one of the principal tasks of economists. Economists have always insisted – and Keynes insists again, by reproducing their ideas – that the most important *agendas* for the State do not refer to those activities already fulfilled by individuals, but to those functions that fall outside the sphere of the individual, to those decisions that are made by no-one, if the State does not make them. The important thing for government is not to do the things that individuals already do and to do them a little better or a little worse, but to do those things that at present are not done at all.

To the old exemplification of this rule, traditionally found in treatises, Keynes adds a few modern ones:

(a) the need for the deliberate control of the currency and credit by a central institution with the aim of reducing the economic harm of risk, uncertainty, and ignorance, and primarily industrial crises and unemployment;
(b) the dissemination, for the same purpose, of statistical data relative to the economic situation (this dissemination, as it is necessary, must be done by law and requires some 'meddlesome' public intervention in private business);
(c) the determination, partially public, of the *quantum* which must be saved by a country and of that which more advantageously should be exported abroad;
(d) public intervention in the determination of the quantity and quality of the population.

It is also settled doctrine among economists that the State is not always the most suitable body to handle these matters, which nevertheless cannot be totally abandoned to private initiative. This has been much debated and Keynes recalls how out of these debates emerged the advantageousness of entrusting some public tasks to autonomous or semi-autonomous bodies such as universities, banks of issue, port authorities (Port of London Authority), licensed railway companies, etc., etc. Against the ordinary socialist doctrine, which is capable only of talking about nationalization or municipalization, Keynes reaffirms the economists' old sympathy for semi-autonomous bodies and corporations. State socialism, which acts through central government bodies, for which ministers of State are directly responsible, is open to criticism

> because it misses the significance of what is actually happening; because it is, in fact, little better than a dusty survival of a plan to meet the problems of fifty years ago, based on a misunderstanding of what someone said a hundred years ago. Nineteenth-century State Socialism sprang from Bentham, from the concept of free competition, etc., and is in some respects a clearer, in some respects a more muddled version of just the same philosophy as underlies nineteenth-century individualism.

I have quoted this biting passage at length in order to clarify the reasons for the great success achieved by Keynes's little pamphlet. Some considered it almost a manifesto of a new period in the history of economics or of the attitude of economics towards the question of the functions of the State. It would seem that until the appearance of the Keynesian manifesto, economic doctrine had been dominated by the principle of laissez-faire and laissez-passer; a colossus with feet of clay, which lived on solely by virtue of tradition and which would crumble thunderously to the ground only now under the frontal assault led by Keynes.

The foregoing exposition, composed largely of Keynes's own words, demonstrates that he knew quite well that this exaltation of the historic importance of his essay is the pure invention of some slapdash reviewers. The principle of laissez-faire was never part of the scientific apparatus of the great classical economists, and it has been the object of long-standing criticism by leading economists from Stuart Mill to the present. The work of economic science, now more than a century old, has always been aimed at discussing, classifying and systemizing the theory of cases of intervention or non-intervention by the State in the management of economic activities. Keynes's contribution to this century-old endeavour is limited to his insistence on some 'cases' of intervention, which have taken on importance in recent years. Even these 'cases' were not discovered by Keynes, nearly all of them being daily objects of discussion in the technical-economic ephemera. Perhaps the only observation that is really new, or at least expounded by the author in a more finely characteristic way, regards the growing socialization of the 'spirit' with which the great joint-stock institutions are governed. What Keynes says about the lack of concern of the Governor of the Bank of England for its own shareholders is very well written, and very insightful. And it could be extended to many other large joint-stock companies, whose managers look on their shareholders as an almost negligible quantity, dedicating much greater attention to their customers, the State, their employees, their workers, the institution itself. There is a certain amount of literature on this interesting aspect of the contemporary economic structure, but Keynes nevertheless deserves credit for giving vivid prominence to the observation.

The true merit of Keynes's book lies in its brilliant style, in the method, often surprising, of its argumentation; in the shrewd expertise of its historical exposition; in sum, in the great artistry of the writer, which had already won him a place in the front rank and afforded him a degree of success with the general reading public unequalled by the current generation of economists. An artistry so great that it even makes the reader reluctant to take note of some of the explicit observations, summarized above, in which Keynes proclaims that he is saying nothing new but summarizing and pursuing the classical tradition, but is led instead to the ingenuous persuasion that he found himself confronted with a *novum* that closes one era and opens another.

Nevertheless, as a diffident reader, allow me to expound a criticism. Why, after battering down, so usefully and brilliantly, a door that has been open for hundreds of years, and once again driven the rule of laissez-faire from the field as a scientific principle, did Keynes not add a few more pages on the current importance of the maxim as a handy rule of practice? Do the few cases that he recalls of public intervention to regulate and guide and limit the freedom of private enterprise, and the others, varying from era to era, from country to country, which could be added to his list, shake the prominent position of the practical rule in the economic world? Has there been a change, from Adam Smith to Keynes, in the respective proportions of cases of 'agenda' and 'non-agenda?' About this Keynes says nothing; although, the point of principle having been settled from time immemorial, this may be the only really interesting question to study. At first glance, the cases of 'agenda', or of intervention by public bodies, appear to have grown in number and importance compared with the cases of 'non-agenda'. Equally, the methods of intervention by public bodies, again as a first impression, appear to be more varied, and Keynes's enumeration of the different kinds of public action, through autonomous bodies, corporations and semi-public companies is certainly impressive. But are we really sure that the first impression corresponds to historical reality? Do we not run the risk of allowing ourselves to be excessively influenced by the obvious knowledge of present methods, whereas we remember less or appreciate less the number, importance and variety of forms of methods of intervention in days gone by? Are we really sure that the cases of 'agenda' accepted by Adam Smith were not, *for the times of Adam Smith*, more important or not less important than the cases of 'agenda' accepted or proposed by John

Maynard Keynes for our times? Here is a fascinating subject of research for an economist with an interest in history. I pose the question without resolving it. And the question could also be posed in this other manner: has the practical importance of laissez-faire as a rule for human conduct really diminished? The proposition that State intervention has become numerically more frequent may be true; but its truth does not prove the decline of the rule of laissez-faire, since it is quite possible that, contemporaneously with an extension of public activity and interference in some branches of economic life, new kinds of activity, in which the old practical rule of laissez-faire conserves its value intact, have multiplied much more. Rather than criticisms, these observations are meant to be simply an expression of the hope that Keynes will find a way to write many more pamphlets that will be just as instructive and pleasant to read and thought-provoking as this one has been.

Part II
Money and Banking

6
On other Pseudo-commercial and Pseudo-bank Containers*

The article begins with a dialogue between a rationalizer and an observer on the relative merits of dispersed or highly concentrated commercial systems. The rationalizer wishes to reduce the number of small shops and sellers, considering an excessive number of intermediaries to be parasitic and an undue burden on the consumers. The observer defends the role of different types of operators in a segmented market. The former argues that prices are high because too many sellers unload on buyers their inefficient additional costs. Einaudi (who is behind the observer) quotes Federico Le Play and Camillo Benso, Count of Cavour, in order to criticize all forms of governmental regulation reducing competition and consumer choice, first in the specific example of bakers in Paris and then he extends the argument to the banking system in the second part of the article.

THE OBSERVER ... No baker, confectioner or grocer is superfluous if he provides a service, sells good things and sells them well, with a pleasant smile and pleasant words rather than ungraciously. They are all too many if they think that just because they exist and have spent a great deal of money on show windows and counters and lighting and shop-assistants, customers will gladly buy inferior goods at high prices. Price-gougers always sound off about the rights of the category being infringed by those who usurp their trade without having the requisite professional training. The new corporations – precisely because they are different from the old guilds recalled by Le Play, which used to harass governments and judges with their incessant lawsuits for trespasses on their game preserves – must have no truck with shopkeepers, industrialists, artisans who, at loggerheads with their customers, would like to reform their tastes; who insist on the need for fair prices – fair for all and such as ensure producers earn a living and nothing more, provided of course the number of producers is right and access is

*First published as 'Di altri scatoloni pseudo-commerciali e pseudo-bancari', in *Riforma Sociale*, XLII, Vol. XLVI, No. 1 (January–February 1935), pp.1–22.

barred to newcomers without training and qualifications. The real backbone of the new corporations consists of people who work and succeed, and who, succeeding, pay taxes to the State and do not ask the State for favours or subsidies. The criterion for telling good members of the corporations from the bad is success. Those whose firms lose money, their own or their creditors', are not proper tradesmen, not proper industrialists and therefore not proper corporatists. Those who actually provide a service to others make money; those who lose money, except for extreme cases of *force majeure* or accident to be demonstrated with the utmost rigour, do so because they are unable to provide others with a real service.

THE FIRST SPECIALIZER The banks must apply the principles of science. Each must ply its own trade. The public must learn to know what will befall the money it entrusts to banking establishments from their very names. Let 'banks' be those that receive sight or short-term deposits and use them in discounting commercial paper, for advances and end-of-month repurchase agreements on goods and securities and other transactions designed to provide working capital to industrialists and tradesmen. Let 'institutions' be those that take long-term deposits or issue 10, 20 or 50-year bonds and use the proceeds for long-term loans for industrial plants, purchases of machinery, agricultural improvements or the construction of buildings. Safety will only be assured when short-term deposits go hand in hand with short-term loans, medium-term with medium-term, long with long. The maturities on the two sides of the balance sheet must match, so that the banker is always ready to return what he has received at the due date.

THE SECOND SPECIALIZER That is not enough. It is necessary to specialize not only by maturity but also by type of credit. The banker must know his customers. The needs of agriculture differ from those of the electricity industry, and these in turn differ from those of heavy industries such as steel, basic metals and mechanical engineering. Someone who serves textile makers does not know chemical companies inside out, and neither can we expect builders to be served well by someone who knows the shipbuilding industry thoroughly, from shipyard to fitting out. Banks must specialize according to the major cycles and branches of production, with the same criteria as those applied to establish the corporations. Indeed, furthering the general process of self-regulation of economic forces, banking must put itself on an ever more objective footing, shedding the antiquated traits that made it such a strictly personal industry. No longer credit granted personally to the individual client, but credit to the industry that is organized and regulated, so that its continuing activity is assured.

THE THIRD SPECIALIZER That is still not enough. The distribution of credit must be not only by maturity and function; it has to be spatial as well. It is not a question of reviving the hoary few-or-many dispute. There are unquestionably too many banks in Italy. All of them have wanted to harvest the same field, the savings of real savers: the landowners, tenant farmers and peasants of the countryside, the clerks, tradesmen and professional people of the towns and cities, large and small. Hence, thousands of banks and waistcoat-pocket banks and thousands of main branches, branches and sub-branches of the major banks and savings banks scattered throughout every village and city district, all of them intent on pumping out money and funnelling it to the handful of large centres. Dispersed, local, small-scale agriculture, industry and commerce are thus left dry, while capital is offered in abundance to large enterprises for investments big and small, with an excess of speculative investment and ensuing bank failures. It is important to replace this irrational competition among many hoping to graze in the same pasture with a rational spatial distribution of banks, so that an orderly intermeshing is created among small, medium-sized and large banks, independent one from another, and small banks seek to use the savings they collect as far as possible *in loco*, turning to the medium-sized regional banks to lend the amount in excess of local needs and for help in the event of abnormal demand for repayments. The medium-sized regional banks must behave in similar fashion *vis-à-vis* the large commercial banks and the latter likewise *vis-à-vis* the central bank of issue, which, freed from the constraint of direct dealings with agricultural, commercial and industrial customers, will be able to perform exclusively, hence perfectly, its function of bank of banks, the supreme regulator of the country's credit and money.

A FIRST THEORIST SPEAKS Does a difference between long- and short-term lending really exist? What is time in banking? If for a moment we suppose a closed market in which there is a single bank, it is hard to conceive what difference there can be between credit with a maturity of 30 years, 5 years, 6 months or 15 days. In that country there is a requirement of, say, one billion lire of capital, of which L400 million in buildings, railways, ports, canals, agricultural improvements and other fixed plant with an average service life of 30 years, L300 million in machinery that can be depreciated in 5 years, L200 million in raw materials, seeds, tools and work in progress producible on average in 6 months, and L100 million in finished products in the storerooms of producers, wholesalers and retailers that will reach consumers after an average of 15 days. On the basis of this proportional distribution among the various types of use of capital in our imaginary market, which we have arbitrarily chosen just for the sake of example, or taking any other distribution that conforms more closely with reality, it is clear that the L100 million invested in the stocks of finished products ready for consumption are just as 'fixed' as the L400 million invested in buildings, the L300 million in machinery or the L200 million in raw materials. If we suppose, as is commonly supposed and according to theorists must be supposed, that the sole entrepreneur or the many entrepreneurs are pure entrepreneurs, i.e., organizers of the capital and labour of others, and that they work with capital entirely borrowed from the single bank, it is clear that the presumed shortness – 15 days – of lending for finished products compared with the presumed length – 30 years – of lending for buildings or ports, railways or canals, is purely an accounting fiction. It is no more possible to disinvest the L100 million invested in finished products – in bread, butchered meat, bottled wine, finished garments, shoes, umbrellas, etc., etc. – than the L400 million existing in the form of canals, buildings, etc. To disinvest would mean not to give the entrepreneur the means to complete the last link of the economic chain, not to transform flour into bread, hides into shoes, felt into hats, cloth into clothing. This can be done, if it is what one wants. But it is well to remember that this also means halting the production of the intermediate products. Who needs flour if it cannot be turned into bread? And it also means not using the L300 million invested in machinery and the L400 million in fixed plant. If the optimal proportions of the different types of investment are 40, 30, 20 and 10 per cent, the last 10 per cent is just as necessary as the others. On pain of arresting the whole mechanism of production, the bank cannot refuse to renew indefinitely its discounting of the bills representing the L100 million of finished products ready for consumption. These L100 million are immobilized neither more nor less than all the other millions making up the total one billion. The difference between what are commonly called long and short-term loans is therefore not their 'duration'. The nature of the problem does not change if there are a hundred or a thousand banks instead of just one. With many comings and goings the whole set of banks must similarly negotiate long- and short-term loans, never immobilizing itself in either those at long or those at short term. Both the former and the latter must 'turn over'. A bank that by virtue of the nature of its deposits is suited to long-term lending will become immobilized if loans are not repaid on time. By the same token, a bank suited to short-term lending will be immobilized if bills are renewed or reduced instead of being honoured when due. A bank thinking it can save itself from locked-up assets, now commonly called 'frozen credits', by making only 'short-term' loans would be badly mistaken; and any theory that tries to differentiate between banks using the criterion of duration has feet of clay.

A SECOND THEORIST SPEAKS Is it logical for banks to specialize according to the industry they serve? Nobody has ever seen a shoemaker hang up a sign saying: 'Shoes sold only to country-folk'. The townsman would pass it by, snickering: 'Good shoes for stone-calloused, earth-soiled rustic feet.' The suspicious countryman: 'He wants to put one over on me, selling me the city's castoffs!' The wise tradesman sells each customer suitable goods after persuading him that those goods are the best goods made specially for the best of customers (who is always the one with whom the tradesman is speaking). It is not in the interest of any industrialist, or of any banker, to limit his customers to a particular social class at any cost. What will happen if the tastes of that class change? What would happen to the unfortunate banker who specialized in lending to wool makers or silk makers or steel makers, only to see the chosen industry hit by a crisis? Unfortunately, specialization is inevitable in some areas, because the area is all wool or all hats or all furniture. But the prudent banker endowed with common sense will have learnt from past experience to set great store by what we vilified theorists call the theory of offsetting risks. To the greatest extent possible, he will have sought customers outside the dominant branch in his area. He will have acquired safe securities in the nearest stock exchange under repurchase agreements. (In the past the best managers of savings banks made great use of this valuable corrective for the unbalanced nature of their investments. But then they were forbidden to continue for some mysterious reason. Perhaps because the expression 'repurchase agreement' has a speculative air about it and the people in the offices see the devil lurking in certain words and have never read in the dictionary that to 'speculate' means to 'look into the future', which for those who succeed is one of the rarest and happiest virtues a man can possess.) Or he will have fattened his current account at an affiliated bank in another region. Other conditions being equal, the more varied the assets, the wiser the banker and the easier he sleeps. Functional specialization, therefore, is a meaningless phase. A banker who takes it seriously digs his own grave.

AN ECONOMIC HISTORIAN INTERVENES The theory that banks must be few, each in its place – the small ones in small towns, the medium-sized ones in medium-sized centres, the large ones in large centres and all of them connected and interdependent, right up to the central bank – goes together with all those economic theories that spring up now and then, become fashionable and then fall by the wayside after a while. Now the makers of historical theories are latching onto corporatism, whose purpose is very different and far higher than that of serving as a coat-rack for these pseudo-historians of economic determinism. They would do better not to forget the misfortune that befell the best of the company of prophets of economic determinism, Karl Marx, who in league with Friedrich Engels predicted that capitalism would come to an end one fine day, blowing up spontaneously by overgrowth. The end was supposed to come around 1890, give or take a year. It was the story of the big fish eating the small. Marx and Engels meant that the big industrialists were devouring the small ones, that the giants – which would come to be called cartels, trusts, etc. – would devour the big ones, until a colossus devoured the giants. The proletariat would then cut off its head or, more mercifully, put the colossus out to pasture, and peacefully establish socialism. All of this was based on theories of what today would be called the greater rationalization or economic efficiency of big business compared with small business, and so forth. Nothing of the sort happened, and if anyone was toppled it was the blimps, the giants, the colossi. For that matter, in the sea it appears the whales are in greater danger of disappearing than the minnows. Size and geographical distribution are only two among the numerous factors that influence the survival of firms, and they act in different directions from case to case, depending on the factors with which they are combined. In banking, sometimes small and medium-sized banks are more economical, sometimes large ones. Sometimes it is the local branch of a large city bank that thrives, at others it is the independent local banker. And it connot be said that it is inadvisable for a bank to open a new branch in a city or an urban or rural district already served by two or three other banks. This is one of the biggest empty containers ever to find a place of honour in the treatises on banking. Precisely where the managers of two or three branches fail to find enough business to cover expenses and send reports back to headquarters on the need for understandings to reduce the overly great number of competing branches to just one, so that each bank can work systematically and rigorously in a particular field without stealing customers from each other, we see a new local banker or a new branch of another bank appear on the scene and thrive. Like any other business, banking is not something that already exists and has simply to be occupied. Though enumerating 'occupation' among the means of acquiring property, jurists have for some time taken pains to point out that it has gone out of fashion, since there is no longer any new land to occupy in civilized countries. Bank rationalizers should deign to learn something from the prudence of the jurists and get it into their heads that banking business is not a cake to be divided; that the slices are not the result of the division of a fixed quantity by a variable number of banqueters, so that if there are three branches and the amount is 30 the quotient is ten, if there are two branches it rises to 15 and if there is just one it jumps to 30. Just as in industry and commerce, business does not work like this in banking. The amount is the end point, not the starting point of the arithmetic operation. Quite possibly, if the number of branches or banks doing business in a place falls from three to one, the amount of business will fall to five and the remaining bank will be worse off than before; and if the number of branches or banks increases instead from three to four, the total amount of business will rise to 50 and, though the new arrival takes 17, the others will see their slices grow from 10 to 11. Hunger makes the mule run faster. Business is a continuous creation. And it is created not by the empty containers of a fair division of existing business, but by the emulation that allows the most capable to create business that does not exist. The only good rule taught by the history of the banks of every age and country is not to stick rigidly to any rule.

THE PRACTICAL BANKER Yes, some rules do exist, but they are as old as Adam and trite as can be. Perhaps the rules could be reduced to just two: 'The banker has only one duty, to his depositors', and 'The banker takes money from everyone, even the bad, but gives it only to the good.' If the banker does not forget these two basic precepts, he may have bad days, anxious days, but, for whatever human predictions are worth, he will pass through the storm unharmed and make port safe and sound.

If the two rules have become flesh of his flesh, the banker is able to give substance even to the formulas, in themselves empty, of long term and short term, of functional specialization and geographical specialization, of bigness and smallness.

If someone tells the banker, 'Your transactions must be long term because your deposits are long term, or your transactions must be short term because your deposits are short term', he will not mistake that piece of advice, which is wise enough within certain limits, for this other one: 'If you have long-term deposits you must *only* engage in long-term transactions because these *are* safe for you, and if you have short-term deposits you must *only* engage in short-term transactions because these *are* safe for you.' He knows that the words 'only' and 'are' are out of place, indeed very dangerous for him.

The banker or the institution that receives long-term deposits or raises funds with bond issues knows many other things instead, among which the following perhaps are worthy of mention:

1 That he cannot lend out 100 per cent of his funds even if he has received them at long term, but must keep a portion in liquidity or invested at short term. Might not some of his customers need new loans at a time when it is not advantageous for the banker to issue new bonds? Might not the annual instalments that he will certainly have to pay on the bonds issued fall due at a time when his debtors should, but cannot, pay their equivalent annual instalments of interest and principal? Since it is not in his interest to make his embarrassed but solid debtors fail and since he himself must pay and wants to pay, it behoves him to keep part of his funds invested at short term.
2 That there are long-term flows of funds that are not renewed at maturity, or that are renewed only after an interval. Time deposits come in waves. At a certain point they diminish, because attractive investments have appeared on the depositors' horizon. Woe betide the banker who, trusting in the renewal of one-year or five-year deposits, has made loans with longer maturities!
3 That alongside the fact of loans that are amortized within *x* years, so that the bank at the end has received repayment from the industrialists and extinguished all the bonds it issued to fund them, one also needs to consider that the industrialist who at the end of year 1 has repaid one-twentieth of his debt finds his machinery depreciated by an amount

equivalent to the debt he has repaid and will therefore have to contract a new debt to renew his machinery and plant. In order to supply the requisite funds, if it is not a propitious moment for bond issues, the banker will have to draw on his liquid reserves or short-term assets.

In turn, a banker who receives short-term deposits cannot, as the story of maturity specialization recounts, put all of them into short-term operations, such as collection and payment services on behalf of customers, bill discounting, current account overdrafts, documentary credit, repurchase agreements, cashier services, acceptance credit, etc., etc. He cannot do this because all this business is remunerative only if deposit rates are zero or very low, taxes light, and administrative overheads and the specific handling costs of each transaction reduced to the minimum thanks to the large volume of business. If the volume of business falls below average, large banks will make a loss. The medium-sized and small ones, with few branches, lean management and the watchful eye of the owner, can make a go of it. Not only may the wise banker not observe the rule of abstaining from long-term lending, but it is not at all necessary for him or in the interest of his depositors and borrowers that he obey it blindly at any cost. No sensible rule can be laid down in general. If the banker receives large deposits from industrialists or tradesmen and these are their working funds that happen to be idle between purchases of raw materials, he must stay alert and stick to liquid assets, preferably discountable at sight with the bank of issue. As long as he was head of Credito Mobiliare, Domenico Balduino was always suspicious of large individual deposits; and when he was not content with the reason for the deposit and the identity of the depositor, Pantaleoni tells us, he went so far as to get rid of both deposit and depositor.[1] If so much suspicion is disagreeable, it is still necessary to stand ready to repay deposits and therefore to avoid long-term loans.

Would anyone dare to say that savings banks have to follow the same rule? Yet they receive mainly sight deposits or short-term time deposits. However, these deposits are individually small or modest, belonging to peasants, household servants, manual workers, pensioners, clerks, annuitants, small and medium-sized artisans, tradesmen and industrialists. They are largely permanent savings, that is, sums that it is intended should not be touched if possible, except in part, when they exceed a certain figure, for the purchase of treasury bonds, consols, perhaps an apartment. The bulk is left there, to take care of illness, the afflictions of old age, weddings and deaths, events that are not an everyday occurrence and some of which may never happen. Should they occur, the orderly and thrifty person – and he will be that if he is a customer of a savings bank – often takes care of them in a different way, without 'touching the capital'. Fortunately, for these good people 'touching the capital' – in their minds capital is any sum that they could have at any time if they wanted but that has not been in their immediate possession for some time, a year, say, and, coming to be enveloped in a sacred mist, has inexplicably ceased to be part of disposable income and mysteriously become capital and hence 'untouchable', which is a good definition, at least as good as all the others offered by economists – is a shameful crime, a mortal sin they would feel it their duty to confess. Why should a savings bank that has gathered in these admirable depositors observe the rule of maturity specialization and abstain from long-term lending? Out of deference to a senseless myth according to which in matters of deposits and assets, the long goes with the long and the short with the short? Rules are to be observed if they are good; otherwise, it is logical to forget them. In my opinion, therefore, the federated savings banks of Piedmont, which at 31 December 1933 had received L3,478 million of deposits, did very well – even though none of them had issued long-term bonds and most of their funds came from short-term deposits or time deposits for a term that strikes common mortals as brief, a year being a short unit of time – to invest 25.39 per cent of their funds in loans, in personal loans secured by pledge of one-fifth of the borrower's salary, in shareholdings that at a glance have every appearance of being long-term investments, and 48.39 per cent in their securities portfolio, which are short-term investments in a manner of speaking that is true enough as long as it is not abused. They say investments in securities are short term, because securities are sold in a flash in the stock market. Now, that flash may work for L100 million, for L200 million. But if one seriously wanted to realize the Piedmont federated savings banks' securities portfolio of L1,683 million, one would have to wait for the market to be ready, that is to say for purchasers to have digested the securities of earlier issues or for new strata of purchasers to have formed. In other words, it is necessary to wait for new savings to be formed, something that won't happen in a day or a month even in a vast, industrious and thrifty region such as Piedmont. Nonetheless, we have no criticism but only praise for the managers of the Piedmont savings banks for the preponderance given to relatively long-term assets. If the market does not offer sufficient safe short-term investment opportunities, should the savings banks, deferring to the maturity myth, reduce to 1 per cent the interest they offer to depositors? To depositors, note, not inclined to commit themselves to keeping their money locked up with the bank for ten years or even five, and most of whom want to 'reserve' the right to have their money turned over to them the next day; but who are basically attached to the savings banks like barnacles and quite rightly keep their money on deposit not for a day or a month or five or ten years but for a lifetime. How many tellers at savings banks have not grown old with their customers, who come like clockwork every year to have the interest 'entered' in their bankbook. 'Entered', not 'withdrawn'; and as soon as the interest is 'entered' it becomes capital, sacred and untouchable. With such worthy depositors, it would be nonsense for the letter to win out over the spirit and for the savings bank, like a bonze before an idol, to renounce thinking with its own head.

From the economic point of view, there is no reason to distinguish here between savings banks and other banks. Both must observe the two rules mentioned above: 'The banker has only one duty, to his depositors', and 'Money, taken from everyone, must only be given to good customers.' If the banker has individually large and fluctuating short-term deposits, he is well advised to steer clear of long-term assets; if he has short-term deposits, but they are individually small and stable, he can and, in the interest of his depositors, he must put a part in medium and long-term assets. How big this 'part' should be cannot be established on a general basis. If the banker knows his trade, if he is careful and prudent, he will come out with the right proportion: 10, 20 or 30 per cent. If he does not know his trade, if he has no nose for business and if he imagines he is doing well by sticking to 10 per cent, even 10 per cent can be too much. Are we certain that discounting bills or offering an overdraft for working capital are really short-term uses? As the 'theorist' recalled earlier, the discount is short term if the bill is withdrawn at maturity, and if new bills presented for discounting have no temporal or causal connection with the one extinguished. But, whether or not the name is the same, if the bill is renewed with straight-line deductions then it is a long-term loan pure and simple. It is up to the banker not to get bogged down in this and, if he has, to work himself free gently, with good grace, with warm words for the customer to whom he wants to say farewell before the customer fails. An overdraft is short term, it is commercial, it is working credit if it goes up and down, sometimes touching the ceiling and sometimes falling below zero, with the customer in credit towards the bank. If the variations coincide with those that can be deemed characteristic of the customer's business, the banker feels safe. But if the overdraft has the bad habit of always rising and never falling, if it stops at the ceiling, this is bad news for the banker. He has fallen into the swamp, and he must think about pulling himself out slowly, without scandal, but firmly. To discourage customers from immobilizing funds, there are the rightly honoured, classic cautionary devices called commissions and forgiveness. By having the customer pay, for example, a commission of 0.25 per cent not on the average amount of the overdraft during the calendar quarter but on the highest amount, the customer is encouraged not to touch the overdraft ceiling. By forgiving the whole of the commission if the customer remains out of debt for more than ten days running, 50 per cent if the position goes from debtor to creditor within 20 days (if the account shows a debtor balance for more than 20 days the full commission is payable), the customer is made to feel that an overdraft is not the same as a loan but is an accordion-like facility to enable him to meet his commitments without embarrassment. It is understood, moreover, not only that the customer can make withdrawals for payments but also, since he collects receipts in the course of business, that he must also make payments to the bank.

Even the rule of being in credit once every ten or twenty days or at least once a year need not be taken seriously. If to move into credit with his bank the customer runs up a debt somewhere else, is it not better that he be in permanent debt, to a greater or lesser extent, with the usual bank? At least the banker will be able to monitor him directly. Moreover, someone who needs the money of others cannot be compelled to make loans to his own bank.

The rules of maturity, functional and geographical specialization must therefore be accepted *cum granu salis*.* The really essential point is not to make mistakes. Investing long term what must be repaid at once is a mistake. But it is also a mistake not to make good long-term investments and to invest badly and unproductively out of a fixation with putting to short-term use sight deposits which it is known are destined to remain in the bank for the depositors' lifetime. It is a mistake to give money to an industry that is not local, not simply because it is different but because, being different or distant, it is not well known. It is a mistake for a banker specialized in dealing with country-folk to lend to townsmen; not because it is not good to lend to solvent townsmen and excellent to distribute risks between country-folk and townsmen, but because this banker, who knows his country-folk through and through, would be swindled by the first city slicker who came within reach of his depositors' millions.

The mistake of mistakes in banking, the worst and biggest mistake of all, is to impose a rigid rule on oneself or – and this amounts to the same thing – to seek to regulate bankers' conduct rigidly. If the regulation really regulates, it only prevents the good transactions and does not prohibit the bad. The only acceptable regulation would be one that ordered bankers to enter only into good transactions. At long-term or short, with country-folk or townsmen, with agriculture or the electricity industry, in Lombardy or Sicily, provided they are good, that is, likely to enable the banker in due time to perform his only duty: to repay depositors. The banker has no other duty and must have no other concern. He renders service to the country only if he knows and feels that he has no other duty. If someone comes to him with talk about the duties of banking towards agriculture or industry or commerce or goes on about carrying the nation's flag through the seven seas, he should let him go on but not give him a penny. Agriculture, industry, commerce and flags do not repay the money lost in cockeyed or unproductive ventures. If the projects are good, if the applicant is serious and honest, these qualities speak for themselves and will make even the most distrustful hand over money. The country is served by opening the purse for serious and honest people, for industrialists who have always honoured their commitments and have eaten bread and water to avoid a bill being

*With a pinch of salt.

protested; and closing it hermetically to beneficiaries of moratoria, to those who have reached a composition with their creditors and haven't even paid the minimum 30 per cent instalment, to the bankrupt, to those willing to pay 10 per cent interest in order to obtain money to be invested at 1 per cent. Those who shower money on these people pave the way for disillusion, ruin and unemployment; rear customers for the public hospitals and convalescent homes, sharpen nails to be driven into the state budget. Those who are unbending towards the undeserving of credit and who, within sane limits, give the money entrusted to them as sacred deposits only to sound people truly cause agriculture and industry to prosper, commerce to multiply and the nation's flag to wave in the most distant seas.

7
Banks with Adjectives*

Some combinations of words, as soon as they are uttered, immediately make one think they were put together by artifice: the words scowl at each other and ill tolerate one another. So it is with the combination 'fascist bank', which was pronounced not long ago as if it were an innovation of the utmost urgency in Italy's existing economic and political landscape.

The combination is not entirely new, since in Italy there are numerous combinations that have a ring like that of 'Catholic bank' and not a few banks that, without bearing witness to their creed in their name, are or were in the hands of the Socialist Party or men of that Party. The socialists preferred to lay their hands on cooperative banks, whose capital was prevalently supplied by the State or by semi-public entities, on which the State could exert pressure; but on some occasions, as in Turin, they founded a savings bank funded by the real savings of ordinary people within their own Cooperative Alliance. In doing so they were imitating the famous wholesale cooperatives of England and Scotland, each of which created a thriving banking business of its own. And in the United States there is a lively popular movement that encourages workers to bring their savings only to banks created by workingmen's associations, so that the workers' savings will not assist capitalist firms but will be used to facilitate the creation of production cooperatives or to provide working capital to consumer cooperatives.

All this is perfectly legitimate and can be advantageous. Those who have a creed must be free to use every available means to make their ideals win out. If a Catholic wants to benefit Catholic tradesmen, farmers and industrialists and not Protestant or Jewish or agnostic ones, let him bring his savings to a Catholic bank. The same goes for socialists or fascists.

---

*First published as 'Banche con aggettivi', in the *Corriere della Sera*, year 49, No. 202, (23 August 1924), p.1.

It is only necessary to set out a few conditions, the first of which is that socialists should indeed be free to bring their money to the socialist bank, and Catholics and fascists likewise, but that nobody should be permitted to use the law or government high-handedness to have the savings 'of others' deposited in his own bank. There was a time when the socialists were criticized in these pages not because they had established savings banks within their cooperatives, but because, thanks to the weakness of the governments of the day, they had succeeded in capturing the savings of the general public and channelling them through self-styled semi-public institutions to the benefit of their own enterprises, both good and bad. In other words: let every Catholic or socialist or fascist be free to deposit his own savings with the bank close to his heart; prohibit everyone from using the arm of the law or government influence to gain control of the savings of those who would wish to deposit their money in a commercial bank or savings bank without adjectives.

It is therefore my incontrovertible premise that the fascist bank, if and when it is created, must be able to receive the voluntary deposits of its own affiliates but must not command even one cent of the billions of lire deposited with the post office savings banks and administered by Cassa Depositi e Prestiti.

Within these limits, the problem of the fascist bank can be treated as one of the many experiments that have taken place in the field of party banks. It is my impression that those Catholic or socialist or workers' banks that have not failed or been liquidated are, at best, no more numerous than the few ordinary banks 'without adjectives' that survive in the struggle to acquire depositors and borrowers. Banking is a very difficult art, and the addition of whatever adjective to the name perhaps serves only to increase difficulties that are already exceptional in themselves.

The difficulties of the art of banking are indeed exceptional. The head of a successful industrial or commercial enterprise is surely a person of value. One cannot create an industrial firm and make it prosper without a good knowledge of raw materials, processing methods, markets and workers, without having taken risks, worked, studied and managed men. But the banker has to know not one industry alone but all of those to which he lends, not one market but many: the storm that will reduce or wipe out the value of the paper he has discounted can come from any point of the globe. The banker has to know the prices not just of one or several raw materials, of one or several finished products, and the wage developments in just one industry. All prices interest him and he must monitor them all. Beyond that, he must have a thorough knowledge of the structure and balance sheet of the firms to which he entrusts money that is not his own.

Now, it is true that bankers today have aids that were unknown to their predecessors. Large modern banks have established research offices and development offices whose archives contain very valuable data, patiently accumulated through confidential relationships, on everyone who might need the help of the bank. What joy for a scholar to be able to read in those archives! What an abundant harvest of unknown information on the economic development of the various countries! A new bank founded today will have to labour for years, perhaps decades, to accumulate the treasure of experience and information that existing banks have acquired through both fortunate and disastrous experiences. The new bank will have to repeat the same experiences, make the same mistakes, before it can safely face the future. But all this – well-ordered archives, accumulated experience, executive personnel selected with a fine sieve – will be useless without the prime factor of a bank's success: the right man.

'He would receive customers on his feet. He would let them talk and in fifteen minutes he took their measure. He never made a mistake.' This is how an Italian, one who brings honour to his country's name abroad, portrayed the head of a large bank several days ago. And this is what I have always read, in almost the very same words, in bankers' books of memoirs. In truth, the banker's duty is to entrust the money of others to able and upright men who know how to put it to work to their own advantage and repay it at the agreed time. Only a fool can think this an easy task; in the economic world there is none harder. All people consider themselves able; and the stronger their conviction, the more they rave about muddled projects, harebrained inventions, and the less is their managerial ability. Everybody declares they are upright, especially when they find pretexts and protest their good faith and their misfortune if they cannot repay. The banker instead has a sole duty: to lend his depositors' money safely.

If he takes pity for a moment, if he becomes groundlessly optimistic or confident, he is lost. That is, his depositors' money is lost. Even an average person can successfully manage a small provincial commercial bank or savings bank, provided he is discerning, attentive and knows his fellow men. But since the fascist bank is, I suppose, to be a nationwide bank, it will have to be managed by men – one alone is not enough in large modern banking organizations – of the highest calibre.

Men of this kind are extremely rare in any country. Lucky are the banks able to procure their services!

In a party bank, whether Catholic, socialist or fascist, the difficulty of finding managers is inordinately greater than in banks without adjectives, since the managers must not forget the cumbersome adjective that would appear to condition the activity of their institution. I am speaking, of course, about large banks operating at national level, not small, almost internal banks that lend to cooperatives affiliated with the same workers' organization.

In countries where politics and banking are less developed, even banks without adjectives may have to pay a tribute to politics. But this concerns a lower or spurious branch of their activity. Whether it is a question of obtaining State subsidies for industries connected with the bank or of hushing up troublemakers who threaten bothersome legislative measures or government action or newspaper articles, I suppose there is a specialist to handle back-room affairs of this kind. All this does not pay, but it does cost. A sum is included among overheads that is disbursed not by the banker but by the hired expert. All this is deplorable, but it does not impinge on the essential duty of the bank.

Beside this percentage of cost, economically comparable, though morally lower, to the percentage of failures, a bank with an adjective must face another risk. The manager has to fight not only against men who are not able and not upright but also against those who, being neither able nor upright, ask for money on the strength of that adjective, because they are Catholics or socialists or fascists. If he gives in for an instant, he will fatally, irremediably, lead the bank to ruin. The newspapers have even recently run stories about Catholic banks that failed for this reason. Before all else, therefore, it is the duty of the manager of a bank with an adjective to repudiate the very adjective with which the men who honour him with their confidence style themselves. Indeed, this repudiation must be a prerequisite for accepting the position. If he does not pose this preliminary condition, we can be sure that he is a man of little value, not worthy of the position. The manager must be ready to go about his job of selecting customers from among Catholics, socialists, fascists as if he always had another word in mind: notwithstanding. When a bank lends only to Catholics, the temptation is irresistible for those in need of credit to declare themselves Catholic even if their faith is weak. And since someone who dons the colour of the side that offers him material advantages is not an upright person, the banker must shoulder the additional burden of discerning the pure, the true believers, from among the many petitioners.

By doing so, he exposes his bank to the danger of leaving its capital idle. The pure, the true believers, the enthusiasts of an idea are not recruited mainly from the ranks of industrialists and tradesmen, who are occupied with their own affairs, ordinarily not too interested in public matters and who wrongly fall in with those who promise them present tranquility. This gives rise to another difficulty for the manager of a bank with an adjective: that of preferring from among the adherents to the adjective those who adhere to it indifferently, in the same way as they would adhere to any other adjective that promised them more favourable discounts than those granted by another bank.

This leads to the ultimate conclusion that a bank with an adjective will have a greater probability of survival and success, the more its managers put the adjective aside and the greater the ability of the banker in selecting from among the petitioners with or without adjectives only able and upright men who are resolved to repay the sums lent to them. Which boils down to saying that, whatever their name, good banks are of only one kind and that the attempt to change their nature by changing their name is vain.

8

Are there too many Banks in Italy?*

1. The report of the Governor of the Bank of Italy for 1929 contains interesting information about the number and mortality of Italian banks. At the end of 1927 there were 4,405 in operation; the number fell to 4,197 at the end of 1928 and 4,097 on 28 February 1930, with a decrease of 208 in 1928 and 118 in 1929 and the first two months of 1930. In reality the reduction was even larger since in the first two years of application of Decrees 1511/1926 and 1830/1926, which established a form of government supervision of banks and entrusted it to the Bank of Italy, many institutions were not caught by the Bank's survey and did not register with the Ministry of Finance. For example, the reduction of 118 banks that occurred in the 14 months from 1 January 1929 to 28 February 1930 was the result of the following changes:

Banks that voluntarily stopped taking deposits		180
Banks that definitively stopped operating		63
		243
Previously existing banks identified in the meantime	121	
New banks	4	
	125	125
		118

The mortality of banks is therefore very high from one year to the next, while for all practical purposes the birth rate can be considered zero.

The reduction corresponds to a tendency that Stringher[1] defined in his report to the 1929 annual meeting as the 'gradual simplifying of the banking organization, which is keenly looked for by those who have at heart the safeguarding of savings'.[2]

*First published as 'Ci sono troppe banche in Italia?', *Riforma Sociale*, XXXVII, Vol. XLI, Nos 7–8 (July–August 1930), pp.356–64.

One has the impression that credit institutions are still too many. At 28 February 1930 they comprised:

1,411	joint-stock banks and bankers;
239	savings banks, pawnbroking establishments, municipal agricultural credit banks, etc.;
2,429	rural banks and other unlimited liability cooperative institutions

In his report to the 1930 annual meeting Stringher noted:

> how the Bank of Italy, in consideration of the excessive number of existing credit institutions, has thought proper to encourage amalgamations whenever the position of the institutions concerned gave evidence of creating thereby a stronger and more vital organization. This not only in order to favour a reduction in the general expenses, but also to check competition in attracting deposits whereby interest rates are affected.[3]

2. What Stringher says in carefully measured words was turned by some commentators into a principle: better a few strong banks than many weak ones.

At this point I want to raise a doubt: is it true that the adjective 'weak' necessarily or generally goes hand in hand with the circumstance that banks are many and therefore small and that the 'strong' banks are the few and consequently large ones? Is it therefore beneficial for banking policy to hinder, on principle, the creation of new banks and to take a favourable view of the amalgamation or merger of existing ones?

I know it is fashionable today everywhere in the world to talk about 'rationalization' and to adopt this ugly word, used to signify the age-old concept of 'reducing production costs', as a synonym of consolidation. Building big appears to be equivalent to building well. Hence the universal mania for cartels, consortia, trusts, giants. It is a mania and it will pass.

3. It is worth rereading Stringher's acute analysis, in his 1929 annual report, of the underlying cause of the series of bank failures that occurred in Italy after 1920:

> The ease with which it was possible to collect deposits at a time of monetary inflation had caused many banks to crop up which either did not have a sufficient supply of actual capital or lacked capable management. It had also induced both old and new banks to expand recklessly in all directions, creating costly branches with the object of collecting money in the form of bank notes, even by offering high rates of interest, raking them in under every description of fiduciary deposits. Thus in many places large sums of money flowed to banks and bankers, which ventured in speculation and tied up capital, often causing serious trouble and losses to the people who placed faith in them.[4]

The Governor does not accuse the large number and small size of banks but, with a happy spirit of observation, states that the cause of the bank failures lay in the misjudgements and blunders committed by inexperienced and reckless people at times of monetary expansion. But misjudgements and blunders can be made by both small and large bankers. Was there not the failure (technically a surrogate of failure was invented, but the substance is the same) of Banca Italiana di Sconto, a giant with widespread ramifications and an incredible number of regional offices, branches and sub-branches, etc., and is it not public knowledge that another large bank, Banco di Roma, recovered its earlier liquidity because the State made the Consorzio Valori, i.e., taxpayers, acquire several billion lire of frozen assets? Faced with these two cases, the burden of proof rests with those who claim that banking crises are due to the large number and small size of banks. To my way of thinking, in a historical perspective this view appears totally unfounded.

4. The correct view is that in this field it is not possible to 'generalize'.

Mergers of two or more joint-stock banks or savings banks do not always produce good results. In response to the usual observations by lay commentators on the merger of what is now the largest bank in the United States, The Chase National Bank, with the Mechanics and Metals National Bank, A.H. Wiggin, the chairman of Chase, noted in January 1927 that

> This merger, together with similar steps on the part of other institutions in the last two or three years, has been made the occasion of comments to the effect that mergers are the order of the day and that the line of logical development is toward fewer and much bigger banks. I am not prepared to subscribe to this doctrine without qualification, and I would not have our merger with The Mechanics and Metals National Bank judged on that basis alone. It is significant that while bank mergers are taking place, new banks of moderate size are also coming into existence and doing well. A merger may bring together organizations which cannot work harmoniously and may combine interests which are not compatible. Each case must be judged on its own merits. Haphazard mergers merely for the sake of large figures do not assure good banking.[5]

Although B.M. Anderson explicitly denies he is claiming that the American system of 25,000 independent banks is preferable to the English system of the big five, of the five suns circled by just a very few planets, he cannot refrain from noting the dangers of mergers put together artificially to avoid the damage of an economic crisis, without their deriving almost spontaneously from the recognition of truly common interests and prepared by the managers having known each other well for years.

5. Mergers can be the indicator of a dangerous method of liquidating industrial crises.

In the United States the cooperation between independent banks, under the aegis of the Federal Reserve Banks, prevented the crisis of 1920–1 from degenerating into a panic. It prevented such an outcome again at the end of 1929. But it did not prevent the *liquidation* of the crisis. Each bank was able to obtain help from the correspondent banks in the larger centres and these from the Federal Reserve Banks; but healthy help, thanks to what in Italy would be called the discounting of sound commercial paper. Each bank had to wash its own dirty linen. No frozen assets offloaded onto stronger shoulders:

> In a surprisingly short time we 'cleaned up' the weak spots, readjusted prices and costs, absorbed our losses, brought liabilities into reasonable relation to assets, and got ready for the next upward move in business. The business tide turned in the third quarter of 1921, and the year 1922 was a year of strong recovery.[6]

In Japan, by contrast, the custom is to hold crises in check, under pressure from a government anxious to avoid bankruptcies and catastrophes. Frozen assets are taken over by banks organized in consortiums, so that industrial firms on the brink of collapse are kept alive until they can be absorbed by so-called great industrial complexes. From 1920 onwards, Anderson notes:

> the stale position, unliquidated, was carried over, despite a partial liquidation at the time of the earthquake in 1923, until the great crisis in 1927, when some great banks went under. Japan endured seven years of business stagnation in the vain effort to avert losses which our system of banking compelled us to take in 1920 and 1921. And Japan is not the only country where banking concentration has unduly delayed necessary liquidation. When many thousands of independent banks must independently meet their obligations at the clearing house every day, it is impossible to carry economic mistakes anything like so far as is possible when only a few great banks dominate the picture. In the interest of the flexibility of our economic life, we must preserve vigorous competition both in banking and in business, and we must have a large number of independent units in order to assure this.[7]

6. Words of obvious good sense, that it is a pleasure to hear repeated by a great expert in banking to all those who childishly believe that the United States, England and Germany became economically powerful thanks to the policy of agreements, understandings, cooperation and consolidation. Yes, all these nice things are factors contributing to success. Up to a certain point, however; as long as they do not hinder the working of the equally necessary factors of struggle, rivalry, competition, of feeling shunned liked the plague when blunders have been committed, of never hoping to shift the consequences of one's own mistakes onto others, the public, taxpayers.

7. Cartels are fine when they serve to exchange information on loans to customers, so that no customer can accumulate debts beyond his solvency by borrowing from several banks that do not communicate. But it is just as fine and fundamentally more secure for each bank, without bothering about what the others are doing, to require its customers to be in the black once a year. In this way the bank ensures that when a customer goes back into debt, it will be for new loans and not to carry over old loans that drag on from year to year and are laboriously reduced by modest percentages. The customer will perhaps be obliged to have accounts with several banks. I see nothing wrong with this. Two, three or five pairs of eyes will be looking at his business and he will have to demonstrate his liquidity to several banks instead of just one. He will not be tied to any one bank and no one bank will be tied to him. The exclusivism that ties an industrialist and a bank together is not to the advantage of either. The likely result is to force the banker to be an industrialist and the industrialist, especially if large and badly off for money, to gain control of the banks. With all due respect for those who, out of a spirit of emulation, are paladins of probably misunderstood German examples, overly close and exclusive ties between industry and banks are a prelude to pathological frozen assets or attempts to take over banks.

8. A network of branches reaching across the whole country from a centre that gathers deposits from each location and redistributes them to where they are invested most profitably is something admirable. The accusation ordinarily levelled against a system comprising a few large and centralized banks – that it pumps savings out of agricultural regions and small centres and channels them to industry in the larger centres and stock exchange speculation – is often unwarranted. If the creation of branches is the result of a slow and healthy development of the central organization and the formation of an expert staff that works well together, and if there is a capable person at the head of the local branch, in moments of need a small agricultural centre may obtain the use of a quantity of savings from the head office that exceeds both the local deposits and the resources that an independent banker would have deemed prudent to invest *in loco*. It is not possible to proclaim dogmas in this field, which is not pure theory but the fruit of concrete contingencies. A large bank with first-class personnel that it knows how to distribute according to their aptitudes in small and large centres, in cities and villages, will not cause anyone to lament the disappearance of the local banker, who knew his customers one by one, helped them within the limits of profitability and prudence, and promoted local initiatives with local savings.

9. Other large and medium-sized banks are unfortunately well known instead for having many branches charged with the task of pumping out local savings with the offer of attractive interest rates and turning them over to the head office. The first and lesser evil produced by banks of this type is the drying up of local initiatives, the use of the money of small savers and

farmers to the benefit of large industrialists and stock market operators, the transfer of the savings of backward regions (the Mezzogiorno in Italy) to more advanced regions (the Liguria–Lombardy–Piedmont triangle). I say that this is the lesser evil because it is often exaggerated and not infrequently it is economically advantageous to invest depositors' money in the most remunerative and secure manner. The greater evil is when the pumping-out of small-scale and local savings is caused by the need to pour the tens and hundreds of millions into the gaping hole of some great initiative in which the head office has become entangled. To cite only examples from the past, remember Banca Italiana di Sconto and the paper castle it erected, with depositors' billions, around the improvised Ansaldo colossus.

10. Local bankers undoubtedly suffer from some disadvantages compared with large banks in terms of the variety and liquidity of their assets. Big banks with many branches can diversify their assets and offset the risks better. Not all industries, not all firms suffer the same misadventures equally and at the same time. Local bankers, instead, mostly deal with only one industry or just a few. Their clients are grape or rice growers, or livestock farmers, or cheese makers or manufacturers of tinned tomatoes. Or else their area is dominated by the wool or the cotton industry. If wool does badly or cheeses do not sell or tomatoes or rice are hit by a severe crisis, local bankers' portfolios may prove to be seriously immobilized.

Very true. But if we look more closely, the fault is not that they are small bankers but that they are stupid or greedy. If we analyse the failures of small bankers one by one, we are forced to admit that greediness and stupidity were the real causes of their ruin. Greediness drives them to invest too large a part of their deposits in advances, let's suppose for apples still in bloom in the orchards in the hope of participating in the speculation on apples. Naturally, since this leads to the production of too many apples, both the farmers and the bankers, turned into bull speculators, go bust. Stupidity made them forget the elementary rules of banking, which advise them not to put all the money, especially the money of others, in just one investment, to hold back on advances when prices are rising and customers gone mad are swearing by a favourite industry. Is it true, though, that only small bankers are greedy and stupid? Do not the mistakes of a big banker produce more grandiosely tragic consequences than the mistakes of a hundred small ones?

If he is a prudent man, a local banker can diversify his assets just as well as a big city bank and certainly better than 20 or 50 years ago. In a few hours he can go to the big city, obtain confidential information, find out which way the markets are moving. Over the telephone he can place large sums short term by entering into blue-chip rollover contracts, through and with the guarantee of very sound stockbrokers (who in Italy as well have now shown that they have not caused their clients any losses, indeed that they have reduced to negligible percentages the losses clients had brought upon themselves by foolishly trading with persons well known to be in dire straits). If he does not expect to gain more than 1 per cent net of expenses on his deposits, our local banker, who has between five and ten million lire of deposits, can – by supplementing the margin on deposits with revenues from the hundred other services involved in collection, bills of exchange, and purchases and sales of securities for customers – earn a reasonable income and render very useful services to his local customers. The trouble starts when he allows himself to be tempted by margins of 3 per cent and 4 per cent and when, instead of being satisfied with modest premises and staff, possessing the necessary comfort and confidentiality for customers, he wants to impress and spends too much on offices, employees, cars and so on. But the problem of an excessively high incidence of expenses and of extravagance also torments big banks today, so that 'rationalization', if it means economy and making good use of money, is rightly a fashionable word for them too.

11. Perhaps there are grounds for supposing that the 2,429 rural banks and other unlimited liability cooperative institutions are too many. Don Cavallotti, the Bagnolo rural bank, its rotten apples and the unfortunate peasants who, when they paid a lira and signed a paper, believed they had countersigned the receipt for the lira but actually became the partners, with joint and unlimited liability, of a megalomaniac. The defect of rural banks is that they must be founded by apostles, willing to work disinterestedly for the good of others. Undoubtedly, there are apostles who have a flair for business, a knowledge of human nature, an understanding of the ways of the world. The names of Cottolengo and Don Bosco spring to mind. What marvellous economic creations, still waiting for the economic historian who will narrate their glorious ventures, were the works that bear the names of these two great saints! To found a rural bank and run it well, it is certainly not necessary to be a saint; neighbourly love and a spirit of abnegation, coupled with common sense and a knowledge of human nature, are sufficient. A rural bank in a small town can do a great deal of good. Our parish priests, most of whom are the sons of peasants, often have common sense and practical abilities. There are not a few, however, who are too kind and easily deceived. Priests and old maids have always been, in every country in the world, the preferred victims of swindlers. With their eyes closed, in the manner of simple folk, trusting in divine providence, with the unshakeable faith that moves mountains they throw themselves into fantastic financial adventures. I do not say this to invoke legislative measures for the regulation of rural banks or particular forms of oppressive supervision. More than in other fields, supervisors must proceed with great tact. It is necessary to avoid shaking the confidence that simple country folk

rightly have in those who nearly always deserve it. It is necessary to avoid strewing a path that is already sufficiently arduous with additional obstacles and red tape. To become friends with the managers, to give lessons on banking without appearing to, between one game of bocce and another, to involve the bishops in good time, before the situation gets out of hand – this is what the *missi dominici** of the Bank of Italy should do. But it is obviously something that cannot be set within the framework of official supervisory action. If rural banks want to continue doing the good that they can do, they must find within themselves, within their own organizations, the moral authority and the means to eliminate the few black sheep and the not many, but more numerous, in their ranks who are too good-hearted and sometimes expose their orders to trials and tribulations.

12. To conclude, large and small banks are not incompatible: in fact, they are complementary. The world is not exclusively for the large or for the small, rather it is for the large, the small and the medium-sized at the same time. There can be an extremely useful circulation among the various kinds of bankers. Why prevent a good officer in the local branch of a large bank, who has come to know the customers of the place well and has their trust, from setting up on his own? He may not have the qualities needed by the manager of a major institution with billions of lire of deposits, but he has the spirit of initiative, the prudence and the know-how needed to make a local bank prosper. Why deny him, on the basis of the ridiculous dogma that small banks are harmful, the possibility of establishing an independent bank? The requirement of a minimum of capital is acceptable, but the requirement of an unreasonable minimum of L5 million, for a bank that may not and does not need to have as many millions of deposits to operate profitably, prevents fruitful energies from finding an opening and producing additional wealth.

On the other hand small independent banks can be very useful for the training of the top management of large banks. Not always do those with promise and talent who join a big bank at a young age succeed in having their abilities recognized. Right from the start they may have been given a specialized job to do and may stay small in that job, sometimes for their whole working lives. The lack of an early opportunity prevents them from being appreciated for what they are worth. In a small or medium-sized bank there are more opportunities to learn and advance. Inevitably young employees end up by having to do a little of everything. Tact, ability and intuition rise to the surface. Since they are only a few, they will sometimes have to do business with managers of other banks, even large ones. Through these contacts the chance of a lifetime may arise. Variety is the

*God's messenger.

spice of life in banking as well. Thus the 1,411 joint-stock banks and bankers, the 239 savings banks and, with the reservations set out above, the 2,429 rural banks in operation in Italy appear neither too many nor few. They are too many all those run by people who are greedy or idiots or amateurs or who wish to engage in banking out of love of their neighbours. They are few in comparison with the thousands of other banks that could usefully operate in rural centres that are without a bank at present, in other centres where there are only branches of big banks busy pumping out money to send to the centre, and in big cities where the existing banks have failed to respond to the needs of social classes that could do with the help of a bank.

9
Debts*

1. I am unable to take seriously people who complain or talk about crisis and yet neither have nor talk about debts, where by 'debts' I mean any obligation whose amount remains fixed or changes little when prices change. As early as June 1930 and again in August 1933 I reduced the substance of the crisis to that concept; otherwise, I observed, the crisis would already have passed (in June 1930!) or would not exist at all.[1] If in 1929 and then in 1930 and every successive moment it had been miraculously possible each time to recreate the economic world on the basis of the existing desires, sentiments, ideas and personal and material capital; if all prices had been perfectly mobile and able to adjust instantaneously to the existing productive factors, why ever should there have been a crisis? Each price would have been perfectly suited to the purposes people desired in every successive moment. All prices being continually mobile, they would have continually been in equilibrium among themselves and with the psychological and technical factors of the economic world. A crisis is an impotent effort to restore a broken equilibrium. It is due to some constraint that prevents one or several elements of the economic mechanism from changing while the rest changes, so that the machine jams or jars or breaks down because the parts fail to mesh. Constraints are necessary to the working of the mechanism, since the latter is operated by man, an imperfect creature unsuited to the terrible, continuous nervous tension of a perfectly mobile system.[2] Sometimes, however, the constraints go beyond what is needed to assure the tranquillity of the great majority of men, who are averse to running excessively large risks. People may have gone too far in digging trenches around the garden of their life. Customs and consortia trenches, perfect or imperfect monopolies constructed by entrepreneurs and by

---

* First published as 'Debiti', *La Riforma Sociale,* XLI, Vol. XLV, No. 1 (January–February 1934), pp.13–27. The occasion was the publication of Irving Fisher, 'The debt-deflation theory of great depressions', *Econometrica,* I (1933), pp.337–57.

workers kill the division of labour, render the earth sterile and diminish production.[3] Debt is a typical form of trench. What if the contract for loans, for personal and material capital did not exist; if it were impossible to invest capital at a fixed rate of interest, and everyone instead collected variable dividends depending on the net income of the firm; if it were impossible to hire labour at a fixed salary or wage, but all intellectual and manual workers were paid instead with a share of the firm's output? In this case, why should there be crises? All would share in the result of production and, whether prices were high or low, each would receive his slice of the cake.

2. It is well known that it would be absolutely impossible for the economic mechanism to function if everything were as mobile as depicted above. Profit-sharing for workers, capitalist and worker shareholding, co-operative systems are properly called 'ideal' schemes for a small minority of savers and workers, who possess the rare qualities needed to run risks. But they are called 'nonsense' for the great majority of savers, who do not know how to select even a halfway decent investment, and workers, who conceive the status of partner in the firm as something that gives the right to command without working. The economic categories of the interest rate, wages, rent and taxes therefore are not inventions of economists but necessities rooted in human nature. The canonists of the Middle Ages had to admit them, even though they regarded them as satanic inventions. The Bolsheviks in Russia, after abolishing them, reinstated them. Both consoled themselves by protesting that 'their' interest rates, wages, rents and taxes were of a different spirit from the vilified ones found elsewhere. The firm does not work if the entrepreneur is not free to move at his ease, at his own risk and profit, rewarding with a fixed price his clerks, workers, providers of capital and suppliers of raw materials. If everyone contributed his own production coefficient in the capacity of partner or shareholder, we would have bedlam not a firm.

3. Naturally, the mechanism works if the fixed component does not kill the mobile one. Interest, wages, rents and taxes are indeed fixed but only for short periods of time, for the time span of man's ability to predict. If the output of a firm is 100, the interest on borrowed capital 20, wages 40 and the remaining 40 sufficient to pay the other expenses and allow a profit; interest can remain at 20 and wages at 40 even if output falls to 90 or rises to 110, because the entrepreneur is in a position to cope with these variations. But if output falls to 70, interest will have to fall below 20 and wages below 40, since it is unreasonable to expect the entrepreneur to work at a loss simply for the pleasure of others. There must be some device or process whereby the fixed claims to a share of the output – what are equivocally called 'costs' – are forced to follow the fluctuations in the value of

the firm's output, albeit with a lag and by steps, each of which has a tread as well as a rise.

4. One such device is for the businessman to work wholly or in good part with his own capital. If he borrows the whole million his firm requires at, say, 6 per cent, he is certain to be bowled over by the first breeze. If his net income falls to L40,000, how will he manage to support his family and pay his creditor L60,000 a year into the bargain? If his plant and inventories depreciate to L800,000, how will he repay the million to his creditor? If, instead, the entrepreneur works with L500,000 of his own and L500,000 of borrowed capital, even if his net income falls to L40,000 he will still be able to meet the agreed interest payments of 6 per cent on the L500,000 loan and will be left with L10,000 of profits: a small sum, but enough for him to keep going if he is judicious and thrifty. The creditor, receiving the interest payments when due, will not call the loan. The crisis, whose causes lie elsewhere, ruins the first businessman and allows the second to wait for better times.

5. Now and then these commonsense observations borne out by ordinary experience have the honour of being theorized by economists, which is fine, and of suggesting remedies, which, as with remedies in general, are not always so fine.

In a recent essay ('The Debt–Deflation Theory of Great Depressions', *Econometrica*, October 1933), Irving Fisher assigns great weight to debt as a factor of cyclical expansion and depression.

In his view, the sequence of events is as follows:

1 New opportunities for profitable investment, stemming above all from new inventions, give rise to investments.
2 Businessmen thereupon contract too much debt.
3 Overindebtedness forces them to liquidate.
4 Liquidation causes prices to fall.
5 The fall in prices or, in other words, the rise in the value of money, reduces businesses' assets by more than liquidation allows them to reduces their debts.
6 Liquidation therefore, in reality, does not decrease the burden of debt but increases it, aggravating the crisis.

From this analysis Fisher deduces the need for 'reflation', i.e., a set of monetary or credit measures capable of 'reflating the price level up to the average level at which outstanding debts were contracted by existing debtors and accepted by existing creditors, and then maintaining that level unchanged' (§ 38). And since 'reflation' is necessary and possible, Fisher adds, it is better to reflate during the third phase of the above sequence than after the fifth.

6. I would like to distinguish between the facts, the analysis of the facts, and the remedies. The facts are certain. Fisher supplies two charts, whose essential data I shall reproduce. Table 9.1 compares the national wealth of the United States in 1929 and 1933 with America's total internal debt at the same dates.

Table 9.1

Year		$ billion
1929	National wealth	362
	Share held by creditors (holders of fixed-income capital)	200
	Residual share attributable to businessmen/debtors (holders of variable-income capital)	162
1933	National wealth	150
	Share held by creditors (holders of fixed-income capital)	160
	Residual share attributable to businessmen/debtors (holders of variable-income capital)	– 10

In the last year of prosperity America's estimated national wealth of $362 billion was divided into two parts: $200 billion attributable to the owners of fixed-income claims (public debt securities, bonds, mortgages and unsecured loans, savings deposits and so on), and $162 billion to the owners of land, houses, shares, private industrial and commercial firms, and other variable-income investments. The trouble was not that $362 billion of national wealth was great or little, or that $200 billion belonged to the holders of fixed-income capital and only $162 billion to the holders of variable-income capital. Not at all, for if each of these two groups had had to hold its share of total national capital in kind, nothing would have happened. The trouble was that the whole $362 billion was attributable according to law to the holders of variable-income capital and that they were under the obligation to repay $200 billion of invariable debt to their creditors, the holders of fixed-income capital. The latter owned nothing; they only held a claim on the others, who appeared to possess everything. Since there had to be some owners who were free and clear of debt, the situation of the debtors was frightening. For many businessmen, perhaps the majority, debts covered more than half the current value of their assets. A gust of wind was enough to topple the house of cards.

When a man's debts amount to two thirds, three-quarters or five-sixths of his assets and he lacks the instinct to sell before the wind changes, he's a dead duck. In fact, in 1933, after the storm had come and, for capital valuations, apparently passed, the national wealth had fallen from $362 to $150 billion. The collapse in the value of land, houses and industrial firms was appalling. True, debts also shrank by dint of repayments, amicable settlements, compositions with creditors and bankruptcies, falling from $200 to $160 billion. This is a large reduction at a time of crisis, but the residual amount is still large and exceeds the total national wealth. Creditors left debtors less than the shirts on their backs, essentially bankrupt. This is the crux of the crisis.

7. The picture is a little less terrifying if we look at national 'income' rather than wealth. National income and fixed charges thereon in 1929 and 1932 are compared in Table 9.2 (amounts in millions of dollars).

Table 9.2

	1929		1932	
	Billion $	**%**	**Billion $**	**%**
National income	85.2	100.0	40.0	100.0
Share of income absorbed by:				
Taxes	9.8	11.5	7.2	18.0
Interest	9.7	11.4	7.4	18.5
Rent	15.7	18.4	7.8	19.5
Total	35.2	41.3	22.4	56.0
Residual share attributable to holders of variable capital income and personal capital (labour)	50.0	58.7	17.6	44.0

The fixed charges do not absorb all the income, even though they include taxes, which go not only to pay the interest on the public debt, and rent, which in truth remunerates a form of capital that was classed under variable-income capital. However, the picture perhaps affords even more insight into what happens in times of crisis. The statistics on national wealth, assets and capital are important, but they do not have a direct bearing on people's everyday lives. It is certainly distressing to lose one's wealth, but to be without income, a daily flow of the means for living, is far worse.

Now, Table 9.2 shows that in 1929 – after the payment of taxes, that is, the sums needed to provide the revenues of the civil service, the armed forces and public creditors, of interest to bondholders and other private creditors, and of rent to landlords – farmers, businessmen, tradesmen, professionals and workers were still left with $50 billion a year to spend. Roughly two-fifths (41.3 per cent) of the national income went to the recipients of fixed incomes and three-fifths (58.7 per cent) to the recipients of variable incomes from capital and labour. The latter, far more numerous than the former, could get by.

In 1932 the proportions were almost inverted; in 1933 the inversion would be complete. The amount of income going to the classes that live on the proceeds of taxes, interest and rent fell from $35.2 billion to $22.4 billion, but their share of the national income rose from 41.3 to 56 per cent. Entrepreneurs (industrialists, farmers, shopkeepers, shareholders) and intellectual and manual workers were left with just $17.6 billion instead of $50 billion, one-third of the previous amount, and just 44 per cent of the total instead of 58.7 per cent. This is the crisis, in terms of its impact on national income. If, as prices fell, every price component had fallen simultaneously and at the same velocity; if, that is, taxes, interest and rent were mobile rather than relatively rigid quantities, it would be indifferent whether $85.2 billion or $40 billion of annual income were divided. Supposing that there had been no change in the quantities of goods produced (an assumption near to the truth) but that only prices had changed, it would be perfectly indifferent whether we named things in terms of dollars or half-dollars. If it is not merely a question of names but of real substance, this is because when prices fall and total national income, the cake to be divided, decreases with them, some participants succeed in obtaining a slice that is the same as before or slightly smaller, leaving the others a correspondingly smaller portion or empty-handed.

The figures are American, but their significance is universal. In every country the crisis of 1929–33 meant an enormous transfer of wealth and income from recipients of variable incomes to recipients of fixed incomes. For this reason it was a crisis.

8. The concept of crisis does not only refer to losses. Some gain from crises, as some gain from inflation. During the past inflation the recipients of variable incomes – entrepreneurs and workers – gained, while the recipients of fixed incomes lost; during the crisis (which in monetary terms means deflation) entrepreneurs and workers are losing and recipients of fixed incomes gaining. In part, such shifts are inevitable and beneficial. This is why the word *crisis* must not only conjure up the idea of doing badly. Crisis also means movement, passage from one equilibrium to another. The economic world has always been in crisis. The end of crisis would mean the end of motion, death. Now and then a thinker reflects on the felicitous nature of a hypothetical 'stationary state'. Famous in the history of economics is J.S. Mill's chapter, 'Of the stationary state' (*Principles*, IV, vi). But the vision, rendered magnificent by the writer's art, does not have and is never likely to have any chance of coming true. Crisis is the eternal law of a world inhabited by men, that is by beings ready to invent, to be fired with enthusiasm and to imitate. Because men are not only inventors and enthusiasts but are also like Panurge's sheep: what one does, the others do too; and if some invent and gain, the others imitate the invention and, multiplying it, lose. In this way crisis, an eternal law of a living, healthy world in movement, from time to time becomes a pathological event. It is reasonable for an entrepreneur to expand his firm by contracting a moderate amount of debts; it is unreasonable for him to go

beyond the bounds of safety by imprudently contracting many debts. Crisis leads to ruin when many entrepreneurs, the majority, unwisely contract too many debts. In stock-market jargon, the position of certain securities, or of securities in general, is called poor if the securities are in weak hands that at the first downturn will be forced to sell, lacking means of their own to cover the differences. In other hands, the current price would be stable; in weak hands, it collapses at the first attack.

9. Analysis of events therefore distinguishes between the following.

1 Crisis as a change in the economic mechanism triggered by changes of taste and by inventions that can satisfy the new tastes or better satisfy old ones. This crisis is eternal, inherent in mutable and perfectible human nature. The analyst is not alarmed if the change causes some pain and friction, for he knows that innovations are not made by the placid and contented but by adventurous optimists, who tend to exaggerate and to make mistakes, which the pessimists will make up for. On the contrary, he is convinced that a periodic succession of upward and downward fluctuations of the economic cycle is beneficial, since the upswing is characteristic of the phases of technical innovation and dissatisfaction with the old, and fosters such technical advances, whereas the downswing serves to correct mistakes and to eliminate incompetents, idiots, schemers, rogues and similar causers of grief.
2 Crisis as an impediment or brake on the movement that ought to occur, hence as a generator of a different sort of movement, destructive rather than creative or corrective.

10. The 'debt' factor can be a condition of the first type of crisis, a condition of movement and progress. If the automobile is invented and the entrepreneur does not have all the capital needed to produce it, debt, if prudently limited, is advantageous. It accelerates the natural movement from the period in which horse-drawn carriages were being made to the period in which almost only motorcars are produced. But if during the transition crisis from the age of the horse to the age of petrol too many get big ideas and contract debts to build 20 or 30 automobile factories in Turin (1900–7), then we have the second type of crisis. Its cause lies neither in the invention of the automobile nor in debt, but in men's mania, their imitative spirit and voracious appetite for swift gains.

During the war and the years immediately following it, which we shall call period I, when currency was depreciating everywhere because too many banknotes were being issued, some people were the first to catch on that it was advantageous to contract debts. They borrowed 100 relatively good lire, bought land, houses and shares, sold these after a while for 150 or 200 depreciated lire and repaid the loan of L100, pocketing the difference. The example soon became contagious, so that even as period I was giving way to period II, during which, with the halt in note issuance, the currency had ceased to fall and was perhaps tending to appreciate, the herd, thinking it had found the easy way to grow rich, set about making debts and buying houses, land and shares, in the hope of selling them at higher prices and turning a profit after repaying the debts. Consequently, instead of stabilizing, the prices of houses, land and shares kept on rising until even the copycats who were late to jump in decided to sell and realize the hoped-for gains. At this point prices collapsed. It was caused not by the debt contracted in period I, which was the fruit of a rational calculation, but by the debt contracted in period II, born of the spirit of imitation and the avidity of people without the flair for speculation.

11. The above analysis of the events demonstrates that the remedy proposed by Fisher is unacceptable. If I understand his line of reasoning, Fisher says that at a certain point businessmen contract too much debt in order to make new investments, that there is the danger of a rush to liquidate assets in order to repay the debts, that liquidation causes the price level to collapse progressively from, let us suppose, 100 to 90, 80, 70, 60 and that the falls in prices can shake the foundations of the economic edifice, burying the innocent under the rubble along with the guilty; he would therefore like to prevent liquidation from the outset by holding the price level steady at 100 with some magic spell. I won't discuss the magic spell, which is monetary in the case in point, so as not to stray from the problem of debt. I shall suppose that an appropriate spell exists, that it is cast by an expert sorcerer and that its success is certain. The price level remains at 100.

If my analysis of the events is correct, it appears that the effective working of the spell should produce the following results.

First, the normal cyclical movement, the crisis I called an eternal manifestation of human nature, continues on its course. There continue to be new inventions, new investments, new prudent debts. But the dross of the preceding cycle is not eliminated. If prices continue to be remunerative, why struggle to reduce costs, to abandon old methods, to scrap obsolete machines? Why should the optimists even temporarily hand over the tiller to the pessimists, the reorganizers, the liquidators of the mistakes that are inevitable in any motion towards the unknown, the preparers of a new rising phase?

Second, therefore, the spell works in the sense that it stabilizes and perpetuates the equilibrium of a past period, retarding adjustment to the equilibrium of the new period. The old investments are preserved along with the old debts, which were prudent in the past period but have become imprudent now that they are overlain by the debts of the new period. The movement that had been normal – and that had not been without its frictions and waste, but this could have been eliminated in due course – now slows down; and its deceleration gradually rigidifies the economic mechanism. Large debts and therefore a heavy burden of fixed interest, high asset values and therefore high inventory costs (wear and tear and depreciation charges), unproductive overheads (worn-out entrepreneurs with their minds turned to the past) pile up and rise exorbitantly. The fixed points of the economic equilibrium increase with respect to the mobile ones. Thanks to the operation of the mobile points the mechanism continues to function, i.e., to move. But when the fixed points, in other words the debts, the inventories, the living dead whose presence hinders those who are truly alive, become too numerous, even the mobile points, consisting in 'new' entrepreneurs, 'free' 'capital', 'fresh' savings, no longer find an opening through which to impart life and motion to the benumbed machine. The machine has bogged down. It doesn't explode, because it is slumbering under the magic spell. But it works more and more slowly and feebly.

12. Which is a lot worse than crisis.

Fortunately, the spell works not only on the normal cycle, slowing and sedating it, but also on the abnormal, pathological cycle.

The madmen and imitators who had contracted debt at the price level of 100 in the hope of realizing land, houses and shares at 120 do not make the hoped-for gains, but neither do they suffer the deserved penalty of losses. Prices remain stationary at 100, and so the imprudent still hope and do not liquidate. Others join their ranks. Just as one sorcerer held prices back on the brink of the abyss, another, it is worth hoping, will drive them back up. The human spirit is annoyed contemplating the divine perfection of the level of 100. Either up or down. And since prices can't go down, let them go up. Didn't the house of cards of shares, land, houses, and debts continue to go up, to rise exorbitantly during the happy times in the United States between 1921 and 1929, when the price level was fluctuating, with minimum deviations, around the miraculous level of 100? In the end, when the bubble reached the limit, it burst, bringing the delayed, violent liquidation, which is nonetheless preferable to slow death.

13. Fisher says that all the sorcerers should have been immediately assembled in 1929 to pump the falling price level back to 100. I reply that the fall that began at the end of 1929 was due to the overlong period of time during which prices, for some still mysterious piece of magic, remained at 100, permitting too many mistakes to accumulate. The longer the period of tranquillity, the less intense the elimination of mistakes, the more frightening the collapse that inevitably, necessarily will come.

In 1929 the sorcerer not only should have pumped prices back to 100. He also should have directed the wind to make some prices fall and others rise; lowered the prices of houses, of land and of shares in sectors where they had risen exorbitantly and raised them in the sectors where they had remained moderate; lowered the prices of goods in relative oversupply and raised those of goods for which supply had remained scant in relation to demand. I do not deny that in the long run this must happen, whatever the general price level, even if it is kept constant through monetary sorcery. In the long run, I say. Meanwhile, the injections of credit permit positions to be held (perhaps the bad ones more than the good), encourage the fools and aggravate the mistakes until the violent explosion. The real remedy lies in withholding credit or increasing its cost for the imprudent, gently inducing friendly liquidations before the mistake has become dangerous.

14. This is the art of the wise, farseeing banker. If such bankers exist, then I too believe in some sort of magic spell that can prevent crises. But the exorcist must arrive *in time*, during the upswing of the economic cycle, before the frightening situation set out in Fisher's first chart is reached.

Fisher is right to say that that the balance sheet situation was absurd in 1933, when the national wealth of $150 billion was more than swallowed up by $160 billion of debt, and he would like to return to the prices and balance sheet situation of 1929, when $362 billion of national wealth was set against only $200 billion of debt. I call them both absurd, but I say that the situation of 1933 was the necessary consequence of the absurdity of 1929. If the hotheads in America had not contracted debts amounting to $200 billion in 1929, the national wealth would not have reached a total value of $362 billion. Beyond a certain point, the values of land, houses and shares are driven up by those who heedlessly buy with borrowed money, which they hope to repay easily with the further appreciation of the item purchased. The real spell therefore should have been cast earlier, between 1921 and 1929; better sooner than later, when prices remained stable on average at the fateful level that in the charts of the *laudatores temporis acti** is today labelled either *zero* or *one hundred*. *Then* would have been the time to give prices a little downward twist every now and again, in order to warn the optimistic entrepreneurs that everything does not always go well in the best of all possible worlds. *Then*, when the central banks of issue might have sensed – what are central bank governors doing if they fail to intuit or sense these elementary facts? – that there was too much credit-based investment; that it was time for them to give a small or large turn of the screw to discount rates and to order especially stringent selection of the bills to be discounted. *Then* it would have been necessary to allow some small or large bank that was badly run or had an excess of frozen assets to sink, and with it the depositors and customers, as a solemn admonition that the hotheads and idiots would be left to stew in their own juice and would find no sympathy or succour from anyone. In economic war, as

* Praiser of past time.

in real war, he who is inexorable is merciful. With timely severity, with a hard heart for the fallen and a fierce face for the whiners, the debts would have remained at $150 billion instead of rising to 200 and the value of the national wealth would not have risen beyond, say, $300 billion. The situation would have been infinitely sounder in 1929; the fall in prices, begun earlier, would not have been so prolonged, and in 1933, instead of $160 billion of debts against $150 billion of assets, the figures might have been something like $100–$120 billion of liabilities and $200–$250 billion of assets. Deflations are inevitable and salutary. The rulers' art lies in keeping them within reasonable limits.

15. Neither should the line of conduct be any different when, despite timely efforts to brake the upward spirals and excessive borrowing, the bubble has burst, sending prices downwards and threatening entrepreneurs with ruin, the good along with the bad. To pump prices back up would be to try to save both the good and the bad. The central bank of issue, which is responsible for preventing a salutary crisis from turning into a disaster, must 'intervene' in the traditional, classic way, taught by experience: to discount 'all' the good paper immediately, without hesitation and without losing a second, so as enable commercial banks and savings banks to meet any demand for repayment, to offer to repay 1,000 to those who demand 100, to extend branch hours for repayment from 4 to 8 p.m.; and not to rediscount bad paper under any circumstances, allowing depositors to make a run on the impaired banks and the latter to be forced to close their doors. In a matter of days, the panic is over; the winnowing process has worked and the deck has been swept clean.

16. But if, unfortunately, discountable paper is in short supply and frozen assets make up nine-tenths of the banks' portfolios, there is but one possible expedient. The only course left is to commend one's soul to God and make the great leap into the void; reading, meanwhile, the famous essay by Maffeo Pantaleoni on the collapse of Credito Mobiliare and the dispute between Attilio Cabiati and Edoardo Giretti in this journal (first two issues of 1933).

The leap will not break the country's back, on one condition: that it does not encourage anyone in the future to repeat the mistakes of the past. To couch the issue in contemporary terms, in the future no industrialist must succeed in obtaining credit lines for investment expenditures from ordinary commercial banks and savings banks, trusting that, should crisis strike before liquidation, the locked-in assets will be taken over by the various convalescent homes to which recourse has been made in the past. Let commercial banks and savings banks stick to their trade and not resort to the central bank of issue except within the rigorous limits of discountable paper. Let investment loans be obtained exclusively through the Istituto

Mobiliare Italiano (IMI) and the Istituto per la Ricostruzione Industriale (IRI) and the technical bodies under them, all of these conceived as permanent, not transient bodies, operating according to the prudential rules that experience counsels for long-term investments. Past experience will be beneficial if it gives rise to a 'permanent' division of labour between banks on the one hand and long-term investment institutes on the other; and if in the future the madmen, idiots and rogues, big or small, along with their customers, are left to sink by the banks and institutes.

17. Probably, my magic spells – which are the classic, traditional ones, valid for all countries, which are all alike when it comes to economic mistakes – are also utopian. I want to confess the reason candidly. The economic sorcerer who should have acted in time, between 1921 and 1929, to exorcise those gripped with the mania for gains was not an omniscient god. He was a common mortal, a man among men. How not to be caught up in the wave of optimism that at times makes men enthusiasts? How to be gloomy in a world where everyone is optimistic? How not to flinch in the face of the possible social repercussions of the closure of poorly organized but grandiose factories? We cannot ask men to operate beyond the limits of mortal strength. We can only hope that, though history is not *magistra vitae**, the accumulated experience of the past will be of some use; and that the drivers of the two economic locomotives, assets and debts, hurtling towards each other at 150 kilometres an hour, know how to apply the brakes some minutes in advance so that the collision takes place at the speed of 50. We can derive a measure of moderate optimism from the study of the past. The current crises are less violent than the crises of the eighteenth century and those of the first half of the nineteenth century, the unemployment and misery less appalling. They are hitting the older countries of western Europe less severely than the new countries. The gravest aspects of the current crisis are not due to economic factors; they are remnants of the wartime mentality and must therefore be cured with non-economic remedies. Without being naively optimistic, we can hope that if non-economic forces do not deter them from doing their duty the central bank governors will in the future be increasingly skilful and timely in applying the brakes of the world economic machine whose controls are in their hands.

* Teaching the ways of life.

10
My Plan is not Keynes's*

Keynes's 'essay' (saggio) ... I use this word not having found a better one for what in English would be a tract or in French a pamphlet. But in reality 'essay' does not convey the concept of a piece penned for the occasion, of a weapon of political and economic contest, which is a feature of the short vehement writings in which practical battles were conducted or theoretical principles set out. The literature of economics, the great literature of economics is typically made up of essays. If someone were to compile a dictionary of economic discoveries, giving the sources in which they were first enounced, they would cite many more short essays than large books. The word libello was once used, very appropriately, for this kind of short and important writings; but this is no longer possible owing to the way it has been misused.

Keynes's 'essay' can be summarized in the following chain of propositions.

I. Let us suppose that the present crisis is due to a failure in the working of the immaterial devices of the mind which lead to decisions and acts of will. That it is a paradox that so many building workers are unemployed when there is so great a need for houses. That the problem is not of means and will to work; that it is not an engineering, agricultural, business, organizational or banking problem. That it is rather a problem of the mind, and resembles the quandary of two skilled drivers of lorries in perfect order who, meeting with plenty of room to pass, cannot get by because, not knowing the rules of the road, they run into each other, not knowing who should keep to the right and who to the left. Today's economic paradox lies in the lack of contact between available factors of production – unemployed men, idle machines, uncultivated land, unused raw materials – and

*It first appeared as 'Il mio piano non è quello di Keynes', *Riforma Sociale,* XL, Vol. XLIV, No. 2 (March–April 1933), pp.129–42. It was a review of *The Means to Prosperity*, by John Maynard Keynes (London: Macmillan, 1933), p.37.

the desire or need for the goods that the unemployed factors would produce if they were employed.

II. Normally, the contact between factors of production and desire for goods is brought about by entrepreneurs in search of profits. The economic machine is set in motion by entrepreneurs, who, by buying factors of production in the market and selling products, play the role in today's society of the paterfamilias in closed patriarchal societies, of the prior or guardian in medieval monasteries, of the minister of production in a collectivist society. But entrepreneurs are operative, that is, assume risks, when they see the chance of a profit, of a positive difference between the price received for the products sold and the cost of the factors of production bought. Once the contact has been established, the enterprise set in motion, the latter is self-sufficient, because the productive factors consume what they themselves produce. Not materially the same goods, because these are exchanged for goods produced by others; but effectively the same goods in a different form.

Today, the contact is not made because entrepreneurs do not hope for profits. The economic machine is blocked. The factors of production, machinery and men, remain unemployed and men's desires remain unsatisfied. Those in work have to pay enormous taxes to keep those out of work alive. We must break the spell blocking the machine.

III. Since the mechanism cannot be unblocked by the normal economic motive of profit, a device must be found. Do we want to give work to a million unemployed? At L10,000 per head,[1] a fund of L10 billion will suffice. If private entrepreneurs do not dare, let the state dare. Of the L10 billion spent, the state is certain to recover, between what it saves on the dole and what it gains from higher tax receipts on taxpayers' increased incomes, at least five.

IV. Let us suppose that the state borrows the fund of L10 billion from someone who possesses it (or creates it); let us suppose that the loan is granted long term and at a modest rate of interest (where modest means probably one of the lowest rates known in history). There it is, a use for the factors of production already existing and available: land to be reclaimed, sea inlets to be turned into ports, building materials to be transformed into houses and unemployed men to be put to work on the land, the sea and the houses. There it is, the miracle of getting the economic machine going again without increasing the prices of productive factors or products ... 'If there were little or no margin of unemployed resources, then ... the increased expenditure would largely waste itself in higher prices and increased imports.' I cite this passage because, after much racking of my brains, I concluded that the gist of the argument was in these few words.

If, instead, there really are unemployed workers and factors of production, the contact made between them does not cause harmful perturbations in other social groups. It would be as if the million unemployed could be transported to a hitherto deserted island and there provide for their own necessities. What harm would this do to the other members of the community? Rather, they would enjoy two advantages: relief from the heavy burden of the dole and a division of the cost of public expenditure (taxes) among themselves and those formerly unemployed instead of just among themselves.

The problem would be more complicated if only unemployed workers were available but no material productive resources, because in this case the new demand engendered by the L10 billion of the state fund would converge on a fixed mass of productive resources and cause their price to rise. The state would compete with private entrepreneurs, upsetting the basis of their economic calculations, with consequences that are hard to foresee. Nothing of the kind in the hypothesis put forward: idle workers, machines, fields, ships, railways and ports exist; they do not produce because they are disconnected. Bring them into contact and with the goods produced the unemployed will feed themselves, without asking for anything from anybody; on the contrary, they will no longer receive alms from others. Indeed, the total output is likely to increase more than proportionately with respect to the additional labour employed. Because if the output is 90 million units where 9 million men work to feed 10 million, where all 10 million work, the more perfect division of labour and the greater incentive to work owing to the unchanged burden of taxes will probably result in the output being 100 + x million units.

V. It thus appears that only one link in the chain is missing in order to resolve today's economic paradox: the fund of L10 billion the state needs in order to create the demand in the market for the factors of production capable of producing the new output.

In old-fashioned countries and among old-fashioned economists such as the writer, the answer to the question: 'Where are the L10 billion to be obtained?' would be: 'From savers'. Until a few years ago when talking about saving what came to mind was the typical *bonus pater familias** who earns 100 every year, month or day and, spending 80, takes the remaining 20 to the bank. If, by piling up 20 on 20, at the end of a year a fund of 10 billion is constituted, here is the expedient, the sought-after device capable of setting the mechanism in motion. Some minor obstacles will have to be overcome: for the state to borrow L10 billion, the fund of new annual savings will probably have to be much more than L10 billion, since it is inconceivable that there should not also be a private demand for

* Dutiful father.

savings, if no other than that of those obstinate people who, even in times of crisis, continue to hanker for a house, a well-tended field or a shop in perfect order and similar anti-economic follies, which, however, are the *raison d'être* of many more people than is commonly believed. To the man in the street and to old-fashioned economists it thus appears absurd to obtain a loan of L10 million if the L10 million have not first been set aside and are not yet available. Without the hare, one cannot make a hare pie.

VI. It appears, instead, that in the advanced countries hare pies are now made with rabbits. In other words I have the impression that for some time English economists have been assiduously engaged in the noble task of looking for rabbits to use in the place of hares. When old-fashioned saving is mentioned, they grimace. Either because so much effort or sacrifice is not needed, since our present ills are not due to famine, earthquakes or wars or even to a lack of resources but to the failure of some cog in men's minds to work properly, or because it is a desperate undertaking to induce men to save with incomes so greatly diminished and taxes so high ('Incomes are so curtailed to-day and taxation so much increased, that many people are already, in the effort to maintain their standard of life, saving less than sound personal habits require'), the fact is that many avant-garde economists prefer to turn their attention to the surrogate of savings rather than to savings in the traditional sense. It is not easy to explain what this surrogate of savings is. It is something nebulous, a mixture of old and plausible concepts and new abstractions. The paternity, involuntary and aimed at a different end, can be traced back to a little known economist belonging to the Ricardian school, James Pennington, who in 1829 (in a letter sent to Tommaso Tooke and published by the same as an appendix to his *A letter to Lord Grenville on the effects ascribed to the resumption of cash payments on the value of the currency*, London, John Murray, 1829) supposedly demonstrated that banks can, with certain limits, create credit. The theory whereby *first* the saver sets aside L20 (or L10 billion among all the savers in the country), *then* he takes them to the bank and *finally* the bank lends them to entrepreneurs, or if they are timid, to the state in order to set in motion the blocked economic mechanism is seen as antiquated or at least inadequate. Alongside it there is another, and in the modern countries apparently much weightier, theory, whereby *first* the bank grants a customer (an entrepreneur or the state) a line of credit, *then* the customer draws cheques on the bank up to the amount of the credit received, *next* the beneficiaries of the cheques pay in the sums to the same or other banks and thus, *finally*, bank *deposits* are created; on average they follow from and are equal to the credit the banks themselves have granted.

VII. Here we have it, we have caught the tail of the rabbit needed to make the pie we want. A way must be found for the banks to grant L10 billion of credit. If private entrepreneurs are loath to ask for credit even at 3 per cent or 2 per cent, because they fear they will make a loss on the ventures they are advised to undertake, let the credit be granted to the state, which does not need to take account of profits and costs, and which can find a gain (smaller unemployment benefits and larger tax revenues) where there would be none for private entrepreneurs.

VIII. But the banks cannot grant credit, either in the old-fashioned way after receiving deposits or in the new way of first granting loans in the knowledge that they will later be covered by deposits, without observing some prudential rules based on experience. For every L100 of deposits only 100 – *y* lire of credit must be granted, where *y* is the reserve in cash (banknotes) or sight deposits with the bank of issue that banks must prudentially hold so as to be always ready to meet the demand for the repayment of deposits. A fault, that of asking to be repaid, common to old-fashioned depositors and to those of a modern ilk. That is to say, deposits and hence loans are a function, a multiple of the reserves held by the banks. If experience advised, for example, a reserve of 10 per cent, the banks would be able to grant short- and long-term credit only up to the multiple of nine times the reserves they hold. Even the theorists of the 'bank which creates credit' admit that its initiatory creative power is not arbitrary.

IX. In turn, the reserve of the banks, consisting of notes issued by the central bank or in sight deposits held with the same, is not an arbitrary quantity. It is a fraction of a country's total note issue, with the remainder to be found in myriad small and large reserves of notes existing at any given time in the pockets or drawers of private citizens or sundry entities.

X. For its part, the total stock of notes circulating in a country is a multiple of the central bank' gold reserve. If experience or laws, which should be crystallized experience, indicate that central banks should hold gold equal to 40 per cent of their notes, the total amount of notes cannot be more than two-and-a-half times this reserve.

Indeed, since experience suggests flexible rather than rigid rules, in times of danger it is desirable to increase the ratio of the reserve to notes. In normal times, if the gold reserve is 10 billion, the notes in circulation can rise to as much as two-and-a-half times that amount, i.e., to 25 billion. In times of crisis, when, in order to meet requests for payments abroad, the gold reserve has fallen to 8 billion and it is feared that it will fall further, the central bank prudently reduces the multiple to two and the stock of notes issued to 16 billion.

XI. If we now work backwards, we will easily discover the expedient, the remedy, the *device* that Keynes proposes:

(a) if the note circulation corresponding to a gold reserve of 8 billion and a multiple of 2, i.e., a proportion of 50 per cent, is 16 billion;
(b) if 4 of the 16 billion of notes in circulation are in the vaults of the commercial banks (including savings banks and other credit institutions) and constitute these banks' note reserve;
(c) if the commercial banks' note reserve of 4 billion corresponds to a willingness on their part to grant credit totalling $4 \times 9 = 36$ billion;

what condition is sufficient for them to *double* the amount they are willing to lend, i.e., to increase their lines of credit from 36 billion to around 72 billion?

The answer is obvious: increase the gold reserves of the central bank sufficiently;

(a) if they rise from 8 to 10 billion, the central bank is less anxious and is ready to increase the multiple of the note issue from 2 to 2.5 and the notes in circulation to 25 billion;
(b) if, of the 25 billion of notes in circulation a quarter, as before, consists of the commercial banks' note reserve, this will be equal to 6.25 billion;
(c) if the ordinary credit banks, encouraged by such a large increase in their note reserve, raise their multiple for the granting of credit from 9 to 12, lo and behold, their lines of credit jump to $6.25 \times 12 = 75$ billion. In other words, more than the desired result.

XII. That, set out above in orderly fashion, is the genesis of Keynes's sensational proposal: let a mass of $5 billion of international gold-notes be created by a world central bank, the Bank for International Settlements in Basel, or some other body. The notes should be accepted in the same way as gold; they should not enter into the active circulation; they would be used exclusively by the Treasuries and the Central banks of the participating countries and would be considered equivalent to the latter's real gold reserve.

The notes would be provided on loan, against gold-bonds for an equal amount and with a very low rate of interest, to those governments that applied for them and undertook to abolish every foreign exchange restriction and every customs duty and quota that had been introduced not because of a given economic policy but exclusively as a defence against imports from countries with devalued currencies or against exports of capital.

Governments and central banks would be able, subject to the removal of foreign exchange and trade restrictions, to use the notes received in the way they deemed most appropriate: to pay urgent foreign debts, restore budgetary equilibrium, expand domestic note-issues on the basis of the increase in the gold reserve.

Each country would have the right to receive a quota of the $5 billion proportional to its holding of gold in 1928, up to a maximum of $450 million. Each country would be responsible, in proportion to its quota, for losses incurred in the management of the new monetary stock.

XIII. Up to this point the reasoning runs straight. Dangerously so, as on a razor's edge, but straight. Suddenly, there is a bolt from the blue:

> The governing board [of the new world central bank] would be directed to use their discretion to modify the volume of the note-issue [above or below the $5 billion] or the rate of interest on the bonds, solely with a view to avoiding, so far as possible, a rise in the gold price-level of primary products entering into international trade above some agreed norm between the present level and that of 1928 – perhaps the level of 1930.

Keynes had in fact dedicated a whole chapter of the essay to describing the ways to raise prices. That it is advantageous, indeed necessary, to raise the general price level is not questioned for a moment by the author, who does not consider it even necessary to give the reasons for such a goal. In an interesting article published in the *Spectator* of 24 March, Sir Arthur Salter declared himself to be in favour of Keynes's proposal, arguing from the point of view of the current situation in England: that a credit expansion is desirable today because the world is at the bottom of the downward phase of the economic cycle; that there have already been three years of credit restrictions, which have reduced prices and costs and eliminated doubtful and bad firms; that prices cannot be allowed to fall any further in the face of a huge burden of debts and fixed costs of every kind; that now or never is therefore the time to give a fillip to prices, with a bold policy of credit and public works; that today, in contrast with 1931, England can afford the luxury of grandiose loans and public works, since the budget has returned to balance and public credit is granitic.

XIV. I do not question the value of the bolt in itself; but I do suggest that it is a foreign body with respect to the reasoning of Keynes, who started from the premise of the existence of available factors of production that had to be set in motion with a device *without touching the general level of prices*. What other meaning can be attributed to the words reproduced above that 'If there were little or no margin of unemployed resources, … the increased expenditure' [whether of private or public bodies does not matter] 'would largely waste itself in higher prices and increased imports'? And earlier he had insisted that the new expenditure (on public works) had to be additional and not merely in substitution for the expenditure that would otherwise be undertaken by private agents; and that, in order to reduce unemployment, the new expenditure had to be directed towards available factors of production. 'If the resources of the country were already fully employed, these additional purchases [generated by the public works] would be mainly reflected in higher prices and increased imports.'

XV. The fall of the bolt is not, I admit, all that important. It needs to be mentioned in order to show how Keynes vacillates between two aims of his proposal: to enable countries, with public loans, to employ the available factors of production, without changing prices, or to give impetus to an expansionary credit policy that will push up prices, restore profits and hence the stimulus for private entrepreneurs to act. Adopting the interpretation most consistent with Keynes's intentions, it is also possible to consider that the bolt is not a foreign body but a second stage of the logical process. In this case the complete chain would be the following:

(a) the new international stock of money is created;
(b) increased in this way, the reserve of the banks of issue permits an expansionary credit policy;
(c) countries first take advantage of this, with loans and public works, to put the unemployed to work and to use the idle factors of production;
(d) as a result of this initial impulse, confidence recovers, prices rise, hopes of profits appear, entrepreneurs wake up. The rusted economic machine, encouraged by the oil of optimism, begins to move, slowly at first and then faster and faster. The crisis is over.

My reconstruction of the thinking of the eminent Cambridge economist is not intended to facilitate criticism of the details of his main proposal. Insofar as this says that in the troughs of the economic cycle a policy of public works pursued by the government is advantageous, it restates a classical theory. With the appropriate precautions regarding the limits of the effectiveness of public works and the need to discontinue them when the economic cycle begins to rise from the bottom of the trough and to climb towards the peak, classical theory is also in agreement.

My aim in carrying out this reconstruction was, instead, to provide a typical example of the dangerousness of walking straight ahead on the razor's edge. The whole chain rests, in its main part, on the truth of the first proposition, that the present crisis is due to the defective working of some immaterial device of the mind underlying human action; and in the additional part (the bolt of proposition XIII), that in order to recreate profits and hence restore, after the initial impulse of state-financed public works, the incentive for the spontaneous operation of entrepreneurs, it is desirable to raise the general price level. If these two premises are true, what follows is true. If the world is upside down because the unemployed cannot make contact with the resources that are available, it is obvious that the push, the expedient, the device proposed by Keynes is sufficient to set it straight, to put it in motion. Whatever the expedient may be – the granting of loans in dribs and drabs by banks or wholesale reflation with an international flood of paper money, it can help. Against a sickness of the mind, against bewitchment, the doctor must turn himself into a witch-doctor and use the same magic arts. Rightly, the production of paper money occupies a high place among spells. Since the masses no longer believe, after the experience of the post-war period, in national paper money, let us exorcise them with international paper money bearing an international stamp. If that helps drive out the demon of pessimism and inertia, let us perform this exorcism.

Is it really true though that the crisis is a sickness of the mind due to such a spell? At the very start of his essay Keynes recognizes that 'If our poverty were due to famine or earthquake or war – if we lacked material things and the resources to produce them, we could not expect to find the Means to Prosperity except in hard work, abstinence, and invention.' He admits this for a moment and as an abstract hypothesis, only to deny that these are the causes of the sickness: 'In fact, our predicament is notoriously of another kind.' And goes on to put forward the proposition described above.

I would say that 'notoriously' the causes of our afflictions are those that he denies: the war and the diseases it implanted into the minds of men, that is greed, the desire for rapid enrichment, impatience with hard work, inability to renounce and save, intolerance of the long wait for the fruit of effort; a spirit of intolerant nationalism that has closed peoples in on themselves and left unused a large part of the existing natural resources, producing the same effects as the famines of earlier times; religious fanaticism in Russia, China and India, religious even if in new communistic, xenophobic and Gandhian forms, which leads men to prefer to go without food and without clothes rather than have dangerous contact with infidels. How can one pretend that the crisis is a spell, and that by pulling some paper switch the spell will be broken when every day, even with eyes that are only half open, it can be seen that the opposite is true? There are, it cannot be gainsaid, some cases to be seen of innocent disaster, of healthy firms overwhelmed by the storm. But innumerable are the examples of deserved punishment! Every time the facts are established when an edifice collapses, they tell us of directors and entrepreneurs who were incompetent, or reckless or dishonest. The firms run by persons who are competent have difficult moments but they survive. The crash of ruins, instead, around those who aggrandized themselves by heaping up debts, planned colossi, dominations, trusts and cartels; around those who, to shore up the paper house, fabricated more paper and sold paper to half the world; around those who, instead of racking their brains to invent and apply new technical devices or better methods of working and organization won applause and profits by inventing chains of companies, emoluments for straw directors, elegant revaluations of assets. There has been a spell and it has not yet been broken; but it is the spell of the stupid, the unscrupulous and the arrogant. To inject paper, even international paper, into a world from which the stupid, the unscrupulous and the arrogant have not yet been chased, except in part, is not the way to cure the sickness but to feed and inflame it. It is not the euphoria of paper money that is needed, but the repentance, contrition and punishment of the sinners, the inventive diligence of the survivors. Outside the catechism of the Roman Catholic Church there is no salvation; the crisis will not be overcome except by abandoning vice and practising virtue.

If only the wizardry of paper money served to recreate profits and thus give renewed impulse to the activity of private entrepreneurs! Alas! here again the chain of the reasoning appears broken! It appears, according to some, that the rings are:

(a) on the basis of the expanded reserves, the banks increase the lines of credit they grant, at a low rate of interest;
(b) the public works carried out using this credit give the first upward push to prices;
(c) the rise in prices recreates profits or the hope of profits;
(d) the renewed hope of profits gives impulse to the spirit of private enterprise.

Proposition (c), *the rise in prices recreates profits or the hope of profits*, is true only on the assumption that the public works carried out using the credit push up precisely those prices that must rise to restore equilibrium. The lack of profits does not stem from the fact that prices are low, but from the very different fact that they are out of kilter. If every price were lowered by 50 per cent – or, for each good, in the proportion necessary to take account of the conditions, changed in the meantime, of production and demand – the crisis would not exist; because it is possible to sell at a profit at 50 in the same way as at 100 if the prices of the factors of production have also fallen to 50. The crisis and the lack of profits stem from the imbalance in prices, from the fact that some prices did not fall or were not allowed to fall; and since prices are revenues for some and costs for others, many lose and especially the entrepreneurs. A rise in prices provoked by public works carried out through the inflation of credit would leave the imbalance unchanged between one price and another, that is between costs and revenues. It might aggravate it.[2]

If it is true, for example, that some agricultural commodities and some mineral raw materials have fallen too far in relation to some industrial products, to the prices of labour and public services (taxes) and to the interest on debt, it would be necessary for the demand deriving from the new spendable resources provided by the creation of the new stock of money to be directed exclusively towards the goods and services whose prices have fallen in relative terms. Is such a programme humanly possible? Do instruments exist that are sufficiently sophisticated to measure the imbalances between the prices of different goods? Do instruments exist that are capable of distinguishing between a price reduction stemming from an imbalance and those due to technical reasons: a reduction in costs, a change in tastes?

Because, if an equilibrium once existed

between different goods	*A*	*B*	*C*	*D*
with prices	10	12	8	15
and the current prices	8	4	7	5

do not allow the producers of *B* and *D* to operate profitably, so that they greatly reduce their demand for *A* and *C*, why imagine that the crisis can be overcome by injecting paper money into the world and increasing prices by 50 per cent to:

12	6	10.50	7.50 ?

The imbalance exists nonetheless; *B* and *D* cannot be produced at the excessively high relative prices (costs) of *A* and *C*. Is it possible to make the injections in such a way as to return to the initial level: 10, 12, 8 and 15? How can the miracle be accomplished? Are we certain the level that was initially balanced is still so? Oh! is it not better to grit our teeth and, as Machlup advises, to force *B* and *D*, with sufficiently high discount rates, to liquidate their overhang of stocks as fast as possible, indeed with further price falls, but with contemporaneous adjustments of the quantities produced; so that, in the end, having cleared the field of the threatening backlog of unsold goods, the prices return to 6 and 8? In the meantime, *A* and *C*, forced to pay a high interest rate and faced with reductions in the demand for *B* and *D*, will also have had to lower their prices. The cartels set up to resist will have laid down their arms and will have been dissolved; and in the end it will be possible for a new equilibrium to emerge at the following prices:

7	6	5	8

At the new level, there is a return to profitability. The crisis is over.

The major obstacle to the resolution of the crisis are prices fixed by law (taxes) or under long-term contracts (interest on public and private debts) or under rigid conventions between social groups (wages and salaries). Ultimately, inflationary mechanisms are contrived with the aim of outflanking and surrounding fortresses that are deemed impossible to take with frontal attacks. Taxpayers, weighed down by an excessive burden of taxes (including the interest on public debts); industrialists and farmers, unable, at a time of falling prices, to pay unchanged taxes, wages and interest, hope for the monetary manoeuvre. If at time *I* the national income was 100 and the share of it absorbed by the recipients of fixed incomes (public employees, interest on public and private debts) was 25 and that going to semi-fixed incomes (private-sector salaries, wages, rents, etc.) was 40, there remained 35 for the recipients of variable incomes (owner-operators, tenant farmers, sharecroppers, industrialists, tradesmen, craftsmen, members of the professions). The situation was more or less in equilibrium.

If at time *II*, when prices have fallen by 35 per cent, so that the national income amounts to 65, the share absorbed by the recipients of fixed incomes remains unchanged at 25 and that going to semi-fixed incomes has fallen to, say, 30, the share remaining for the recipients of variable incomes, those who run the risk of obtaining more or less, is clearly just 10. They, and they are many, complain that they can no longer live.

If all prices were fluid, they would all fall by about one-third: to 17, 27, and 21. Since such fluidity is opposed by laws, controls, customs, powerful pressures of strong social forces, the recipients of variable incomes, crushed between the anvil of fixed or semi-fixed costs and the hammer of falling prices, convinced of the impossibility of obtaining tax reductions, amicable compositions with creditors, agreements to lower wages from trade unions, invoke with anguish the expedient that will allow prices and incomes to be raised back up from 65 to 100, with the minimum friction and universal content. Keynes prescribes for the purpose the remedy of the $5 billion gold-notes printed to supplement the gold reserves.

By now, however, the original equilibrium has been destroyed. Who says that we must return to the original proportions of 25 for fixed incomes, 40 for semi-fixed incomes and 35 for variable incomes? When paper money is printed, the intention may well be to proceed with courtesy and justice. But in the grab grab of the world of the $5 billion gold-notes, the smartest win; and it would be no surprise if taxes and creditors succeeded in raising their share from 25 to 35; wage-earners and other recipients of semi-fixed incomes theirs from 30 to 40, so that the recipients of variable incomes were left with the remaining 25; better than 10, but not as much as might appear since the 10 were out of 65 and the 25 out of 100. Moreover, would all the recipients of variable incomes perhaps participate equally in the abundance or would the preference go to the smartest?

Those who remember that the social disorders of the post-war period were due not to the war in itself but to the inflation that, albeit not inevitably, accompanied it[3] will be dismayed by the possible social consequences of a new experiment with paper money so soon after the recent experience. Such experiments can be repeated, although at very great risk, only at intervals of a century: the European war of 1914–18; the French assignats of 1790–6; Law's system of 1715–20. To repeat the experiment today could imply the collapse of western civilization.

We know the response of the inflationists, or reflationists as they prefer to call themselves today: the reflation will be prudent, limited to what is necessary to raise prices not from 65 to 100, but to no more than 80, surrounded by binding guarantees. All told, I believe that the recipients of variable incomes run less risk in making the best of a bad lot than in resorting to expedients. The monetary device is like trying one's luck at Monte Carlo. It may work but it may revive the disorders of 1918–20. New unwarranted enrichments and new undeserved impoverishments would cause the fire of social hates and envies, which appeared to be dying down with difficulty, to flare up again. As always in history, the cheats, the profiteers and the parvenus would know how to save themselves in time. The victims would be the innocent, the industrialists, the farmers, the upright and judicious shopkeepers, who have so far resisted the impact of the crisis.

No. There is less risk in paying high taxes and unchanged interest rates. It is better to resign oneself to not having income, to leaving one's share to be temporarily enjoyed, as a sort of premium for the insurance of social peace, by office and factory workers. In the long run those who succeed in paying the interest agreed will see their credit increase. Governments and individuals will be able to convert their debts, as soon as this is legally possible, from 8 to 6 per cent, from 6 to 5 per cent, from 5 to 4 and to 3 and perhaps to 21/2 per cent. Scrupulous respect of the word given, even if this involves putting up with what is, or appears to be a major injustice, is still, and will continue to be for some time, the best guarantee of success in life for individuals and nations.

11
The Concluding Remarks of the Governor of the Bank of Italy for the year 1946*

During his tenure as Governor of the Bank of Italy Einaudi transformed the Annual Report of the Bank into an exercise quite different from a mere description of the activities of the Bank. It became a full account and analysis of economic transformation, and the Final Considerations, read aloud in the presence of all the political and economic establishment of the country, became a permanent occasion for complete reassessments of governmental economic policy by an independent technical body. In 1947, Einaudi described a country emerging defeated from World War, trying to recover confiscated resources and occupied territories, dealing with reconstruction but burdened by debt, deficit and an inflated paper circulation. Einaudi's analysis of the difficulties of reconstruction and of the growing inflation anticipated a vigorous shift in economic policy. Only a few months later Einaudi introduced, as budget minister, a plan to combat inflation through both a banking restriction and budget cuts, and successfully implemented it.

Gentlemen,

A survey of the economic conditions in Italy during the year 1946 gives the impression of an uneven improvement reached, with great difficulty, in spite of marked contrasts as to the way production should be organized and the social product distributed, which contrasts have not prevented, however, the full life of the single initiatives and have not hindered their creative power.

---

*First published as *Annual Report of the Governor of the Banca d'Italia to the Shareholders of the Bank, at the Ordinary General Meeting held in Rome on March 31st, 1947, on the Bank's Activity for the year 1946* (Rome: Printing Office of the Banca d'Italia, 1947). The text was originally translated into English in an abridged version by the Bank of Italy and only the final considerations have been reproduced here, without the analysis of the balance sheet and the ordinary activities of the Bank of Italy.

However, this survey also shows that the monetary uncertainty has penetrated, as a disturbing element, or as a risk – to be neutralized and used as a source of profit – into the consumer's and the producer's calculations with the result that the production and the exchanges received disorderly stimuli and shocks, while the salary problems got confused and dangerous self-amplifying processes took place.

It is a duty both for you and myself to find out on the present occasion, through an examination of the Bank's balance-sheet, what the origin of such a situation is and to be guided accordingly in the future.

Final considerations

... It is now essential to investigate the facts that have occurred, by way of what I shall call a 'moral-economic' analysis.

How did it happen that the Governor of the Banca d'Italia watched, without reacting, the circulation rise between the end of May 1946, and 20 January 1947 – at which date the subscriptions to the Reconstruction Loan were closed – by an amount of L103,817 million, which corresponds almost exactly, barring the L10 billion subscribed by the Institute of Deposits and Loans, to the L102 billion subscribed in cash to the loan? The first impression these two figures give is that on one side the Italian Treasury had the opportunity to enrich its current account with the Banca d'Italia with L102 billion, and that the latter having issued during the same period almost L104 billion worth of additional notes, a L206 billion fund was thus created and should be at the Treasury's disposal for the reconstruction. We already know that from an accounting viewpoint this did not happen.

Using for a while a language pertaining to the concepts of fault and of responsibility, we find the following.

1 That the State Treasury has no direct responsibility whatsoever for the increased circulation: the Treasury's debt towards the Bank – for various items including the ordinary and extraordinary advances, the former special transactions of the *Consorzio Valori* (which were a particular type of loan to the Treasury), the cover of AM lire issued (another form of loan to the State on the part of the Bank) and miscellaneous minor services – was L502,604 million in May 1946, and L503,401 million on 20 January 1947. The difference (of L797 million as an absolute figure and of just slightly over 1 per cent in relative proportion) is indeed too small and so easily explained by the overlap of the enormous number of debit and credit entries between the State and the Banca d'Italia, to allow a claim of responsibility to be brought against any Minister of the Treasury.
2 That the Banca d'Italia, as an institution operating, by its nature, the business of banking, has no responsibility either for the increased circulation. Between May 1946, and 20 January 1947, it received L11,327 million

more of deposits under various forms and employed out of that sum only L8,577 more, thus withdrawing L2,750 million from circulation. The Governor of the Banca d'Italia is therefore at least as innocent as the Minister of the Treasury for the increase in the circulation.

Could the Banca d'Italia, first of all, refuse to supply the Allies with funds in notes, which they previously procured by issuing AM lire? Under the 24 January convention it was obliged to; and that convention seemed – and was indeed – advantageous for the country, as it enabled the Bank to control the circulation efficiently. Our Institution could certainly not refuse to furnish notes of its own, when the corresponding dollar credits in the United States are precisely subject to such a delivery. Between May 1946, and 20 January 1947, the deliveries have risen from L11,834 to L22,492 million, with an increase of L10,658 million.

Could the Bank refuse to rediscount the bills pertaining to the compulsory pools of cereals and other products considered of prime necessity? The law appoints the Consortiums for operating such pools and imposes upon them to find the means for paying the price of the wheat to the farmers immediately through advances on the part of institutions authorized to finance such transactions. But as these institutions do not have sufficient funds, they are obliged to rediscount the bills with the Banca d'Italia. In the aforementioned period, the amount of rediscounts to the compulsory cereal pools (the rediscount of the voluntary deliveries of products, being an ordinary commercial transaction, was included among the usual banking transactions) increased by L31,377 million.

Could the Bank refuse to pay to the Italian Exchange Office the sums needed for purchasing from the Italian exporters the dollars, pounds, Swiss francs, pesos and other first-class free currencies (at present 50% of the amounts coming in to them) which the exporters are bound by the law to surrender to the Exchange Office at the official rates? It would be the same as saying that the exports are prohibited; because the Italian manufacturers, when exporting, need the lire equivalent of the exported goods for covering the cost of the raw material, the salaries, their general and sundry expenses. In the same aforesaid period – May 1946 to 20 January 1947 – L27,607 million were thus paid out by the Bank. To suppose the Bank could act differently would mean that it was free to suspend the activity of the export industries, to leave hundreds of thousand workers jobless, to deprive the country of most important credits in foreign currencies, which are essential for our economic life.

Furthermore, could the Bank, the depository by law of large deposits from the banking institutions, refuse to reimburse the latter when they in their turn had to face withdrawals on the part of their customers? Just to mention a typical example, how could the owners of savings accounts subscribe to the Reconstruction Loan if not by withdrawing a part of them? Between May 1946 and 20 January 1947, the deposit accounts of the banking institutions decreased from L125,447 to L90,986 million a reduction of 34,461 million.

Finally, could the Banca d'Italia, as the State's Treasurer, refuse to pay to the State the sums standing to the latter's credit in its current account with the Bank? The Bank, which on 31 May 1946 had a balance of L45,598 million to the credit of the Treasury, paid out to the latter, or by its order, funds totalling L4,556 million the balance being thus reduced to 41,042 million (see Table 11.1).

Table 11.1

	L million
Supply of funds to Allies	10,658
Rediscount to compulsory pools	31,377
Purchase of foreign currency	27,607
Deposit accounts reimbursed	34,461
Diminution in Treasury's current account	4,556
Together	108,659

Table 11.1 shows that the total amount of outgoing notes explains more than amply the increase of L103,817 million in the circulation.

We must go on in our analysis and find out what caused the condition of necessity the Bank found itself in of issuing in seven months and twenty days L104 billion lire of additional notes.

Let us take an example: the compulsory wheat pools. Out of L31.4 billion of extra bills pertaining to the compulsory agricultural pools, not less than 28.7 originated from rediscounts covering the wheat pools. Adding the rediscounts already made on 31 May and still existing on 20 January 1947, the rediscount to the wheat pools amounted to L32.9 milliard for Banca d'Italia alone. A further L30 billion must be added for wheat pools bills discounted by banks and not presented yet for rediscount to Banca d'Italia. Altogether, at the above mentioned date of 20 January 1947, over L60 billion have been advanced by the Italian banking system and not returned to it so as to allow the regular transfer of the wheat from the farmers to the consumers. To whom was the sum of over L60 billion advanced? It is to be noted that in the 1946/47 campaign the mills are paying the wheat to the pools at a rate of L900 per quintal; and as the pools are operated in the interest of the State, all the latter gets back for the sale of wheat are these L900 a quintal, just a little more than what is needed to cover the cost of operating the pools (L240), the expenses of the UNSEA, National Statistical Economic Office for Agriculture, (L175), plus transportation (L400). If we add the cost of grinding and baking, we may say that the State does not even get back the actual cost of the transformation and distribution of wheat, so that the average price of L2,700 per quintal paid to the producer remains entirely at the government's charge.

What do these figures mean from the banking angle?

We must consider two elements: the 'compulsory pools' and the 'political price of bread'.

The former element, if not combined with the latter, would only mean more work, with interest and commissions artfully credited, by law, to the banks. When the pools did not exist, the transfer of wheat from the producer to the consumer was taken care of directly by the farmers, the millers and the bakers. The farmer gradually sold his stocks and, instead of an interest in their value, enjoyed a psychological benefit, originating from the contemplation of the wheat stored in his barns and from the feeling of security given by such food supplies, as well as another benefit, of a pecuniary nature, consisting in the hope for a rise in prices. The compulsory pools replaced such forms of compensation with the security for the farmer to get the proceeds immediately; whereas the banks earn interest and commissions on the handling of the corresponding money.

The second element, however, the 'political price of bread', has added to the first one further aspects which are to be carefully considered.

Be the price of bread the economic or the political one, the entire amount paid by the State and by the consumer to the parties involved in the production of bread (the L2,700 given to the farmers, the L2,300 and more per quintal paid for transportation, for operating the pools, for grinding, for baking) is being spent by the farmers, the millers, the bakers, the employees of the various offices and administrations concerned, for purchasing consumption goods and instrumental goods. The entire sum of, say, L5,000 per quintal is thus placed again in circulation, except those very small quantities which the peasants are again hoarding, as they used to before the years 1944–45; and once such sums are placed again in circulation they have an influence on the prices.

What influence? Here arises the difference between the economic price and the political price systems.

When the price of bread is the economic one the entire sum of about L5,000 per quintal of wheat turned into bread and macaroni would be reimbursed by the consumers and, after deduction of the portions due to the intermediate stages of production, would go back to the bakers, the mills, the carriers, the pool organizations; from here, reduced to the L2,700 originally paid to the farmers, it would return to the financing institutions and, with respect to the rediscounted bills, to the Banca d'Italia. In connection with the economic price system, the circulation reaches therefore its yearly minimum towards the end of the wheat campaign. In the 1940–41 campaign the rediscounts to the wheat pools started in August with L901 million, reached a maximum of L1,603 million in October and gradually came down to L82 million in June 1941; in the 1941–42 campaign the respective figures are L496, L1,296 and L218 million; similarly in the 1942–3 campaign, such rediscounts started with L1,067 million in August, went up to L1,768 million in October and down again to L410 million in next June. It was a regular cyclic motion, which allowed anyone to make anticipations.

In 1945–46, as a consequence at first of an accumulation of arrears and then owing to the sudden return of the political price of bread – which system the late Minister of the Treasury, Soleri, in vain tried, for a second time in his life, to abolish – the minimum is L2,701 million in May, 1945, and the year's maximum is L6,054 in November, which then decreases very slowly. In May, 1946, for wheat alone we have only come down to L4,220 million.

After that it is a non-stop *crescendo*. The rediscounts to the compulsory pools, existing with Banca d'Italia, reached the totals shown below.

5,097	million	at the end of	May	1946
5,332	"	"	June	"
12,064	"	"	July	"
19,022	"	"	August	"
23,494	"	"	September	"
24,994	"	"	October	"
25,711	"	"	November	"
33,229	"	"	December	"
36,474	"	"	January	1947

What has happened is clear enough. Out of the sum of about L5,000 per quintal of wheat paid to the various parties involved in the production, perhaps only one-half is paid by the purchasers of the bread and, owing to the various expenses to be covered, fails to go back as far as the banking institutions which advanced the cost of the wheat. The L2,700 remain a debt on the part of the State. The notes do not come back. Supposing, but hoping for the contrary, that the political price system should still be maintained in our country, the present debt of the State towards the Banca d'Italia and the other banks, which is L63 billion (33 + 30), would increase every year. Circulation would only augment in connection with every wheat campaign, without ever decreasing.

The notes that would thus be put in circulation without coming back would inevitably affect the prices and give an impulse to the devaluation of money. It is therefore imperative that the intentions on the part of the present Government to put an end to the political price system and to do so radically without leaving a chance for a relapse and without making any exception for one class of people or another – which exception would soon become the rule – be realized promptly. *Periculum est in mora**.

After what I have said about the rediscount to the compulsory agricultural pools there is no need to comment extensively on the other two

* Danger is in delay.

causes of the issue of notes: the supply of funds to the Allies (balance on 20 January 1947, L22,492 million, including the amount existing in May 1946, plus the subsequent additions) and the purchase of foreign currency (L36,925 million on the same date). The notes stagnate and accumulate, the Treasury being unable, as in the case of the wheat pools, to collect either through taxation or from the monetary market (long- and short-term loans) the funds it needs for covering the cost of the foreign currency purchased from the Italian exporters and at present also the expenditures made in the country by the Allies, with notes furnished by us.

The considerations we made regarding the rediscount to the pools stand good also for these other causes of money issue, with the difference that here we can say there is collateral. Against the Treasury's L63 billion for the wheat pools, in fact, there is nothing, the bread having already been consumed and the consumers having paid the price charged them; whereas against the lire furnished to the Allies and to the exporters of Italian goods stands the first-class foreign currency credited to us. The difference is a fundamental one; but in order that circulation may derive from it a beneficial effect, the foreign currency secured should be exchanged for essential goods so that the proceeds of the latter could then be used for reimbursing the lire advances received from the bank of issue. Even if the reimbursement took place with some delay and even if the stagnating of notes in the circulation produced its usual bad effect, the damage would not be permanent and the prices, after temporary fluctuations, would tend to return to the old level.

There are, however, two risks in the return process which takes the form: lire–foreign currency–foreign goods–lire realized by selling those goods.

The first one is that the foreign goods, purchased with the foreign currency secured, be sold not at the economic but at the political prices, the exchange being figured not at the rates corresponding to the reality of the moment when the foreign goods are sold in Italy, but at historical rates: for example, with respect to the dollar, at 100 or 225 instead of 400. In this way the Treasury does not collect lire suitable for paying salaries and supplies at the rates of the day or for covering the cost at that time of new Italian exports. The result is a loss for the public treasury or for the domestic economy, which somebody will have to bear.

The second risk is that the lire collected by selling the foreign goods be used not for reimbursing the bank of issue, which advanced the Italian money, but for covering current expenditures. If this happens, the originally temporary issue of lire becomes a permanent one and, as a dead weight, definitively causes prices to go up.

Last year, after going through the survey for 1945, the prospects were brighter. It is true that the circulation of Banca d'Italia notes and AM lire had increased from the L312,485.1 million in total at the 1944 year end to L382,049.9 million at the end of 1945, with a difference of L69,564.8 million. But we could state, with pride, that for the major part of the increase were to be blamed the Germans, the neo-fascists and the expenditures not reimbursed yet at that time by the Allies. The responsibility for the increase on the part of the free legitimate Italian Government was so small that it could be neglected. To day we cannot feel so bright. Until all public expenditures, including those appearing as investments, are not covered without making recourse to the issue of notes, the ghost of inflation will not be driven away.

The means for driving it away are well known. In the matter of finance there are no new miraculous remedies. By performing little tricks on paper, by changing the name of things and bits of paper no substantial results are attained. Substance has only two names: taxation and loans. Real taxation, not a deceptive one. Loans coming from the nation's savings, and not as a result of book-keeping manipulations. If the State and the minor administrations need L800 billion a year, the citizens must give the State L800 billion a year out of their income, that is out of the yearly gross earnings of their labour, their industries and their capital. The name given to the different types of taxation makes no difference, whether it is a tax on the income, on the capital or on consumption; today even the form of the loans is irrelevant, whether they are perpetual or redeemable or with a fixed term, long or short. What counts is that the Italians are giving the needed billions, through taxation or loans, by drawing on their current income. The survey we are making is not the proper occasion for discussing the right proportion between taxes and loans. The ideal would be to take care of the current expenses with the taxes and to use the loans for expenditures apt to yield directly or indirectly the means for the services involved; but even if the ideal proportion could not be maintained in our disturbed days, the damage would not be a very great one. The main thing is to keep to the principle that fresh domestic earnings are alone to be used.

As far as taxes are concerned, the prospects are good (see Table 11.2).

Table 11.2

		Index numbers	
	Actual receipts (L million)	**Of actual receipts**	**Of wholesale prices**
Monthly average of first half-year	14,267	100	100
July	4,655	33	103
August	20,527	144	108
September	16,866	118	117
October	26,660	187	124
November	23,940	168	131
December	30,869	216	142

We gather from the figures in Table 11.2 that the tax receipts have increased not only as absolute quantities, the rapidity of their increase being even greater than that of the price rise. The increase is a considerable one in the nominal yield, but there also is a substantial rise in the quantity of goods and services which can be purchased with that yield.

Such is not the case regarding the loans' yield, meaning by loans everything the monetary market has furnished to the Treasury at a long or short term. In the second half year of 1946 we see in fact a marked decline in the yield of the means put at the Treasury's disposal by the money-savers of their free will (see Table 11.3).

Table 11.3

	First half-year 1946 (L billion)	**Second half-year 1946 (L billion)**
Actual cash yield of the Reconstruction Loan from 20 November to 31 December 1946	–	56
Proceeds of Treasury Bills paid in as subscriptions to the Reconstruction Loan	–	10
Treasury Bills	61	15
Increase in balance of current account with Treasury of the Cassa Depositi e Prestiti and of the Social Security institutions	34	27
Increase in balance of current account with Treasury of the Banco di Napoli and other banking institutions	22	–13
Increase of banking institutions' deposit accounts with Banca d'Italia	6	–25
Subventions to Treasury by the Institutions authorized to finance the agricultural pools	–	30
	123	100

(Naturally, the reconciliation does not include the Reconstruction Loan's further yield in the first part of January 1947.) Within the given period, the synopsis proves that the monetary market presents a unity; and that the so-called 'loans' have not and cannot have the object of giving the Treasury financial means it would be unable to secure through other channels; but that they have another equally important object, of consolidating the placement of funds which would be made all the same but in a precarious and insecure way. The subscribers who from 20 November to 31 December gave the Treasury the Loan's L56 billion in cash have not actually given fresh or new money. They drew on their banks and the banks in order to comply with the customers' orders had to reduce by L38 billion (13 + 25) the balances of their current accounts with the Treasury itself and with

Banca d'Italia. What counts is the total amount of funds placed at the Treasury's disposal: L123 billion in the first half-year of 1946 and 100 in the second.

This fact is explained by the great change that occurred in 1946 in the consideration the money-savers have for public investments, as compared with their attitude in the years 1940–43, which was partially maintained until 1945.

During the 'fascist' war the so-called 'capitals circuit policy' prohibited or strongly limited all investments in real estate, in shares, in new industrial enterprises, compelling the savings to converge to the Treasury Bills or to bank deposits. On the other hand, it was very difficult to secure commodities and instrumental goods either abroad or in Italy. The government loans were therefore contributed to by the proceeds of the sale of merchandise stocks or by funds reserved for the amortization or upkeep or repair of property and which could not be invested in industrial, agricultural or commercial enterprises. Not to refill the stocks of merchandise, not to replace or repair machinery, not to take care of the upkeep of the houses does not mean to be saving, but to turn the invested capital into liquid funds; it means not to reinvest that part of the product which should be used for securing the preservation of the existing capital. And, if that money, through the Treasury Bills or the bank deposits, goes to the State and is used for the war, the pre-existing capital lessens, without being reconstituted, by a similar amount. In substance, the country is being impoverished; but the impoverishment assumes the appearance of a more abundant yield of the monetary market in favour of the public Treasury. The question so frequently put, 'How is it that the Treasury, which spent so lavishly during the war, suddenly becomes unable to provide for the most moderate reconstruction expenditures in peace time?' is answered: 'yes, to go on in the same way could be possible, but it would be a Sisyphean job: on one side it would mean consuming a part of the existing and invested private capital and on the other there would be the attempt to reconstruct another private or public capital'. It would mean 100 would be destroyed for reconstructing 50 or 20 or even less; because what is lost by destroying is often worth more than what is recovered by reconstructing. Yes, if only it were possible to indefinitely abstain from replacing and repairing machinery, from rebuilding the houses, from refilling the exhausted stocks. But as all this does not belong to the world of possible things, it is clear that once the moment is over of the capital's consumption on account of the war, it is a matter of necessity to expect the new savings to become the source of the State's extraordinary expenditures as well as of private investments. Once the dimensions of the fund are reduced and the private investments make their reappearance, competing with the State, it is obvious that there comes a moment, which for us was the year 1946, when the monetary market's contribution to the Treasury must suffer a decline.

The Treasury's temporary enrichment during the war and immediately after was helped also by the rationing and the impossibility of spending money. The black-outs, the air raids, the evacuations imposed a secluded and frugal life. As it was impossible or useless to spend the income's excess over the cost of the rations, that excess found its forced outlet in the bank deposits and in short-term government securities. In all parts of the world the year 1946 marked a revival of money-spending, which was a crazy one in some countries but was not unknown in ours as well. The rising receipts of the cinemas and of the entertainment and gambling places show the decrease in saving and consequently in the voluntary flow of money to the Treasury.

Another factor has contributed, more obscurely but perhaps more powerfully, to the formation of available funds: the slow, gradual swell of circulation. Profits, as a marginal element in the distribution of the income deriving from enterprises, are the first to take advantage of the introduction on the market of a new purchasing power, which, instead, causes the labour income to suffer temporarily – as the latter can adjust itself to it only with a certain delay – and permanently affects the income of the big and the many small creditors of fixed monetary amounts. Among the parties thus affected are the State, as a creditor of taxes, the public and semi-public administrations, the companies operating public services, all of them, owing to their nature or to the controls they are subject to, being slow in registering changes in their receipts.

Within the limits in which such a redistribution brings an advantage to the financial situation of private concerns, or provides with extra funds the classes that are more inclined to save, or lightens the taxation burden, it may be the source of more money available for investment in public loans.

The very effort made by the creditors of fixed sums to reconstitute their property's real value, which is corroded by inflation, may work in the same direction; at the same time when that erosion makes saving easy for their debtors.

However, like a curve flattening as it approaches its asymptote, this sequence of effects gradually exhausts itself. The advantage which the debtors of taxes and of fixed sums may derive from a protracted inflation declines proportionally to the reduction the real value of their debts underwent as a result of the previous inflation. The debtor of L100 has a profit of 50 if the purchasing power of the L100 goes down to 50 per cent; but if through further devaluation that original power declines to 25, 10, 5, 3 per cent, his profit will only be 25, 15, 5, 2.

Regarding equipment and stocks, there comes at a certain point the problem of replacing and refilling them. The working classes' forced saving has a limit in life's minimum needs. And on top of all this, the signs of inflation come to the attention of the union leaders and of the heads of enterprises, so that through the application of the sliding scale or otherwise, the adjustment of salaries to the devaluation of money takes place immediately and sometimes, in the beginning, manages even to improve the real value of the workers' pay. Finally, should inflation be perceived also by the public, people will avoid holding money or credits in money. If the malady's spread is not promptly stopped, this is the beginning of the end.

However, we know that the end of the lira must *not* come. We know it because the data of the problems we have examined lead us to the logical conclusion that there is a possibility – and therefore a duty – to put a stop to inflation. Let us summarize these data.

The first element is the ratio between the increase in the circulation and the increase in the yield of taxation (actual receipts). In the second half-year of 1946 circulation rose by 28% as compared with the end of the first half-year; but the actual receipts were in December 116% higher than the first half-year's average.

If we see to it that also in the future the increase in the tax yield exceeds the swell of notes, an efficient barrier will be put against the spread of inflation.

Taxation is not enough, however. For a good many years to come the yield of taxation will obviously be insufficient for covering the total amount of the expenditures. A part of it, which we may call extraordinary, will still have to be covered by debts. But here we face the contrary fact: the sums furnished the Treasury by the monetary market, (i.e., the fresh savings) are declining. Some of the reasons are advantageous for the collective interest: the end of the consumption of the existing capitals and the revival of the industrial, agricultural and commercial enterprises; others are not, and for these, inflation itself is responsible. In the long run, the inflation that has already taken place destroys the propensity to save. Why save if the product of saving volatilizes as far as purchasing power is concerned? I am positively sceptical about the concrete value of the modern theories which lead one to surmise there are countries and circumstances where saving may prove harmful, for I believe that the essence of truth contained in those doctrines is nothing other than the old and fully accepted theory relating to the expedience of looking for the best proportion between consumption and saving. But in Italy today there is a probably unanimous opinion that the proportion between consumption and savings, between the production of consumer and of instrumental goods, must now be modified in favour of the saving and the instrumental goods.

The need for reconstruction is so strong that money-saving (that is, the production of instrumental goods) must be favoured, subject, of course, to the requirements of physical health and moral life.

However, saving is a function of the confidence in monetary unity. The monetary market will give the Treasury the sums needed for filling the void between the taxation yield and the total government expenditures only if the production of savings – which is a production like any other, being the result of man's voluntary acts – is considered by the money-savers as a proposition interesting enough for them to feel induced to manufacture savings in quantities sufficient for private and public investments. Normally these people perform the voluntary act of saving only if they expect to derive from it some sort of moral or economic satisfaction. They might be content – and they usually are – with an interest of 0, of 2, or 3 per cent, but it is doubtful whether they are greatly stimulated to save money by threats of expropriation, by abuse and by prospects of facing a firing-squad. Regarding currency they are positively discouraged by the fear of devaluation and they identify devaluation with excessive public expenses, which excess causes a further issue of money. The examination of the Bank's balance-sheet has proved that the identification is correct: during the period from May 1946 to 20 January 1947, there was a L104 billion increase in the circulation against L108 milliard worth of notes issued in connection with public expenditures (supply of funds to the Allies, rediscount to agricultural pools, purchase of foreign currency, reduction in the banks' deposit accounts and in the Treasury's current account).

The concern on the part of the money-saver has proved correct also under another respect, however. If we consider the increase in the direct and indirect payments by the Treasury during the first and the second half-year of 1946 we obtain the results shown in Table 11.4.

Table 11.4

	First half-year (L billion)		**Second half-year (L billion)**
Direct payments for actual expenses	207		244
Indirect payments:			
for discounts to agricultural pools	–	60	
for purchase of foreign currency	7	24	84
	214		328

These are actual payments on account for engagements taken as against the year's operation and against the carry-overs of the previous years, as well as, with respect to the indirect payments, on account of extra-budget expenditures. And in fact, as far as prices are concerned, the actual expenditures are of greater importance than the engagements, the effect of which is to be noticed only in the future. The index numbers of the examined facts are as shown in Table 11.5, taking as a basis the first half-year of 1946.

The fate of the lira depends on the respective speed of the various competitors in the race: on one side the public expenditure, which from one half-year to another rises from 100 to 153 and is stimulated to a wild race by the rapid growth of the allotments of funds, luckily not always followed

Table 11.5

	First half-year 1946	Second half-year 1946	December 1946
Indirect payments	100	118	144
Total of direct and indirect payments	100	153	
Actual receipts	100	144	216
Means furnished by monetary market	100	81	
Circulation	100	116	132
Wholesale prices	100	121	142

by an actual disbursement; on the other side the receipts, some of which, those coming from the monetary market (loans and current accounts), show signs of weariness by coming down from 100 to 81, whereas the actual receipts rise from 100 to 144 and show an increasing speed, reaching 216 in December.

At the point we have reached, however it is no use depending only on increased zeal on the part of the public in paying the taxes due. It is imperative to take at the same time an action for stopping the ascending rush of the expenditures.

It is not the Bank of Issue's job to suggest how to increase taxation and to reduce expenditures. The choice of the taxes to be augmented and of the expenditures to be reduced belongs to the politician.

It will suffice to remark here that, by going on with inflation, the State annuls its efforts to augment the real weight of the taxes and that there can come a moment when the increase in the circulation causes a more than proportionate increase in prices, so that the more the State spends, the less it gets. It is the beginning of the precipice; of what is called today a 'nose-dive'. The State is taken in the coils of money's declining purchasing power and anxiously tries to avoid a catastrophe by way of new issues of money. And the more monetary units are issued, the lower is their purchasing power. The moment comes when unpronounceable totals of the circulating monetary units have an infinitely small, almost null, purchasing power.

In Italy we are today still far from the moment of indifference, as may be called that moment when all new monetary issues are useless and give no more advantages to the public Treasury. But we are at a cross-roads. There is a hard road leading up and another easy and flat one leading down to the precipice. The top and the abyss are not visible yet but we feel them. The choice of the road to follow is up to us. Nothing except our own will prevents us from choosing the hard road leading up. The country is working and producing, the manufacturers are brightly reviving their initiatives, the middle and the rural classes have not completely lost the habit of saving, the workers are asking for work and, well organized, are ready to cooperate in the common toil. The effort we are to make is not even a material, substantial one: what we must do is to waive all unnecessary expenses, all delayable disbursements, all expenditures coming last in the order of urgency and productivity.

It is imperative that a stop be put to the request for funds coming in to the public Treasury from regional and municipal administrations and from groups anxious to be first or afraid to be second in the assault on public money. It is imperative that the manufacturers stop applying to the government, under the pretext of the danger of unemployment, asking for subsidies and loans which, as they very well know, are useless, being granted in the form of paper money. It is imperative that the union leaders perceive the danger arising for all classes, especially for the workers, from the recourse to an increase of the circulation. It is imperative that our vision of reality be not disturbed by premises not corresponding to the truth. In the matter of salaries a point is reached where every nominal increase causes a diminution of their real value. If the flow of the actual products does not grow, the rise in salaries, as a result for instance of the automatic application of the sliding scale, has no other effect than to augment the misery of the more unfortunate, who live on a fixed income or whose earnings increase at a lower rate than the average rise provided for by the sliding scale. Under such conditions, the sliding scale is an instrument of privilege for a minority and of impoverishment for the majority. The union leaders, misled by a mirage, are under the illusion of promoting everybody's welfare and instead they actually cause social injustice to be emphasized. They commit again the error which, after the glorious period of the last decade of the past century and of the first decade of ours, placed the labour organizations – which played such a great part in Italy's economic and social progress – under the power of the monopolists and of individuals whose practice is to assault public wealth or to produce a discord between regions or between South and North.

While the danger is not over and a fairly long stretch of the steep road leading to safety and greatness is not covered, all classes must submit themselves to their common fate. Let the middle and the upper classes pay without complaining, along with the usual imposts, also the new tax on patrimony which has just now been announced; and let the workers and employees stop asking for raises which are bound to vanish before they are enjoyed.

At the end of the easy road which comfort and a desire for popularity invite us to follow, awaits the chasm of monetary unity's destruction and of social chaos. But no particular will-power is necessary to refrain from following such path which leads to the enchanted gardens of inflation. All we have to do is to repeat what the men of the past generation did in other times. Do you remember the figures of the deficits after the First World War? When you pronounce them they seem small: 23 billion in 1918–19,

11 in 1919–20, 21 in 1920–21, 17 in 1921–22. Very small indeed if compared with the deficit our present Minister of Treasury, Mr Campilli, announced for this year, L610 billion.

However, let us translate those sums into lire having the same purchasing power of the present lira, so that a comparison may be made: and we find out that the deficit was 784 billion in 1918–19, 331 in 1919–20, 539 in 1920-21 and 481 billion in 1921–22.

And yet a few years later, in 1924, the fascist government's minister proudly announced that his government had again balanced the budget. That was a false boast, because, practically, the balance already existed on 28 October 1922, when the new regime began. And it existed because the governments that followed one another after the World War aimed at the liquidation of the inheritance the war left us and endeavoured to free the country's budget from all permanent burdens which would have also at that time driven the currency towards disaster.

Marcello Soleri, in Giolitti's government, was in 1921 successful in convincing Parliament to abolish the political price of bread and thus to lay the foundations for balancing the budget.

Gentlemen,

I believe and I have faith in free regimes, in which freedom of discussion plays a leading role. The Italians of today will tolerate no more that a new tyrant, availing himself of the result of their efforts, should boast about having again balanced the budget and saved the lira. The lira was saved by them, the Italians, in 1920–22, and they will do the same today. They must not expect the lira to be saved by any Messiah or by any would-be thaumaturgus, even if he were in charge of the management of money. They must not believe that salvation can come from anybody else but themselves. Salvation is certain and unfailing. All that is needed is an act of willpower: the determination to waive all superfluous expenses, which means today all such new expenditures – already approved or to be suggested in the future – which do not prove absolutely, I could almost say physically necessary; and the determination to bear all the necessary tax burdens. I do not even want to put the question: 'Are we going to find that willpower?'. I do not put it, because there is but one answer to duty's categorical imperative: 'I obey!'.

12

The Theory of Imaginary Money from Charlemagne to the French Revolution*

1. If one reads the books on monetary subjects that were written in the period from the sixteenth to the eighteenth century, one frequently encounters the concept of 'imaginary money'. Other terms used are 'ideal money', 'political money', *moneta numeraria*, 'money of account'. What these terms meant was not very clear even to contemporaries. The most authoritative writer among the historians of French monetary vicissitudes, François Le Blanc, resigned himself to defining as imaginary any kind of money which, 'properly speaking, is but a collective term comprising a certain number of real moneys'. The imaginary money which almost everywhere was called 'pound' or an equivalent term such as 'livre', 'lira', 'pond', was, in Le Blanc's words, 'never changing in value; in fact, we have used it since the time of Charlemagne, and it has always been worth 20 sous (shillings), and each sou, 12 deniers (pence)'.[1] It is called 'imaginary' because of the fact that it has never been coined; 'because we have never had a real specie which has consistently been worth 20 sous or one worth 12 deniers'. Although from time immemorial

---

* A translation, by Giorgio Tagliacozzo, of 'Teoria della moneta immaginaria nel tempo da Carlomagno alla rivoluzione francese', *Rivista di storia economica*, 1936, I, 1–35. The essay is printed here with the permission of President Einaudi, who has approved the translation. The editors acknowledge the valuable assistance of Raymond de Roover in the preparation of the manuscript.

With the approval of the author, paragraphs 31, 32, 33 and 35 were omitted from the translation. Paragraph 34 of the original is number 32 in the present version; to preserve the continuity of the argument President Einaudi has made a brief addition to this paragraph. The notes of the original article have been included a few notes added by the translator.

men have neither seen nor touched any imaginary money, nevertheless, in the remote past it was something real, 'since if we go back to the time when in France people began to count in pounds, shillings, and pence, we shall find that these imaginary moneys owe their origin to a real thing'. According to Le Blanc, Charlemagne really coined silver shillings, 20 of which weighed a Roman pound of 12 ounces.[2] Thus the silver shilling was a real currency, and 20 of them weighed 1 pound, while each of them was divided into 12 pennies. The pound, however, was never coined; yet from then onward people acquired the habit of counting in pounds of 20 shillings with each shilling divided into 12 pence. Later on, according to Le Blanc, the shilling, along with the penny, deteriorated more and more, so that it ceased to be the twentieth part of the pound-weight; but the public went on counting in pounds, shillings and pence despite the fact that the pound tale, as Le Blanc observed, weighed in his time (1690) – or was supposed to weigh – only 7 pennyweights and 3 grains, less than 3 per cent of the original weight at the time of the restored Roman Empire (800).

> These changes, I [Le Blanc] admit, are surprising because if there is anything in the world which ought to be stable, it is money, the measure of everything which enters the channels of trade. What confusion would there not be in a state where weights and measures frequently changed? On what basis and with what assurance could one person deal with another, and which nations would care to deal with people who lived in such disorder? Nevertheless, this has not prevented money, which is the most precious and most important of all standards, from changing its value in France almost as often as our clothes change in fashion.

2. The practice of counting in pounds, shillings, and pence – already sanctioned by the glory of Charlemagne – became even more venerable when, in 1226, Saint Louis coined the groat, or gros tournois, which had a weight and fineness equivalent to that of the sou or shilling of the imaginary pound. For a time the sou, instead of being imaginary, became real, visible and tangible.

> This is the great epoch for the value of our sou and consequently for that of the livre. The people became so strongly attached to that established value that in subsequent reigns, whenever the money was debased ... they always asked that it be restored to the same goodness as it had formerly in the time of Saint Louis. [Perhaps] it was an effect of the veneration which the French had for everything this saintly monarch had done.[3]

3. The idea of a form of money which for centuries remained invisible exerted a powerful influence on the human mind: 'Two kinds of money', wrote Dutot:

> are the soul and the moving force of Trade: one Real and the other Ideal. Real money is of gold and silver. It was introduced to facilitate commercial intercourse, and it caused sales to replace barter by becoming the price and measure of everything which is the object of trade. But since the shipping of specie from one country to another was so embarrassing as to constitute a serious obstacle to trade, bills of exchange were resorted to as a means of transferring funds from place to place. To facilitate the making of bargains and computations, people invented moneys of account or of exchange, such as the livre, the sou, and the écu in France; the penny, the shilling, and the pound sterling in England; the groat, the shilling groat, and the pound groat in Holland. This kind of ideal or imaginary money which, properly speaking, consists of collective terms comprising also a certain number of real moneys, will be called Political Money.[4]

He speaks of a 'collective term', evidently regarding ideal money as if it were some kind of compound, equivalent to a certain number of real moneys. His strange definition does not specify the kind and the number of real coins that the imaginary money is supposed to represent.

4. The Italian writers are no more helpful than the French. According to the Italian economist, Giovanni Antonio Fabbrini:

> money is called imaginary in so far as it has no substance, being a mere idea or product of our imagination. It is called 'of account' because it is helpful in keeping accounts and, unlike real coins, it stands firm and cannot arbitrarily be cried up or down. Since real coins are all variable, imaginary money performs for coins the same function which money in general performs for other goods, that is, it expresses the idea of a fixed value.[5]

Although Ferdinando Galiani (1728–1787) did not believe that 'in this world, one can hope for ... perpetual stability and stagnation', and although he was convinced that 'a constant and unchangeable measure need not be desired or sought', since perpetual stability 'is wholly repugnant to the ordering and genius of nature itself', still he did not deny the logical possibility of an imaginary money that would be stable. He wrote: 'If imaginary money were a term for a definite number expressing an idea of price, and if this idea were fixed in our minds and so detached from everything that it would not be affected by any disturbances, then it would certainly be invariable and constant'.[6]

5. An idea, a product of imagination liberated from the legislator's arbitrary action, a numerical expression, an idea detached from everything and unaffected by any disturbances – all such terms and concepts were, according to the stern verdict of the impeccable Messedaglia, 'evidently the consequences of rather inaccurate and confused notions on the subject'.[7] Luigi Valeriani had an easy time discrediting and denying the concept that money of account was something 'impassive, independent of all human

values'. This absurd notion grew out of the fact that people, as they played with the words 'imaginary', 'ideal', 'of account', 'fixed', came to believe that money of account was a mere idea, whereas 'it is very improperly called imaginary or ideal, there being nothing imaginary in it but its derivation, by mental division or multiplication, from moneys which are said to be real'.[8]

6. No, money of account was not the mere idea of money, as Fabbrini believed. An idea cannot be a standard of value, or an invariable term of comparison for evaluating commodities, even if, as Galiani corrected, the idea is fixed in our minds. In that case we must assume not only that this idea is detached from everything and from all disturbances but also that man himself is invariable in his wants and in his tastes and that the goods themselves are invariable in quantity and quality. But neither was the money of account an uncoined multiple or fraction of a coin in actual circulation, as Valeriani contended, since a double or half of a gold florin, even though it did not happen to be coined, would be real money no less than the florin itself.

7. Pompeo Neri, the clearest among the Italian monetary writers of the eighteenth century, finally identified the imaginary pound as equivalent to the result obtained by dividing or multiplying a specific current coin by a given number. In order to express a valuation, one could even use a number without specifying the unit which was used; for instance, by saying 'that a philippus dollar was worth seven and a half, the sequin fourteen and a half, the doblon twenty-five and a fourth, and so on', except that 'the public was accustomed to the words' pound, shilling and penny, 'and was scrupulous in preserving the identity of the word pound in sound rather than in value'. The number in question did not remain unchanged, mainly because it was not related to a stable currency. Because of men's malice and princes' needs, the pound was at any time linked to the worst moneys in circulation:

> The unit of value designated by the name of pound having steadily decreased in the estimation of the public, a forever greater number of these units became necessary to evaluate the same quantity of metal. In the same way, to ascend a tower, it is necessary to climb more steps if the steps are low than if they are steep, although the height of the tower does not increase, as some naively believe. They are deceived by the same illusion which misleads the eyes of anyone who, leaving the shore in a boat, thinks that the shoreline is moving rather than the boat.[9]

Even though Neri's definition, 'imaginary money is the result of dividing or multiplying a real coin by a given number', comes closer to reality, it is still unsatisfactory. This definition contradicts what it is supposed to define. The pound, quotient of the division of the gold florin by a variable number, is indeed variable, but it is no less real than the florin. Why then call it imaginary and oppose it to the florin, a real currency, as if it had an entirely different nature?

8. The difficulty in finding a satisfactory definition for 'money of account' results from its history. Money of account was not created by decree but grew almost spontaneously out of men's habit of keeping accounts in monetary units, some of which corresponded in the time of Charlemagne to real coins.[10] Later on it happened from time to time that the money of account was pegged to a real coin which was equivalent to a pound, shilling or penny. Such a correspondence was accidental or, if deliberate, did not last long. Except for the penny, the name given to the real coin was different. The coexistence over long periods of time of a penny in money of account and a penny in coin, one equal to the other, does not prove, as Landry (*Essai*, p.13) rightly observes, that the two systems, that of imaginary and that of real money, were linked or soldered together. It is not correct to say that through the penny both currency systems were based on a real coin. In addition to the money of account – the pound of 20 shillings and the shilling of 12 pence – were there not also coins such as the gold mouton, the silver groat (gros tournois), and the silver penny? It was possible that at a given moment one silver penny was equivalent to one penny in money of account. But the relation between the mouton, the silver groat and the silver penny was not so stable as that between the pound, the shilling and the penny since, in terms of money of account, a pound was always 20 shillings and one shilling was always 12 pence. Besides, even when the groat was rated 1 shilling, it does not follow that it contained twelve times as much silver as did the penny.[11] Little by little – and this happened during the fourteenth and fifteenth centuries – the penny in coin lost its equivalence with the penny in money of account and was coined first in vellon (that is, an alloy composed mainly of copper mixed with a little silver) and then in pure copper.

9. Sooner or later, but generally at the beginning of modern times, the different monetary systems in various European countries reached a state in which they were governed by a seemingly very odd principle, very different from our modern conception.

Today each country has only one monetary unit: the lira, franc, mark, pound sterling, or dollar. This is the system established by the French assemblies at the end of the eighteenth century. In Italy, for example, the present monetary unit is the lira, defined as a given weight of pure gold, namely (1936), 0.07919113 grams.

It is possible that a real coin containing that quantity of pure gold, and having the legal fineness of 90 per cent, is not in actual circulation. If such is the case, its multiple of 20 or 50 or 100 lire will exist. If not, the fact does not change the principle. The silver coins or bank notes in circulation are representative money, convertible in gold because the owner of silver or paper money is entitled to have it exchanged for gold at the central bank, or for drafts on a foreign bank which will deliver the same quantity of gold. Furthermore, if in the country in question convertibility is temporarily suspended, such a suspension does not cause the monetary unit to lose its quality of real currency. The note of the Bank of Italy today (1936) is a promise to pay, at an indefinite time in the future, 0.07919113 grams of pure gold for each lira. Perhaps the market will cause that promise to be valued at a discount in order to transform it into present gold. The fact remains that the monetary unit is defined as a real physical quantity of gold, silver, some other metal, or perhaps even another commodity. On the basis of that monetary unit or on the basis of representative coins or notes, we make bargains, accept obligations and settle debts. We promise to pay 100 lire and discharge this obligation by delivering a note of 100 lire. The note of 100 lire is real money.

10. Prior to the French Revolution, the monetary system of most European countries was based on altogether different principles. Contemporary authors could take these principles for granted and did not have to explain them to others. Their strange terminology causes us, who live in another world, to wander for a while in a dark forest.[12] By and by, we finally understand the tacit assumptions of their discourses. The key, needed to interpret the apparent confusion of the monetary treatises written prior to the eighteenth century, is the distinction between a monetary unit used as a standard of value and of deferred payments, and another monetary unit used as a medium of exchange.

11. There was, then, a monetary unit used only as a standard of deferred payments (promises to pay) or for the purpose of keeping accounts. This was the function of a money of account, an imaginary or ideal money. The public made contracts, kept books, established mortgages, or stipulated rents in pounds, shillings and pence. In the time of Malestroit and his 'Paradoxes' (1565), an ell of velvet was valued at £10 tournois; a measure of wine, at £12; a pair of shoes, at 15 sous; the daily wage of a labourer, at 5 sous; the annual rent of a gentleman, at £500; and a town-house or farm, at £25,000.[13]

Although it was possible to make contracts or to keep accounts in imaginary money – that is, in pounds, shillings and pence – it was impossible to make actual payments in these monetary units, since they had not been coined for several centuries. Payment was made in real currency, that is, in gold coins, white money or silver coins, black money or low-grade silver, vellon or copper coins.

The coins in circulation had a great variety of names:

Gold: florins, ducats, sequins, angels, nobles, crowns, sovereigns, French and other écus, moutons, gold louis, doblons, guilders.
Silver: Philippus and other dollars, pieces of eight, reals of Spain, silver louis, testoons, blanks, guilders (originally gold), ducatoons, etc.
Vellon and black money: farthings, obols, Dutch stivers, French douzains, Tuscan crazie, etc.

In the time of Malestroit, a customer could pay a shopkeeper for an ell of velvet, priced at £10 tournois in money of account, by giving him 4 écus du soleil rated at £2 10*s*. each. Similarly, the buyer of a barrel of wine, costing £12, could give in payment 20 testoons current at 12 sous per testoon. A shoemaker would be satisfied if he received 15 douzains in black money, at 12*d*. per douzain, for a pair of shoes selling at 15*s*. In the same way, a journeyman, whose wage was 5*s*. per day, would be content with 5 douzains in currency. A gentleman would collect his rent of £500 tournois in the form of 200 écus du soleil; and the one who had sold a house or a farm for £25,000 would give quittance to a buyer who had paid him 10,000 écus at £2½ per écu. If there was a change in the ratio between real and imaginary money – for example, if the rates of the currency in terms of money of account were doubled or reduced by half – the number of coins to be paid in discharge of a debt would vary inversely. For example, if we assumed that prices remained the same, either 2 or 8 écus, respectively, instead of 4 would be needed to pay for an ell of velvet priced at £10 tournois. The workman would receive either 2½ or 10 douzains instead of 5; the gentleman would collect either 100 or 400 écus instead of 200; and the seller of a house would receive either 5,000 or 20,000 écus, instead of 10,000.

12. The essence of the concept of imaginary money is not, therefore, the idea of a collective term (Le Blanc and Poulain), or of a fixed value (Fabbrini and Galiani), or even of a result obtained by using a variable divisor or multiplier (Neri). Early writers were correct in making a distinction between imaginary and real money, but their definitions of the former show that they were not sure of the basis of that distinction.

Imaginary money – here is my thesis – is not money at all. It is a mere instrument or technical device used to perform some monetary functions.

13. Let us assume the monetary unit to be the gold franc weighing 0.29 grams of pure gold (0.32 grams at the fineness of 90 per cent). Let us further assume that gold pieces of 10, 20 and 100 francs were coined; for medium-sized and small transactions, silver species of 5, 2 and 1 franc; nickel coins of 50 and 20 centimes, and copper coins of 10 and 5 centimes.

However, the silver, nickel and copper coins contain so little metal that, if melted, they cannot be sold at a price equal to the nominal value inscribed on the coin. Therefore, those coins circulate only as representative money, as tokens of the gold coins into which they are legally convertible. Let us further assume that only gold coins can be minted freely and are full legal tender for all debts. The other coins are minted by the state only and are legal tender up to a certain amount, which is somewhat larger for the silver coins than for the inferior nickel and copper coins.

In this system, that of the pure monometallic standard, there is no place for imaginary money, even if the monetary authorities should wish to introduce imaginary money for the purpose off stabilizing the currency. Keeping accounts and stipulating contracts in imaginary livres and at the same time making payments in real francs would not present any advantages and, besides, would necessitate the establishment of a legal ratio between the livre and the franc. If this ratio were 1 to 1, the two denominations would be identical. If another ratio were chosen, for example, 2 to 1 or 1 to 2, the livre would become either a fraction or a multiple of the franc. The introduction of an imaginary money would in this case only complicate matters and would serve no purpose, not even that of keeping the subsidiary coins in circulation. They would stay in circulation simply because melting them down is unprofitable, their value as bullion being so much less than their monetary value.

The device of an imaginary money is also unnecessary to prevent the overvalued subsidiary coins from driving the gold out of circulation.

They cannot do so as long as they are not coined in excessive quantities and are not full legal tender. If the rules are not observed, disturbances may occur, but they will be the result of the government's monetary policy, and the creation of imaginary money will not prevent their occurrence. This analysis, of course, presupposes the existence of rational rules and their rational application.

14. Now let us assume that the monetary system is that of the bimetallic standard. The monetary unit is still the franc, defined as being equivalent to either 0.29 grams of pure gold or 4.5 grams of pure silver. The denominations actually coined are gold pieces of 10, 20 and 100 francs and silver pieces of 1, 2 and 5 francs. Let us disregard for the moment the existence of token coins for the smaller denominations, since the remarks made above would apply to them. If left to themselves, the two kinds of francs – gold and silver – would be two different monetary units. There is no reason why the market should permanently consider 0.29 grams in gold, the weight of the gold franc, as the exact equivalent of 4.5 grams in silver, the weight of the silver franc. Such an equivalence, if it existed, would be merely accidental and ephemeral. As a natural consequence, a double standard is accompanied by a double price system: the same commodity may have one

price in gold francs and another price in silver francs. Thus one hundred loaves of bread may conceivably sell for 40 gold francs or for 38 silver francs. This is not bimetallism, but duometallism, and it would be extremely cumbersome.

15. A duometallic standard with two monetary units and two price systems can be changed into a bimetallic standard with only one monetary unit and only one price system, if certain requirements are fulfilled. These requirements are: (1) that both gold and silver coins are full legal tender; (2) that there exists free coinage for both metals, so that anyone bringing gold or silver bullion to the mint will receive the same weight in gold or silver coins of the desired denominations (in order to avoid minor complications, let us assume that this transaction involves neither expense nor delay);[14] (3) that there exists a fixed legal ratio between gold and silver. For example, this legal ratio was 1 to 15½ in the countries adhering to the Latin Monetary Union, which means that 100 silver francs weighed 15½ times as much as 100 gold francs.

16. For the bimetallic standard to operate properly, it is further necessary that the market ratio be equal to the legal ratio or, in other words, that the price ratio between gold and silver ingots or bars in the bullion market be the same as that established by the mint. As long as this requirement is fulfilled, it is indifferent to a debtor whether he effects payment in gold or silver francs, because they have the same value in bullion as in currency. For this reason, both kinds of currency will remain in circulation, and one will not have the tendency to drive the other out.

17. The accidental identity of the legal and the market ratio may last for a long time. If the mints absorb most of the gold and silver bullion offered on the market, the mint price (that is, the amount of currency supplied by the mints in exchange for a given weight of bullion) tends to dictate the market price for industrial uses, so that the bimetallic system sometimes gives the impression of lasting stability. If, however, there should be an appreciable change in the production of either one of the two metals, or in the tastes of the public for jewellery and plate, or in the preference of hoarders for gold or silver, or in the demand for gold rather than for silver coins, then the market ratio would tend to deviate from the legal ratio. While the latter remains fixed at 1 to 15½, the former may rise to 1 to 16 or drop to 1 to 15. In the first case, gold is worth more as bullion than as coin. Silver, being overvalued by the mint, will be delivered by the public to be coined. The silver coins thus obtained will be exchanged for gold at the legal ratio of 1 to 15½. This gold will then be resold at a profit on the bullion market, with the result that all the gold coins will soon disappear from circulation and their place will be taken by heavy and inconvenient silver coins. In the second

case, silver instead of gold is at a premium and is worth more as bullion than as coin. Therefore, it is now silver that will be hoarded or exported or sent to the melting pot. The country will be reduced to using gold coins, beautiful, indeed, but inconvenient for petty transactions. Soon the public will complain about the lack of small change, and the officials will resort to makeshifts: they will be forced to allow the circulation of tokens or of dirty scrip, having the disadvantage of conveying contagious diseases. Thus the bimetallic standard is bound to become an alternating monometallic standard, swinging from gold to silver and from silver to gold, to the great annoyance of the public.

18. To prevent these swings, it is possible to use two devices, while still keeping the bimetallic standard in operation. One of them is seigniorage, but it is effective to a limited extent only. The reason is that seigniorage in recent times has been very moderate. In Italy the mint charges are only 2 per thousand to cover the expense of coinage. At any rate, seigniorage is to a certain extent a check against the practice of selling coins in circulation for their value as bullion, whenever the market price of bullion has risen above the mint price. On the other hand, let us assume that silver has fallen in price because of an increase in production. If the coinage were free of charge and not subject to delay, it would be profitable to take silver to the mint as soon as the price of the quantity of bullion contained in 100 francs dropped, even by a very small percentage, below the amount of 100 francs. If there is a coinage charge of 2 per thousand, the price of the same quantity of bullion has to fall below 99.80 francs before it becomes remunerative to bring bullion to the mint. As long as the drop in the price of bullion on the market does not exceed the seigniorage, it is unprofitable to coin more silver and to melt down the gold coins.

19. It must be admitted that today seigniorage, because it is either nonexistent or insignificant, can hardly be considered an effective check against the disruption of the bimetallic standard. This was not true of former centuries. From Charlemagne to the French Revolution, seigniorage was much higher than it is today, although it varied greatly from one country to another, from one period to another, and from one denomination to another. But in those times seigniorage did not always serve as an effective device of monetary policy, stabilizing the existent standard. The rulers considered the mint as a source of income, and in a period of financial stress increased seigniorage in the hope of thereby increasing their revenue, whether or not such a measure was called for to protect the standard at that particular time. The rulers also were reluctant to increase seigniorage on gold coins. The gold coin was a symbol of their sovereignty, and rulers rarely tampered with it; they were more inclined to make

seigniorage high for the silver coinage and still higher for black money and vellon. It happened that they increased the seigniorage when they should have lowered it; they sometimes lowered it inadvisedly for the very coins which were being culled out to be sent abroad or to the melting pot. Accordingly, seigniorage cannot be used today and was not used in the past as an effective instrument of policy to prevent the breakdown of the bimetallic standard.

20. The second device available to governments to preserve the bimetallic standard is to change the legal ratio in accordance with the variations of the market ratio. Unfortunately, this device, too, is clumsy and difficult to use. If the market ratio increased from 1:15½ to 1:16, gold would disappear from circulation unless the legal ratio was also changed and made to conform to the market ratio. This might be done in two ways, either by increasing the weight of the silver franc from 4.5 to 4.645 grams of pure silver, while the contents of the gold franc (0.29 grams) remained unaltered, or by reducing the weight of the gold franc to 0.28 gram without changing the weight of the silver franc. In both cases a recoinage, either of all the gold or of all the silver that was in circulation, would be necessary. If changes in the market ratio were frequent and appreciable, one recoinage would follow on the heels of another, and the currency would always be in a state of flux and confusion. As Ferdinando Galiani stated with reference to the disequilibrium between good and bad money, 'to withdraw it [one of the two, and he was thinking of the good money rather than of the bad], to recoin it and to put it back into circulation, takes too much time' (*Della moneta*, ed. by Nicolini, p.181).

21. In past centuries the device used to remedy monetary disturbances was precisely the money of account or the imaginary pound. It was an instrument of extraordinary flexibility which had been slowly developed in the ten centuries after the reign of Charlemagne. Its full possibilities were realized neither by the Revolutionary Assemblies, which eventually abandoned it, nor by the monetary authorities, who during the ten preceding centuries had failed to take full advantage of it and had diverted it to dangerous uses. Apart from the imaginary pound or livre, divided into shillings (sous) and subdivided into pence (deniers), in which prices were set and contracts established, there were also real moneys. These real moneys could not be reduced to two types (with their several denominations), as is the case with the bimetallic system; on the contrary, there were several types, and each of them was a unit or denomination independent from all the others.

At the time of Cesare Beccaria (1738–94), a famous economist and criminologist of the eighteenth century, the following coins were current in the Duchy of Milan:

GOLD

National Milanese: doblon (25.5.-)[15]

Foreign

Spanish: doblon (25.10.-), another doblon with two columns (25.-.-)

French: the old louis (25.10.-), the doblon called merliton (24.12.6), another coin with the sun and two shields (31.-.-), another coin with the cross of the Holy Spirit (37.2.6), another coin with four escutcheons (26.2.6)

Venetian: sequin (14.10.-)

Genoese: doblon (25.7.6)

Florentine: doblon (25.15.-); sequin (14.10.-)

Roman: doblon of Clement XII (25.-.-)

Savoy: doblon (25.-.-) ; sequin (14.7.6)

Mantua: doblon (25.5.-)

Portuguese: old lisbonina (41.-.-), new doblon with effigy and border (110.-.-)

Viennese: ongaro (14.5.-)

Chemnitz: ongaro (14.7.6); Roman sequin (14.15.-) ; Genoese sequin (15.-.-)

SILVER

National Milanese: ducatoon (8.12.-); philippus dollar (7.10.-)

Foreign

Roman: ducatoon of Clement XI (8.2.6); new testoon (2.5.-) ; new paolo (-.15.-); half-paolo (-.7.6)

Savoy: ducatoon (8.9.-) ; new écu of Piedmont (7.12.-) ; old lira of Savoy (1.10.-)

Venetian: ducatoon (8.8.-) ; giustina (7.7.6)

Florentine: ducatoon (8.7.6) ; livorina with the tower (6.19.-) ; same with the rose (6.12.6)

Mantua: ducatoon (8.9.-)

Genoese: genovina (10.5.-)

French: old écu (6.19.-); écu with the three fleurs-de-lis (17.11.-); écu with the two L L (6.-.-); écu with three crowns (7.16.-); écu del popone (6.5.-)

Burgundian: ducatoon (8.7.6)

German: ducatoon (8.5.-)

Bologna: écu (6.4.-)

Spanish: piece with the arms of Castile (6.17.6); half-piece (5.8.9); another piece with column and globes (6.16.-); half-piece (3.8.-); écu of St. John the Baptist of Genoa (6.-.-)[16]

Beccaria does not list the black moneys and copper coins which circulated at the same time. Their inclusion would only have strengthened the impression that the currency of the small Milanese duchy was in a disorderly state. Disorder did reign, but not because of the multiplicity of monetary types in circulation; there circulated no less than 22 gold coins and 29 silver coins, most of which were foreign. What really matters, however, is that all these types, with one or two exceptions, were independent monetary units. Table 12.1 shows how they may be classified according to their value in money of account.

Table 12.1 Rates of the gold and silver coins current in Milan (1762)

Gold					
Number of coins	**Rate in money of account *£ s. d.***	**Number of coins**	**Rate in money of account *£ s. d.***	**Number of coins**	**Rate in money of account *£ s. d.***
1	110. 0.0	2	25.10.0	1	14.15.0
1	46. 2.6	1	25. 7.6	2	14.10.0
1	41. 0.0	2	25. 5.0	2	14. 7.6
1	37. 2.6	3	25. 0.0	1	14. 5.0
1	31. 0.0	1	24.12.6		
1	25.15.0	1	15. 0.0		

Silver					
Number of coins	**Rate in money of account *£ s. d.***	**Number of coins**	**Rate in money of account *£ s. d.***	**Number of coins**	**Rate in money of account *£ s. d.***
1	10. 5.0	1	7.11.0	2	6. 0.0
1	8.12.0	1	7.10.0	1	5. 8.9
2	8. 9.0	1	7. 7.6	1	3. 8.0
1	8. 8.0	2	6.19.0	1	2. 5.0
2	8. 7.6	1	6.17.6	1	1.10.0
1	8. 5.0	1	6.16.0	1	0.15.0
1	8. 2.6	1	6.12.6	1	0. 7.6
1	7.16.0	1	6. 5.0		
1	7.12.0	1	6. 4.0		

Source: Cesare Beccaria, 'Del disordine e de' rimedi delle monete nello Stato di Milano nell'anno 1762', in *Le opere*, Vol. I (Florence: Le Monnier 1854), pp.470–1.

As Table 12.1 shows, there was only one instance in which three coins were current at the same rate. There were only eight instances in which it happened that two pieces were rated the same. Except for these few cases, no other two coins had the same value. Moreover, none of the 51 coins listed by Beccaria, with one single exception, had multiples or sub-multiples. The exception refers to the case of the paolo rated 15*s.* and the half-paolo rated 7s. 6*d.* There are a few other instances of coins which were double the value of other coins, but this is purely accidental, since the types in question were issued by different foreign mints without any attempt being made to issue doubles or halves.

How could a coherent system be built with different monetary units? How could they be counted, and in which of the 50 units? This difficult problem was solved by using the imaginary livre. This was the abstract unit which was used to evaluate all the coins in actual circulation and to bind them into one system. By saying that the Spanish doblon 'with the two columns', the Roman and the Savoyard doblons – all three of them gold coins – were worth £25 di imperiali, one stated simply that they were equal in value; and by saying that the sequin of Genoa, actually coined in Chemnitz, was worth only £15, one stated that this coin was worth three-fifths of the doblons mentioned above and was rated twice as high as the Milanese philippus current at £7 10*s*. di imperiali.

22. It was possible that wrong rates were set for coins of the same metal, as, for example, when two coins having different gold or silver contents were made current at the same rate in money of account. In fact, Beccaria shows that, of the three doblons, all rated £25, the Spanish doblon contained $117\frac{9}{16}$ grains of fine gold, the Roman doblon $117\frac{13}{90}$ grains, and the Savoyard doblon only $112\frac{6}{16}$ grains. The Savoyard doblon, being much lighter than the other two, was consequently overrated to that extent. Such errors in rating, once they were ascertained by assaying, could easily be adjusted when the coins in question were all of the same metal, be it gold or silver.

23. The problem of setting accurate rates and of establishing a workable monetary system was much more difficult and complex when the coins in circulation were of two or more different metals. In this case, the setting of proper rates in money of account for all the current coins depended not only on the skill of the assayer but also on the ability of the mint officials to keep in touch with the conditions prevailing in the bullion market and to follow closely any changes in the price ratio between the metals that had monetary uses.

24. In order to simplify matters, let us assume that there are only two coins – gold florins and silver scudos – which are full legal tender and to which the mint extends the privilege of free coinage. Let us further assume that the market ratio between gold and silver is 1 to 12, which was actually the ratio in the second half of the sixteenth century, a fact recognized by both contenders in the famous Malestroit–Bodin controversy. With these assumptions in mind, let us suppose that the gold florin, weighing 120 grains of fine gold, is current at the rate of £24 in money of account. What, then, should be the rate of the silver scudo having the same weight

of fine silver? Evidently, £2, or one-twelfth of the rate given to the florin. For our monetary system of florins and scudos to be in equilibrium, the proportion between the rates, £2 and £24, set by royal proclamation, has to be the same as the ratio, 1 to 12, existing in the bullion market between the price of a silver ingot and that of a gold ingot of equal weight.

Now let us suppose that the market ratio changes from 1:12 to 1:11½. In the case of the bimetallic system, as it existed during the nineteenth century in the United States and in Europe, adjustment would have been difficult to achieve unless all the gold or all the silver in circulation were recoined. Before the officials of the mint had even begun to make the necessary arrangements, all the undervalued coins would most likely already have been sent abroad or to the melting pot. In former centuries, however, an adjustment could have been made very promptly. It would have sufficed to issue a royal proclamation crying up the silver scudo from £2 to £2 1*s*. 9*d*., that is, to a number obtained by dividing £24, the rate of the florin, by 11½ instead of by 12.

And what if the market ratio changed from 1:12 to 1:12½? In such a case, the normal procedure would have been to cry down the silver scudo from £2 to £1 18*s*. 5*d*., that is, to a figure obtained by dividing £24 by 12½.[17] [18]

25. The function of imaginary money in a country that had adopted the bimetallic standard was consequently that of keeping the monetary system in equilibrium. This objective was achieved by the simple process of crying the currency up or down, that is, by increasing or decreasing the current rates in money of account of the real coins. If this were done carefully, the legal rates would at all times be in accordance with the ratio between the prices of gold and silver, as determined by market conditions.

The instrument called 'imaginary money' has the following connotations.

1 Expressions in 'imaginary money' are abstract numbers, notwithstanding the denomination in terms of pounds, shillings and pence. People used these terms in their enumerations in remembrance of the historical fact that, in the past, pounds, shillings and pence had actually existed in concrete form.
2 Expressions in 'imaginary money' are not absolute numbers. Instead of saying, 'The gold florin is worth £24'. it is possible to assign to the same coin another value, provided that other coins got new rates accordingly. The rate, in 'imaginary money', of the silver scudo should be a function of the rate of the florin; and, to be precise, this functional relationship should reflect the market ratio between gold and silver.
3 It is a matter of indifference which coin is chosen as the one whose rate is fixed, while the value of all others may vary. Both can conceivably be allowed to vary, but only on condition that the rates reflect the market ratio between gold and silver.

4 According to historical experience, it was, however, more expedient to keep the rates of gold coins fixed, while the rates of silver coins might, if necessary, be altered. Since gold coins were regarded as a symbol of sovereignty, rulers were reluctant to damage the prestige of this symbol by alterations. Not only the rulers but also the subjects believed that gold coins should circulate at stable rates; they were convinced that an invariable archetype should serve as the standard of value. Both myths, that of the royal symbol and that of the unvarying standard, were the outcome of unfortunate experiences; the current rates of the real coins, as expressed in terms of money of account, were often manipulated for purposes other than the preservation of the bimetallic standard.

26. The discovery of 'imaginary money' as an instrument of monetary policy was not the work of a theorist, but the result of a long process of historical change (see paragraph 8 above). However, if, among many contingent factors, one wanted to indicate which one came closest to being determined by deliberate choice, one should mention the longing of medieval men for the eternal, the immutable, the universal, accompanied by an abhorrence of the transitory, the mutable and the particular. They stubbornly looked for an invariable standard of value and called it the pound; they pretended that it was immutable in the monetary chaos in which abraded, clipped, and adulterated foreign as well as domestic coins circulated side by side. Eventually they discovered that imaginary money could be used as an instrument of monetary policy, in order to obtain certain results. Legislators and economists after 1789 scorned this discovery. Far from realizing its potentialities, they failed to see its true import, considered only its passing attributes (cf. below, paragraphs 43ff.), and then forgot all about it. If the great advocate of universal bimetallism, Enrico Cernuschi, had meditated upon the solution offered by the age-old experience of European nations, he would have exclaimed: 'Eureka!'

27. Another reason why legislators and economists misunderstood, despised and forgot this monetary device is that the concept 'imaginary money' was surrounded by the thick mist of a strange terminology, repellent to the layman and conducive to deceitful practices. We have already pointed out how difficult it is in times of monetary devaluations and revaluations to persuade men that prices have not changed but that the monetary yardstick has become longer or shorter. Yet today the terms of comparison are only two: the monetary unit, e.g., the lira (in Italy), and one unit of a given commodity, e.g., a kilogram of bread; and there is only one ratio: between the monetary unit and the unit of a commodity. Whether a change in this ratio occurs because of a change in one or the other of the two variables should therefore be easily ascertainable. At the time of imaginary money three units had to be correlated: the imagin-

ary monetary unit (the pound), the real monetary unit (the scudo), and a unit of an economic good (e.g., a kilogram of bread). As a result, there were also three ratios: pound to commodity, pound to scudo, and scudo to commodity. Upon reflection it is a simple proposition; yet it is apt to confuse casual observers as well as more profound thinkers. When individual or class interests were at stake, endless disputes were certain to arise. The point of the great controversy between Malestroit and Bodin was that Malestroit contended that a change in the pound-to-commodity ratio had been cancelled by a contrary change in the pound-to-scudo ratio, with the result that the scudo-to-commodity ratio had remained constant. On the other hand, Bodin considered only the scudo-to-commodity ratio and declared that it alone had changed.

If we assume that the price of bread had increased from £1 to £2 and that, at the same time, the rate of the scudo had increased from £2 to £4, then the price of bread had remained unchanged at ½ scudo. The public, used to counting in pounds, shillings and pence, complained about the rise in prices, but Malestroit demonstrated that 'the general rise in prices, about which everyone today complains, is only a delusion, a way of counting without consistency or substance' (Malestroit, *Paradoxes*, ed. by Einaudi,). The learned man was right, because the pound was a mere numerical expression, and the scudo a real silver coin. However, the people whose incomes were fixed in imaginary pounds, shillings and pence were not wrong either. They were damaged if they did not succeed in getting their 'abstract' incomes raised, because only then did they receive the same number of scudos as before. After the great monetary devaluations following the First World War we have become accustomed to the idea or variability in the monetary standard. Since prices are sticky, either because it is their natural tendency or because they are regulated by the government, we all suffer or benefit, as the case may be, whenever there is a change in the symbols of wealth without a change in the reality. Today monetary devaluations or revaluations attract immediate notice only through the fluctuations of the foreign exchanges in which only those few who have dealings abroad are directly interested. But this was not so in the past; then the public became immediately aware of monetary disturbances because of fluctuating domestic exchange rates, indicating current rates of real coins in terms of money of account. If the ratio between the precious metals changed from 1:12 to 1:11½, the market, being very sensitive, often anticipated the ruler's proclamation. The rate of the silver scudo priced officially at £2 (as compared to the gold florin priced at £24) rose little by little in the market until it reached £2 1*s.* 9*d.* Such an unofficial quotation was called in Italy *in abusivo* because it was an abuse of the law, and hence strictly prohibited; coins were supposed to be current at the rate fixed by the monetary ordinances. Nevertheless, it frequently happened that the change in the market rate, although illegal, was only a prelude to a change in the official rate, to be proclaimed sooner or later, depending upon the alertness of the monetary authorities.

28. With reference to monetary matters, the language used in former centuries was so confusing that the public was befuddled as to what was actually going on. Today this same terminology is so unfamiliar to economists that it constitutes a serious obstacle to the understanding of early monetary literature.

Prior to the French Revolution, the expression 'enhancement of the currency' (Fr. *augmentation*; It. *aumento* or *alzamento*) meant that the real coins were cried up, that is, that their rates were raised by proclamation, as, for instance, the silver scudo from £2 to £2 ls. 9*d*. However, insofar as people reckoned and stipulated contracts in pounds, shillings and pence, such a rise of the current rates corresponded to a weakening (Fr. *affaiblissement*; It. *indebolimento*), deterioration (It. *peggioramento*), or debasement of the money of account. By 'crying up' the money, a single legislative act devalued the money of account and revalued the currency, that is, the real coins. Usually the result was that, after a while, prices were raised as expressed in pounds, shillings and pence, although they remained constant if measured in revalued gold and silver currency. Contrary to what a modern economist would expect, 'crying up' (Fr. *hausser la monnaie*; It. *alzare*) was synonymous with debasement or with a shift from what was called 'strong' money (Fr. *monnaie forte*; It. *moneta forte*) to 'weak' or 'base' money (Fr. *monnaie faible*; It. *moneta debole*).

29. Conversely, the expression 'abatement of the currency' (Fr. *diminution*; It. *sbassamento*) indicated that the current coins were cried down, that is, that their rates were decreased, as, for example, when the silver scudo was called down by proclamation from £2 to £1 18*s*. 4*d*. Consequently, 'abatement of the currency' was synonymous with an improvement or strengthening (Fr. *renforcement*; It. *rinforzamento*) of the imaginary money of account, which was the standard of value. By such an act, the money of account was revalued, and the currency devalued. After a while, prices in pounds, shillings and pence tended to fall, although they often remained on the same level if measured in gold or silver. 'To abate the currency' (Fr. *diminuer les monnaies*; It. *sbassare*) was, therefore, a shift from weak to strong money. Often it meant a return to good money (Fr. *retour à la forte monnaie*) which had been allowed to deteriorate.

30. As today, so also between AD 800 and 1800, people had their minds fixed on the mirage rather than on reality. Therefore, they protested especially against the enhancements of the currency and approved of abatements. Those who complained the most – and they formed the majority – were wage earners, pensioners, and all recipients of revenues fixed in

pounds, shillings, and pence. They were hurt by enhancements, and the resulting curtailment of their purchasing power, through the rise in prices as expressed in money of account. This same group naturally gave its support to the abatements, which tended to lower the price level.

31. In a monetary system based on the use of imaginary money, the banks did not and could not issue notes promising to pay in money of account instead of in real currency. What would it have meant for a bank to be a debtor of £24 million toward the bearers of circulating banknotes? Insofar as people used imaginary money as a standard of deferred payments, but made payments in scudi and other real coins, the said bank, in case of enhancement of the scudi from £2 to £4, could have discharged its obligations with 6 million scudi instead of 12 million, thereby gaining the difference. On the other hand, if the scudo were cried down from £2 to £1, the bank would have been compelled to repay with 24 million scudi the original 12 million for which it was obligated, and thus would have been reduced to a state of bankruptcy. Perhaps it is possible to find a bank which failed for this reason but, if so, it was an accident due to a mistake in the conduct of business. This mistake must then also be attributed to the halo of mystery which for a thousand years surrounded the concept of imaginary money and caused it to be mistaken for something different from what it really was. Even the careful Pompeo Neri missed the truth – as so many other writers did – when he listed the pound-banco (*lira di banco*) among the imaginary moneys. As a matter of fact, his own description contradicts this classification.

According to Pompeo Neri, the pound-banco (*lira di banco*) was created:

> by taking as its measure a given weight of silver, or even an unadulterated coin, and by determining its contents in pure gold or silver, without giving any consideration to subsequent adulterations introduced by custom or law. Then the values of the imaginary pound-banco and scudo-banco would be fixed, so that they would be regulated by a standard independent of arbitrary legislation or public catastrophes. As a result, contracts would be made stable, and this standard of value, being perpetual and incorruptible, would be a convenient yardstick for measuring the value of all sorts of merchandise and real money.
>
> ('Osservazioni', p.153)

Thus the pound-banco was a promise made by a bank which had received, let us say, 10 grains of pure gold, defined by the bank itself as a 'pound', to restore to the owner an ingot of identical weight and fineness. However, this was not imaginary money but real money, and even the best of the real moneys, since it was immune from clipping and from frauds in weight or fineness. It was easily transferable from person to person, or even from place to place, and independent of variations in the name, the substance, or the rates of other currencies.

32. During the thousand years of its history the monetary system based on the coexistence of the imaginary pound and real moneys could and actually did perform the following functions in a more or less efficient way and with more or less comprehension on the part of princes, bankers, and contracting parties.

1 This system allowed every state to have its own unit of account, the pound, which might be equal to the unit of other states, but not necessarily so; in most instances equality soon disappeared.
2 This system also allowed every state to coin one or more real moneys: of gold only, of silver only, or of both metals. A state might even have no mint of its own, if it pleased the ruler to give currency to foreign coins. Beccaria – and Verri agreed with him – gave excellent reasons for advising a prince, especially a small one, against minting his own currency. Except in some particular cases, 'the coinage of money is but a comedy of transformations accompanied by an unnecessary waste of metal in minting; it is a public burden which only profits the projectors, men who conceal their gains under the cloak of a pretended benefit to the sovereign, and hence to the entire nation'.
(*Del disordine*, Florentine ed., p.478).

This single unit of account – the pound and its fractions – made it possible to use for payments any number of coins or real moneys, gold as well as silver, domestic as well as foreign – upon the sole condition that their rates were fixed in proportion to the gold or silver contents of the coins; moreover, the official ratio and the market ratio between gold and silver bullion had to be equal.

The principal shortcoming of this system was that the official rates set by proclamation were slow in adapting themselves to changes in the market ratio. In order to overcome this defect, Ferdinando Galiani, by far the best Italian economist of the eighteenth century, proposed in his book, *Della moneta* (written in 1750, when he was 23 years of age) a practical remedy: the current or proclamation rates should no longer be compulsory. Instead, the current rate was simply to become an optional price (*prezzo di voce*), effective only in the absence of any agreement to the contrary. Does the state fix the prices of commodities in general? It does not. Why, then, should it fix the price of currency?

> The prices of wheat, of wine, and of oil are much more important [than the currency rates]. Those of land, of buildings, of rents, of interest, and of foreign exchange are still more important, and yet those prices are not regulated by any other law than 'the consensus of the public'.
> (Della moneta, ed. by Nicolini, pp.159–60).

Ferdinando Galiani's proposal to make the unofficial rate legal would have compelled the prince to revise promptly the proclamation rates whenever they were out of line with those practised in the market. By following this policy, he would have avoided the inconveniences and the lack of stability inherent in the modern bimetallic system and would have supplied the public with currency in the desired quantity and of the desired denominations.

Since each state was already provided with its own standard of value or imaginary pound, and since the creation of paper money representing mere numbers is and was inconceivable, a bank, even if it were a national bank, necessarily assumed in those times a supranational character. The pound-banco, representing a given weight of pure gold or silver, was itself a universal currency, which, like any other of the real currencies, could be rated in the money of account of each state and which was more suitable than hard coin for the purpose of making international transfers. The bank moneys of Venice, Genoa and Amsterdam were used in traffic all over Europe, owing to the confidence which these moneys enjoyed, because of their convertibility into invariable weights of gold and because they could easily be made current abroad. In the Christian community of medieval Europe it was possible for each nation to adopt any foreign currency as its own, by simply giving it a rating in domestic money of account.

33. If these were the functions which actually were or might be filled by imaginary money, it does not seem that a conscious effort was ever made to use it as a means to achieve a purpose – supposing this purpose were desirable and possible – for which it was particularly well suited. That purpose is the utopian idea of price stability, which must be called 'utopian' for a number of reasons.

1 An acceptable definition of the concept 'the general level of prices' does not exist, since it is uncertain which goods should be included in the preparation of a satisfactory index. Only finished products, or also raw materials and unfinished products? Only tangible goods or also services? Only consumer goods or also capital goods? Furthermore, economists and statisticians are not in accord as to the criteria which should be used in constructing an index for measuring the price level itself, and all are sceptical about the possibility of adhering to those criteria, once they are chosen.
2 The idea that it is desirable to stabilize the general level of prices – a naive and undemonstrable idea – does not have to be accepted. Why should invariability of prices exist in a world where everything else continuously changes? Should we also aim at the invariability of each single price, which is manifestly absurd? Why intend the invariability of something as abstract as the general level of all prices? One should, however, recall that medieval man was inclined to look at the world in the light of eternity and immobility. The modern popular desire for a general price level that would be constant may be a fossil remnant of that medieval state of mind.

3 The possibility of reaching that end by means of a monetary policy which consists in decreasing or increasing the volume of money in circulation, as prices go up or down, especially if those variations are undesirable, is questionable. The success of such a policy depends entirely upon the assumption that everything else remains equal. If it is true that nothing, absolutely nothing, changes in the economic world except the quantity of money, then prices, by definition, will vary with this quantity. If nothing varies, except that the quantity of money is doubled, the person who has £10 instead of £5 will spend £10 instead of £5, because, if he is not willing to do so, his desire to build up monetary reserves will have changed, which is contrary to our assumption. If nothing varies, the same amount of economic goods is offered for £10, no more and no less. Consequently, one unit of an economic good priced at £5 must necessarily go up to £10. The assumption that other things remain equal is extremely useful for purposes of analysis, but does not work out very well in practice. Everything changes with the change in the volume of money in circulation: the cash reserves of the individuals, and consequently the velocity of circulation; the production of economic goods, and consequently also their supply. Monetary policy has to operate with a very delicate and complex mechanism. In order to be successful, the policy-maker must combine an analytical mind with a quick appraisal of the imponderable factors.

34. Whether one considers stability of the price level possible or utopian, desirable or naive, does not matter much; what I wish to emphasize is that the attainment of this goal might have been, and still might be, greatly facilitated by using imaginary money as a tool of monetary policy.

Today such a policy, intended to counteract undesirable price fluctuations, requires that the monetary authorities take either one or the other of the following steps if, let us suppose, prices go up and are to be brought back to their former level: (1) either the volume of bank credit and the circulation of bank notes has to be contracted, or (2) the metallic currency has to be withdrawn and recoined with a higher content in fine per monetary unit, whereby, as a result, the number of units that can be coined from the existing stock of precious metal is reduced.

On the other hand, if prices fall and the monetary authorities want to raise them to their former level, the appropriate measures to be taken are: either (1) an expansion of the volume of bank credit and the circulation of bank notes or (2) a devaluation of the monetary unit by reducing its gold or silver content, whereby the number of units that can be coined from a given stock of precious metal is increased.

The trouble is that all these measures are very cumbersome and slow and that they are liable to cause violent and unpredictable reactions which will disturb equilibrium conditions, if such exist, in other sectors of the economy.

The use of imaginary money as a tool of policy, on the other hand, offers a tempting solution to the difficulty. Let us assume that the index of general prices is at 100; that the gold florin is current at £24 and the silver scudo at £2. Let the index now rise to 111.11. In order to adjust the matter, all one need do is to cry down the currency by one-tenth, to reduce the rate of the florin from £24 to £21 12*s*., and that of the silver scudo from £2 to £1 16*s*. The transaction resembles what is called 'a monetary deflation'. The amount of currency in circulation is unchanged, but its purchasing power is automatically cut down by one-tenth. Everyone owns the same number of florins and silver scudi as before the proclamation, but everyone has one-tenth less in imaginary pounds. Since buying and selling is done in money of account, the reduction of its volume by one-tenth, by virtue of the quantity theory of money, will bring prices down again from 111.11 to 100.

And what to do if the price level drops to 90? In order to raise it again, all that the monetary authorities have to do is to issue a proclamation crying up the currency by one-ninth: the florin from £24 to £26 13*s*. 4*d*. and the silver scudo from £2 to £2 4*s*. 5⅓*d*. Such a transaction resembles what is called a 'monetary inflation'. Although the volume of currency remains the same, its purchasing power is raised by one-ninth by legislative fiat. Everyone now possesses one-ninth more in money of account, and, since this is the standard of value, prices must go up again from 90 to 100.

35. It is conceivable that the normal sequence of events may be the following.

1 The production of precious metals increases.
2 As a result, the volume of currency in circulation, florins and scudi, increases too.
3 This increase automatically causes another increase in the number of imaginary pounds, as long as the current value of the florin and the scudo remains fixed at £24 and £2, respectively.
4 Since the quantity of economic goods that are offered for sale remains steady, as do all the other data of the problem, except the volume of money, prices tend to increase.
5 However, the prince, by crying down the currency at the opportune moment, prevents an increase in the volume of imaginary money, despite any increase in the volume of actual currency.
6 Therefore, prices, too, are prevented from rising. The problem created by a decrease in the production of precious metals and by a tendency of prices to fall, while the production of economic goods continues to grow, is solved by reversing the procedure described above.

36. It is not easy to understand why Irving Fisher, who examined with such care the historical precedents for his managed and invariable dollar,

failed to mention the system of imaginary money. To those princes of past centuries who were eager to secure for their subjects the benefits of price stability, this system could have rendered great service. Illusory stability, to be sure, because stable prices in imaginary pounds would nevertheless result in the payment of a greater or lesser quantity of florins or scudi. But did Pompeo Neri not teach that 'the public was scrupulous in preserving the identity of the word pound in sound, rather than in value' ('Osservazioni', p.110)?

37. In the same formal way, another troublesome problem of modern times, that of foreign exchange, might have been considered solved. But it would have been solved by being transferred from the international to the national scene. The monetary adviser, anxious to preserve the prestige of the domestic currency, could have reasoned as follows:

'In the system of imaginary money, by hypothesis, two national moneys exist side by side, one imaginary and the other real. Among the latter, we have supposed that there was a gold florin weighing 120 grains of pure gold and having a value of £24 in money of account.

'If the prince was careful to maintain the weight of the florin at 120 grains, the foreign exchanges, expressed in florins, would remain stable. A foreign prince might reduce the weight of his sequin from 120 to 100 grains of pure gold; in that case the domestic florin would be at a premium of 20 per cent over the sequin: a perpetual reason for national pride and prestige.

'If, later on, the prince decided to cry up the florin by one-tenth and to increase the current rate from £24 to £26 8*s*., this was a domestic matter which affected only the 'internal' exchange, or the relation existing between the 'national' moneys : the real florin and the imaginary pound. The foreign exchanges between the real currency of one country and the real currency of another country were unaffected. What did it matter to foreigners, if someone chose to modify the basis for the settlement of debts between citizens of the same state?'

This analysis leads to one important observation: whereas the present system of real money is likely to arouse emotions, because it creates the false impression that foreigners are to blame for any devaluation of the national currency, the ancient system of real and imaginary money made it clear to everyone that monetary devaluation was mainly a domestic matter, important only in the relations between classes and individuals within the same nation. In domestic trade, contracts were stipulated and accounts were kept in imaginary money, while in foreign trade prices were usually fixed in gold florins.

38. The rate at which a coin was officially allowed to circulate was called *corso di grida* the current rate by proclamation. There existed also a *corso di*

voce or *corso in abusivo* which, as the names suggest, was the unofficial or market rate. These two conceptions, curious as they are, are to be found at every step when one goes through the monetary tracts, treatises and proclamations before 1800. At first, one is perplexed by these terms, then the matter becomes somewhat clearer, and finally one is attracted. Is it possible that the legislators of the French Revolution were, through their eagerness to return to the true and simple, actually opening the road to mystery and complication? What they wanted to make clear to the public was that the monetary unit was a disc of silver weighing 4.5 grams, or a disc of gold of 0.29 grams. Thereby, they erroneously assumed, people would never again fall into the error of looking at the monetary unit as perpetually endowed with a fixed value of its own. That these enlightened legislators were wrong is shown by the fact that in our days the link between various monetary units, such as the mark, lira and franc, has again been broken. From these monetary names all precise connotations disappeared when it became no longer possible to convert the corresponding units into specific weights of precious metal; and at present convertibility is neither unconditional, prompt, nor certain. Thus, after one-and-a-third century of fixed metallic equivalents, people are again debating attempts to give a fixed meaning to the monetary names which correspond to nothing but signs or tokens.

Legislators before 1800 had solved the problem by clearly separating money as a token or sign and money as a commodity (metal). The former was called 'imaginary money', the other was the real currency. Now the theory of 'imaginary money' could lead to the reality of dealing with money as a marketable good, not different from other commodities. While their contracts were made in pounds, shillings and pence, people thought of the gold florins or silver scudi in which they would be paid; and by thinking in this way they were constantly reminded of the fact that florins and scudi had no miraculous virtues of their own. These coins, therefore, in spite of their name, had no permanent value or other characteristics but were priced as were, for instance, wine, wheat or a farm. From the Middle Ages down to the end of the eighteenth century, men saw much better than we do that money is a negotiable commodity like any other. Because we exchange money only at national boundaries, it appears to us, at least inside a country, to be a supercommodity whose value is stable. One lire is always one lire, one franc is always one franc, and one mark is always one mark. In former times, because of the existence of money of account, men every day set a price on the florins, scudi, écus, doblons, sequins and testoons which they received and paid out. Every day, in every single transaction, it was made clear to their minds that the money with which they paid, even bank money or paper money, was a commodity like any other, that its price was governed by the market and, like any other price, was the result of an infinite number of economic and non-economic forces which determine the general equilibrium of all prices.

39. In the language of the Enlightenment, my present study would have been called 'an apology for imaginary money'. After this attempt, which I believe to be the first one of its kind, a 'philippic against imaginary money' seems superfluous. Such attacks, virulent as philippics usually are, can be found in all writings dealing with debasements and monetary disturbances, as, for example, in the historical summary given by Francesco Ferrara in one of his classic introductions.[19]

40. The myth of the immutability of the monetary unit, which could be used in the harmless game of keeping the price level stable in terms of imaginary money (but variable in terms of real money), or of stabilizing the foreign exchange (while allowing fluctuations in the domestic exchange), lent itself also to other, less innocent uses. The influence of what was a pure ideal allowed the sovereigns to engage in counterfeiting.

41. A sovereign often could not resist the temptation to tamper with the coinage, especially when through the expenses incured in foreign and civil wars he was under compulsion to raise additional revenue, without being able to collect larger taxes from his subjects. One favourite method was recoinage: the sovereign decried or banned the old coins and forced the public to bring them to the mints so that he could deduct the seigniorage for the coinage of the new moneys.[20] The seigniorage was usually deducted in kind from the bullion or from the decried coins brought to the mint. This procedure allowed the prince to take away 10 or 20 per cent of the precious metals owned by the public. He was able to get more revenue without having to ask for a benevolence from the Estates General, who gave financial aid only grudgingly. It is no wonder that the mint was regarded as a source of revenue in a time when an adequate tax system had not yet been established and when revenues from the royal domain were no longer sufficient.

The system of the imaginary pound was useful in making the tribute somewhat less felt. If it had been the practice of the mint to pay 7 ounces in coin for one mark of precious metal, consisting of 8 ounces, it would have been obvious to the public that the prince retained one ounce for seigniorage. But such was not the practice. Let us suppose that the mint price was £480 for a mark of pure gold. A merchant who delivered bullion to the mint would consequently receive £480, or 20 florins of £24 each, for one mark of bullion. From this one mark of bullion the mint coined 22.85 florins instead of only 20 florins, current at the rate of £24. In so doing, the mint gained 2.85 florins on each mark, a seigniorage of exactly one-eighth. Afterward the price of bullion, expressed in new florins of £24, was likely to increase and to rise even above the mint price. If the operation was not too frequent and if the public had time to forget previous experiences, it could succeed.

High seigniorage, open or concealed, fell into disuse at the beginning of modern times. It was less easily concealed and, when in later ages regular taxes were established, princes were no longer impelled to use this device.

42. Accusations of counterfeiting, such as the one which Dante hurled at Philip the Fair, King of France (1285–1314), were in many cases justified by the facts. The prince surreptitiously coined florins or scudi which were reduced in weight, in fineness, or in both, while he continued to call these adulterated coins by the same name as before and continued to make them current at the same rate: £24 for the florin and £2 for the silver scudo. By weighing and assaying the new coins, the public soon discovered them to be deficient in weight and fineness, and then became offended.

43. Instead of tampering with the real coins, princes could perform their operations through the instrument of 'imaginary money'. A florin which hitherto had circulated for £24, or a newly coined florin of the same weight and fineness, could simply be 'called up' to £30. Thereby nothing was changed, except that the circulating medium was raised by one-quarter in nominal value. This would please large numbers of people because with the same number of florins in their purses they had become richer by one-quarter; in imaginary pounds, it is true. A prince who had received £24 million in the form of a million florins of £24 each could now repay his debt with only 0.8 million florins of £30 each. His debt was diminished, and he consequently gained (by 2 million florins).

44. Ferdinando Galiani justified enhancement of the currency in his theory by defining it as follows: enhancement is 'a profit which the prince and the state derive from the slowness with which the majority of people change their ideas with regard to the value of money and the prices of goods'. Even at present no better definition of devaluation, today's name for 'enhancement of the currency', could be given. Galiani insisted that his definition had no malicious intent: 'Are not the sale of noble titles, the award of honours, and a large number of other customs actually based simply on deep-rooted associations which cannot easily be changed?' And Galiani continued:

> If a prince ennobles all his subjects, he does not give them added honour but takes away some honour from the word 'nobility.' The meaning of 'nobility' is changed. Similarly, if in establishing a new decoration for merit he does not confer this decoration first upon people who are already admired and illustrious, which fixes the value of the order in peoples' minds, but gives it to his lackeys, then the decoration will simply be regarded as a livery for servants, whatever its design.

Similarly, enhancement of the currency

> does not produce a change of things but merely of words. The prices of commodities, in order to remain the same in reality, must consequently be changed in name. If this occurs on the same day on which the currency is enhanced and if everything is changed simultaneously and proportionately, then enhancing the currency will have no more effects than would a law giving Latin, Greek or Hebrew, instead of Italian, names to the different coins. If there is a change in the words by which prices are expressed, and nothing else, things remain as they were. If, on the other hand, the words remain unchanged, then things themselves change. We are being told that an enhancement of prices is a remedy for enhancement (of the currency).When everything has been readjusted, the effects of the enhancement may be said to have vanished as the morning mist is dissipated by the rays of the sun. Disturbing effects of any enhancement of the currency must therefore be the result of the fact that prices are slow in adjusting themselves. The delay occurs because people who are accustomed to paying one-ducat for a certain dish expect to be able to buy the same dish as long as they pay something called a ducat. They complain about the avarice of whoever denies the dish to them, or they foolishly accuse others of having caused the dearth of all things. It must be noted that a prince who would repeat enhancement every month would necessarily destroy any association between a given commodity and its price, and thereby the device of enhancement would become perfectly useless and ineffective (as an instrument of monetary policy). What normally could be accomplished by an enhancement of the currency would subsequently have to be done by other means.
>
> (*Della moneta*, ed. by Nicolini, pp.186–7).

45. Galiani had already demonstrated that enhancing the currency favoured debtors by lessening the burden of private and public debts. It would bring about a temporary reduction of wages and salaries and taxes, thereby encouraging industry. Galiani was impatient with the defenders of those who were hurt:

> Nor should one call for help and try to arouse pity with the words 'orphans', 'widows', 'virgins', 'pupils', because they are very few. The true orphan, the true pauper, is the industrious peasant, the craftsman, the mariner, the merchant. These should be pitied, and they are those who, being accustomed to paying on leases and rents, will benefit from enhancement of the currency.
>
> (*Della moneta*, p.209)

46. Galiani's subtle praise is more devastating than the virulent philippic of Ferrara. In the long run, people prefer security; they prefer it to the advantage obtained at the expense of others. Through monetary devaluation or through the invisible reduction of wages owing to the fixity of popular associations regarding the value of money and the prices of commodities, debtors obtained, as in a Hebrew jubilee, partial remission. Imaginary money was a splendid instrument invented during the infancy

of European nations for performing certain tasks of public policy which today are performed by other methods. However, this instrument destroyed all certainty. Instead of a crude but certain monetary unit, such as the grain or gram of pure gold, it established an abstract unit which the public fancied to be stable. Princes could manipulate this monetary device for their own advantage, although they acted as if it were for the benefit of the public. When the instrument was misused, the drawbacks outweighed the advantages. The device of imaginary money was consequently discarded at the end of the eighteenth century and was replaced by a real monetary unit which was fixed beyond doubt to a weight of fine gold; thus the gram of gold became the standard of value. Under this principle people lived and throve for more than a century. But with the coming of a universal monetary deluge (since the First World War) the monetary universe entered into a period of fluidity in which the long-forgotten imaginary money made its reappearance, namely, in the writings of those who proposed what in effect amounted to a pallid imitation of the device of earlier days. What has been attempted in these pages is not the advocacy of its reintroduction. We only have tried to demonstrate that what certain modern authors advocate is a monetary device which, after having been perfected over the centuries, was abandoned in the period of the French Revolution.

13
Noise*

The explanation of *fuge rumores* helps to explain some of Donato Menichella's[1] rules of conduct ... The Governor of the Bank of Italy, with the agreement or cooperation of the Minister of the Treasury, can use two effective weapons to control the lira, the exchanges, the country's industrial and commercial activity: they are changes in the discount rate and changes in the percentage of deposits commercial banks have to hold with the central bank.

Changing the discount rate is a traditional weapon that has existed almost since time immemorial. When businessmen go mad, get too big for their boots and buy securities without a thought to the price or the return, or build factories without end, invest without discretion, build up stocks of fuel and raw materials, produce for the warehouse, the central bank raises what is known as the price of money. From 3 per cent the discount rate goes to 4, to 5, to 9, to 10 per cent. Commit follies if you will, behave as if the devil were at your heels and a minute lost in the race to buy and to borrow would be your ruin; but you will pay dearly for your excesses. It also happens, but not always, that if the commercial banks and the savings banks follow the example of the central bank and money becomes expensive in the country as a whole, footloose capital will arrive from abroad in search of profitable investment, to the advantage of the balance of payments.

When, instead, businessmen are in a bad mood, depressed and, for a variety of changing reasons, unwilling to undertake new initiatives and to carry on with their old work, a reduction in the official discount rate might encourage the undecided if the cost of money, helped by the abundance of bank deposits, comes down everywhere. If with an official discount rate of 6 per cent, which along the way becomes 8 or 10 per cent at the banks,

---

* First published as 'Rumore', *Corriere della Sera*, year 85, No. 235 (1 October 1960), p.1.

there is nothing to be gained from new factories or machinery that can be hoped to earn a return not exceeding that same 8 or 10 per cent, there may appear to be something to be gained if the official discount rate is lowered to 4 per cent and the cost of money to 7 or 8 per cent. The effect is not certain, but if, with the contribution of other factors, the depression can be overcome, lowering the discount rate is undoubtedly beneficial.

In countries in which the market for short-term securities, such as Treasury bills, is vigorous and broad, use is made of what are known as 'open market' operations, whereby the banks, acting on the advice of the central banks, sell short-term securities from their portfolios at times of euphoria and by this means reacquire the deposits deemed to be in excess and raise the cost of money for the overadventurous entrepreneurs; or, on the contrary, they buy short-term securities in the market and thus provide money to a market that is languishing for lack of business.

In Italy the market for short-term securities is not so broad and lively as to permit purchases and sales in sufficient quantities to exercise a significant influence without the value of the securities collapsing. This is why preference was given, in 1947, drawing on an American experience that was followed only this year by the Bank of England, to the expedient of requiring commercial banks to place a part of their deposits with the Bank of Italy. Initially, the proportion of deposits was 25 per cent, but the idea was that it should be increased when it was deemed desirable to prevent commercial banks from granting excessive advances and discounts to over-optimistic customers and decreased when, instead, it was deemed desirable to allow the commercial banks to have more funds and increase their loans to customers, encouraging them by cuts in the cost of money.

None of this happened. During Menichella's governorship, changes in the official discount rate were few and far between and the proportion of the commercial banks' deposits held with the central bank remained virtually unchanged at the initial value of 25 per cent.

Wishing to find the reason for this conduct, apparently in contrast with what had been expected, I again came to the conclusion that the Governor, now honorary, of the Bank of Italy did not like 'noise'. Silence is part of the Bank's tradition. Staircases, rooms and corridors are silent and clean. The ushers are few, properly attired and courteous. People don't talk loudly; irksome noises are not to be heard.

Menichella applied the tradition to the management of the discount rate and the compulsory reserve ratio. An increase in the official discount rate from 3.5 per cent to 4 and then 5 and 6 per cent and, if necessary, higher still generates 'noise'. Newspapers blow up the news, stir up public opinion; financial commentators come close to prophesying chaos, crisis. Predictions are made of falls on the stock exchange, of its being impossible to obtain advances or discount bills. Those who have a line of credit hurry to use it all up so as to be safe against a credit squeeze, even at the risk of depositing the funds elsewhere at a low rate of return. If, instead, the discount rate is lowered from 6 per cent to 5, to 4 and then to 3.5 per cent, it is as if lucky times had come. The cautious do not move yet; but already men of lower quality begin to be a nuisance. Bankers are hard put to keep them out from under their feet. Political commentators rage on about why no-one is investing. Why are investments not being made? And the investments must be 'massive'; otherwise they count for nothing. If individuals in the private sector do not make up their minds, why does the State not intervene to absorb and put to use the billions that are 'lying idle'? Is the South of Italy not in need of, and avid for, investment? Let one or two hundred billion be committed to the construction of a factory, a colossal one. What does it matter that the workers employed will be few in comparison with the many more who would be employed in less striking initiatives decided by someone who if need be would also risk his own money? Speed is of the essence: the billions are there and what is important is not to let them 'lie idle'. Somewhere in Italy the war led to the extraction from the bowels of the earth of a bad quality of coal that has a low yield, less even than the advantage of its low price, that ruins the grates of furnaces with its sulphur, that nobody buys unless forced to by some calamity, such as war. The loss is a heavy one, some billions of lire, borne as usual by the taxpayers. But, since the reduction in the discount rate or, and the effect is the same, of the percentage of compulsory reserves that commercial banks must hold with the central bank, indicates that the billions are there, let us hurry to invest them in some plant that will use that wretched coal to produce electricity; and since nobody on the spot would buy it all, let us invest other billions to carry it somewhere else, even overseas. What does it matter if the employment created will be minimal in comparison with the billions invested? What matters is to make 'massive' investments to utilize the billions 'lying idle'.

If these things happen or threaten to happen in Italy even when the discount rate and the compulsory reserve ratio are still and remain unchanged, just imagine what would happen if they were deliberately moved up and down! Who stands to gain from the uproar, the babble of voices, the articles? It sufficed that – through years of strenuous efforts, starting from the day he and I were in London in 1947, painfully obliged, in order to fill an awkward hole, to beg a few million dollars from the US Secretary of the Treasury – Menichella succeeded in building up a gold reserve sufficient to cope with the ever present possibility of temporary needs in the balance of payments and the coffers of the state, for proposals to multiply as to how to invest, or waste, part of that reserve in far-flung parts of the world and on the rashest projects.

For these reasons Donato Menichella does not like 'noise'. He preferred, I imagine, to receive the managers of the banks, friends of his or persons devoted to him, the heads of firms large and small in his study. Which is silent, where visitors are introduced by ushers with a dignified bearing, through vestibules and along corridors free from the dust and cobwebs that are or were to be seen in some ministries and public offices. In the Governor's study orders are not given, there is discussion, the situation is examined, the intricate knots are disentangled, and advice is given. Instead of raising the discount rate, why not politely reduce some overdraft limits, why not increase the interest rates on facilities whose restriction is desired? In addition to counsel and advice, which nonetheless amount in practice to orders, help is provided: if in some cases, in some circumstances, the 25 per cent compulsory reserve ratio is high for a bank, the amount of central bank rediscounting in favour of the needy bank can be increased. Without 'noise', without bringing journalists rushing in, situations are discussed one at a time and the appropriate solution sought for each.

Sometimes the difficulty of a particular situation is the fault of the managing director or the general manager of a small commercial bank, or a savings bank or a rural bank. The Governor of the Bank of Italy is informed before anybody else of misdeeds, omissions, faults and sometimes crimes. His inspectors have given him the list of all the improper transactions carried out by that bank; an accurate list with names and surnames, with an exact description of each irregularity.

There is a serious dilemma. According to one, questionable, interpretation of some article of the Penal Code, combined with that of another article of the Banking Law, the Governor has a duty to report the facts to the public prosecutor. *Fiat justitia*,* above all. Come what may. Unfortunately what would come, by observing the law, would be disaster. Credit is that extremely delicate thing based on silence, on trust, on invisible and impalpable factors. Bad news of money lost, of favouritism, of the granting of excessive credit leaks out, nobody knows how. It just leaks out. People talk, the local newspaper insinuates. Depositors rush to make withdrawals, first a trickle then a flood. If a commercial bank closes, the neighbouring savings bank becomes suspect, and the run on deposits spreads.

Must the Governor of the Bank of Italy, who knows all these things in advance, report them in observance of the principle that above all kingdoms save themselves by rendering justice? Or is it not morally and socially preferable, instead, to run the risk of violating the law, to avoid 'noise' and to try to find a timely remedy? Cannot the guilty general manager or managing director be called to account and, if he is unable to prove his innocence, above all be made to pay and make his wife and relations pay? If there is guilt, and it is evident, is it not better to pay? Together with him, even if not responsible, let his chairman and other directors, blockheads or cretins, be required to pay. If all that is not enough, the associations of

* Let justice be done.

commercial banks and the federations of savings banks have an interest in intervening with life belts. Since the failed bank nonetheless has a tradition, depositors and borrowers who are worth something, the central bank may recommend a merger with a sound bank, which sacrifices something and in exchange acquires goodwill, deposits and customers. By avoiding 'noise', the guilty are forced to disgorge whatever they still have, credit is saved, the depositors do not even notice the risk they ran. Is it better to overcome difficult situations in this way, if possible, or to pay homage at all costs to the commandment 'let justice be done'?

Sometimes the race to arrive first – whether the attempt to make a beneficial rescue in the common interest or an anonymous report reaching the public prosecutor's desk; whether to save the depositors or to pay homage to pure justice – is a close one. If in the end the depositors are out of danger and a minute later the anonymous report lands on the public prosecutor's desk, justice is done and at the same time the public interest is unharmed.

If the doctrine of *fuge rumores** was really that applied by Donato Menichella, let it be a lesson for those who are entrusted with the most delicate of all responsibilities, that for public credit.

---

* Keep away from rumours.

Part III

Public Finance

14
Contribution to the Quest for an 'Optimal Tax'*

Precedents and the occasion of this study

1. This study follows several others of mine, brought forth from time to time in obedience to the need the scholar occasionally feels to put his thoughts on paper even before they have been distilled into a final form, compact and consistent in all its parts.

In the first version of what has always remained a stenographic transcription of university lectures, for fear of its becoming a treatise on finance, affirmed that the fundamental problem of tax studies consisted in investigating the concept of the object of taxation and that this, whatever its apparent form, could all be reduced to the continuous flow of income. In that first version (*Lezioni*, 1911[1]) there was the enthusiasm of the neophyte who aspired to frame the whole matter of taxation in a single basic concept: in essence, a prohibition on taxing any portion of income differently from any other portion. I endeavoured to demonstrate that this principle, or postulate, was the logical conclusion of the historical evolution of tax systems in the past and the sole idea that could unify the motley conglomeration of taxes now on the statute books. In that first version there was also the idea of the existence of a 'natural tax', the tax which would have been established if the persons delegated to allocate the public burden had succeeded in perfectly translating into a compulsory rule the voluntary judgement of citizens, capable in turn of consciously appreciating the importance of public goods *vis-à-vis* private goods. The subsequent versions or editions of the 'lectures', the second published in 1914, the third in 1916 and the fourth in 1926, do not deviate, albeit with changes in the details, from the fundamental idea of the possibility of constructing a logical

---

* This is the introduction of a text first published as 'Contributo alla ricerca della "ottima imposta"', *Annali di Economia*, Milan, V, 1928–29, pp.7–244. It was republished in the collection of essays, *Saggi sul risparmio e l'imposta*, 2nd edn (Turin: Giulio Einaudi Editore, 1958).

system of taxation, coordinated by a single principle, immune from all the contaminations that can result from the contingencies of the moment, from class or particular interests or from that factor of such great importance in this field, the 'fantasy' of the lawmaker stimulated by the urgent needs of the treasury.

2. However, it was not so much a fully realized work as an attempt, not pursued beyond the point of stenographic reproduction, to achieve the clarification that a teacher must make, for himself and his students, when he lectures on the principles of his subject. I do not know whether I shall ever get around to the definitive book.[2] The following paper is one of its preparatory chapters. Other chapters appear in the first three essays of this volume.

Only the first essay (*'Intorno al concetto ...'*) gained a certain notoriety, owing to the thesis of the exemption of savings from taxation, to which its content was very summarily reduced. It gave rise to quite an abundant literature, which is listed in a review of Fisher by Fasiani and, in part, in the bibliographical note at the end of this volume.

Although provoked by the polemics that, between 1913 and 1915, had such illustrious and brilliant champions as Loria, Ricci, Prato and Griziotti, I did not return to the specific issue of the exemption of savings, finding that the arguments adduced by my critics had been validly refuted first by Borgatta and then by Fasiani. But in the second and third essays I sought to analyse an essential point for the discussion begun in the first, that is to say the variations in the interest rate and the method of studying them.

3. This time I return to the starting point: that is to the so-called problem of the exemption of savings.

I fear unhappy terminology played no small part in the poor reception the thesis received when it appeared in Italy. Since 'exemption' means the privilege or permission not to pay what would be justly due, and since exemptions are to be avoided in a correct tax system, a thesis presented terminologically under the name of 'exemption' had to appear worthy of condemnation *a priori*, even though its substance clearly was not a proposed exemption but a study of the means to avoid a case of double taxation, perhaps the most insidious and subtle case of double taxation known.

4. My returning to the point was occasioned principally by my reading in 1923 and rereading in 1928 Antonio De Viti De Marco's *Lezioni di scienza delle finanze*, in 1928 re-titled *I primi principii dell'economia finanziaria*, whose author can only be faulted for allowing his work to circulate in an offset version for decades before giving it suitable typographical form.[3] The consequence was that the reader who finds offset reproduction irritating, and who like the writer, for this reason could never bring himself to read

the rare lectures of Ferrara even though he keeps them jealously among his books, had no knowledge of what De Viti thought, if not through the partial analyses contained in *Il carattere teorico dell'economia finanziaria*;[4] whereas the industrious persons specialized in searching for unpublished material in that particular species of book-in-the-making that is the university lecture text were able, without citing him, to profit abundantly from the teaching of the greatest of our living theorists of finance.

Now that De Viti's limpid pages have seen the light of day, everyone knows how precise, luminous and synthetic is his concept of finance. If in a future edition De Viti should decide to eliminate what for him is obviously a dead weight due to academic exigencies, leaving the treatise on Italian positive law to others and retaining only those pages that illuminate a theoretical problem, his work would appear even more clearly to be what it already is today: a book of 'principles' in the classic style, emulating the very few *Principles* that we have in the field of finance.

De Viti starts out from the conception of the state as a cooperator in the production and hence a participant, on an equal footing with all other producers, in the division of social income. According to De Viti, every particle of income produced in each successive moment in society is born burdened by the debt of tax, because every particle was produced with the collaboration of the state and would not exist without the state.

What is income? This is the fundamental question of taxation, to which De Viti answers with an unforgettable analysis that will be set forth below: 'the output or income of society consists of the volume of first-degree goods produced and consumed annually'. Since first-degree goods are also called 'direct goods', that is to say goods which unlike capital goods, are not used to produce other goods but serve directly to satisfy men's needs, and since De Viti added that the tax base is, precisely, social income, it is not surprising that, as I read, the old thesis of the prohibition on taxing savings twice returned joyfully to my mind. Since in the production process savings are identified with 'capital goods', which wait to be transformed into direct goods, it occurred to me that De Viti's thesis contained a striking demonstration of the truth that to tax first capital goods (savings) and then direct goods (income produced and consumed) was to make the mistake of double taxation.

How great was my disappointment and my discomfort when, upon turning the page, I read De Viti's peremptory condemnation of the Millian principle that the taxation of savings duplicates the taxation of income from savings (pp.216–25)! That disappointment engendered the present study, which does not intend to go back over the whole discussion of the major problem but only to examine some points that seemed important to me in reflecting on De Viti's central pages. And since De Viti's fundamental principle that 'every particle of income is born burdened by a corresponding tax debt' is referred to by Ricci in a recent essay, which returns to and perfects a previous writing of his, here and there I took both of these works into account insofar as the argument they contained had a bearing on the order of ideas considered here. I further want to remark that, precisely because it was my intention here to study the problem of what kind of tax best implements the principle that every particle of income is born burdened by the related tax, in other words that no part of income must escape being taxed and none must be taxed twice if all the others are not likewise (on the identity of these propositions see De Viti, p.213), I have not been able to return to the content of my previous studies in order to highlight the changes proposed here with respect to my former propositions. Besides, I think it is impossible to return to the mental position one had the first time one discussed a given subject. For this reason first editions are different from second editions if these are truly such, i.e., a rethinking of the same subject studied earlier. Rethinking means thinking with a fresh mind, without necessarily being bound by the results arrived at previously. In the present case the results are the same, though they are obtained through a different procedure. Accordingly, this new paper does not supersede but supplements the previous ones.

5. It was not only because of the disappointment I suffered that I have preferred to choose De Viti's treatment as a hat-rack on which to hang my criticisms and constructions. For polemical purposes, other writings, and Ricci's in particular, might have offered some advantages. From his first and lengthiest essay on 'income and taxation', Ricci had the great merit of clearly basing the problem of the taxation of savings on a sharp distinction between static societies[5] and dynamic societies, and of showing that it was especially characteristic of dynamic societies.

As taxes, in reality, are paid by individuals and not by society, with respect to taxes it is individuals and not society that are stationary or progressive. When stationary or progressive or decadent societies are discussed below, the reference implicitly is to societies composed of a single individual or else to societies in which only individuals having the indicated characteristics of being stationary, progressive or decadent will be considered active and relevant for the purpose of the discussion. Real societies are a conglomerate of individuals having diverse and opposing attitudes, and their characteristics result from the prevalence of the dominant characteristic.

In the first part of his essay Ricci treats general economic problems, on which it is not necessary for us to dwell in the present study, which concerns finance. In the second, financial, part of his essay, he declares himself to be overly agnostic with respect to the premises of finance, professing that the essential aim of finance is 'to procure money for the state by taking it from the pockets of taxpayers; but once the total amount required to satisfy public needs has been determined, it can be allocated in infinite ways' (p.78). Anyone who starts out from such an agnostic proposition can reach the conclusions he likes best, and the construction of a logical system becomes impossible. In reality, Ricci too adopts a premise (see below, §§ 7 and 8); but since it is not demonstrated in his discussion it will behove us to take it – in practically identical terms – from De Viti, who derives it logically from the general conception of finance that he expounded as early as 1888 in *Il carattere teorico*. In De Viti the concept of taxable income is examined and re-examined from the perspective of its utilization for purposes of taxation and of a general conception of the state. It therefore is more suited to the discussion of finance than any other. But other conceptions will also be considered when the opportunity arises.

Methodological premises

6. Before coming to the heart of the subject, some preliminary terminological notes are desirable. The first regards an erroneous interpretation that could be made, and I believe has been made, of De Viti's principle that 'every particle of income is born burdened by a corresponding tax debt', so that 'if one particle does not pay its debt, another must pay more than its debt' (*Principii*, p.215). If I am not mistaken, the principle, which De Viti demonstrates with a superb analysis of social gross income and its decomposition into individual net incomes (pp.209–16), is equivalent to that which I adopted in 1912 – demonstrating it elsewhere (*Lezioni*, 1912, pp.430–45, and *Lezioni*, 1926, pp.116–22)[6] as deriving from a historical analysis of the necessary passage from one type of distribution of taxation to the subsequent type – with the name of postulate of equality: 'two equal amounts of wealth must be equally taxed, so that if one lira is taxed with ten cents, every other lira, of whatever income it is part and to whomever it belongs, must likewise be taxed with ten cents ('Intorno al concetto').[7]

7. If, therefore, De Viti's principle appears to me incontrovertible, not least owing to the similarity of formulation reached by independent paths, not equally convincing is a translation of the same principle some make in writing: the law of taxation observed in all the countries of the world and in all eras distinguishes between the production of income and its disbursement. Tax must fall upon the income 'produced' in a given financial year, without interfering with the use the taxpayer then wishes to make of it, whether consumption or saving, reasonable use or dissipation. If the taxpayer saves a part of his income and in the subsequent year another income is born, the latter is a new income that needs to be subject to a subsequent tax without fear of double taxation.[8] Where the sophism consists in saying that the 'further [post-production] transformations of income (consumption, distribution, capitalization) are subsequent and extraneous to the concept of income in finance'; that is, in affirming that inasmuch as the existing tax systems have constructed a concept of taxable income captured

every year at the moment of its production and separated from the subsequent moments of consumption and capitalization, that concept, so constructed, must become an idol that cannot be subjected to critical analysis.

Historical experience deserves serious consideration, but while it provides valuable material for the construction of theory, it is not itself theory. The point is to know whether the concept of income embodied in legislation is rational and logical, whether by chance it might not give rise to instances of double taxation; instead, we are told that the path to analysis and criticism is barred because legislation defines income in such and such a way and that definition must be adopted as fixed and unquestionable! The point is to know whether the division of time into annual cycles is logical; instead, we are told that because legislation established the division into annual cycles it must be adopted as a rule for every analysis!

The author in question confuses two very different types of investigation: the first consists in constructing the system of tax law in force in a given country, the second in constructing a theoretical system of principles of taxation.

The first investigation necessarily must be conducted within the limits established by the legislator. If the legislator has defined income in a certain way, and Italian law, for example, starts out precisely from the concept of production in a given year and does not consider the subsequent phases of the income produced, the investigator must start out from that definition and build on that base.

His field of study and critical inquiry is vast, his task being to examine what inferences can be logically drawn from the fundamental legislation in the different sectors and applications of tax law; what deviations from the norm may have been brought about by special provisions or court interpretations; what reforms are needed to give harmony to the body of tax law. A noble and fertile field of study, in which those who are not only economists but also have a good knowledge of the law excel.

The second type of investigation is not bound by any limit imposed by any lawmaker. Its task is rather the opposite: to investigate that which is rational in positive law, to identify that which is universal and permanent and that which instead is transient and destined to be replaced by more perfect rules, better suited to the conditions in which positive tax law exists and by whose changes it is perpetually stimulated to change. While this may remind philosophers of law of the necessity of a 'natural' law standing above 'positive' law, we students of finance can state the content of the second type of inquiry as follows: 'the fair rule is that whereby income is defined in such a way that all of it is taxed and every part of it is taxed equally'.

Thus, the definition of income is not a starting point and is not necessarily the one adopted by a given lawmaker at a given moment. Rather, it is a point of arrival, the ultimate result of the choice, from among different methods of taxing income and hence from among different definitions of income, of the method and the definition which satisfy the required conditions of universality and equality. The point of arrival may accord with the current definition of income as the wealth produced in a given year without regard to its disbursement, but it may not. And if the conclusion is otherwise, we shall derive arguments from it in order to subject the existing tax systems to criticism and to indicate, approximately and with all the caution due in such delicate matters, the paths for their necessary, progressive transformation.

8. Umberto Ricci does not invoke the legislative maxim, since, correctly, he does not confuse the two types of inquiry and his is a study in pure financial economics. Nonetheless, he too makes an idol of income and worships it. There is no double taxation, he says (see the succinct exposition of his theory in *La tassabilità*),[9] if the taxpayer first paid 2,000 units of tax on 10,000 units of income and then pays 200 units of tax again on the remaining 8,000 units that were saved and converted at 12.50 per cent into an annuity of 1,000 units. The taxpayer did not have 10,000 units but only 8,000, the other 2,000 belonging to the state for the quota it contributed to the common production. If the 8,000 saved yields 1,000 a year, the latter amount must likewise be divided into 200 belonging to the state and 800 belonging to the taxpayer. In every round the state appropriates 'its' quota in respect of the common production and leaves the taxpayer free to do as he chooses with the part remaining to him. 'In short, the state *must* take the tax on all the income *before* it is allocated between consumption and saving. The division between consumption and saving comes *afterwards*.'

Here, again, the question is solved by being formulated apodictically in a given way. It is said: 'Income is *first* the amount of 10,000 produced in period I and *then* the amount of 1,000 produced annually in period II and the subsequent periods; the state *must* therefore tax first 10,000 and then 1,000.' If this were true, there would be little need for lengthy discussion. But the unknowns that need to be determined are, precisely, the income of period I and the income of period II. In seeking to determine them we cannot disregard the indisputable fact that period I is linked with period II, as are the quantities of income of one period with the quantities of income of the other. Obviously, for practical reasons the state needs to divide time into slices called years, but this practical necessity must not, in pure theory, make us fall into the mistake of disregarding the continuity of time and the links between the economic events of one period with those of the next. All income is taxable, but what income is cannot be established with an arbitrary definition of the unit of time. Why adopt one year and not three years or ten as the unit of time? Postulate different units of time and the results will differ greatly, as we shall see (§§ 84f.).[10] To be sure, the state *must* tax *all* income, but we must not solve the question *a priori* by affirming that all income is the amount consumed plus the amount saved, or, alternatively, only the former or only the latter. What income is, to be taxed in its entirety, can be known only at the end of the investigation; it is absolutely necessary to reject whatever proposition that says the state *must* at all costs act in this or that manner.

It is admitted that the state must tax all income and tax it equally, because this rule corresponds to that minimum of arbitrary power, that absolute impartiality, that the state observes today in allocating taxation. In the past it may also have been possible to postulate unequal treatment and construct a tax system on that premise. Not today. Apart from this premise, no other is needed.

9. Above all, it is inadmissible, in pure theory, to assume that income and its periodicity must necessarily be defined in the way it pleases this or that investigator. Arguments based on such gratuitous premises are without value, and Ricci's argument against Mill's demonstration of the double taxation of savings and of the yield of savings actually has the following form.

1 The state must tax the income produced in period I and then the income produced in period II, without trying to find out whether the latter income derives or is obtained as a substitute for the former.
2 The income saved is produced in period I and the yield of savings is produced (or received or earned) in period II.
3 Hence, there is not double taxation when the tax falls first on the income saved in period I and then on the yield of savings in period II.

If the premise is admitted, the argument is impeccable. But why should the premise be admitted? It is logical to start out from it if one intends to build on the basis of the existing rule. But in pure theory, when the point is precisely to discover the foundations of the existing rule, the premise must be demonstrated, not assumed.

10. Another circular argument of the same type is made when one wants to demonstrate that the taxation of all income, consumed and saved, does not diminish the value of the part saved more than it diminishes the value of the part consumed. Take someone who in year I has an income of L10,000 and divides it exactly in two, L5,000 allocated to immediate consumption and L5,000 to be saved. The L5,000 consumed are reduced by 10 per cent tax to L4,500 and everything ends there, the tax and the residual income being consumed (i.e., destroyed). The other L5,000 are first taxed at 10 per cent, with L500 and reduced to L4,500, and the latter amount, invested at the current rate of interest of 5 per cent, gives rise to an annuity of L225, taxed in turn at 10 per cent and reduced to L202.50 net. However, since at a 5 per cent interest rate an annuity of L202.50 cor-

responds to a present value of L4,050, it is demonstrated, as Mill said, that the share of income saved is taxed much more heavily than the share consumed. Denoting income as *r* and the tax as *i*, we have:

for the part of income consumed

$$i = \frac{r}{10}$$

and, in the example mentioned:

$$i = \frac{5{,}000}{10} = 500$$

for the part of income saved

$$i = \frac{r}{10} + \frac{r - \frac{r}{10}}{10}$$

and, in the example mentioned:

$$i = \frac{5{,}000}{10} + \frac{5{,}000 - \frac{5{,}000}{10}}{10} = 950$$

No, responds Ricci, because a tax of 10 per cent, which is *general on all incomes*, reduces the yield on all capital and hence the rate of capitalization, i.e., the interest rate, from 5 per cent to 4.50 per cent. And so, capitalizing the net annuity of L202.50 yielded by savings at the *new* interest rate of 4.50 per cent, we obtain a present value of L4,500, neither more nor less than the residual value of the consumed part of income after the first tax has been paid (see *La taxation*, pp.878–9).

Setting aside the fact that the problem of double taxation would remain in its entirety even if Ricci's argument were correct,[11] the argument is not convincing as it rests completely on a syllogism of the following type:

(a) the general, uniform tax on income reduces the interest rate by a proportion corresponding to the ratio of the tax to income (for example, if the tax on income is 10 per cent and the interest rate was initially 5 per cent, the latter is subsequently reduced to 4.50 per cent);
(b) the tax under discussion is general and uniform;
(c) therefore, in the example given it reduces the interest rate from 5 per cent to 4.50 per cent;

where both the greater and the lesser are unacceptable propositions.

A first note to my study of 1912 and my entire essay *Osservazioni critiche* seek to demonstrate that is it not true that a general, uniform tax on income has the effect of making the interest rate diminish by the same proportion as the ratio of the tax to income, and that it can instead have the most diverse effects depending on the nature of the tax and the use made of it.[12] Section IV of the same essay sought to make it clear that the very concept of a general, uniform tax is nebulous and deserves to be clearly defined. So deserving, in fact, that one may legitimately argue that the tax Ricci refers to, which falls upon both the consumed part and the saved part of an income considered to have been produced in period I (financial year), is not at all uniform and general. Here, again, the uniformity and generality of a tax is not a first datum, known and immobile, that can be taken as a point of departure; rather, it is a point of arrival that is determined according to the characteristics of that tax and its effects. In that note I said that a 'general' tax is a 'neutral' tax, one that leaves the judgement of every man unchanged with respect to every unit of income. In more detail, here I would say that a tax is 'general' or 'neutral' or 'fair' when it does not give rise to double taxation. With this definition I intend to clarify that it is not sufficient to define a general tax in a given way in order to infer that it therefore does not give rise to double taxation; but that, instead, a tax may be called general only when it is constructed in such a way as not to give rise to double taxation. Whether that is or is not the effect of the tax cannot be determined *a priori* with a definition; it must be demonstrated with reasoning.

In the note I just mentioned I endeavoured to show that a tax that is truly 'general and uniform', or 'neutral' or 'fair', far from being a curiosity, an isolated fact in the economic and financial world, is part of a whole, an essential element of a political life in which the state performs its proper tasks perfectly and, because the use of the proceeds of the tax is therefore perfect, private wealth grows, the volume of the flow of income increases, saving increases, the interest rate falls and capital values increase by proportions that have no relationship with the tax rate.

11. In this study, I do not, however, have to address general problems of political, tax and economic equilibrium such as those discussed in the study referred to above. The scope of the problem is limited.

We are faced with different types of tax that are in competition one with the other.[13] Each tax claims to be the 'fair' tax; not only the tax on earned income (which taxes consumption and savings) but also that on consumed income and that on produced income. All three are born at a time when there is a given amount of income, defined in the ways set out above, and a given interest rate. Precisely because they differ one from the other, the three types of tax probably have a different influence on the future of income and the interest rate. What is it? We cannot say *a priori*. In order to discover what is the *specific* effect of the type of tax chosen, which is separate from or added to the generic effect that all three types can produce, insofar as they are a tax, we must suppose, for example, that the use made of the revenue from the three taxes is identical; in short, that they differ one from the other only in that one is levied on income defined in one way and the others on income defined in different ways. What is the specific influence that each of the three types of tax has on the interest rate, as a consequence of their different respective objects of taxation? This is the inquiry to undertake, which is not performed by imagining that the tax, owing to some magic quality, has a direct influence of any kind on the interest rate. Between the 'tax' and the 'interest rate' there are many intermediate links that cannot be simply ignored. Turning back to the earlier numerical example, we know only that the tax on the L5,000 saved has immediately reduced that amount to L4,500. For the moment nothing else is changed. The taxpayer, who did not come from the moon, knew that his L10,000 would in any case have been reduced to L9,000 by the tax and had decided to divide them into L4,500 consumed and L4,500 saved. The interest rate consequent on the division made was 5 per cent, and the perpetual annual return on the L4,500 saved amounted to L225.

At this point the two types of tax intervene; I say two because those on produced and consumed income can be considered identical, since their effects are equivalent. One is levied again at 10 per cent on the L225, reducing them to L202.5, and the other leaves them intact at L225.[14]

What is the 'differential' effect that the two types of tax produce subsequently? It is not yet a question of an impact on the interest rate, which, if nothing else changes, would have no reason to move. Why should it move if the taxpayer still divides the L9,000 available after the first tax is levied into L4,500 consumed and L4,500 saved?

For the interest rate to move, it is necessary for the two types of tax, which leave the taxpayer with a net annual return of L202.50 in one case and of L225 in the other,[15] to have an impact on the behaviour of savers and induce them to increase or decrease the supply of savings or not to change it at all. For different taxpayers, according to the circumstances, opposite effects may be produced. The outcome may be a change in the interest rate as a consequence of the application of the one or the other type of tax; a change due to the way the taxpayer reacts, in the one case and in the other, after thinking over what it is advisable to do.

12. The taxpayer, it is true, comes rapidly to the conclusion, after thinking through the effects that the market reveals to him as already evident and finished of the action taken by him and by many others, who, reasoning and acting in various ways, cause, without waiting for long, the action to accompany and almost precede the reasoning. But for us, who analyse and anatomize the motives of human actions, it is Hobson's choice to take one step at a time and follow the taxpayer in the successive phases of what he does when:

(a) he receives L10,000;
(b) he pays the tax of L1,000 on them;
(c) he divides the L9,000 remaining into two equal parts: L4,500 to be consumed and L4,500 to be saved;
(d) he ascertains that on the L4,500 to be consumed no further tax is to be levied;
(e) he ascertains that, at 5 per cent, he can convert the L4,500 to be saved into a perpetuity of L225;
(f) living in a certain country, *M*, he also ascertains that, under the type of tax in force, he will not have to pay any tax on the perpetuity of L225;
(g) living, by hypothesis, in another country, *N*, equal to *M* in everything except this particular, he ascertains instead that, under the type of tax in force, he will have to pay a tax of L22.50 per year on the perpetuity of L225.

No link in the chain of the taxpayer's actions having been forgotten, I believe, the question is: will the taxpayer behave in the same or a different way in the two countries, *M* and *N*, or in the different periods in which, all else unchanged, the two types of tax are in force in the same country? Of course, the expression *rebus sic stantibus* forces us to suppose to be possible what is instead absurd; it not being possible that if one circumstance – the type of tax – changes, all the other circumstances remain unchanged. On the other hand, it would not be possible to proceed further in the reasoning in any other way, without ceasing to reason at all and resigning oneself to the depressing conclusion that nothing will ever be known in the field of economics,[16] and, if it is supposed that the value of the changes in the tax are very small compared with all the other circumstances that are kept unchanged, the error committed is also very small.

13. When in the earlier study of 1912 I put forward 14 proofs to demonstrate that lawmakers of modern states, although protesting their attachment to modern theory, which calls for the taxation of all earned income (consumed and saved), in practice, by means of special provisions, excluded savings from the object of taxation, by exempting forests (fifth proof), or a presumed quota of savings (first proof), or insurance premiums (fourth proof) or buildable land (last proof), or profits allocated to reserves (thirteenth proof) or those accumulated abroad (fourteenth proof), what was the gist of the demonstration? This:

> *that regardless of and, sometimes, contrary to his expressed will,* the lawmaker *tends* increasingly to exempt savings from taxation. [I did not dream] at all of putting forward Mill's principle of equality as a principle *just in itself* that *must* be the lawmaker's aim and goal and that *condemns* the taxation of earned income. On the contrary, the postulate is for [me] a simple *tool* of research: a lens that permits

close examination of the facts. It is a touchstone that does not serve to divide lawmakers' financial acts into good and bad but simply to establish the common elements of a series of facts, common elements that make it possible to group and coordinate the facts, so as to establish a regularity in their occurrence, a law governing their happening.[17]

14. Those who wondered that I should have postulated, without any demonstration,[18] a so-called principle of justice and declared that one should not invent but accept instead the principles of tax justice that can be observed in the public's conscience, failed to see that there was nothing arbitrary in postulating a principle in that way, that it was only a way of beginning the analysis and that the essential thing was that this be consistent in all its parts, the reasoning logical, the premises adopted and the conclusions drawn of help in explaining the facts considered and the facts considered and explained relevant, probative and universal. Never ever! cries our friend Ricci:

> to admit that the only essential requirement of a tax system is the perfect logical consistency of the various components is to proclaim the failure of the art of finance, reduced to a plaything for the erudite. It would be sufficient to formulate a principle, no matter how bizarre, extract all the consequences with impeccably rigorous reasoning, and then confront critics with this little speech: 'dear critics, accept my principle as a postulate and tell me only whether the premises are correctly deduced from the premises'. It is obvious that in this way there would be no criterion for preferring one of the various systems excogitated by the finance experts: they would all be equally good provided they constituted as many logical systems.[19]

15. A criticism to which I had already replied: 'let others try to postulate a principle that explains a greater abundance of facts than the one I have put forward and that leads to the construction of a system that is more logical and consistent in its parts'.

In the preface to his *Principii* De Viti expresses a similar concept when he states that he intended, 'following a general order of ideas [he had] established in 1886–87', in *Il carattere teorico*, 'to set out a positive exposition of the financial theories that, starting from those premises, arrive, by virtue of their intrinsic merit, at the logical conclusion'. Scientific progress is not made in any other way but this: by substituting provisional hypotheses that explained a given number of facts[20] or relationships between facts with other hypotheses, still provisional, that explain a larger and larger number of facts.

It had appeared to me that the postulate of equality, with its corollary of the exclusion of savings from the object of taxation, explained many facts, including those usually adduced to demonstrate other interpretations of the same principle; and neither does it appear to me that progress has been made beyond a peremptory negation based on the *ipse dixit** of the current systems of taxation, taken as a yardstick admitting of no contradiction. The dispute therefore remains suspended and cannot be renewed until others demonstrate that the postulate of equality, with the opposite corollary to mine of the inclusion of savings in the object of taxation, explains reality to a greater extent and better than my hypothesis.

Content of the paper or choice of the type of distribution of taxation that gives rise to a stable equilibrium

16. In the meantime I want to add to the hypothesis put forward a feature that I had left on the sidelines in 1912.

To the best of my knowledge, nobody observed, as a criticism of my thesis, that at a certain point Mill's demonstration, repeated by Fisher and by me, required a follow-up.

Remember the man who, with an income of L10,000, consumes L5,000, paying L500 in taxes, and saves L5,000, paying L950 in taxes. I had stopped at this point, content to have shown:

(a) that the system of taxation just described, known as the taxation of earned income, led to the unequal treatment of two portions of identical income or of two taxpayers who distributed their income differently between consumption and saving;
(b) that lawmakers, although pretending not to want to know anything about it and claiming at every turn they wanted to tax all the L10,000, in many cases actually taxed or tended to tax only the L5,000. In doing so, it is true, they pulled every kind of face and put forward numerous pretexts, one more ridiculous than the other. They did not resign themselves to recognizing the truth of the principle or to using the entirely valid argument, not theoretical but based on the observation of human psychology, that Mill himself had offered them to avoid translating the principle as it stood into a statutory provision; that is, the danger of fraud.[21] Instead, they bent over backwards in order to burn incense before the idol, rendered venerable by age, of the taxation of earned income, and explained the obvious, numerous deviations from the commandments of the idol as 'exceptions', explainable on political grounds, or on grounds of human compassion, class, prudence and so on. They did not see that, by dint of exceptions, they deprived their principle or concept of earned income of any substance and engendered the desire to replace that mutilated object with another principle that would have, as the more perfect definitions or postulates must have with respect to less perfect ones, a greater unifying power.

* He said so.

Ending the demonstration here, a certain undeniable result had, in my opinion, already been obtained: that of having put forward an instrument for interpreting and unifying tax rules that was more elegant and fruitful than those that had normally been adopted in the past.

17. There remained one step to take; and the demonstration that the tax on earned income faced a man with the choice of paying, if the tax rate was 10 per cent, L500 on the L5,000 he decided to consume and L950 on the same L5,000 if instead he decided to save them, should have led to the step in question being taken.

I am not aware of that step having been taken. Critics and defenders of the theorem of the double taxation of savings persisted in arguing about whether the theorem was true or not, whether the L5,000 saved did or did not pay L950 instead of L500; $\frac{r}{10} + \frac{r - \frac{r}{10}}{10}$ instead of $\frac{r}{10}$; and I have already shown above that the negations of the theorem were based on premises that were theoretically non-existent (the *ipse dixit* of the universal lawmaker) or highly questionable (the immediate proportional fall of the interest rate).

18. The real question that deserved to be posed regarding that dilemma was not, 'Does it exist or not?', since clearly no substantial doubt could be raised as to its existence, but, 'Can it last?' Is an economic situation stable that offers the taxpayer a choice between owning and enjoying L4,500 (L5,000 income – L500 tax) or L4,050 (L5,000 income – L950 tax)? Isn't the situation created by a tax law that proposes to subtract from two equal incomes two different amounts of tax, and that leaves it up to the taxpayer to choose to pay the greater or the lesser tax, manifestly an unstable situation that cannot last? If it cannot last, what are the effects of the law imposed by the legislator on the economic equilibrium? What is the definitive tax structure which, through a series of temporary equilibria, tends to establish itself, whatever the initial rule declared by the law?

This study intends to give an initial answer to this truly fundamental question. The conclusion is that the tax on earned income:

(a) not only violates the principle of equality and is in fact held in low regard by legislators who affect to repute it the only equitable tax and therefore, it is an idol with feet of clay (a truth demonstrated in the first study);
(b) but it is also the shadow of an idol, a vanity that has never existed and that cannot exist. The taxation of earned income is such that it leads to

> an unbalanced economic situation that cannot last and that gives rise to successive situations until it transforms itself into something that could even turn out to be its opposite.[22] This is the further truth, which following the inevitable premises and some apparent digressions, is the new conclusion meant to be reached in the pages that follow.

This is the only way to demonstrate the non-arbitrariness of a postulate. If, that is, a postulate is not arbitrary, not only must it contain in itself the greatest number of minor truths, not only must it not leave uncovered too many extravagant cases, called 'exceptions', but it must be alive and vital. It must be such that, when applied, it leads to a situation that is stable, permanent, to an equilibrium, which does not have within itself the causes of its dissolution. If, on the other hand, the postulate posited is arbitrary, not only does it give rise to numerous unexplained exceptions but, in the attempt to implement itself, to live, it negates itself, and transforms itself into its opposite.

Here, then, is another definition of the 'equitable' or 'optimum' tax. It is a tax that lasts, that leads without frictions, to a situation of equilibrium; a tax that can be implemented without negating itself.

19. Economists working in the field of finance have always conducted studies of tax equilibrium when dealing with the displacement, repercussion and evasion of taxes and their effects in general. But, for the most part, studies on the displacement and effects of taxes were an accessory in treatises on finance, traditionally included in them but without any logical connection with the other parts of the argument. The authors would limit themselves to saying that often the legislator's desire suffers the same fate as the good intentions that pave the road to hell, without highlighting the profound effect that the laws of economics, of price, of interest and of equilibrium have on the tax system and the great advantage that could be derived from studies of these reactions in choosing among the various kinds of taxes.

Only a few saw the relationship between economic forces and a legal distribution of taxation, which does not take account of the economic forces. Among those who realized the importance of such studies was De Viti in the book that provided the occasion for the present essay. 'The combined action', he writes, 'of the economic forces of displacement, diffusion, evasion, and consolidation pushes toward a return to an equilibrium dominated by the action of economic forces, where the equilibrium was broken or modified by a conflicting legal distribution' (*Principii*, p.135). And later on: 'The reaction of economic forces, set in motion by the legal distribution, tends toward a financial equilibrium, not different from the one to which the natural play of the forces in play would lead in a private economy.' Therefore,

> in order to break down a legal distribution which has not taken them into account, the action of economic forces must generally overcome a series of obstacles, that is, a set of frictions. Consequently, the phenomena of repercussion, diffusion, evasion and elision or consolidation of the tax, require a longer or shorter period of time to prevail. The equilibrium is established only at the end of a certain period of time, during which the legal distribution may fully achieve its short-term goals.

In his thirteenth chapter entitled, 'The Political Theory of Proportional and Progressive Taxation' (pp.175–94), De Viti gives a splendid example of the process through which the old equilibrium, disturbed by a strongly progressive tax, re-establishes itself, but only 'for new savings, new production, new buyers and owners and new generations' (p.153).

20. The move from one kind of tax distribution to another is determined primarily by the legislator having to adapt the tax system to the changing conditions of the economic environment in which the system must live. The time comes when the kind of tax imposed in relation to a given system or economic equilibrium is no longer suitable to a new economic equilibrium, which has been taking shape while the legal rule has remained unchanged. Internal forces arise that force the tax to change, to change its nature, to adapt to the changed environment. Permit me to reproduce here some pages from my course (*Lezioni* 1926, pp.117–20, and even earlier *Lezioni*, 1911, pp.429–39) in which, in language appropriate to their didactic purpose, I explained the transition from a primitive kind of tax distribution based on surface area to that of the tithe and the reasons for the latter's collapse.

21. It can be stated that, in an earlier historical period, wishing to render proportionate the tax on the wealth of taxpayers, land extension was taken as an index of wealth, and for the sake of brevity the surface area of land was taxed for the purpose of taxing the income of taxpayers. This corresponded to a historical period in which people lived in a pastoral economy. Naturally, finance has developed in parallel with economic transformations, and just as there was a pastoral period in the economy, so there also existed a method of taxation suitable to that period. Surface area was a fair enough method for establishing the income of individuals, in that people, moving around continuously in their migrations and having large expanses of land at their disposition, did not need to use all of the land but limited themselves to trying the land and using only the best parts, looking after, therefore, the surface area that was actually put to use. There being, therefore, little difference between one pasture and another, surface area could serve as a rough criterion suitable to evaluating the incomes of pastoral families and populations.

22. With the transformation from a pastoral to an agricultural economy, however, this system gave rise to serious problems. At the moment in which people cease to live as nomads, land extension may become an erroneous index of incomes, insofar as all land is not equally fertile. Equal amounts of land may produce 10 in one case and 5 in another. To require payment of the same proportion of tax, in such cases, is the cause of inequalities among taxpayers.

Neither is this even the most serious problem, since basing taxation on the extension of land can lead to the formation of rents to the benefit of favoured owners.

The classic theory of rent is well known. In a certain country there are, at any given moment, different lands used for cultivation. There are fertile lands that yield 20 quintals per hectare, and for which the cost of production is L10 per quintal, average land that yields 15 quintals with a cost of production of L15 per quintal, and land that yields 10 quintals, each of which costs L20. The last type, which are called *marginal lands*, because they are at the margin of cultivation, are the ones that determine the market price of the commodity, in that, if on these third-class lands the cost of producing each quintal of wheat is L20, it is evident that the market price of wheat cannot be less than this figure because, if it were, the wheat, or the commodity, whatever it might be, would no longer be cultivated on that land. And if the amount of wheat produced on marginal lands is necessary for the consumption that takes place at L20, then L20 will be paid for all the wheat on the market. This price of L20 is not only the price of wheat from marginal land but of wheat from all kinds of land, by virtue of the law of price indifference, whereby the same goods cannot have two different prices on the same market at the same time. Therefore, since the price of 20 also applies to the wheat produced on second-class land at a cost of L15, and on first-class land at a cost of L10, the second-class producer will have a rent of L5 and the first-class producer a rent of L10 for each quintal of wheat produced, so that in total the second-class producer will have a rent of L5 on 15 quintals = L75; and the first-class producer a rent of L10 on 20 quintals, or L200.

Let us suppose that a tax is imposed on the basis of land extension at, for example, L10 per hectare. We have assumed that each third-class hectare produces 10 quintals. In this case, what will be the after-tax cost of production for each quintal? Obviously, L20, the old cost of production, plus L1 of tax. Consumers will also pay L21, since we are dealing with a necessary commodity. The price, therefore, will have to go up to L21 for third-class land; but then, for the same reasons as mentioned above, it will also become L21 for wheat from the other classes of land. Those who produce at the new cost of L21 for third-class land will have a rent of zero as before, because they produce at a cost of L21 and sell at a price of L21. The second-class producer, on the other hand, also sells at the new price of L21, or 1L more per quintal than before, because the market price is the same for everybody. Since he produces 15 quintals, he makes L15 more; and since he pays only L10 in tax, he thus has an increase in income of L5. This is an extra rent, to be added to the L75 that he had before.

The first-class producer also sells at the new price of L21. By selling 20 quintals at 1L more per quintal, he makes L20 more. He spends L10 in tax, and makes L10. This is an extra rent in addition to the L200 that he had already received.

> Here is the damage done by the method of taxation: consumers pay the landowners 1L more per quintal, or L45 more for 45 quintals. But the landowners pay only L30 to the state. The difference of L15 goes to the owners of first and second-class lands.

This extra income owing to the form of the tax could appropriately be called an extra income from taxation; and it is one of the not infrequent cases of rent attributable to the work of the legislator.

23. The problems described here brought about an advance in the art of taxation. Income was no longer held to be proportional to land extension. The new method is well-known under the name of the *tithe*.

On a production of 20 quintals of grain, for example, two went to the state and 18 to the taxpayer. This system represented an improvement because it is certain that more fertile land normally yields greater quantities of production than more sterile land, and so the tax came to correspond better to the agricultural wealth of the taxpayers. This type of tax is still in use in less advanced societies such as China, Turkey and India and is relatively easy to collect. There is no need for complex calculations to determine income; the amount produced from the land is measured and a certain share of it is taken to pay for the expenses of the state.

24. However, this system is also inequitable and is the cause of economic damage. It is inequitable because gross income is not net income and therefore is not always proportionate to net income, which can be demonstrated with a numerical example.

Let us suppose a tract of land 'No. 1', whose gross production is 100. It is land under extensive cultivation and so does not require a lot of expenditure, where gross production is not very high, and net income is small in absolute terms but conspicuous as a proportion of gross. For example, out of barely L100 of gross income, net income can be calculated at L80. This system corresponds to the social era in which capital is very scarce and agriculture is carried on in primitive conditions. Let us now suppose an era of intensive cultivation, with a large application of capital and the achievement of much greater gross production. This is tantamount to comparing the grasslands of the Roman countryside or the Maremma to the irrigated lands of Lombardy or Piedmont. Here expenses are much higher, but so is gross production. Instead of L100 we will have L500, but in order to produce them we must spend L300, leaving a net income of just L200, which is certainly greater than L80 in absolute terms, but amounts to just two-fifths of gross production, while in the case of extensive cultivation net income came to four-fifths of gross production.

It is obvious that when the tax takes the form of a tithe it results in inequity among the various taxpayers. In the first case the tithe is 10 out of 100, in the second 50 out of 500; but if we calculate the tax in terms of net income, 80 and 200 respectively, the proportion of the tithe to net income in the first case is 10 out of 80 or 12.50 per cent, in the second 50 out of 200, or 25 per cent, and is therefore much greater in the second case. In proportion to net income, those who own land under intensive cultivation pay more, while those who own extensively cultivated land pay less.

The tithe also produces substantial negative economic effects. There is a law called the law of decreasing returns, which states that in agriculture, beyond a certain point, it is not possible to obtain a higher return without making proportionately greater capital expenditure.

Great productivity cannot be achieved without great expenditure, since what is necessary are buildings, levelling of the land to improve water runoff, spending for personnel, which could be done without in extensive cultivation, periodic reaping of standing grasses, as often as nine times a year as in the water-meadows of Lombardy, etc. All of these expenses greatly increase the cost of production. Accordingly, the proportion of net income to gross income is higher in extensive cultivation. As was explained in the preceding example, the tithe tax, in the case of extensive cultivation, amounts to 12.5 per cent of net income, and in the case of intensive cultivation to 25 per cent of net income. Thus the tax exacted with the tithe system is inequitable and causes economic damage, so that this form of taxation is almost a reward for extensive cultivation and delays the transformation and progress of agriculture toward improved and more intensive methods of cultivation. The tithe thus becomes unsustainable in historical periods in which population growth makes it necessary to move to intensive cultivation. And it was abandoned in all developed countries, except in some special cases, in which it still survives today, as for example in Italy owing to the tax on buildings, which is a true tithe. In fact, the tax on buildings is 10 per cent of net income, but net income always amounts, by law, to 75 per cent of gross [now 66.66 per cent]. The tax of 10 per cent on so-called net income therefore amounts to 7.5 per cent [now 6.66 per cent] of gross income. It is thus, like all tithes, unequally distributed and imposes greater taxes on old and working-class houses, where expenses are higher, compared to new and luxurious houses, where expenses are lower.

25. The essential content of the excerpt reproduced here is this: that any system of taxation has its own logic and cannot survive when it is placed in conditions that are repugnant to that logic. Taxation of surface area or gross production can be logical and vital systems when the rest of the economic system is suited to them; they cease to be such, not because they have changed, but because they are no longer in equilibrium with the other givens of the general situation. They were alive when the taxpayers, paying taxes in conformity with the rules imposed on them, actually paid tax in proportion to their net income, to the amounts of direct goods that they were able to take from the earth and, less costs, employ to their own satisfaction. But when the economic structure changes and the tax is paid without any relation to net incomes, when it gives rise to instances of parasitism, like those that I have called – whether the first to do so, I don't know – extra income from taxation, a condition of instability is created, which in the long run makes it necessary to change the kind of tax imposed. The old tax, having become unbalanced, gives rise to a new system, whose existence is sustainably compatible with the changed economic system.

26. We are only at the beginning of the construction of the theory of tax equilibrium, which will in turn have to be grafted on to a broader theory of financial equilibrium, both of them being part of the general theory of economic and social equilibrium. This construction has been hindered by the panic that struck the hearts of researchers when they heard Pareto and his followers enunciate the thousands of unknowns and equations that it would be necessary to consider and resolve in order to move on from the first stage of approximation, from the study of the equilibrium in the most general sense to the second stage and further approximations. Since this is not now and perhaps never will be possible, a sort of *hiatus* set in somewhere between the general theory and the particular theories; and while the first became more and more refined and improved, the others went ahead on their own, without regard for the general theories, relying on old methods of reasoning, the isolation of factors, causes and effects, common logic and so on. Yet it appears that, though not the same technique used in the theory of general economic equilibrium, the method of reasoning and the general conception of that theory can also be useful in particular fields.

As for the question that is of particular interest to us here, the dispute between proponents of the tax on earned income and those of the tax on consumed income, it could go on for a long time if it were limited to a debate over social preferences, for the rich and the poor, of equity and inequity, of miserliness and profligacy. Umberto Ricci, with his mischievous verve, could win the contest by making his readers smile at the figure of poor Hetty Green, the New York millionairess who lives poorly, like the lowliest working woman, in just two rooms of her very own skyscraper and, to the great scandal of the general public, should not, if Mill's theory were applied, have to pay any tax because she saves all of her income.

The problem, addressed on the basis of rules fallen from the sky that one should, without knowing why, blindly obey, or of sentimental or invidious considerations, would remain insoluble.

In terms of an equitable, well-balanced and stable tax, the problem of Hetty Green, avaricious millionairess and saver of almost all her income, should be stated as follows: is it possible to tax Hetty Green on the income that she saves? I say that the tax that one would like to impose on her tends not to achieve its objective and ends up somewhere else and more precisely on the consumption of someone other than Hetty Green. Moreover, the attempt tends only to produce harmful effects for the collectivity and mostly for those for the relief of whom the proposal was made to impose a tax on the poor millionaire in the first place.

The ultimate needs that must be satisfied by a system of tax laws are probably the demands of imperative duty. The state must act in accordance with the commandment to be just and honest. But it is also probable that, in order to achieve this purpose, sentimental impulses for and against the rich, for or against the poor are not very helpful. If moral evil is to be short-lived and moral goodness is to triumph, it is probable, in the present state of our knowledge, that in attempting to achieve good it is more helpful to examine which, among the possible systems of taxation, possesses the requisites of maximum stability and permanence. It is not certain, but it is possible, perhaps probable that a stable system, suited to the collectivity, also embodies the commandment to do justice.

27. In any event, it is worth the effort to examine once again – after the attempt made in the essay *Intorno al concetto* – the problem, which is substantially the same as that which vexes investigators in all fields of scientific inquiry: to search for unity where before there was duality, to find common elements in apparent dissimilarities.

A stage of scientific inquiry in which:

(a) the science of finance is something different from the law of finance;
(b) the legal rule is different from the economic rule;
(c) taxes hit people other than legally targeted taxpayers and other than those whom the legislator intends to target;
(d) taxes instituted by law are entirely different from the taxes that exist in fact;
(e) each of the various chapters of the science of the legal distribution of the tax burden and its actual distribution goes its own way;
(f) upon the writing of each new chapter or new division of the subject matter, upon enactment of each new tax a new principle or justificatory pretext enters into play – it is a grossly primitive, intolerable situation.

The pages that follow are an attempt to contribute to the revision of the doctrines of finance informed by the dominant concept in economic theory of the interdependence of forces, which, through reciprocal action, determine, through varying degrees of oscillation, a stable equilibrium. The budgetary needs of the state, the kinds of distribution of those needs among taxpayers, the interest rate, the flow of present and future incomes are all quantities, none of which is given but which are all determined as a function of the others.

28. And another way of giving substantial and not merely formal unity to the subject under study is to try to find – as will be done in the conclusion – the source of savings primarily in 'rents', the extra income that some are able to obtain beyond their ordinary income. This location of the source of savings in 'rents' gives unity to tax theory because:

(a) if it is believed proven that the taxation of savings gives rise to double taxation;
(b) and therefore savings are excluded from the field of taxation;
(c) if it is also believed that savings are drawn from 'rents' and can be substantially identified with the latter;
(d) one can conclude that 'rents' should be excluded from the field of taxation;
(e) and that taxation should be limited to ordinary income.

Or rather, put another way, a new basis is given for the classic theory according to which taxation should be based on ordinary income (§ 143);[23] and an equally new formulation is given of the link between tax and income, between state services and their remuneration, by replacing the formula, accepted but in contrast with the universal experience regarding the remuneration of all the other factors of production, with a more rational formula (§§ 149–51).[24]

29. This attempt to find an 'optimum' type of distribution of the tax burden (see below, §§ 31–4 for the characteristics of the optimum type) is made possible only by the abandonment of the idea of interest as consisting in something that is 'produced' by another thing called 'capital'. Here, instead, reference is made always and only to a 'rate of interest', as a link that joins and equalizes things that are apparently equal and actually different, separated by time. Being a simple link between things and values separated by an interval of time, it is not one of these things or values, does not take concrete form in them, and must not be confused with the shares of income assigned to creditors, investors and capitalists (see § 65).[25] The observation of the errors caused in the field of taxation by confusing a concept of simple linkage between values separated by an interval of time with a completely different concept of new wealth produced during the same interval of time is another blow in the work of dismantling the old symmetrical architectures with which economists separate incomes into

interest, wages, rents, profits and taxes and it appeared that what did not appear in one column was in the others and all of the things stuck in the various columns derived from an activity called 'production'. The whole thing is an architecture, which, if one looks behind it one sees a vacuum or, if you prefer not to speak of a vacuum, a disconcerting darkness.

The uselessness for purposes of finance of an economic concept may not be sufficient reason to hold that concept erroneous in economic theory;[26] but it is a fairly clear indication of the need to define the concept and to limit the field of its fruitfulness. It is possible that a concept that is fruitless in one field is also, on closer inspection, fruitless in others, in which case it reveals itself to be a trifle lacking even theoretical interest.

30. De Viti's book tries to pull the science of finance out of this situation of inferiority. De Viti has a well-defined conception of the state, producer of public services and therefore collaborator in the production of direct goods, used for the satisfaction of human needs. In this capacity, the state participates in the distribution of social income, on a par with the other collaborators in production, with labour, with capitalists, landowners and entrepreneurs. No part of the perennial flow of social income must be exonerated from paying tax to the state, because it has contributed to the production of the entire flow of income, no particle excluded.

De Viti constructs his system starting from this simple hypothesis, which could be defined as an arbitrary postulate even by those willing to accept from time to time the innumerable and gaily-coloured idols of justice which are alternatively recommended to the adoration of lovers of finance.

De Viti shows little respect for the idols of progressivity, the psychological analyses with regard to the sacrifices of the taxpayers, the subjective discrimination between income and income. Everything that falls outside his simple conception of tax as a share of gross social income, which is equal to the sum of individual net incomes, is not welcome under his roof. His building turns out, therefore, to be schematic, eurhythmic, able to explain a vast number of tax institutes, probably most of the tax institutes now in existence.

Is not the simplicity, the eurhythmy, the logical coherence of the building so constructed the only possible proof of the nearness of De Viti's theory to the truth? If in the pages that follow I advance some criticism of a particular point of his theory it is not because I believe that the method of starting from a hypothesis of the state and following out each of the many consequences that can be derived from the perspective of taxation is mistaken, but because I believe the method is susceptible to being applied with greater logical rigour.

If there is a criticism of a more general nature that might be made of De Viti, let it be said that his system is not sufficiently 'naked', not sufficiently free of references to third and fourth level politically, historically, and socially contingent approximations. He too is subject, like everyone else, to feeling regret at not being able to explain, in addition to the fundamental 'facts', all of the other little factoids obstructing the field of taxation and that can be destroyed only by negating them, thus denying to the legislator any theoretical pretext for translating into a compulsory rule whatever product of his political imagination.

Features of the 'equitable' or 'stable' tax

31. The objective I wish to achieve in these pages with the aid of the writings cited in them is this: to determine the nature of the tax with which the economic system will remain in equilibrium and will not be pressed to change by some force derived from the tax itself. We will call this tax:

(a) *equitable*, should we care to use this qualifying adjective taken from the vocabulary of the law;
(b) *neutral*, should we want to place special emphasis on the idea that, by adopting it, the legislator wishes to abstain from using the tax to obtain economic, moral, political or social effects and intends to obtain from it only the remuneration for the state's contribution to the production of social income;
(c) *typical* or *optimum*, if we should wish to highlight the fact that the tax is such that it will allow the state to obtain, with a minimum of friction and the greatest possible immediacy, the tax revenue needed to maximize the economic power of the society, including the state.

Qualifying a tax as 'neutral' – or 'fair' – is not in contrast with qualifying it as typical or optimum if by neutral we mean a tax fashioned in a way suited to its proper purpose of procuring revenue for the state and not in a way suited to achieving moral, political, social or economic objectives other than those of a fiscal nature (see *Osservazioni critiche*, § 4). This is not to deny that there also exist taxes which have other ends, that, for example, are not intended to bring in money for the state but to take money from *X*'s pocket and put it in *Y*'s pocket. But these are pseudo-taxes, which, having been fashioned in opposition to the proper nature of taxes, push the existing equilibrium towards change so that the tax itself is negated and its objective thwarted. The neutral or typical or optimum tax is that which, whatever the objective the state wishes to pursue, does not in itself disturb the existing equilibrium, or, since the tax is in any case a factor in the existing equilibrium, it allows an equilibrium to take shape while the tax remains unchanged as regards the structure and the impact desired by the legislator.

32. Among all the qualifying adjectives of the tax we are looking for, I would give preference to 'optimum', which, ever since Cannan, has acquired the right of citizenship in the language of economics.[27] The

optimum tax is not necessarily high or low, and a tax of 20 per cent can be optimum and preferable to a tax of 5 per cent. The optimum tax is that which, in a given time and place, obtains the greatest satisfaction of public needs compatibly with the production of the most abundant flow of national income. The optimum tax, or better the optimum tax increment is that which best adapts itself to the pre-existing economic equilibrium and which disturbs it least, with the least friction and with the maximum yield for the state and the maximum increase in private income. The optimum tax does not diminish but increases the amount of national income compared to what that amount would have been without it. In 1919 I discussed at length the characteristics of the optimum tax, which I then called neutral, and demonstrated that its essential characteristic is its achievement of a *maximum* result. The optimum tax is something more than the tax that imposes the minimum sacrifice on people. 'The assignment', I said then,

> of a certain share of wealth to tax and precisely of that share which proves to be most conducive to wealth by application of the law of distribution is a necessary condition for maximizing the fruitfulness of man-made wealth. ... In the same way that it is not thinkable or possible, except perhaps in an initial dose, to satisfy the need for food without satisfying the need to drink, to be clothed, to have a house, so it is not thinkable or possible to live, to raise children, to save in a way that is appropriate for people unless the state guarantees the conditions for a civil society and prepares the way for better conditions in the future. In theory, the allotment of a certain fraction of overall wealth to taxation and its conversion into public goods is, except for the infinitely small amounts at the margins, no more and no less fruitful than the allotment of the same fraction to private uses. This amount, if the calculation were done correctly, is the allotment that yields the maximum conceivable result. Allotting to taxes a greater or lesser amount would be an economic mistake.
>
> (See *Osservazioni critiche*, § 6)

The theory of the optimum tax is not a masked version or a repetition of the erroneous theory of the 'benefit' or 'reproductive' tax. 'The state', as I also explained in 1919,

> acts as a productive factor in conformity with its own identity, not, that is, as an industrialist or as an organizer of production, but as a political entity: soldier, magistrate, educator, defender of the general interest, conducting those enterprises which would otherwise not be conducted at all or would be conducted badly by private entrepreneurs. In this guise it has contributed to the achievement of the objective, which is the maximum production of material and spiritual goods, to the greatest elevation of the people. The action of the state is not always aimed at the enrichment of individuals; on the contrary, the opposite is often the case, that with respect to some individuals the state gives little and takes a lot. The objective of taxation is not equality in what is taken from or given to individuals but rather the maximum elevation of the collectivity.
>
> (See *Osservazioni critiche*, § 7)

33. From this economic conception of taxation, as opposed to political or sociological conceptions, I inferred the irremediable error of theories which, with regard to the effects of taxes, considered taxation as something that 'diminished' the income of taxpayers. Posing the question in this form: 'What is the cost, what is the sacrifice imposed on taxpayers by taxation?' is legitimate only for special purposes, to study differences in behaviour between one kind of tax and another;[28] it is legitimate for tallage, receipts of which are allotted primarily to the embezzlement of oppressive governors and to the oppression of subject peoples;[29] it is partially legitimate for taxes inferior to the optimum tax, which give rise to costs owing to friction and adaptation; it is not legitimate for the optimum tax.

'The application of wealth', I wrote also in 1919, 'to the payment of taxes is a particular instance of the general rule of the distribution of wealth'. This law

> is not only an abstract truth, which is so deformed by individual egotism and by the struggle between political groups and classes that it seems never to happen concretely, but it is an objective which people are striving to achieve. Experience is persuading people more and more of the necessity of subjecting themselves to a common law; and furthermore they are being persuaded of the necessity to work consciously and voluntarily on the creation of this common law, on its execution, on the procurement of the means able to make it active and fruitful. If this political awareness is not very widespread among the general public, felt by most people only in exceptional moments, it is undeniably growing, taking root in the human spirit and increasingly becoming an inspiration for the actions of elected officials and also for those of the governed multitudes. From an abstract scheme, useful as a guiding light for researchers and suited to classifying human actions, it is becoming, little by little, an objective to be achieved, a rule consciously desired and obeyed.
>
> It is the permanent rule that historically has always existed, although it has only gradually become able consciously to direct human actions. In comparison with it, the other rules of conduct seem transient, variable from time to time ... If this is the fundamental and permanent truth to which one is invariably led when the theory of the optimum distribution of wealth between public and private aims is put to the test of historical experience, it must logically be concluded that paying taxes does not diminish but actually increases the amount of income at men's disposal. Taxes increase the flow of present income, because they maximize the fruitfulness of savings invested in production, maximize labour productivity, maximize the spirit of enterprise and the human capacity for invention ... There is *one* distribution of income between public and private goods, *one given amount of taxes*, which is capable of obtaining the maximum result. Within the limits in which the scheme is implemented in reality – and everything indicates that it has been implemented for the most important components of the public budget and in proportions much larger than most people believe – this tax system causes the flow of newly created wealth to be a maximum. The tax system does occasionally contract the flow of present goods, because it directs people's work toward the production of future goods – roads,

bridges, railways, schools – but the contraction is temporary, and soon gives rise to a new expansion which brings the collective income to a higher level.

(See *Osservazioni critiche*, §§ 9 and 10)[30]

34. The 'optimum' tax whose characteristics I thus tried to outline ten years ago is not something that is historically or ideally fixed; that can be identified once and for all. The world inhabited by the state changes, the state's objectives change, and with them the optimum tax. Rather, the optimum tax never exists completely in any given moment. Because of the legislator's slowness in keeping up with the variations in the economic, social and institutional equilibrium in which the tax must live, the tax laws are always behind with respect to the world. The legislative rule is still fixed at the point it had reached in an earlier economic phase, and its fixedness causes frictions and costs and pain to the people. Researchers are pushed to investigate and to discuss the echo of this pain which the by now unsuited tax inflicts on the people, and they discover new kinds of distribution of the tax burden more appropriate to the world as they now see it, improved incarnations of that ideal of the optimum which they pursue. But before the newly conceived tax takes concrete form in a legislative rule, the world, although not much, has already changed. So that when the new rule is born it is already the cause of pain, and the people have already begun to call for it to be changed again.

The prophet said:

> Il n'y a que violence dans l'univers; mais nous sommes gâtés par la philosophie moderne, qui a dit que *tout est bien*; tandis que le mal a tout souillé, et que dans un sens très-vrai, *tout est mal*, puisque rien n'est à sa place. *Tous les êtres gémissent* (Saint Paul, Romans, VIII, 22) et tendent, avec effort et douleur, vers un autre ordre de choses.[31]

If the ardour to discover the truth that inspires even the humble students of taxation in their apostolate could from time to time manage to shorten for just an instant the duration of the painful effort that people perennially make to achieve a new better order of things, their labours will not have been in vain.

15

On the Source of Saving and the Taxation of Normal Income as an Approximation of the Exclusion of Income from the Tax Base*

161. While I was meditating, with great delight, as happens with good books, on the pages of De Viti's *Principii* and trying to follow with my mind the transmutations of capital goods into direct goods and the consequent tax vicissitudes, I happened to read, in the hours in which the mind loves to rest, one of the most pleasing and deservedly successful novels from the other side of the Atlantic, *Maria Chapdelaine*, by a writer, unknown yesterday but famous today, Louis Hémon, who died young before the glory of his one book could be obscured by those that would perhaps have followed.[1] It is the powerful poem of the pioneer in French Canada, the revelation of why a handful of men, no more than 80,000, abandoned by their mother country in 1763, should have multiplied (to about 2,750,000 in Canada alone, without counting the numerous offshoots in the United States), populated provinces and now become the most prolific, compact, traditional and lively people of North America. Reading that book, one feels the deep-rooted reasons that move men to conquer the earth, that produce families, and great and lasting races. One also sees clearly, and that is why I remember the book, the phenomena of labour, wages, profit and saving not obscured by monetary superstructures or verbal conventions. The land stretches out vast, without limits, before the eyes of the pioneer, but covered with firs, pines, scrubs and bushes of every kind, without roads, but crossed by rivers and buried for seven months of the year under a thick blanket of snow and ice. Samuel Chapdelaine is a pioneer, who has an inclination for the unknown, the far off. One after the other he has cleared three or four fields. Alone, with the faithful companion of his life, he halted where the pasture allowed him to feed his two cows and where it was possible to 'clear the land'.

---

*First published as 'Della fonte del risparmio e della tassazione del reddito normale come approssimazione alla esclusione del risparmio dalla materia imponibile' as a conclusion of *Saggi sul risparmio e l'imposta* (Turin: Giulio Einaudi Editore, 1958).

> From dawn till dusk I swing my axe, without ever returning to the house, except for lunch, and she, during the whole day, keeps the house, tends the animals, looks after the pens, cleans the stable, toiling without cease. Three or four times a day, in front of the door, she stops a moment to look where I, down at the edge of the wood, with all my strength was clearing the ground of bushes and trunks with my axe to make it arable.

When in July the springs around the house dry up, eight or ten times a day she goes down to the stream and brings up water for the cows, carrying the buckets in her hands or on her shoulders. Years and years of toil and 'misery' follow; and then come children and the work begins again on new land, better able to meet the needs of the larger family. When the children are still small, the pioneer hires a hand to help him 'clear the land'; when they have become able to work, the hired hand, no longer necessary, is not dismissed, but in winter when the land is covered with snow goes with the two oldest children to earn his keep as a woodcutter, paid by one of the companies that at an even higher altitude produce timber for construction and raw material for paper mills.

162. Where is the income? It is the wheat, the milk, the cheese, the butter, the wool, the meat that every year is obtained from the cleared land.

Where is the saving? It is in 'clearing the land', cutting down trees, making them into beams and planks and using these to build the house, the stable and the stockades.

It is the rearing of a first cow and then of many on the pastures that have also been cleared, with the trunks and stones removed and divided into fields.

What is the tax levied on? Or better, what in our opinion should it be levied on for Samuel Chapdelaine to consider it fair? On the wheat, the milk, the cheese, the butter, the wool, the enjoyment of the house he lives in; on the direct goods that the household manages to procure in growing quantities as time goes by.

The tax is not levied on the clearing of the land, the building of the house or the rearing of cows and heifers, because the land that is cleared, the house that is built and the cows that are reared are capital goods and Samuel Chapdelaine would immediately feel that the tax fell on him twice: first on the land he clears and then on the wheat that comes from the cleared land, first on the house that he and his sons put up trunk by trunk and then on the shelter they will enjoy against the snow and wind of the long winter.

163. And where does the saving come from? Not from a wage, which is not paid, not from having denied the hired hand – who for eleven years, at every return of summer, has come back to the farm – a cent of what he is owed for his work. It comes from the toil and the 'misery' that Samuel

Chapdelaine and his family have endured for so many years. It also comes, although he is not even aware of this, from his ability as a pioneer, from his love for the new land, never inhabited before, from the ambition to make the land increasingly arable, a place where at last his children can put down roots. Another, his neighbour, is unable to live on land that has already been cleared. Three Frenchmen have arrived nearby recently from France, three men with the hands of townsmen, who speak a sophisticated French very different from the simple French of the seventeenth century and who are regarded by these uncouth Canadians with amazement and admiration, almost as if they were men of another race. Their neighbours and they themselves are convinced that failure awaits them. The land, although already cleared, is not able to provide even a wage to those who cannot love it, make it fertile and wait. It will devour the old savings that the newcomers have brought from France and cast them back on to the streets of the city they have come from.

164. This is the same everywhere. In the same way as the saving of the pioneer does not go by itself to him, does not derive from a wage that is not paid and does not consist in the wheat, the milk and the wool that he consumes or sells to procure other articles to consume but comes from the work of material effort, planning and organizing from which he expects a return (wheat in years to come, a dwelling for the next winter); in the same way the saving of the entrepreneur in our complicated society is not created with the expenses incurred to buy raw materials, pay clerks and workers and rent the capital needed to set up the factory. All these expenses have also been incurred by others, they have also been incurred by the projector who has thrown himself, without the necessary qualities, into the same venture and who is forced by the market to pay, on a par with the entrepreneur, the whole salary to the worker, the entire interest to the capitalist and the full price of the raw materials to the supplier. But the entrepreneur obtains a profit and can save, whereas the projector loses, and the profits obtained by entrepreneurs, like the losses of projectors, fall within a positive and negative range that goes, in both directions, from zero to limits that cannot be established.

165. The problem that the tax must resolve is extraordinarily complicated.

1 The tax must apply to the whole mass of direct goods that are produced and consumed during the year, in proportion to each taxpayer's contribution, net of expenses, to the total quantity of such goods.
2 The tax must not apply to the land that is cleared, the capital goods that are created in the period or year considered and that have not yet been transformed into direct goods. Taxation at this stage would be a duplication of the taxation of the direct goods into which the capital goods are subsequently to be transformed.

3 The tax must apply to the land that ceases to be arable, to the capital goods that are consumed in the period or year considered, because the depreciation of the land, the consumption of the capital goods signify their transformation into direct goods, without renewing the part consumed. If the depreciation of land and capital goods is not taxed, as is the case today,[2] a part of the direct goods produced during the year would escape the tax.

166. The only lawmakers to resolve the question in the manner concretely closest to the fairness it was desired to achieve were those[3] 'great economists who, unknown to Europe, governed the destiny of Lombardy in the last century [the 18th]'. They discovered the method of taxing normal or ordinary income, also known as cadastral income, whereby no attempt is made to discover the truth about individual taxpayers' actual gains and losses, but what is investigated is the income that, given a specific piece of land with a certain fertility, position and crop or given specific factory equipment, the normal entrepreneur would succeed in obtaining. The tax falls on that normal income, which is more than the low incomes obtained by incapable entrepreneurs and the losses of projectors, and less than the high incomes achieved by capable and lucky entrepreneurs. Elsewhere,[4] I have examined the economic and technical characteristics of the cadastral method, which set it well above the 'barbarous' methods (as Cattaneo called them) with which fines are imposed in 'cultured countries' on the activity of taxpayers, which are fashionable today under the name of taxes on actual income. In those studies I also showed all the drawbacks and difficulties associated with the taxation of individuals' excess incomes or actual incomes.

167. Here, developing an argument referred to on other occasions, it is important to highlight how the method of taxing ordinary income is also a device that very satisfactorily meets the needs of taxing only direct goods while excluding increases in capital goods.

In truth, what is ordinary income if not that obtained by the entrepreneur and in general the average taxpayer who uses the factor of production he possesses with the ability of a good paterfamilias, that is in accordance with an average or normal ability, neither superior nor inferior? In every field normal income is obtained by the taxpayer I would call representative, if it were not clearer to keep to the now established terminology of marginal taxpayer.[5]

If an entrepreneur, he is a marginal taxpayer if he pays workers the current wage, capitalists the market interest rate and suppliers the current price for raw materials and machinery and earns for himself the ordinary return due to men endowed with the managerial and organizational abilities normally required for his function.

If a worker, he is a marginal taxpayer if he performs the normal work in relation to his ability and receives the corresponding wage.

If a member of the professions, he is a marginal taxpayer if he uses his professional abilities in such a way as also to obtain an income corresponding to them.

If a landowner, he is a marginal taxpayer if he keeps his land in a state of normal efficiency according to the customs prevailing and the technical rules normally observed in his area and obtains an income, variable from plot to plot, that does not exceed or fall below that ordinarily obtained in those conditions.

If a capitalist, he is a marginal taxpayer if he does not look for particularly adventurous investments but is satisfied with the return that can be earned on savings invested with the security that suits the prudence of a good paterfamilias.

And so on. Marginal taxpayers are those who do not consume the land but do not clear it either, those who do not increase the initial endowment of capital goods but do not allow it to diminish either by failing to make good wear and tear. They are taxpayers who conserve their assets, who keep them intact, who are careful to restore but unable to create. If all taxpayers were marginal taxpayers, and obtained neither more nor less than the income needed to remunerate their work, whether manual or intellectual, whether executive or organizational, whether investing capital or using their land, economic society would not change over time. Every year a constant flow of direct goods would be made available to men and would be consumed; every year a fraction of the cleared land would become overgrown again, a fraction of the houses built would fall down, a fraction of the machines, ships, roads and stocks would depreciate and turn into direct goods; and every year, like patient ants, men would restore the factors destroyed, so that, with no change in the endowment of capital goods, the flow of direct goods would remain constant.

In this imaginary situation the state would levy a fraction of the direct goods produced annually and would respect the endowment, perpetually renewed and conserved, of capital goods.

168. Real society is not the same as this imaginary society. There are those who rise and those who fall. There are sub-marginal taxpayers, who do not succeed in earning the normal wage, the normal fees, the ordinary entrepreneurial profit, the ordinary income from the land. However, for psychological reasons of imitation, for their unawareness of their below-average abilities in relation to the task they have assigned to themselves,[6] they consume more of the income in direct goods than they actually produce, thus bit by bit eroding the endowment of capital goods they had inherited from an earlier period. And they also erode it since, not being able to use it efficiently, the wear and tear caused by time and use is not

offset by an output that is sufficient to provide normal quotas of maintenance, repair work and replacement.

And there are super-marginal taxpayers, who from the same endowment of capital goods, and for workers we can consider the innate or acquired abilities as capital goods, succeed in obtaining more than the normal wage, the ordinary entrepreneurial profit, the ordinary income from the land. If, as often happens, their consumption needs do not increase immediately just because their incomes have increased beyond the normal, they can devote the part in excess of the normal, ordinary amount that is sufficient to maintain their earlier standard of living to the production of new capital goods, in addition to those serving to replace those that already existed at the beginning of each subsequent period.

169. If capital goods are seen as works of reforestation and mountain area management, strengthening the banks of rivers, building networks of irrigation canals, from the largest to the smallest, and levelling land, we can say that in a society of marginal men all these works are maintained in a good state but are not improved. The same volume of water is channelled, the same fields are irrigated, the same quantity of direct goods is produced from year to year.

In a regressive society made up of sub-marginal men the mountain areas are neglected, the river banks are not looked after, the irrigation ditches clog up little by little. The degradation is imperceptible. In each year men obtain produce from the land that is nearly equal to that of the previous year; nearly, but not quite the same. After ten years, after twenty, the difference is appreciable. After a hundred years, where there used to be fertile fields full of men, malaria is rife and buffaloes graze.

In a progressive society made up of super-marginal men the mountain areas are managed better and better, reforestation is extended to the highest altitudes, the land is protected from erosion with defensive works, with barriers, with artificial lakes, the river banks are made unbreakable, the flow of water is regulated and used to irrigate an ever larger cultivated area. The produce of the land grows from year to year and maintains a growing number of increasingly prosperous people.

170. What approach should taxation take in the presence of these three types, which are not really types of stationary, regressive and progressive societies but types of conservers, squanderers and creators within the same society; types on whose varying prevalence depends the stationary, regressive or progressive state of the society as a whole?

The great economists, whether they were called Don Vincenzo De Miro, Pompeo Neri, Gian Rinaldo Carli, Cesare Beccaria or Pietro Verri, gave this memorable answer to the question: 'Behave, oh state, in distributing taxation as if all the men of your country belonged to the marginal or normal type. Ignore the existence of sub-normal and super-normal men.'[7]

171. Indeed, why should the state consider the existence of men who do not know how to make normal use of the capital goods with which they are endowed or of those who use them exceptionally well? Has it not provided its services equally to all? Has not its army protected all in the same way, have not its magistrates and its officials protected the goods and physical integrity of all to the same extent? Has it not given all an equal opportunity to learn and improve themselves? Why should the state suffer the consequences of the bad management of others or participate in the gains deriving from particularly good management of which it does not have the merit? Why should it allow its services to languish just because some taxpayers are unable or unwilling to use their means of production? Why should it intensify and increase its services as soon as a taxpayer plants a tree on the mountain and not wait, as do the men of its country, to expand its tasks, to spend more until, as a result of mountain reforestation, the land on the plain has begun to produce more?

If the state wants, as it sometimes must want, to be the top super-marginal entrepreneur of its country, if it wants to shift the focus of production so as to produce, for the time being, a smaller quantity of direct goods ready for immediate consumption and a larger quantity of capital goods; if, that is, it wants to levy taxes to implement itself those works of reforestation, strengthening of river banks, recovery of submerged and swampy land; if, accordingly, it intends to reduce the incomes consumable today to increase those consumable in the future, why ever should it levy these extraordinary taxes in such a way as to exempt sub-marginal taxpayers, the squanderers of the existing endowments of the marginal goods that it wants to increase, and tax more heavily those who, in view of their super-marginal aptitude, already cooperate spontaneously in its drive to increase the country's economic equipment? Will not the results of the state's work potentially benefit all producers, including the sub-marginal? If the latter do not succeed in deriving an advantage, why must super-marginal taxpayers be saddled with the loss caused by their inability or indolence?

172. At this point we can change the rule laid down by De Viti, which says that:

> everybody, consuming general public services in proportion to their income, must pay tax in proportion to that income

into this other one:

> everybody, consuming general public services in proportion to their normal income – to the income that the normal producer or worker would ordinarily have had in relation to the means of production possessed – must pay tax in proportion to that normal income.

173. The rule laid down by De Viti is an attempt to give an answer to the question: 'What is the individual consumption of general public services?' As noted above, every factor of production receives a remuneration corresponding to the value of its contribution. There may be frictions, errors and social losses as a consequence of the ways in which the market fixes the remuneration of each factor, and a very important branch of economics is that which studies those frictions, errors and losses and indicates remedies. The normal rule is: the remuneration of labour depends on the value of that labour, not on the value of another factor of production, of capital or land or entrepreneurial talent; the remuneration of entrepreneurs depends on the value of their contribution and not on the value of some other contribution, such as labour or land. Only the state sees its remuneration depend not on the value of its contribution to the common output but on the income of taxpayers, that is on the remuneration of every other factor of production.

In a field that is obscure and destined to remain obscure for ever, this is the best approximation that exists to the unknown truth. But let it be clear that is a highly imperfect approximation. Why should the contribution of the state depend on the value at different times of the contribution of the other factors of production, of capitalists, workers, entrepreneurs? None of the contributions of these other factors is measured in this outlandish way. Workers' wages are not a constant proportion of entrepreneurs' profit, or vice versa. The proportions vary from case to case and are determined by the principle of giving to each factor what it merits, whatever the consequent proportions may be.

174. It seems to me that the addition of the adjective 'normal' to De Viti's proposal leads to an improvement in the criteria for assessing the contribution of the state. Without that addition, the rule would leave it up to the other factors of production to decide whether to pay or not to pay the state, depending on the success of each in collaborating in the common venture. The incapable, the presumptuous, who lose, would pay nothing; the capable and hardworking would pay a lot. The state would be a sort of parasite that would adapt itself to recognizing that its contribution is worthless if that of the other collaborators is of no value and acquires value only if this is given by the others. This is a theoretically unsustainable position. Each factor is worth what it is worth, not the value passed to it by others in relation to their own earning capacity. Workers certainly do not think that their work is worth nothing because their entrepreneur unfortunately fails. The rule that requires workers, of equal ability, to be paid equally by entrepreneurs whose fortunes differ is a powerful spring driving economic progress and contributes to the elimination of unfit entrepreneurs and to the victory of the best.

The aim of the addition of the adjective 'normal' is to put the state in the same position as the other factors of production. Let the state be paid, since no better rule can be found, in relation to the value of the other factors of production and not to its own value, but let it be paid by all in relation to the value that each individual factor normally has, abstracting from individual success or lack of success. Public services are provided to all, and it is not the state's fault if the other factors do not know how to use the productive forces they possess.[8]

175. Neither is it any more difficult to calculate the 'normal' social income and distribute it, without gaps or duplications, among the components of society than it is to calculate and distribute the 'actual' income or, in other words, the sum of the normal and exceptional losses and gains applicable from one moment to the next to each individual taxpayer. Indeed, this second operation is a practical impossibility, the source of unfairness and endless gaps and duplications, whereas the first type of calculation is commonly performed by appraisers for various purposes and in fact is preferred by tax officials for the allocation of incomes that are not clearly documented.

176. The commandment to divide taxation according to 'normal' income is not identical to the rule that logically follows from the demonstration in this and my earlier writing: 'Do not take account of saving when it is accumulated and tax it when it is turned into consumption.'[9] I wish to insist on this declaration of non-identity, since in the whole of this controversy it happens all too often that the reservations put forward by the expounder of the main thesis are elevated to the dignity of objections discovered by the critics. I have pointed out repeatedly that it is one thing to establish a principle and another to examine the limits of its practical application. The principle of excluding saving from the tax base cannot be applied in full because, and as long as, men are what they are; that is, unfailingly drawn, at all times and in all countries, not to pay taxes, as soon as they find a way to avoid doing so. The lawmaker who abstracted from human nature or presumed to remedy it merely with the threat of punishments, even very heavy ones, would be imprudent. The best remedy is the lawmaker's ability in drafting legislation, and above all in devising expedients by means of which to apply the principle without danger for the Treasury and without arousing the envy of those who do not know how to save or who save less than others.

177. The principle of taxing normal income is something more than an expedient. On a par with the exclusion from the tax base of new trees added to woods until they are fully grown and cut down, of the increase in the

value of buildable land until rent for the house built on it is received and of life insurance premiums, and on a par with the temporary exemption of the income from new houses and new industrial enterprises, the taxation of normal income appears to be a practical application of the principle of excluding saving from the list of things that can be taxed, an application that comes closer to meeting the needs that a legislative formula must satisfy in order to take account of the moral, sentimental and political factors that the lawmaker must consider. Those who would disdainfully dismiss the so-called exemption of the saving of the rich accept and applaud the exemptions granted to those who, by building new houses, provide lodgings for the multitudes, and to those who, by improving their land or setting up factories, provide workers with jobs. The disdain and the applause are equally lacking in theoretical significance. Nonetheless, the lawmaker, who must give great consideration to human sentiments, does well similarly to pretend disdain and to do what earns him applause. By acting in this way, he diminishes the opposition to his wise action.

178. The taxation of normal income is the closest and probably the best approximation that is known to the principle of excluding saving from the tax base. As noted earlier, sub-normal taxpayers, who lose or gain less than what is commonly considered the normal retribution for their labour or the investment of their capital, are almost never able to save; indeed, they normally consume the saving they or others had previously accumulated. By taxing sub-normal taxpayers on income they do not produce, the tax on normal income obeys, as far as is possible, the theoretical rule that saving should be taxed when it is consumed, capital goods when they wear out without being replaced.

The grey area of marginal taxpayers, who earn the normal income or thereabouts, includes those who gain and spend in accordance with the current standard of living and who, not having, as producers, the courage of the pioneer or the creator, do not diverge, as consumers, from the customs of the times they live in. The tax falls on them in full. Since on average there is no practical scope for saving, the theoretical rule is observed in most cases.

179. Super-normal taxpayers are the only ones to have practical scope for saving. Pioneers save who clear land in the deserted regions of Canada, in addition to their normal work of producing direct goods; peasants save who in Sicily and Monferrato break up the hard soil and plant vines; workers save who do piecework and earn the bonuses paid to the most diligent and whose wives keep a small shop or take in work to do at home in their spare time; members of the professions save who attend to their clients with special care and cause them to be faithful and enlarge their number; entrepreneurs save who know how to organize the factors of pro-

duction well and, while paying the same wages and prices as their competitors, gain where others lose. Where a differential, super-normal income exists, saving is possible. This possibility is not equivalent to actual saving, but it is a good approximation. The generations that spend all the income produced are not the generations that create capital goods. Those who clear the land or set up a business do not have the time, the desire or the inclination to spend more than the normal income. They will be followed by a second generation of conservers and a third generation of squanderers. For the time being the generation that creates, that increases the endowment of capital goods will perhaps spend less than normal or at most a little more. The exceptions occur at times of monetary and economic revolution, of parvenus whose wealth is the result of a stroke of luck. Normally, for those who have created affluence or wealth with tenacity, with hard work and ability, the excess income with respect to the normal income corresponds roughly to saving. Their spending increases, not immediately but prudently after the wealth has been consolidated, when they begin to enjoy the fruits of earlier sacrifices. The tax that applies to the normal income is an excellent approximation of the ideal tax that exempts saving.

180. Lastly, it conforms with the needs of the life of the state, which, if the state is vigorous tend to increase. By taxing ordinary income and implicitly exempting saving, the state fosters its own grandeur with the wealth of private individuals.

> The long interval between one revision of the land register and the next [I wrote in *La terra e l'imposta* with regard to the infrequency of such revisions] produces a beneficial effect. Farmers, encouraged by the exemption of income in excess of the ordinary cadastral income for the remaining years of the thirty-year interval, improve their agricultural methods, raise the productivity of their fields. Experiments with innovations, first isolated, multiply. At the end of the thirty years the land is transformed and the methods of cultivation, the products and the men are different. What was the 'ordinary' product at the time of the previous revision has become the low output of the most ignorant or least capable farmers. Average farmers, good patresfamilias, find themselves pushed much higher on the productivity scale and the 'ordinary' product is now equal to what was the dream of the most daring experimenters. Here at a stroke the state reaps the fruit of its wise and prudent pursuit of exceptional incomes. Here we have the demonstration that applying the tax to the actual fruits of the land, variable from man to man, instead of to the normal fruits, is not only, as Carlo Cattaneo exclaimed, a barbarous economic error but also a major financial error.
>
> (*La terra e l'imposta*, p.139)

It is not always technically possible to apply the theoretical principle with the admirable approximation found in the cadastral taxation of the normal income from land. But always, whatever the expedient adopted, if it has the effect of implementing the rule of taxing the whole flow of direct goods produced and nothing else, no privilege or exemption will have been granted nor any mistake of double taxation made. The tax on squanderers is not doubled when they are required to pay tax on the assets destroyed. They pay, as they must, on the capital goods they convert into immediate enjoyment. No immunity is granted to creators when they are not taxed on their saving. If they were taxed, they would pay twice, first on the capital goods and then on the direct goods into which these are transformed. The rule that only direct goods are to be taxed is the only one that permits economic progress and eliminates the tax frictions that slow it down.

16

The Optimal Tax as a Neutral Tax, in the Physiocrats, in Smith and the Italian Catastisti of the Eighteenth Century*

Do taxes exist?

183. The question may appear paradoxical but it isn't. I said earlier that public debt (§§ 134 and 135)[1] and taxation (§§ 15–18) sometimes appear alive but are dead. They are the vendettas of reality for the arrogance of the avengers. These would like men to suffer from taxes and continuously to compare one man's sacrifices with another's and to add sacrifice to sacrifice and to make sacrifice proportionate to pleasure; or they would like taxes to take away every year a constant or variable part of a certain mysterious accounting item called profit. Reality mocks the avengers' plans and regularly upsets them. No sooner has the doctrinaire devised a system whereby all those who find themselves in a given situation must pay, for example, a tax of L1,000 lire on L5,000 of income, than inexorably, day by day, time erodes the work of the learned lawmaker. For some years X pays the L1,000 on the L5,000 of income from his house and suffers, as the avenger wished. As for all human suffering, the suffering of taxation diminishes with time and habit makes it appear less. The time comes when X sells the house and goes his way with L80,000, the market price at 5 per cent of a house yielding L4,000 net. He has endured the amputation of L20,000 compared with the L100,000 the house would have been worth if the tax had never existed. If time has not yet dimmed the memory of the incomes and prices of old, he may well be the only one at this point to suffer from the tax of L1,000. But nobody thinks of him, the seller, when the tax of L1,000 on the house is mentioned. He is a wanderer, lost in the distant mist, heading towards other taxes, no longer remembering this one that pained him in the past. Does the buyer suffer when he pays the annual tax of L1,000? No, because he

*First published as 'L'ottima imposta come imposta neutra, nei fisiocratici, in Smith e nei catastisti italiani del Settecento', in *Miti e paradossi della giustizia tributaria* (Turin: Giulio Einaudi Editore, 1938).

receives the annual income of 5 per cent, or L4,000, on the capital of L80,000 lire invested in the house. The tax is there, the state treasury receives it and nobody feels the pain. In one of his writings Benvenuto Griziotti found an illuminating metaphor to describe the fact: the tax is like a ray that impinges on the pupil of our eye and appears alive, but it comes from a far-off star that has been dead for centuries. The ray has travelled in the firmament for years, centuries and finally reaches us and shows us how the star was alive that instead is now dead. That is how certain taxes are. They appear alive; men perform the rites of paying and collecting them, but he who was hurt by them may well have died years or centuries ago and no longer feels anything. And nobody suffers in his place. Writers have used the term 'amortized' for these taxes, which have caused a loss or an amortization of the capital value of the thing taxed. I do not know the etymology of the word 'amortization', but by chance those writers chose an expressive word. An amortized tax is a tax that is dead in the hearts of men, that no longer causes them to feel pain or regret. Many taxes are dead.

184. The paradox of dead taxes irritated the avengers. It appeared an affront to justice. It is necessary to abolish the taxes that are no longer felt by living men. A tax that at every instant does not cause men to feel the pain of divine judgement – thou shalt work with the sweat of thy brow to pay the tax – does not fulfil its purpose. A system is wanted under which the pain of the tax is inevitably perpetual and lancinating. I confess that I am unable to enter into such a perfect state of tax satyriasis. The paradox of dead taxes makes me suspect that meaningless words may have held even greater sway than I have already shown. Have we perhaps allowed ourselves to be influenced by the empty sound of words? Impost brings to mind something that is placed on top and is a burden. A tax on income or on capital appears to be something that logically weighs down, curtails, reduces income or capital or both.

185. In the last century economists were guilty of aggravating the propensity to interpret the word 'impost' in the sense of weight or pain by unhappily placing the discussion of taxes in the fourth part of their treatises, for reasons of harmonic design. Production, distribution, circulation and consumption of wealth: this is the classical four-part division of the economic drama enshrined by Jean-Baptiste Say. The first three acts of the drama were the creative acts: men create wealth by toiling, trading and distributing. The last act was devoted to the destruction of what had been created. The economists of those times, not having discovered the laws of utility or marginalism and not having yet learned to reverse the order of the notions, were desperate. Reluctant to fill the pages of the treatise on consumption with teachings drawn from the writings of Agnolo Pandolfini

(or Leon Battista Alberti?) on the good management of the home, they really did not know what to put into the fourth part. Three wings of the edifice were high and large, but the fourth? Taxes came to the rescue. Since private consumption offered little matter, the discourse turned to public consumption. Taxes were thus theoretically linked to the idea of consumption, of destruction. In the four-part economic drama men produced, transported, traded and distributed wealth. Then came the flood. Consumption destroyed, and in the act of consuming there was an internecine struggle between men, who expected to consume everything they had produced, and the state, which wanted to take a part away from them to provide for public consumption.

Two driving ideas sprang from this academic architecture: that taxation is destruction and that it is destruction of what others, private individuals, had created.

186. The sun has set on the architecture of the treatises of Jean-Baptiste Say. No modern economic treatise is constructed on that model. The driving ideas, born from what was a mere expedient of scholastic exposition of the science, have remained.

If I go back to the memories of my youth, between 1890 and 1900, I am struck by the idiomatic phrases, resembling those of taxation, that were commonly used then. In that period the industrialist used to say 'I, who give bread to a hundred, a thousand workers ...', and most people found his manner of speaking to be natural and the workers who expressed dissatisfaction with their benefactors to be 'ungrateful'. Today, in his heart of hearts, the industrialist may sometimes still think this way, but he no longer dares make his thinking known and it would no longer appear reasonable to his listeners. The worker does not maintain the employer, or the employer the worker; neither gives alms to the other. Each lives on the fruit of his own work and his own creation. The work of both is made fertile by their mutual collaboration, but both benefit from collaborating. To say that the worker is maintained by the industrialist is just as grotesque as saying that the baker maintains his customer because he provides him with bread. Just as there is equivalence between bread and money, there is equivalence between work done and wages. Both must be grateful to the other, because their union has allowed the worker to produce a higher wage and the entrepreneur a larger profit.

Cost and compensation are two sides of the same coin. The managing director of a newspaper before 1900 used to complain every day of the rising cost of the paper consumed by the printing presses. We all laughed because that was a sign of the growing success of the paper. For him the turning of the rolls of paper was an act of destruction, for us it was the precondition of creation.

187. The same is true for taxes. It is untrue and grotesque to say that they imply destruction. They are the means whereby the state creates new goods: security, justice, defence and national grandeur, culture, health and unity of the men living on the national territory. Thanks to taxes, the state creates the legal and political environment in which men can work, organize, invent and produce. What would men be if the state did not exist? Miserable savages, wandering on the earth, without defence against the wild beasts, uncertain of their food and life, armed the one against the other. This is not to say that the entire social product, the entire national income pertains to the state. It means only that there exists an optimal distribution of the annual national income; a distribution thanks to which the state receives taxes, the worker wages, the saver interest, the entrepreneur profit and the landowner rent. And each receives what is his, what was created by him, what is necessary for his participation in the common task to be the maximum and the most effective.

188. In the ideal distribution, the ideal or perfect state therefore does not weigh on anyone. It receives its due, all its due and nothing more. The idea that taxes are withdrawals from something man created is radically, profoundly wrong. Man and state – or, to speak concretely, man operating in the various ways offered to him, as an individual, as freely associated with others (associations and companies) and as mandatorily associated with all the others (the state) – together produce, by means of a highly complicated mechanism, an endless flow of new goods. That flow would diminish in the absence of any one of the forms of human effort: the individual, the voluntary collective or the mandatory collective. The individuals and the bodies that participate in the production of the flow of new goods have the right to participate in the enjoyment of the flow and to obtain the means for the continuous renewal of their efforts and hence of the flow and hence of their participation in the enjoyment thereof.

Mercier de La Rivière had already written:

> very unwillingly I give public revenue the name of impost: a word which is always taken badly, which announces a burden to be borne; whereas public revenue on the contrary ... is in no way grievous, and traced back to its origins can be seen to be the fruit of its utility.
>
> (*L'Ordre naturel et essentiel des sociétés politiques*, 1767, II, 40)

And Dupont de Nemours:

> [in its perfect form] the greatest possible public revenue, increasing daily, is the most profitable one possible for all members of society, is onerous to no one, costs nothing to anyone, is paid for by no one and takes nothing from the property of whomsoever.
>
> (*De l'origine et des progrès d'une science nouvelle*, 1768, 1910 edition, 28)

Words forgotten, that had been revived by this writer[2] before meditating on the pages of the Physiocrats and from which it is necessary to draw the last logical inference.

189. Which is the ultimate condemnation of the attempts that have been made by so many and with so little success to discover the perfect, absolute and everlasting rule of the 'just' tax on the basis of the 'real' 'pain' felt by men in paying the tribute.

Utilitaristi and *contabilisti* (utilitarians and those who follow an accounting approach) – the two large branches into which the innumerable sects of tax avengers are divided – have vainly striven to find the perfect tax. Having entered a blind alley, they could not find the way out.

When the worker asks for the wage that appears 'just' to him, does he perhaps say: for me the measure of justness is the boss's gain? If he gains a lot, my wage must be high, if a little, low; if he loses, I must resign myself to working for nothing? He does harbour the idea that the wage must increase if the industry prospers, but underneath this idea and much more firmly rooted there is another: that the wage must be given to him because he works and in proportion to the value of his work. Each person is the measure of himself. Wages, interest, profits are the remuneration of work, of capital, of the entrepreneurial function; and they are commensurate to the value of the contribution of work, capital and enterprise. It doesn't come into anyone's head to pay the worker according to the value of the capitalist's contribution, the capitalist according to the value of the worker's contribution and the entrepreneur according to the value of the contribution of the other two and of the owner of the natural agents of production. There is discussion on how to measure the value of the various contributions, but nobody has tried to shuffle the cards by proposing to remunerate one factor according to the value of the contribution of one of the others.

And yet the idea, which if it were enunciated in the ordinary affairs of life would appear grotesque and laughable, is accepted as pure gold when men begin to discuss and rave about the affairs of the state. Instead of paying the state for what the state does, for the value of its contribution to the common interest, it is deemed natural, obvious to pay it according to what others do, not according to the greater or lesser perfection of its work, but according to the greater or lesser success of the work of others. From the lazybones and the incapable, taxation must require little because, poor thing, he has not wanted or has not been able to produce much; from the hard worker and the capable taxation must require much because he wanted and was able to produce much. This is common sense turned on its head. What would be the reaction to the baker who gave away bread to all the down-and-outs who came to his shop and sold it for 50 cents a kilo to all those shabbily dressed or armed with a certificate of poverty, and for L5 a kilo to the rich? It would be agreed that the baker had gone off his rocker and would end up bankrupt in the almshouse. Unless men are irrational, good bread is paid for as good bread by one and all, at the same price. Even in besieged cities and states the custom is to ration bread, to make it last longer, but to sell bread of the same quality for the same price. In the same way the state provides moral and spiritual goods of the highest quality to all those who are in a position to benefit from them. What fault is it of the state if Tom and Dick, equipped with the same economic means, benefit differently from the services it provides in equal quantity to both? Why, if the first gains and the second loses, should the state make the first pay and let the second get off scot-free? Is not such conduct illogical, incomprehensible? The state has done its duty, has performed its function when it has created the environment of peace, justice, culture and coordinating social institutes in which both can use the means they possess to the same degree. Logic and common sense require the state to make both pay equally for its services. The success or lack of success of the two taxpayers' enterprises does not concern the state. Whether they lose or gain, whether they lose a lot or gain a lot is none of its business. Just as the worker wants to be paid an equal amount by two businessmen for the same amount of work, just as the saver demands an equal amount of interest if he has lent the same amount of capital, the state, which has provided the same services, wants to be paid an equal amount.

190. Note that the equality of wages, interest and taxes for the same input provided by the worker, the saver and the state is a necessary condition for social order, progress and prosperity.

If entrepreneurs had to pay high wages when they gain and low wages when they lose, if they had to pay 10 per cent on borrowed capital in the case of success and had the right not to repay principal in the case of a loss, we would be on the brink of chaos and the ruin of society. Why strive to be enterprising and prudent, hard-working and careful, if those who succeed see wages and interest increase at their expense and annul the recompense due to their ability? What punishment would be inflicted on the incapable and the lazy if the more they lost and worked badly, the larger the decrease in their wage bills, their interest payments and, why not, their raw material costs?

Nevertheless, conduct that in the ordinary affairs of life appears immediately to be insane and ruinous inexplicably becomes right, obvious and indisputable when we turn to the affairs of the state. Utilitarians and *contabilisti* outbid each other in proclaiming that the state must get itself paid for its services on the basis of others' income and capital, must try to align taxation with the enjoyment, the benefits others obtain. The focus is always on what others do, what they enjoy, what they suffer and never on what the state gives. As it would for individuals, this insane rule of conduct produces dire consequences. A state that acts according to this doctrine rewards the incapable, the bunglers, the losers and persecutes the hard-working, the capable, the winners.

191. Societies have not yet gone to the wall because in practice lawmakers and administrators of the public finances have been wiser than the doctrinaire avengers. They have paid lip service to the supreme principles of justice invented by the latter; they have recited the customary prayers before the altar of equality of sacrifice, of proportionality that is constant or rises in relation to income or capital; and then they have acted as best they could, as dictated by the instinct of the need to govern, to cover expenditure and not make taxpayers too dissatisfied or vociferous. For all its being uncertain and wavering, the work of the lawmakers is worth more than the teaching of the avengers.

We must decide to take a step forward, to cast the bad counsellors of so-called fiscal justice out of the temple of the state. We must have the courage to say that the so-called supreme rules of sacrifice, with the logical inferences of proportionality with respect to personal and overall income, are hollow phrases, words lacking common sense, indeed having no logical significance. The priests of the nothing that appears to be the word need to be whipped.

192. The priests will cry out that I want taxes to be paid in the same numerical monetary measure by rich and poor alike and that I want to revive the poll tax. Not true. Nowhere in these pages is there a word justifying such an interpretation.

What was said and shown was only:

(a) that taxes cannot be rationally allocated by applying any of the principles of sacrifice, because a principle whose meaning is not known cannot be applied (see §§ 159–62);[3]
(b) that taxes cannot be rationally applied in proportion to the 'actual' income of individual taxpayers, because such an allocation of the tax is illogical and pernicious (see §§ 187–9).

In the propositions just set out there is not one word suggesting that rich and poor must pay the same taxes. The tax allocated in accordance with the rules referred to above cannot claim to be rational. At most it can boast that it follows the dictates of ratiocinative reasoning, which means unreasonable reasoning. If, more modestly, instead of claiming to be the only rational tax, it confesses that it is an expedient recommended by common sense, by the feeling of solidarity between classes, by the criterion of economic efficiency and so on, it will become an expedient not unlike other expedients that rival it on an equal footing and therefore deserve to be examined calmly. First, away with arrogance.

Yes, if we go from imposts to tailles

193. The optimal tax to which lawmakers aspire is that which we already know does not burden, does not weigh down, does not take away anything, indeed increases taxpayers' wealth. And this cannot be called an impost. Conversely, a real impost is that which really burdens, takes away, imposes a levy, is that taken by the state which takes away a lot and gives little back to citizens. And this we shall call 'taille'.

194. In modern times men hardly know any longer what a real taille is. It is necessary to go back to the writers of the seventeenth and eighteenth centuries to read a living page on this subject.

A hundred years before the revolution, La Bruyère described French peasants thus:

> One sees certain wild animals black, livid, and burned by the sun, male and female, bound to the soil, which they dig and turn over with indomitable perseverance. They have something like an articulate voice, and when they stand upright, they show a human face and, in truth, they are men. They retire at night into dens, where they live on black bread, water and roots. Since they save other men the toil of ploughing, sowing and harvesting, they deserve not to lack of the bread they have sown.

Of the causes that led Saint-Simon to say of the greatest European king that he was also the king of the destitute, one is highlighted by Alexis de Tocqueville: the arbitrary uncertainty of taxes.

> The tax-gatherer who has the misfortune to allocate the taille among the taxpayers of his commune is at the same time tyrant and martyr. Since he is responsible with all his fortune for the sum assigned to the commune, everyone avoids the ruinous job and everyone is forced to do it in turn. 'This service', writes Turgot, 'is the despair and almost always the ruin of those obliged to perform it; all families in easy circumstances in a village are thus successively reduced to want.' Reduced to ruin himself, he holds the ruin of all the others in his hands. 'The preference for his relations,' says the provincial assembly of Haute-Guyenne in 1772, 'for friends and for neighbours, the hate, the desire for revenge against enemies, the need for a protector, the fear of offending a well-to-do citizen who provides work struggle in his breast with the sense of justice'. Terror takes every sense of pity from the tax-gatherer. In some parishes the tax-gatherer does not go about unless accompanied by soldiers and bailiffs. No taxpayer pays, however, unless the soldiers have not first lodged in his house. The peasant waiting, like an ass, to be beaten before paying is shrewd. 'To flee violent and arbitrary taxes, as late as the eighteenth century the French peasant acts as the Jew of the Middle Ages. He shows himself to be poor in appearance, even if by chance he isn't really. For good reason external prosperity frightens him. In its report for 1761 the agricultural association of Maine narrates that it had toyed for a moment with the idea of distributing cattle as a reward and encouragement. It was dissuaded from doing so by the thought of the painful consequences that spiteful

jealousy might have brought down on those rewarded, subject to the oppression of increased taxes in the years that followed.'[4]

The taxpayer, fearing to see his taxes increased in the future if he were to pay punctually, prefers to bear the cost of forced execution rather than show himself capable of paying.

> 'Every one subject to the taille', says the provincial assembly of Berry, 'dreads to expose his riches; he avoids any display of these in his furniture, in his dress, in his food, and in everything open to the view of others'. M. de Choiseul-Gouffier desired, at his own expense, to roof his peasants' houses, liable to take fire, with tiles. They thanked him for his kindness but begged him to leave the huts as they were, telling him that the tax-gatherers would have increased the taille if they were covered with tiles instead of thatch. If I earned any more, exclaims a peasant, it would be for the collector.[5]

Le Pesant de Boisguilbert, a century before the revolution, had clearly seen the causes of the evil. The ruin of France is mainly due

> to the uncertainty of the taille, the rate of which, being completely uncertain, has only this certainty: the poorer one is, the more one pays ... The lesser harm of the taille for the populace is having to pay something to the king; it is so perfect that it ruins both those who are crushed by the burden and fall and those who succeed in avoiding it ... The number of those who can be subjected to the taille decreases every day; and today thirty have to pay what yesterday was paid by sixty ... Since it is necessary to avoid any show of wealth, one does not dare, for fear of paying double the tax, possess, even when one could, the necessary cattle without which the land is not enriched, as would nonetheless be the desire of those who know that such enrichment is the soul of agriculture and the cultivation of crops.[6]

195. Arbitrariness had produced the same effects in Italy. We can read the solemn pages of the 'Report on the present state of the universal census (registration in the cadastre) of the Duchy of Milan in the month of May of the year 1750', the wisest document that the history of finance has produced in Italy and outside Italy.

In contrast with the dictum of Roman law: '*Is vero, qui agrum in alia civitate habet, in ea civitate profiteri debet, in qua ager est; agri enim tributum in ea civitate debet levare, in cuius territorio possidetur*';* that is, against the rule of universal taxation of things in the place where they are situated, the privileged classes waged a long war, victorious for them, disastrous for the public good.

---

*A man who possesses land in another community must declare it in the community in which it is situated. For land tax must relieve that community in whose territory it is owned.

> The law of the territory, a clear and immutable law, cannot be abandoned without falling into a thousand absurdities and a sea of uncertainties, because wishing to describe and census goods, not according to the rule of the place where they have always been and will be in eternity, but according to any other rule founded on the personal qualities of the owner, every rule will be upset by the daily changes that follow in these personal qualities and in the transfer of the goods from one name to another, so that the cadastre is permanently vacillating and communities are deprived of that natural wealth from which they must receive help to meet their needs.
>
> (p.30)

196. Endless disputes arose in Lombardy between 1559 and 1718 owing to the arbitrariness of the criterion of personal taxation: townsmen against countrymen, countrymen against townsmen; towns that, with the pretext of taxing all the income of their inhabitants, no matter from what source obtained, stole, as far as taxes were concerned, the land from villages; rural communes, which, in order to survive the consequences of depopulation, due in turn to oppressive and arbitrary taxes, invented imaginary taxpayers and, through them, tormented the real living ones. I don't know whether the financial literature contains a page that can be compared with this classic one that Pompeo Neri dictated in the report on the Milanese census:

> Since such arbitrary practices [in the allocation of taxes on goods, on persons and on mouths that at the time were variously distinguished one from the other] have for the most part tended to increase the burden on persons, to the point where in some places, partly owing to the harshness of the taxes and partly because of other calamities, depopulation followed, so that to make good the loss due to the fugitives a remedy was invented that certainly has never served to populate any village and this was to imagine that there should be people where there were none and that the rods of land that normally served for the work and maintenance of one head, that is of the head of a family, should constitute a fictitious head, that was known as a dead head, obliged to pay what in the communal annual taxes was payable by a living head and two living mouths. And the owners of the land were made responsible for such payment on behalf of the dead head, so that not only did they find it abandoned by the workers but also found it fecundated by this new tax, which it was believed would encourage the landowners to take greater care of their workers and remedy the avarice of some, who, to avoid the personal tax, had their lands cultivated by workers from elsewhere; but when workers abandon the land, because of military incursions or exorbitant taxes, as has happened more than once in this domain, experience has taught us that the village is not repopulated by means of dead heads and that if they are not given something to live on the living heads do not come back.
>
> (pp.45–6)

197. Arbitrariness wrecked the whole tax system during the Spanish dominion. The prince pressed the state, the state turned to the provinces and these to the communes. As long as the sum required was paid to the exchequer, no one troubled to see how it was allocated and paid.

> The obscure and unequal method of allocation ... makes it possible for the administrators of the community not to reveal in the taxes the true sums corresponding to the particular need, since the members of the community, unable to know with certainty the amount of their quota, cannot know whether they have been overburdened and must blindly trust their administrators ... The joint obligation of the community to pay for the insolvent, which cannot be done without adding their burden to that of the solvent, gives administrators the pretext to impose such surtaxes as they like, a pretext that cannot be disputed by the taxpayers because they can complain that the burden is heavy but can never produce the figures to show it is unfair, and it cannot be disputed by those above them, to whom they deliver the money, because the justification of the extra burden is too difficult and because it is deemed prudent and just to facilitate those who bring in the money in every way, so that they can put it together without difficulty.
>
> (pp.72–3)

Quotas, solidarity, allocation by interested parties are words that are becoming fashionable again. Do those who are bringing them out remember the dark shadows that accompanied them in the past? The tax assessor, a state official, is perhaps an imperfect substitute for the magistrate. Together with the soul of the judge, he has the old soul of the representative of the royal tax authorities, and he not only defends his own wealth against the assailants but wishes at all costs and by any means to increase it at the expense of private individuals. Deep down in the soul of the tax assessor there lives, however, awareness of the public interest and is born the germ of the impartiality with which the judge allocates what is due to the state and what is due to the individual. It is necessary to strengthen the good germs and make them grow; it is necessary to assign the ultimate settlement of all tax disputes, *de facto* and *de jure*, to an independent magistrate, and it is necessary that he, having nothing to fear from men and nothing to gain and knowing that he has to answer for his work only to his conscience and to God, feels himself, and is, truly independent. To assign to colleagues, companions, even if members of an association, the task – jealously reserved to the father, the head, the king and by them delegated to the magistrate, who, although incarnating them, is required to obey their commands only when they are handed down in accordance with the law – of allocating taxes would be to go back hundreds of years, to abandon the scales of justice in the hands of the strong and the cunning, to the great misfortune of the weak and the honest.

198. Don Vincenzo De Miro, chairman of the first commission of the census, chose 80 communes at random, ten for each of the eight provinces of the state, and calculated the amount of the 'royal' tax burden, assuming that three-quarters fell on property and one-quarter on persons.

Amazing inequalities were found. One scudo of capital value of land and other cadastral goods appeared subject to a tax that varied enormously in the same province and even more so between different provinces. It was found that in the countryside around Milan the land of the least heavily taxed commune paid on average only 8 denari and 5 punti per scudo, whereas that of the most heavily taxed commune paid 2 soldi, 5 denari and 3 punti, four times as much; in the countryside around Cremona the lightest burden was 6 denari and 5 punti and the heaviest 4 soldi, 7 denari and 9 punti, with a difference of more than one to eight; and in the entire state of Milan the least heavily taxed commune of the 80 chosen at random paid only 1 denaro and 9 punti, whereas the most heavily taxed was weighed down by a tax of 13 soldi, 5 denari and 1 punto for each scudo of estimated value, more than 92 times the lightest burden.

Inequalities on just as large a scale were also found for the 'personal tax burden'; they can be summarized by saying that the average head of the least heavily taxed commune paid 13 soldi, 11 denari and 1 punto, whereas the average head of the most heavily taxed commune paid 36 lire and 9 punti, 51 times as much.

Prudently, De Miro notes that 'The disproportions and inequalities found in these eighty communes also occur in all the others communes of the state and in many there will be a greater disparity than that found in those referred to above' (p.49). How could the inequalities be less, in light of the summary attempted below of the description that, with the indignant soul of a jurist, De Miro gave of the confusion and obscurity surrounding the methods for allocating taxes?

Mouths and heads; mouths and half-mouths; halves and quarters of heads of women and the halt and the blind; living, dead and counterfeit heads; heads of husbandmen and heads of sharecroppers' eighth part; heads distinguished according to Holy Communion or marriage; heads of families, of married men, of bachelors, of widows; civil, ecclesiastic and forensic rods; points of rods, men and hearths. This is the language used in the collections of Milanese proclamations designed to achieve the 'fair' allocation of taxes. After making the calculations and reducing the results to simple units of account, poll and scudo of estimated value, it turns out that Don Vincenzo De Miro found inequalities of up to 1 to 51 for poll taxes and of up to 1 to 92 for property taxes. Are we really sure that with today's highly acclaimed systems, improved to the *n*th degree, we have not arrived, always in deference to the goddess Justice, at inequalities that are much more serious and inexplicable than those that amazed the jurist of the eighteenth century?

199. Consequently, the cry of all the writers on finance in the seventeenth and eighteenth centuries was for certainty more than justice. Justice was desired above all to protect peoples against the harm wrought by arbitrariness. Adam Smith, in his second maxim with regard to taxes, summarized, with his customary conciseness, the experience of centuries in just a few sentences:

> The tax which each individual is bound to pay ought to be certain, and not arbitrary. The time of payment, the manner of payment, the quantity to be paid, ought all to be clear and plain to the contributor, and to every other person. Where it is otherwise, every person subject to the tax is put more or less in the power of the tax-gatherer, who can either aggravate the tax upon any obnoxious contributor, or extort, by the terror of such aggravation, some present or perequisite to himself. The uncertainty of taxation encourages the insolence and favours the corruption of an order of men who are naturally unpopular, even where they are neither insolent nor corrupt. The certainty of what each individual ought to pay is, in taxation, a matter of so great importance that a very considerable degree of inequality, it appears, I believe, from the experience of all nations, is not near so great an evil as a very small degree of uncertainty.
>
> (*The Wealth of Nations*, 5, II, 2, II)

The nineteenth century, and perhaps even more the twentieth, forgot that lesson and chased after the myth of absolute justice. For most of the way justice and certainty do not conflict; indeed, the one promotes the other, since fair taxes can be collected more easily, with less resistance on the part of taxpayers, than unfair taxes. The point is nonetheless reached where the progressive search for justice oversteps the mark and becomes incompatible with certainty. Justice in the distribution of taxes is measured by the rough-and-ready scales of the eye and the hand, not with the delicate scales of the goldsmith. When lawmakers attempt to use fine scales, it is necessary to remind them of Adam Smith's solemn conclusion: 'a very considerable degree of inequality, it appears, I believe, from the experience of all nations, is not near so great an evil as a very small degree of uncertainty'. Uncertainty destroys the tax base. The command *pereat mundus, sed fiat justitia** is of no help here where the aim of justice is to keep the earthly city alive through taxation.

* Let the world perish, but justice must be done.

Part IV
European Economic Integration

17
Why we need a European Economic Federation*

The absurd anachronism of the economic sovereignty of modern states

Alongside the tenacity with which peoples, small and large, yearn to conserve and perfect their own spiritual, cultural and political autonomy, we have the opposite tendency of the economy towards unity, not merely of large areas, but of the entire world. Not just small states but large ones too have become economically anachronistic and absurd. The modern states, those of 1914 and 1939, are just as absurd today as were the many communal republics of central and northern Italy at the end of fourteenth century, or the small Italian principalities at the close of the fifteenth century, or the several tiny states into which Italy was fragmented in 1859. In the past, roads, gunpowder, the discovery of America, the growth in literary and epistolary communications had rendered obvious the incongruence of closed borders between city and city, principality and principality, state and state. People yearned to move about freely, to contract and trade unhindered; they could no longer remain shut inside the old, cramped borders. A formula for mediation between small homelands and great territories was not found and the small homelands were submerged. In his large volume on the question of Italian unity, [Raffaele] Ciasca gathered thousands of eyewitness accounts of the fervour with which, between 1800 and 1859, the needs pushing toward Italian unification were expounded, debated and championed. Today, someone with equal desire and patience could gather analogous testimony about the causes that are pushing towards the economic unification of the world. Let us recall, in a quick list, the main ones:

---

*First published as sections IV, V and VI of Movimento Liberale Italiano, *Per una federazione economica europea* [Rome: without publisher] 1 September 1943. Republished in *La guerra e l'unità europea*, 2nd edn (Milan: Edizioni di Comunità, 1948).

(a) the invention of railways, navigation without sails, and aeronautics, which has eliminated distances and brought faraway lands and peoples into contact with one another;
(b) the spread of automobile transportation, which has eliminated the connection between rapid transport and costly and limited fixed installations, making the former possible wherever there are roads or thoroughfares;
(c) the invention of the telegraph and the telephone, now rendered partially independent of the materiality of wires and cables;
(d) the invention of the radio, which makes it possible for people and peoples to contact each other instantaneously, notwithstanding the limits of borders and political prohibitions.

If the governments of states endowed with absolute sovereignty had not been assiduous in nullifying the advantages of low-cost land and maritime transportation by customs duties, prohibitions on imports and exports, quotas, foreign exchange monopolies, bilateral clearing arrangements between states; if governments, after building ports and railways, after driving tunnels through the Alps at the cost of billions, did not exert themselves daily in the imposition of all kinds of limitations on the use of ports and railways and mountain tunnels; if governments, after allowing and promoting postal, telephonic and telegraphic exchanges, did not do their utmost, by the jealous control of the same and the irksome difficulties of passports and visas, to impede people from enjoying the means of communication which human ingenuity has devised; if governments, by limitations and prohibitions on immigration and emigration, did not prevent people from moving about as suggested by their advantage, the world would be a single market today and people and goods would go from one point on the globe to another, allowing everyone to enjoy the best opportunities for work and production available on earth, in the places best indicated by economic advantage.

The tragic choice: destructive war or the economic unification of the world

In the conflict between technology, which is unifying the world economically, and the artifices with which governments are attempting to break up that unity, who will the victory go to? To the truth and reality given by technology, which eliminates mountains, crosses seas, shortens distances, or to governmental artifice, which is opposed to economic progress?

The answer does not appear to be in doubt. Victory will go to technology and not to artifice. If men of state fail to find the formula for mediation between small, spiritual homelands and the unity of the economic world, the former, and not the latter, will be destroyed.

In 1914 and 1939 Wilhelm II and Hitler were the instruments of historical necessity. The economic world moves towards unification; and if the artificial, delaying obstacles interposed by the governments of the small modern states – all states, even the largest ones, are small in the face of technical and economic forces that in a second allow men to communicate, from Rome to Tokyo, from Washington to London, from Sydney to San Francisco, from Cape Town to Stockholm – are not removed through voluntary agreements, they will be abolished by rivers of blood to the profit of whatever nation invents and puts to use the means of subjugating the others. The wars of 1914–18 and 1939–194(?) are the tragic manifestation of the historical necessity of world unification.

The attempt, having failed in 1914, does not appear to have much probability of success this time. Spiritual needs, which desire that the small states be kept alive and that the most varied species of civilization, religion, language, literature and customs be exalted, have tenaciously resisted material forces, which would like to reunite under one command first Europe and then, by logical necessity, the entire world. The small states will survive intact today's grandiose struggle; but by means of how much destruction of material and moral values, how much bloodshed?

Neither must we delude ourselves that the attempt will not be renewed. As long as the dispute has not been settled, it will loom menacingly over the world and render ineffectual mankind's aspiration to a higher material and spiritual life. Wilhelm II and Hitler have posed a question that will have to be resolved. In 20 or 30 years, as soon as the horrors of the present war have become a memory that has not been lived by the new generations, who will then be between 20 and 40 years old, someone is bound to try again. If that attempt also fails, despite the deaths of tens of millions of people and the destruction of glorious historical cities or even entire continents, it will be repeated, as many times as it takes, with the extermination of modern civilization, until the unification of the world has been achieved under the heel of some dominant nation. Those who talk today of the Bolshevik threat, as they did yesterday of the yellow peril, have shut their eyes to this threat, which is not hypothetical but a necessary consequence of manifest and powerful causes.

The way out: not Leagues of Nations but economic federation

Neither must we hope to save the world with words alone, with agreements, with new leagues of nations. Those who fought against and denied the viability of the League of Nations from its foundation as early as 1918 were arguing from historical experience, from the failure of all the leagues of nations attempted in the past, from the Hellenic Amphictyonic league to the Holy Roman Empire, from the American confederation of 1776 to the Holy Alliance. Leagues of nations always failed miserably:

(a) because they did not have their own revenues, but were dependent on financial contributions from the member states;
(b) because they did not have their own army, but were dependent on armed contingents dispatched voluntarily by the allied states against the aggressor state;
(c) because they did not have their own legislative body and their own executive authority, but were dependent on the unanimous vote of the member states.

A political body that is born impotent cannot live and is the cause of disputes and tinder for wars. The common will is easily scoffed at by the lawless bully who knows that the others will never agree to put him back in line. The impotence of the common will is an encouragement to offence and war. The latter is better impeded, in the presence of empty shells of impotent unions, by partial accords among the few that, feeling themselves threatened, join together to oppose force with force, threat with threat. Much better the old European balance of the Triple Alliance and the Triple Entente than the union of all states rendered powerless by the *liberum veto* of each one.

If we wish to rid ourselves of the nightmare of the total extermination of humanity and the ruin of civilization, we must therefore try another way. To safeguard the spiritual values of small national states, we must resolutely recognize that small economic markets shut inside the political borders of individual states are an anachronism and must be abolished. To safeguard the spiritual we must renounce our jealousy of the material. I say the *jealousy* of the material and not the material itself, which on the contrary will be increased and enhanced by our renunciation. What evil will we suffer if we are able to create an organization that is able to guarantee mankind:

(a) that mountain tunnels and railways and ports and ships and aeroplanes and maritime canals really serve to transport unlimited quantities of goods and people at the lowest possible cost?
(b) that the postal, telegraph, and telephone services help to put people rapidly and instantaneously in contact with one another without the hindrance of police and censorship?
(c) that the radio will become an instrument for the free dissemination of truth, and of competing principles to the advantage of all and not for stuffing minds with self-glorification and contempt for others?
(d) that it will be possible to implement the unification of systems of weights and measures, of currencies, of industrial and literary property that will facilitate the exchange of goods and ideas and new inventions?

Not evil but great good will follow for the wealth and economic power of individual states from the renunciation of narrow-minded selfishness and particularistic material jealousies.

It is worth repeating the principle that what is involved here is unifying some economic matters, not renouncing the political independence of individual states. It would be premature and damaging to put on the table today the question of the suppression of individual states in favour of a federation, whether small or large, European or worldwide. Our spirits are not ready for that; and many, among whom is the compiler of the present memorandum, would be decidedly averse to it. The starting point is exactly the opposite: states must renounce their sovereignty over some well-defined and enumerated economic matters in order to safeguard their sovereignty over what is most precious to them, over matters that really touch the spiritual, moral, social and civil life of their peoples. The states must renounce not to lower themselves but to raise themselves even higher.

18
The Economic Tasks of the Federation*

Avec le principe sacré de la liberté du commerce, tous les prétendus intérêts du commerce disparaissent. Les prétendus intérêts de posséder plus ou moins de territoire s'évanouissent par ce principe, que le territoire n'appartient point aux nations, mais aux individus; que la question de savoir si tel canton, tel village doit appartenir à telle province, à tel Etat, ne doit être décidée que par l'intérêt qu'ont les habitants del tel canton, de tel village, de se rassembler pour leurs affaires dans le lieu où il leur est le plus commode d'aller.[†]

Turgot

1. Need for an exclusive list of tasks

From an economic point of view, European federation means the assignment to the federal authority of some economic tasks defined on an exclusive basis in the document constituting the federation, defined, that is, in such a way that the federal authority has the power to attend only to the tasks included in the list, all the other tasks not on the list remaining

*First published, under the pseudonym *Junius*, as part one of 'I problemi economici della federazione europea', in *L'Italia e il secondo risorgimento*, Lugano, year I, Nos 18–19–20, 26 August, 2 September and 9 September 1944. Republished in the collection *La Guerra e l'unità europea*, 2nd edn (Milan: Edizioni di Comunità, 1948).

† Thanks to the sacred principle of freedom of trade, all pretended interests of commerce disappear. The pretended interests to control more or fewer territories vanishes thanks to this principle: that territories do not belong to nations but to individuals, that the question to know whether such a canton or such a village shall belong to such a province or to such a state, must not be decided otherwise than by the interests of the people of the said canton or village. Let them meet for their own business in the place which is more convenient for them to go.

within the competence of the individual federated states. It is useful, therefore, with a view to attenuating the suspicions and fears of large bodies of opinion or of strong interest groups, to reduce the number of tasks assigned to the federation at the beginning to the indispensable minimum. With time, experience and growing popular consensus will allow the list of tasks to be expanded, in accordance with the formalities prescribed for the approval of amendments to the federal constitution; formalities which will certainly not be easy to observe: a special majority, greater than half the votes of the two chambers of the federal parliament, a special majority of the federated states expressed through an *ad hoc* procedure. If the obstacles to approval of the amendments are overcome, this will be because the expansion of the tasks of the federal authority will have become part of the consciousness of the great majority of the citizens of the federation and of most of the federated states, persuaded of the benefits obtained in the light of experience. It is fitting, therefore, that the initial scope be restricted to those tasks without whose performance the federation would be practically non-existent.

2. Postal, telegraph and telephone services, international transportation by rail, sea and air and on canals and rivers: the question of waterpower?

Some of these tasks are of a technical nature and have already been internationalized or, where they have not, the absence of internationalization indicates, with the force of the intuitively obvious, how anachronistic is the persistence of individual sovereign states in the contemporary world: postal, telegraph and telephone services, the regulation of cross-border transportation by rail, by navigable rivers and canals, by sea and by air. A federal postal, telegraph and telephone administration can obviously manage these services, of a clearly technical nature, much more economically and in a much more effective way than separate administrations can. And it is also clear how the management of the Alpine lakes, of large rivers such as the Danube, the Rhône, the Elbe, the Rhine and, by way of the Ticino, the Po, can be better regulated by a federal authority, able to take account of all the special interests and carry out the necessary public works in the most suitable places, than by individual states that are the jealous custodians of local interests not always coincident with the general good. The political problems connected with the management of straits and the air space over national territories are much more easily solved at federal level than through wrangling among individual sovereign states.

One controversial issue is likely to be whether the regulation of waterpower should be a federal matter; and it seems obvious that the regulation of waterpower deriving from or closely related to the management of cross-border lakes and rivers must be assigned to the federal authority. For other sources of waterpower, opinions may be in discord, the advantages inherent in the possibility of fully utilizing, with appropriate exchanges, waterpower having its origin in different countries and different periods of seasonal peaks and troughs being outweighed for some by the desirability of not overly offending the feelings about priorities and property of the populations in which the waterpower is located. And the latter therefore argue that it is better, in order to avoid local opposition, to postpone the federalization of waterpower, apart from the exception mentioned above, to some future time.

3. Money and monetary surrogates; advantages of transfer to the federation

Devolution to the federation of the regulation of money and money surrogates appears to be uncontroversial. The current disorder of monetary units in all the countries of the world, the difficulties for trade deriving from the uncertainty of exchange rates between one country and another and even more from the impossibility of carrying out such exchanges have opened everyone's eyes to the advantages that would derive from the adoption of a single monetary unit throughout the territory of the federation. If, in all of Europe or at least in the federated Europe, we were to think and calculate and fix the prices of goods and services in, for example, to adopt a neutral term, gold lire, how much simpler, how much easier it would be to make payments, transfer funds and settle balances!

If the federal authority intended to return to the gold standard, that would mean the authority arrogating to itself the right to adopt the single new gold monetary unit and the necessary fractional units of silver, nickel and copper for the payment of minor items, and the right to institute a single central bank or bank of issue charged with issuing banknotes convertible on demand into gold. If it did not intend to return to the gold standard, the federal authority, while again reserving to itself the right to mint gold coins, would still have the exclusive right to mint fractional coins in silver, nickel and copper and to issue banknotes of the central bank expressed in the new currency unit, the gold lira let's say. In other words, the right of individual federated states to coin their own money with their own denominations, weights and names, and to institute central banks with the independent right to issue banknotes would be abolished. The only exception that might be allowed would be for the mint or the central bank, possibly through local branches, to stamp coins with different designs for each state, but with uniform denominations, weights and names. It would be quite clear that this diversity was of a purely sentimental nature, that the notes and variously designed coins would be issued exclusively by the federal authority, in the quantity this and not the individual states fixed, and would all have to be mutually interchangeable with no obstacles whatsoever.

The advantage of the system would lie not only in the calculation and convenience of cross-border payments and transactions. Although very considerable, that advantage would be small compared to another, much greater one: the abolition of the sovereignty of individual states in monetary matters. Those who recall the misuse that many states made and make of the right to print money can have no doubt of the urgent need to deprive them of this right. It has boiled down in substance to the right to falsify money (Dante would have put all of these modern rulers of states and banks into his inferno, together with Master Adam), that is to the right to impose the worst of all taxes on peoples, the worst because unperceived, weighing much more on the poor than the wealthy, a source of enrichment for a few and of impoverishment for most, the yeast of malcontent for each social class against all the other classes and of social disorder. The devaluation of the Italian lira and the German mark, which ruined the middle classes and fomented malcontent among the working classes, was one of the causes that gave rise to the bands of unemployed intellectuals and ruffians who handed power to the dictators. If the European federation makes it impossible for individual federated states to pay for public works by printing more banknotes, and forces them to raise the necessary funds solely with taxes and voluntary loans, it will have accomplished, by that alone, a great feat. An achievement of healthy and effective democracy, because the rulers of the federated states will no longer be able to deceive their peoples with the mirage of works completed without cost thanks to the miracle of banknotes, but will have to demonstrate that they provide citizens with real services to obtain acceptance for new taxes or credit for new loans.

4. Concerning certain theoretical doubts about federal monetary management

The transfer to the federation of the exclusive right to mint coins and issue notes will not by itself achieve the miracle of ensuring the peoples have sound money. Miracles never happen in economic matters. But the possibility of falsifying the monetary unit diminishes with the decrease in the probability of wars and violent social upheavals; it therefore diminishes in a federal system, which removes the causes of such events or at least makes them less powerful. The great publicity given to the debates in federal assemblies, the opposition of regional interests, and the vigilant oversight of the representatives of the individual states all contribute to the same result.

In the face of which some doubts must fall; particularly those advanced by a group of mainly English theorists, of whom the best known and most representative is Lord Keynes, and which it is not the place here to discuss in detail. In short, these theorists say that, at certain times, especially during a crisis, it may be advantageous for an individual state to devalue its currency (variable foreign exchange rates) and keep domestic prices unchanged rather than maintaining the value of the currency (constant foreign exchange rates) and leaving domestic prices to fall. It is said that the first method is softer and blander than the second, because if nominal domestic prices do not fall it is not necessary for nominal wages to fall. Nothing changes in the substance of things since it is merely a question of two different methods of obviating or limiting the damage in times of crisis. As Robbins has well said, it is not necessary for federalists to take a position on such a delicate and difficult matter. If, as it must be, the management of monetary policy is left to the federal authority, this will be able, in particularly serious cases, to resolve to make special issues of banknotes or to enlarge the availability of central bank credit only in the country where such a cure appears likely to be beneficial and, in that case, it will also be able to establish special exchange rates between banknotes whose circulation is limited to a single state and those in general circulation. But this doubt is noted only for the sake of completeness, it being practically certain that in a large federal state such a method of dealing with crises will undoubtedly appear inadvisable compared with other more effective ones, and that the crises themselves will be less serious than they are in a world divided and afflicted by international jealousies.

5. On the taxes to be assigned to the federation; customs duties and excise taxes; exclusion of state contributions and federal surtaxes on state taxes; the federal tax on total net income; exclusion of a federal inheritance tax

There is much more uncertainty concerning the assignment to the federation of the right to levy taxes. The rule that the federation must have only those powers that are explicitly assigned to it in the constitutional charter must be approved with regard to this matter as well. While it is easy to agree on the principle that the federation must be able to levy only certain listed taxes and no others, it is not as easy to answer the question: which taxes should be listed? With regard to one group there is no doubt: since, as will shortly be seen, the federation has sole authority to regulate international trade, so, as a logical consequence, only the federation can exact customs duties on goods imported from abroad within the new enlarged customs line and possibly those rare exit duties on goods exported abroad and any of those still rarer transit duties which are kept or introduced. On a par with customs duties, equal recognition must be given to all rights over statistical records, registries, railway, port, river and air surtaxes imposed on the transportation of goods from one state to another and abroad, which can be used to mask hindrances to cross-border trade. To the federation alone belongs the authority to regulate this matter with duties and taxes. By equally logical inference, the federation alone has the right to establish taxes on the domestic production or manufacture of goods (excise taxes). Customs duties on foreign goods and excise taxes are like Siamese twins, so that where the former are present the latter inevitably appear. If a customs duty of L1,000 per quintal is applied to sugar imported from abroad, an equal excise tax must be applied to sugar made domestically; otherwise, if the excise tax were only L800, no-one would buy foreign sugar and the state would lose the revenue from the higher duty; and if the excise tax were L1,200, no-one would make sugar domestically because everyone would buy foreign sugar. So the federation will be able to establish, as it wishes, excise taxes of L1,000, L800 or L1,200 but it alone and not the federated states must be the master of decisions in this field, unless we want each of the federated states arbitrarily to nullify the effects of the economic policy decided by the federation.

Although it has been shown that revenues from customs and excise taxes were sufficient in the past to support the needs of some federations (the United States of America and the Swiss Confederation), it has to be acknowledged that they no longer suffice today and that there are no grounds for affirming that they must suffice in a future European federation. One method it appears necessary to exclude is that of contributions from the federated states, measured so as to make up for the shortfall between federal expenditure and the yield from customs duties and excise taxes. The experience of the Australian federation and that which, in analogous matters, can be recalled concerning relationships between state, communes and provinces in the Kingdom of the Two Sicilies and Tuscany, demonstrate the difficulty of adequately providing for federal needs in this way without fomenting discontent and resistance in the federated states. And neither does it appear advisable to give the federation the right to superimpose, in tenths or hundredths, surcharges on state taxes, because the distribution of taxes on *European* citizens would vary from state to state according to the weight of the tax burden and the assessment methods used in the individual states. In one country, where the state tax system is highly progressive, the rich would pay more and modest taxpayers less for a federal public service, while in another, where state taxes are proportional or mildly progressive, the rich would contribute less and the modest more for the same service, offending the principle of equality among all the citizens of the federation.

In the end, the solution which imposed itself in the largest federations (USA) and which it would be well to adopt from the outset in the European federation, appears to be the assignment to the latter of the right to establish, in competition or contemporaneously with the individual federated states, its own tax on the most generalized possible basis, which nearly universal consensus identifies as a tax on the total net income of citizens. Nothing bad will happen if the federation and the individual states, in adopting the same tributary instrument, apply it with different criteria with respect to its graduation (progressivity), the minimum amounts exempt, the deductions for family expenses, insurance and debt, and the assessment methods. The varied experience that will thus be gained and emulation in the search for and assessment of taxable items will not fail to produce the good effect of gradually indicating to the federation and to the federated states the best common road to follow.

Given the elasticity and huge base of the tax on income, it does not seem advisable to give the federation the right to collect other taxes; not even those on inheritances, which should be reserved to the states, so tight are the bonds tying them to family law and the law of inheritance, which each state will continue to regulate according to its own historical traditions and social ideals.

6. Federal regulation of the transportation of goods and persons; its double content

More lively doubts have been raised concerning the implementation of the fundamental postulate: to the federation alone belongs the regulation of the movement of persons and goods between one federated state and another and between the federation and foreign countries. This postulate contains two affirmations. In the first place, the federation alone has the right to conclude trade, navigation and emigration treaties with foreign countries. In the second place, individual federated states are prohibited from imposing any restrictions on the cross-border movement of persons and goods through prohibitions on immigration, restrictions on domicile and residence for citizens belonging to another of the federated states, by entry, exit or transit duties, by discriminatory tariffs on rail, river, lake, maritime or automobile traffic, by industrial monopolies, tax stamps, permits, demurrages, licences, medical examinations and limitations with regard to infectious diseases and all other pretexts of whatever kind. The entire question of the cross-border movement of persons and goods is to be regulated solely by the federal authority.

7. Assignment to the federal authority of foreign trade; federation is synonymous with a single customs territory

There is no substantial controversy on the first point. Free-traders and protectionists agree that whatever system is deemed most advantageous for the federated Europe as a whole to adopt towards the rest of the world must be decided by the federal parliament and not by the parliaments of the individual states. The federal parliament must have the authority to decide whether Europe should surround itself with high customs barriers against imports from Russia, the United States, Asian and South American countries and Australia or whether it should adopt a policy of moderate protection or customs duties which are purely fiscal. The federal parliament alone will have to decide what customs policy to adopt in relation to colonies belonging to the individual states or the federation. To the federal parliament alone belongs the decision as to whether emigration and immigration will be free or subject to quotas; and which treaties are to be stipulated with countries of destination. Is the federal territory perhaps not one and one alone? Are customs duties not revenues reserved to the federal treasury? The only effect of a variation in duties along the various sections of the international frontier would be to make goods flow to ports with the lowest duties, from which they would then radiate throughout the federal territory. The necessity of a single federal customs system is so evident that no controversy has ever arisen concerning it. First and foremost, federation means a customs league, a single customs territory.

8. Prohibition on obstacles to cross-border trade; the obvious necessity thereof to remove a powerful cause of war

The necessity of the second part of the economic postulate, the prohibition on the individual federated states from placing any impediment, under whatever pretext or whatever name, to the cross-border movement of persons and goods within the single federal territory, is just as obvious, but it is precisely this evident necessity that is the greatest obstacle of an economic nature to the federation.

The latter is wanted in order to remove the possibility of wars; and since customs barriers between countries, all other impediments to cross-border trade and the various forms of autarchy are a powerful cause of war, it is necessary that the barriers between one federated state and another be abolished and a territory constituted within which persons and goods can move freely. Switzerland would not be a federation if the canton of Geneva could close in on itself and protect its own *national* industries by establishing customs duties on goods coming from the canton of Vaud or Fribourg or Bern, and if every other canton could do likewise, every canton being a sovereign state, against the goods of all the other cantons. The United States of America would not be a federation if the state of New York could protect its agriculture by prohibiting the introduction of meat coming from the slaughterhouses of Chicago or wheat from the states of the Mid-West; or if each of the states wished to create its own automobile industry and therefore imposed heavy customs duties on automobiles made by Ford, merely because this company has its factories in Detroit, in another state.

It is precisely because a federated Europe means a single customs territory, open, with no impediments apart from the natural ones of distance and the related differences in transportation costs, to the importation of goods coming from any other point of the federated territory, that the suspicions and the doubts and the criticisms are multiplying.

19
The Instruments of the Federal Administration*

A common army

The federation would be an empty name, would amount to a useless and damaging league of nations, if it did not have a force of its own, capable of defending federal territory against external aggressions and preventing wars among its members.

This is certainly the most delicate aspect of the proposed change in the system of states. But all the rest would be in vain if we did not recognize the necessity of a clear division of tasks between state and federation. To put it in terms familiar to Italians, the military police (*carabinieri*) and the police for the maintenance of internal public order would be under the state, while the army, the navy and the air force would be under the federation. Without this clear distinction, whatever might be done would be idle chatter. The federal armed forces should never be composed of state contingents, but would be recruited individually, just as happens today for national armed forces. There would be no Italian, German or French soldiers and their respective commands; but only federal soldiers and officers. Time and practice would resolve questions that now seem very difficult, such as the language of command. Moreover, the solution of the many problems connected with the formation of a federal army would be facilitated by the fact that a single army would not be the sum of today's state armies but would normally be made up of a much smaller number of soldiers. Whereas, in times of peace, 10 independent states keep under arms 10 times 1 million men, for the federation an army of 2 million men would be sufficient, a fifth of the total that would be considered necessary for the sum of the member states.

---

*First published as paragraph VII/2 of Movimento Liberale Italiano, *Per una federazione economica europea* [Rome: without publisher] 1 September 1943. Republished in *La guerra e l'unità europea*, 2nd edn (Milan: Edizioni di Comunità, 1950).

The federal judiciary

The competence of this would obviously be restricted to the matters assigned to the federation. A *supreme court* chosen in accordance with special guarantees and in whose selection member states should have a voice, would decide as to the nullity of laws enacted and acts performed by the federal authority that exceeded the powers explicitly assigned to it.

The federal police

Under which title are included all executive bodies serving to enforce measures regarding federal matters; all other aspects of administration remaining entrusted to the states.

Diplomatic representation

As a logical consequence of the transfer of powers of war and peace and the regulation of commerce, the railways, waterways, postal services, etc., to the federation, the latter should maintain its own diplomatic representation to non-member states. This representation should regard only the matters transferred to the federation and would not imply the dissolution of diplomatic and consular representatives of single states for all other purposes. Time would gradually resolve problems arising from the double nature of international relationships thus established. In doubtful cases it would be wise not to try to resolve at the outset all the problems that logically might arise. Let us allow experience to provide the solution.

Federal legislative and executive bodies

No-one can predict what these bodies will become in half a century or a century. They will have the prestige that they will have been able to acquire through their accomplishments. What is important today is that formal prestige remain with state bodies. The federal authorities must be simple bodies of economic administration, capable of attracting men esteemed above all for their technical competence, not eager to shine in political speeches. To express the idea in concrete terms, federal administrators should resemble the members of the Swiss federal council more than the prime ministers of modern states. Moreover, an appropriate division of labour between the political leadership of the federation and the states would work itself out on its own, reflecting the federation's authority over defined matters, of an economic nature, consolidated services scarcely susceptible to reform; whereas the states would continue to be assigned all other public functions and therefore all those more subject to change and capable of attracting to themselves men endowed with a combative political temperament.

Having said that, it should be noted that historical experience demonstrates that the bodies under discussion, must be, where it is desired that they be vital, composed more or less as follows:

(a) a council of states, in which each state should have an equal number, one or two, of representatives;
(b) a legislative council, to which the citizens of the member states should send their own deputies, one per million or half-million or other suitable number of inhabitants.

The two councils would exercise the federal legislative power; and, in order to be considered such, laws would have to be approved by both councils.

The right to propose laws and the federal administrative power would belong to a federal council (ministers) named by the council of states and the legislative council meeting in joint session. By turns, one of the council members would be designated as president, whose office would therefore lack, a necessary prerequisite, the prestige conferred upon heads of state by popular election or hereditary succession.

The contemporary existence of the two councils, state and legislative, is required, on the one hand, in order to ensure smaller member states against the possible dominance of the larger states, and on the other, to provide a way for the will of the citizens in general, not of the Italian or French or German group, to make itself felt. Through the right to make themselves heard directly by means of their deputies in the legislative council, people would gradually become conscious of the common federal citizenship, perfectly compatible, given their different ends, with the jealous conservation of national citizenship.

Notes

Editors' Introduction

1 Luca Einaudi wrote Sections 1, 2 and 5; Riccardo Faucci wrote Section 4 and Roberto Marchionatti Section 3.

2 For an extensive biography, see R. Faucci, *Einaudi* (Turin: Utet, 1986). For a recent assessment of his impact, see R. Marchionatti 'Luigi Einaudi, economista e liberale', in Centro Studi di Storia dell'Università di Torino, *Maestri dell'Ateneo Torinese dal Settecento al Novecento*, Renata Allio (ed.), (Turin, 2004), pp.61–84.

3 Piero Sraffa (1898–1983), economist, left Italy after a confrontation with Mussolini on the Italian banking system. Fellow of Trinity College, Cambridge, for many years, founder of the neoricardian school and editor of the complete works of David Ricardo. See J. P. Potier, *Piero Sraffa, unorthodox economist, a biographical essay*, (London: Routledge, 1991). See also two essays connecting Einaudi and Sraffa, A. D'Orsi, 'A child of Cultura Positiva: Turin and the education of Piero Sraffa', and N. Naldi, 'Piero Sraffa's early approach to political economy: from the gymnasium to the beginning of his academic career', both in *Piero Sraffa's Political Economy. A Centenary Estimate*, T. Cozzi and R. Marchionatti (eds), (London: Routledge, 2001). Antonio Gramsci (1891–1937), founder of the Italian Communist Party and Marxist theorist, wrote *Quaderni dal carcere*; see A. Gramsci, *Prison notebooks*, J. A. Buttigieg (ed.); Vol. 1, (New York: Columbia University Press, 1992). Piero Gobetti (see also footnote 11), *On Liberal Revolution*, edited and with an introduction by Nadia Urbinati; (New Haven; and London: Yale University Press, 2000). Carlo Rosselli (1899–1937), socialist intellectual and politician, theorist of liberal socialism, one of the founders in exile of the anti-Fascist movement, 'Giustizia e Libertà', murdered in France by the Fascist secret organization *La Cagoule*. See C. Rosselli, *Liberal Socialism*, Nadia Urbinati (ed.), (Princeton: Princeton University Press, 1994). Palmiro Togliatti (1893–1964) succeeded Gramsci as Secretary General of the Communist Party in 1926 and held the position until his death.

4 Giovanni Giolitti (1842–1928) was prime minister in 1893–94 and in 1903–05, 1906–09, 1911–14 and 1920–21 in the years of Italian industrialization. He was open to concessions in favour of moderate Socialists but his use of prefects against the opposition, especially during elections, was considered anti-democratic by some opponents (see G. Salvemini, *Il Ministro della malavita*, Firenze, Edizioni della Voce, 1910). Einaudi also criticized him because he did not achieve a fiscal reform adequate to the needs of growth. Both Einaudi and Salvemini reconsidered their hostility to Giolitti after they had experienced his successors.

5 Einaudi's articles in *The Economist* have been republished in *'From our Italian Correspondent'. Luigi Einaudi's Articles in the Economist, 1908–1946*, Roberto Marchionatti (ed.), two volumes (Florence: Leo S. Olschki, 2000).

6 'Conoscere per deliberare', the opening article in L. Einaudi, *Prediche Inutili*, Turin: Giulio Einaudi Editore, 1956.

7 L. Einaudi, *Dei diversi significati del concetto di liberismo economico e dei suoi rapporti con quello di liberalismo*, in B. Croce and L. Einaudi, *Liberismo e liberalismo*, Paolo Solari (ed.) (Milan and Naples: Ricciardi editore, 1957), pp.124–5.

8 See his economic programme for postwar Italy written in 1943 for the Liberal party, now in L. Einaudi, *Riflessioni di un liberale sulla democrazia* (Olschki editore: Florence, 2001), pp.4–16.
9 First published as 'Che cos'è un mercato' (Locarno, Tip. F.lli Molè, 1944); republished as Chapter 1 of *Lezioni di politica sociale (*Turin, Giulio Einaudi Editore, 1949), under the title 'Lezioni sul mercato'.
10 First published as 'La bellezza della lotta', *Rivoluzione Liberale*, Turin, II, no. 40, 18 December 1923, pp.161–62; republished in L. Einaudi, *Le lotte del lavoro (*Turin, Piero Gobetti Editore, 1924).
11 Piero Gobetti (1901–26) was the most promising young intellectual of Italian progressive liberalism after the First World War. He animated the Italian cultural debate between 1919 and 1926. Gobetti set up his first journal when he was seventeen, the review *Rivoluzione Liberale* when he was 20, and his publishing house at 22, mobilizing Liberal, Socialist and Catholic intellectuals. He died at the age of 24, an anti-Fascist refugee in Paris.
12 The debate was collected and published in Croce and Einaudi, *Liberismo e liberalismo*, Paolo Solari (ed.), (Milan and Naples: Ricciardi editore, 1957). The correspondence between the two men is in Luigi Einaudi and Benedetto Croce, *Carteggio (1902–1953)*, Luigi Firpo (ed.), (Turin: Fondazione Luigi Einaudi, 1988).
13 Benedetto Croce (1866–1952) was a liberal philosopher, historian and literary critic, editor of the journal *La Critica*, Minister of Education before Fascism 1920–1, president of the Liberal party in 1943–7. He was a towering figure in Italian philosophical and historical thought in the first half of the twentieth century and the most prestigious Italian liberal thinker, but followed a more historicist and Hegelian line of thought, of German descent.
14 First published as 'Dei diversi significati del concetto di liberismo economico e dei suoi rapporti con quello di liberalismo' in *La Riforma Sociale*, March–April 1931; republished as 'Liberismo e liberalismo' in various collections of essays in 1933, 1954 and 1957.
15 Schumpeter provides a definition of 'Economic Liberalism' and 'Political Liberalism' close to Einaudi's idea of *liberismo* and *liberalismo*. Economic liberalism indicates an action conducted

> in the spirit of laissez-faire, that is to say, ... the theory that the best way of promoting economic development and general welfare is to remove fetters from the private-enterprise economy and to leave it alone. This is what will be meant in this book by Economic Liberalism... By Political Liberalism, which must be distinguished from economic liberalism ... we mean sponsorship of parliamentary government, freedom to vote and extension of the right to vote, freedom of the press, divorce of secular from spiritual government, trial by jury, and so on, including retrenchment and pacific, though not necessarily pacifist, foreign policy.

See J. A. Schumpeter, *History of Economic Analysis* (1954) (London and New York: Routledge, 1994), p.394.
16 Schumpeter, *History of Economic Analysis*, p.855.
17 See L. Einaudi, 'Teoria e pratica: di alcune storture intorno alla equazione degli scambi', *La Riforma Sociale*, September–October 1931, and 'Della moneta serbatoio di valori e di altri problemi monetari', *Rivista di storia economica*, June 1939.

18 In 'The Theory of Imaginary Money from Charlemagne to the French Revolution', in which Einaudi shows his vast erudition in the field of monetary history, he notes that 'people love certainty'.
19 See his Preface to *Cronache economiche e politiche di un trentennio*, Vol. V (Turin: Einaudi, 1959).
20 Printing Office of the Banca d'Italia, 1947.
21 Attilio Cabiati (1872–1950), Professor of Economics at the University of Genoa, a follower of Pareto, was forced to give up his university posts for his anti-Fascist attitude. See the articles collected in A. Cabiati, *Crisi del liberalismo o errori degli uomini?* (Turin: Einaudi, 1934) and his book *Fisiologia e patologia economica negli scambi della ricchezza tra gli stati* (Turin: Giappichelli, 1937).
22 J. M. Keynes, *The Means to Prosperity* (London: Macmillan, 1933).
23 'Il mio piano non è quello di Keynes', *Riforma Sociale,* March–April 1933.
24 'Riflessioni in disordine sulla crisi', *La Riforma Sociale*, January–February 1931, and 'Nuove riflessioni in disordine sulla crisi', *La Riforma Sociale*, November–December 1931.
25 L. Einaudi, 'Della non novità della crisi presente', *La Riforma Sociale*, January–February 1932.
26 In 'My plan is not Keynes's' Einaudi quotes with admiration an important article published by F. Machlup in *Zeitschrift für Nationalökonomie und Statistik*, and maintains that the Austrian economic journals were at that time better than the British and American ones.
27 L. Einaudi, 'Fondo disponibile di risparmio e lavori pubblici', *La Riforma Sociale*, May–June 1933, and 'Risparmio disponibile, crisi e lavori pubblici', *La Riforma Sociale*, September–October 1933.
28 The public works issue is also discussed by Einaudi in his 1933 review of Keynes's *Essays in Biography*, published in *La Riforma Sociale*.
29 'Debiti', *La Riforma Sociale*, January–February 1934.
30 'Il contenuto economico della lira dopo la riforma monetaria del 21 dicembre 1927', in *La Riforma Sociale*, January–February 1929, and 'Dei metodi per arrivare alla stabilità monetaria e se si possa ancora parlare di crisi di stabilizzazione della lira', in *La Riforma Sociale*, May–June 1930.
31 Respectively: 'Banche con aggettivi', *Corriere della Sera*, 23 August 1924; 'Ci sono troppe banche in Italia?', *La Riforma Sociale*, July–August 1930; 'Di altri scatoloni pseudo-commerciali e pseudo-bancari', *La Riforma Sociale*, January–February 1935.
32 In F. C. Lane and J. C. Riemersma (eds), *Enterprise and Secular Change*. Homewood, Ill.: Richard D. Irwin, 1953. First published as 'La teoria della moneta immaginaria da Carlomagno alla rivoluzione francese', *Rivista di storia economica*, March 1936.
33 'Rumore' was one of Einaudi's last articles in the *Corriere della Sera* (16 June 1960), in which he comments on the interventions of Donato Menichella, Governor of the Bank of Italy.
34 See the recent appraisal of this tradition in D. Fausto and V. De Bonis (eds), The theory of public finance in Italy from the origin to the 1940s, *Il pensiero economico Italiano*, 11, 2003, 1.
35 L. Einaudi, *Studi sugli effetti delle imposte* (Turin: Bocca, 1902).
36 In his own copy of *Studi sugli effetti delle imposte*, F.Y. Edgeworth annotated that Einaudi gave proof of good sense in his treatment of the elasticity of demand for dwellings: see I. Magnani, 'L'economia di Luigi Einaudi, ovvero la virtù del buon

senso', in *Luigi Einaudi: istituzioni, mercato e riforma sociale* (Accademia Nazionale dei Lincei, Rome 18–19 February, 2004).

37 This approach, which linked economic with political theory, was very favourably commented on by the philosopher Giovanni Vailati, a pioneer of the introduction of pragmatism in Italy, and a colleague of Einaudi's at the Cognetti de Martiis Laboratory.

38 L. Einaudi, *Saggi sul risparmio e l'imposta,* 2nd edition, Turin: Giulio Einaudi editore, 1958, p.xiii. The Introduction to 'Contributi alla ricerca dell' "ottima imposta"' and the Conclusion to the volume are in this collection.

39 M. Pantaleoni, 'Contributo alla teoria del riparto delle spese pubbliche', *Rassegna italiana,* 15 October 1883; republished in Franco Volpi (ed.), *Teorie della finanza pubblica* (Milan: Franco Angeli Editore, 1975).

40 *Saggi sul risparmio ...,* p.13.

41 See Pigou's review of Einaudi, *Economic Journal,* June 1913; and Young's review in *American Economic Review,* September 1914. On Ricci and Einaudi, see D. da Empoli, 'La doppia tassazione del risparmio nella polemica di Umberto Ricci con Luigi Einaudi', in P. Bini and A. M. Fusco (eds), *Umberto Ricci (1879–1946) economista militante e uomo combattivo* (Florence: Polistampa, 2004). Griziotti and Einaudi had an interesting correspondence on the double taxation of savings. See L. Firpo (ed.), 'Lettere di Luigi Einaudi a Benvenuto Griziotti (1900–1936)', *Annali della fondazione Luigi Einaudi,* I, 1967.

42 L. Einaudi, *Osservazioni critiche intorno alla teoria dell'ammortamento dell'imposta e teoria delle variazioni nei redditi e nei valori capitali susseguenti all'imposta,* Atti della Reale Accademia delle scienze di Torino (Turin: 1919, vol. 54, carte 1055–1131).

43 Here Einaudi seems to have switched to the opposite position to the one he held in his early studies: a tax which forces landowners to build before the 'right time' is wasteful, since it disturbs the investment projects and therefore the achievement of the 'natural' economic equilibrium (*Saggi sul risparmio...,* p.129).

44 *Saggi sul risparmio ...,* p.181 (my emphasis).

45 L. Einaudi, *La terra e l'imposta,* Annali di economia dell'Università Commerciale Bocconi, 1924.

46 As an economic adviser and, later on, Senator of the Kingdom, Einaudi participated in fiscal reform projects that included not only personal taxation, but also a levy on capital. Both were justified by the difficulties Italy faced after the Second World War. See his *Interventi e relazioni parlamentari,* Vol. 1, (Turin: Fondazione Einaudi, 1980).

47 Note that the welfare approach in taxation, leading to the so-called 'sacrifice principles', was generally contrasted by Einaudi, since it could pave the way to progressive taxation. Cf. L. Einaudi, 'I sommi principi utilitaristici e l'imposta', *La Riforma Sociale,* 1933, pp.474–85. Einaudi reviewed Pigou's *A Study in Public Finance* in very respectful terms, but voiced dissent on crucial points, such as the distinction between 'exhaustive' (consumptive) 'expenditures' and 'transfer expenditures', the effects of public debt and the unearned income increment taxation. See L. Einaudi, 'Cronache e rassegne', *La Riforma Sociale,* 1928, pp.159–87. In a letter, Pigou minimized the importance of the dissension (see Fondazione Luigi Einaudi Archive). On Pigou and Einaudi, see F. Forte, *Introduzione* to the Italian translation of Pigou, *Uno studio sulla finanza pubblica* (Milan: Giuffrè, 1959), pp.xxvi–xxviii.

48 A very simple example is a tribute for the maintenance of an occupation army (*Saggi sul risparmio ...,* p.184).

49 L. Einaudi, 'Contributi fisiocratici alla teoria dell'ottima imposta', *Atti della R. Accademia delle scienze di Torino*, 1932; 'La teoria dell'imposta in Tommaso Hobbes, Sir William Petty e Carlo Bosellini', ibid., 1933. Also in L. Einaudi, *Scritti economici, storici, civili*, R. Romano (ed.) (Milan: Mondadori, 1973).
50 See Faucci, *Einaudi*, pp.269–71.
51 'Ipotesi astratte e ipotesi storiche e dei giudizi di valore nelle scienze economiche', *Atti della R. Accademia delle scienze di Torino*, 1942–43, in *Scritti economici, storici e civili*, p.393.
52 *Contributo alla ricerca dell 'ottima imposta'* (1929), now in *Saggi sul risparmio...*, p.271.
53 Antonio de Viti de Marco, *Principii di economia finanziaria*, (Turin: Giulio Einaudi editore, 1934).
54 *Saggi sul risparmio...*, p.379. In Einaudi's most mature works the subject of 'normal' income gets the upper hand over the subject of the exemption of saving (S. Steve, *Sul concetto di imposta generale*, in *Scritti vari* (Milan: Angeli, 1997), p.118).
55 L. Einaudi, *Miti e paradossi della giustizia tributaria* (Turin: Giulio Einaudi editore, 1938).
56 Today, the extraordinary power of 'persuasion' deriving from control of the mass media gives Puviani's theory a degree of truthfulness that it did not have when it was conceived.
57 See, among others, N. Kaldor, *Papers relating to 'An expenditure Tax'* (London, Allen and Unwin, 1955), favourably commented on by Einaudi in his Preface to *Studi sugli effetti ...*, pp.xxiii–xxx.
58 Junius, 'Il dogma della sovranità e l'idea della Società delle Nazioni', *Corriere della Sera*, 28 December 1918, re-issued in Luigi Einaudi, *La guerra e l'unità europea*, 1st edn. (Milan: Edizioni di Comunità, 1948), p.33.
59 R. N. Coudenhove-Kalergi, *Pan-Europa* (Vienna: Pan-Europa-verlag, 1923). R. N. Coudenhove-Kalergi, *Europe must unite* (Paneuropa Editions: Glarus, 1940).
60 P. Stirk (ed.), *European Unity in Context, the Interwar Period* (London: Pinter, 1989), p.17.
61 J. Pinder, 'Federalism in Britain and Italy: Radicals and the English Liberal Tradition', in P. Stirk (ed.), *European Unity in Context*, pp.201–24.
62 Ernesto Rossi (1897–1967), co-author of the 1941 federalist Manifesto of Ventotene (where he was in prison as an anti-Fascist), had kept alive a debate with Einaudi in the 1930s and encouraged him to start writing about it again as soon as he was released from Fascist prisons. Altiero Spinelli and Ernesto Rossi, *Il Manifesto di Ventotene [Per un'Europa libera e unita, progetto di manifesto]*, 1941. See also C. Cressati, *L'Europa necessaria, il federalismo liberale di Luigi Einaudi*, Turin: Giappichelli, 1992 and U. Morelli, *Contro il mito dello Stato sovrano. Luigi Einaudi e l'unitá europea* (Milan: F. Angeli, 1990).
63 Movimento Liberale Italiano, *Per una federazione economica europea* (Rome, 1943). Republished in *La guerra ...* .Sections IV, V, VI and VII are in this collection.
64 L. Einaudi, 'I problemi economici della federazione europea' (Lugano: Nuove edizioni di Capolago, 1944). Republished in *La guerra ...* . Section I is in this collection.
65 *La guerra ...*, p.38.
66 *La guerra ...*, p.40.
67 Luigi Einaudi, 'La unificazione del mercato europeo', in F. Parri, P. Calamandrei, I.Silone, L. Einaudi and G. Salvemini, *Europa federata* (Milan: Comunità, 1947), p.61.

68 Isolated authors had mentioned the question of a common or single bank of issue, including Joseph Garnier in 1869, Raphael George Levy in 1895 and Hans Fürstenberg in 1932, but without any echo and without an overall economic programme for the federation. See Luca Einaudi, 'The generous Utopia of yesterday can become the practical achievement of tomorrow: 1000 years of Monetary Union in Europe', *National Institute Economic Review*, no. 172, April 2000, pp.90–104.

3 The Beauty of the Struggle

1 See note 11 of the Editors' Introduction.

4 Economic Liberalism and Political Liberalism

1 Adam Smith, *An Inquiry into the Nature and Causes of the Wealth of Nations*, edited, with an introduction, notes, marginal summary and an enlarged index, by Edwin Cannan (London: Methuen, 1904), Vol. I, pp.419 and 421.
2 See Einaudi, *Liberismo e liberalismo*, p.43.

6 On other Pseudo-commercial and Pseudo-bank Containers

1 Maffeo Pantaleoni, *Scritti vari di economia* (Rome: Lib. Castellani ed., 1910), Vol. III, p.377.

8 Are there too many Banks in Italy?

1 *Editors' note*: Bonaldo Stringher (1854–1930) was General Director of the Italian Treasury from 1893 to 1898, Undersecretary and Minister of the Treasury in 1900 and 1919. He directed the Bank of Italy from 1900 to 1930, first as Director General (1900–28) and then as Governor when the position was created in 1928.
2 *Annual Report of the Governor of the Banca d'Italia – Year 1928* (Rome, 1929), p.34.
3 *Annual Report of the Governor of the Banca d'Italia – Year 1929* (Rome, 1930), p. 29.
4 *Annual Report of the Governor of the Banca d'Italia – Year 1928* (Rome, 1929), p.32.
5 Citation taken from Benjamin M. Anderson, 'Bank consolidations in a period of speculation', *The Chase Economic Bulletin*, Vol. IX, No. 5, p.5. See also by the same author, 'Branch banking throughout Federal Reserve districts', *The Chase Economic Bulletin*, Vol. X, No. 2. Anderson is the 'economist' of the Chase National Bank and his writings are always notable for their acute spirit of practical observation and solid theoretical foundation.
6 Benjamin M. Anderson, 'Bank consolidations in a period of speculation', *The Chase Economic Bulletin*, Vol. IX, No. 5, p.11.
7 Ibid.

9 Debts

1 See 'Dei metodi per arrivare alla stabilità monetaria e se si possa ancora parlare di crisi di stabilizzazione della lira', *La Riforma Sociale*, May–June 1930, and 'Nuovi vagabondaggi intorno alla crisi', *La Riforma Sociale*, July–August 1933.
2 On the psychological need for constraints, see 'Bardature della crisi', *La Riforma Sociale*, September–October 1932.

3 See 'Trincee economiche e corporativismo', *La Riforma Sociale*, November–December 1933.

10 My Plan is not Keynes's

1 I have translated Keynes's calculations roughly into lire, without giving the details of his demonstrations. Readers should note that in other respects as well, this is a not a literal summary of Keynes's pamphlet. I have left out many of his arguments, which appear to me, although perhaps not to him, to wander from the main point. I set out the latter as I have reconstructed it in my own mind, with some amplification that is unnecessary for adepts but necessary for those who wish to retrace every step in the reasoning. It is possible that by reducing and amplifying in this way I have altered the sense. Naturally, the summary and the criticisms refer not to Keynes's pamphlet but to my reconstruction.

2 On this point and in general on credit management it is worth reading an essay, which I do not hesitate to call stupendous for its classical force and straight reasoning, by Fritz Machlup, 'Zur Frage der Ankurbelung durch Kreditpolitik', in *Zeitschrift für Nationalökonomie*, Vol. IV, No. 3, pp.398–404. Reading this and other essays published by the Viennese review gives me the impression that today the palm of excellence among economic journals, which for some years after 1890 appeared to be won by Rome and then to have moved to London and Cambridge (USA), is now being disputed, with the outcome uncertain, by Vienna. This essay has the merit of reproducing Machlup's lapidary judgement, in contrast with the widespread view, echoed also by Keynes, that a sharp lowering of the discount rate helps to overcome crises:

> The discount rate policy of central banks undoubtedly has great importance in the downward phase as well. According to the view of the majority, its importance lies in an easing or alleviation of the crisis by means of a rapid and resolute lowering of the discount rate. In my view its importance lies in a deferment of the resolution of the crisis, in a prolongation of the state of depression owing precisely to the facilitating reductions in the discount rate. If it is true that overcoming the crisis consists in re-establishing an equilibrium between costs and prices that once more permits a production which covers costs and leaves a profit, if it is also true that the equilibrium in prices is reached all the sooner the faster stocks of unsold goods are liquidated and the faster the costs of the factors of production and labour are pushed down, if, lastly, it is true that a higher discount rate accelerates the emptying of warehouses and the fall in prices, then the rapid reduction of the discount rate is obviously likely to prolong the crisis. Compassionate reductions in the discount rate bring relief. They encourage the maintenance of high prices, which in the end must be abandoned; they permit the temporary continuation of forms of production that will ultimately have to be stopped; they make it possible to prolong rates of return that in the end will prove unsustainable; in short, they produce a deferment of the resolution of the crisis. Alleviating the crisis means prolonging the cure.

Machlup therefore arrives at the following elegantly paradoxical propositions:

> Whereas a premature increase in the discount rate during the upward phase of the economic cycle shortens the expansion (and therefore attenuates the subsequent crisis), a premature reduction in the discount rate during the

downward phase is likely to prolong the depression. Whereas a tardy increase in the discount rate during the upward phase prolongs the expansion (and therefore aggravates the subsequent crisis), delay in reducing the discount rate during the downward phase is likely to shorten the depression.

3 I have tried, with reference to Italy, to demonstrate that the war was not responsible for the social ills that followed it and to recount the stages and causes of the post-war disorders in *La condotta economica e gli effetti sociali della guerra italiana*, published in the Collection of papers for the Carnegie Foundation for International Peace (Bari: Laterza, 1933).

12 The Theory of Imaginary Money from Charlemagne to the French Revolution

1 *Translator's note*: Up to the time of the French Revolution the pound system, which still survives in Great Britain and parts of the British Commonwealth of Nations, existed in most countries of western Europe, including France, Italy and the Low Countries. The pound (Fr. *livre*; It. *lira*; Dut. *pond*) varied in name and value from one country to another. In England, it was called the 'pound sterling'; in France, the 'pound of Tours' (livre tournois); in the Low Countries, the 'pound groat' (livre de gros or pond grooten). In Italy there was a great variety of pounds: lire di grossi, lire di imperiali, lire di piccioli, etc. Everywhere 12 pence (Fr. deniers; It. denari) were equal to 1 shilling, and 20 shillings (Fr. *sous*; It. *soldi*) to 1 pound. The universally used abbreviations for these three units were £, *s.*, *d*. The different pounds should not be confused any more than American, Canadian and Mexican dollars are. During the period under consideration, the relation between real and imaginary money was always closer in England than on the Continent. The reader should bear in mind that the expressions 'pounds, shillings and pence' as used in this study do not refer to English money only, but to money of account in general, unless otherwise specified in the context.

2 *Translator's note*: The truth is that Charlemagne never coined a silver shilling but only a silver penny or denarius. Two hundred and forty of such pennies were made from a pound weight. Originally, the pound weight and the pound tale were thus the same, since they both contained the same number of pennies. The shilling or solidus was uncoined and was merely a numerical expression for twelve pennies.

3 François Le Blanc, *Traité historique des monnoyes de France* (Paris, 1690), pp.xxi, xxv, and *passim*.

4 Dutot, *Réflexions politiques sur les finances et le commerce* (The Hague, 1754), Vol. II, pp.4–5.

5 Giovanni Antonio Fabbrini, *Dell'indole e qualità naturali e civili della moneta* (Rome, 1750), p.93.

6 Ferdinando Galiani, *Della moneta* (Naples, 1750), pp.99 and 101 (ed. by Nicolini, Bari, 1915, pp.87–8).

7 A. Messedaglia, *La moneta e il sistema monetario in generale* (Rome, 1882), ch. 7, p.1.

8 Luigi Valeriani, *Ricerche critiche ed economiche ... sulle monete di conto* (Bologna, 1819), Pr. I, pp.150–1.

9 Pompeo Neri, 'Osservazioni sopra il prezzo legale delle monete', in *Scrittori classici italiani di economia politica*, Vol. VI, ed. by Custodi, pp.109–10 and 154–6.

10 Not in all three denominations: pounds, shillings, and pence. According to Le Blanc (*Traité*, p.xxii), as we have seen, only silver shillings were coined; according to Adolphe Landry, *Essai économique sur les mutations des monnaies dans l'ancienne France de Philippe le Bel à Charles VII* (Paris, 1910), p.11, only the penny (denarius) was coined.

11 Translator's note: This was especially true in the Low Countries, where weight, alloy and seigniorage varied from one denomination to another.

12 A typical example of a tangle is Marquis Girolamo Belloni's *Lettera in riposta ad un quesito propostogli sopra la natura della moneta immaginaria* (Rome, 1727), p.27, which the complacent editors, the Paglierini, praise as written 'with such method and clarity' that it leads 'the reader easily and gradually to a true understanding of imaginary money'. The letter is reprinted in Vol. II of the collection, *Scrittori classici italiani di economia politica, parte moderna*, edited by Custodi, 1803.

13 The present study was undertaken as a result of the recent publication of a hitherto unedited memoir by the Seigneur de Malestroit, author of the paradoxes made famous by the Réponse de Bodin. For the convenience of the reader, the text of the 'Paradoxes' and a second reply by Alexandre de la Tourette to the memoir of Malestroit are republished in the same volume; *Paradoxes inédits du Seigneur de Malestroit touchant les monnoyes avec la réponse du Président de la Tourette*, ed. by Luigi Einaudi (Turin: Giulio Einaudi, 1936).

14 In fact, today the cost of minting is very small, little more than two per thousand in those countries that still charge seigniorage. In countries such as the United States which have free coinage, there is still the loss of interest for the time required by the minting. For the importance of these charges, see below, paragraph 18.

15 The figure between parentheses, after the name of each coin, indicates the current rate in Milanese lire di imperiali. Thus, 'doblon (25.5.-)' means that the coin called a doblon was rated currently, or officially, £25. 5*s*. 0*d*. di imperiali, the imaginary money used in Milan.

16 Cesare Beccaria, 'Del disordine e de' rimedi delle monete nello stato di Milano nell'anno 1762', in *Le opere*, Vol. I (Florence: Le Monnier, 1854), pp.470–1.

17 In decimal fractions, those new values corresponded, respectively, to £2.087 and £1.92. The old system of counting in pounds, shillings and pence allowed the use of figures which corresponded more closely to currencies in actual circulation.

18 Translator's note: These adjustments are based on the assumption that the monetary authorities did not wish to alter the rate of the florin. Otherwise, the same result might have been obtained by crying down the florin from £24 to £23, if the market ratio changed from 1:12 to 1:11½, or by crying up the florin from £24 to £25, if the market ratio changed from 1:12 to 1:12½.

19 'Della moneta e de suoi surrogati', Introduction to Vol. VI of the Second Series of the *Biblioteca dell'economista*, 1857, pp.xxxv–liv; republished in F. Ferrara, *Esame storicocritico di economisti*, 1891, Vol. II, Pt I, pp.324–44.

20 It should be observed that seigniorage was not necessarily higher on coins of base metal. There could be a low seigniorage on an inferior coin with much alloy and little silver, if it were not overvalued according to its current rate in money of account. On the other hand, there could be a high seigniorage on a fine coin of nearly 24 carats, if it were overvalued and made current at a high rate (in money of account).

13 Noise

1 *Editors' note*: Between 1934 and 1944 Donato Menichella (1896–1984) was General Director of the IRI, the industrial and banking conglomerate formed by the government to save from bankruptcy Italy's main firms during the Great Depression. Menichella was called by Einaudi to become General Director of the Bank of Italy in 1946 and then succeeded Einaudi as Governor in 1948, becoming honorary governor in 1960.

14 Contribution to the Quest for an 'Optimal Tax'

1 Luigi Einaudi, *Lezioni di scienza delle finanze* (Turin, 1911).
2 Naturally, 'definitive' books are, fortunately, not written. This was the case of the one imagined here (*note added in 1957*).
3 Antonio De Viti De Marco, *Scienza delle Finanze e diritto finanziario, Lezioni dettate dal prof. A. De Viti De Marco, raccolte e compilate da Ottavio Pavia e Amilcare Mussa,* Regia Università di Roma, Anno Accademico 1893–94 (Rome: Lit. L.Laudi, 1894). Antonio De Viti De Marco, *I primi principii dell'economia finanziania,* 3rd edn. (Rome: Sampaolesi, 1928).
4 Antonio De Viti De Marco, *Il carattere teorico dell'economia finanziaria* (Rome: Loreto Pasqualucci Edit., 1888).
5 As a terminological 'convention', it is perfectly legitimate to apply the adjective 'static' to one type of society, in contradiction to another – progressive – type of society. But since the adjective 'static' is frequently used to indicate the stage of a society in a given moment, and the society one studies may be progressive or regressive or stationary, I have preferred to use the adjective 'stationary' to indicate a society of a different type from those that are moving in one direction ('progressive') or the opposite direction ('regressive' or 'decadent'). On the meaning of the adjective 'stationary' used as an abbreviation or shorthand, see § 48. It needs to be added that the use of this adjective does not imply any affirmation as to the possibility of the existence of such a society.
6 Luigi Einaudi *Lezioni di Scienza delle Finanze, raccolte e pubblicate a cura del dott. Achille, Necco,* 3 vols. (Turin: Tip. E. Bono, 1912). Luigi Einaudi, *Corsó di Scienza della Finanza,* 4th edn (Turin: Edizione della rivista *La Riforma Sociale,* 1926).
7 Einaudi, 'Contributo alla ricerca dell' ottima imposta', p.12.
8 This, in summary, is the translation of the principle as rendered by Ettore Lolini, 'Un sofisma finanziario: la doppia imposizione del reddito risparmiato', *Economia,* November 1928, pp.403–19, and especially p.415.
9 Umberto Ricci, 'La tassabilità del risparmio', *La Riforma Sociale,* Fasc. 3–4, March–April 1928.
10 Not in this volume.
11 This is Mauro Fasiani's contribution to the discussion of the problem with his article 'Sulla doppia tassazione del risparmio', *Riforma Sociale,* March-April 1928, pp.123–40, §§ 6 et seq.
12 In Luigi Einaudi, *Osservazioni critiche intorno alla teoria dell'ammortamento ...,* 1919, I cited and summarized the Italian literature on the question, which runs from Jarach's essay (Cesare Jarach, 'Gli effetti di un imposta generale ed uniforme sui profitti', *Atti della Reale Accademia delle Scienze di Torino,* Vol. 46, which I presented to the Turin Academy on 12 February 1911), to my observations in

Luigi Einaudi, 'Intorno al concetto di reddito imponibile e di un sistema di imposte sul reddito consumato, saggio di una teoria dell'imposta dedotta esclusivamente dal postulato di eguaglianza', dated 23 June 1912 (essay I in *Saggi sul risparmio e l'imposta*, Turin: Giulio Einaudi Editore, 1958), to Gino Borgatta, *L'economia dinamica, studio critico sui problemi dinamici dell'economia pura* (Turin: Utet, 1915), to Benvenuto Griziotti, 'Teoria sull'ammortamento delle imposte e sue applicazioni', in *Giornale degli economisti e rivista di statistica*, January 1918, pp.1–37, February, pp.57–87 and April, pp.181–207, to the above-mentioned Einaudi, *Osservazioni critiche* of June 1919. In keeping with the bibliographically backward state of economics, there is no handbook of the point reached by the discussions on a certain number of theoretical problems that are considered essential. If such a handbook on, say, 500 problems were updated continually and revised to include the new problems posed, its compiler would gain everlasting glory. Above, I mentioned the names of those who, to my knowledge, have dealt with the problem of the effect on the interest rate of a general tax, in chronological order of the contributions published. But how many others, in Italy and abroad, have probably touched on the subject! And although at least some few have addressed it, how many approach it, as indicated by the text, in a way that suggests that the discussions of it so far have not minimally shaken the orthodox opinion that the general tax must necessarily reduce the interest rate in proportion to the general tax rate! Naturally, in order to be useful the handbook would have to be 'reasoned' and 'limited' to writings that contain interesting developments or insights on each individual problem, so that one would know the occasion of the debate, who posed the problem, who took it up for further treatment and the phases of the subsequent discussion. Full bibliographies, with the titles of all the books and essays touching on a given problem, are very useful in a second phase of scientific elaboration for those who are already familiar with the subject and intend to delve deeper and be sure they have forgotten nothing. By contrast, they disorient and mislead those who confront the problem for the first time; and since they are compiled from the point of view of a systematic classification of the existing material, their divisions are based on the chapters and sections of the literature and not on the problems that were alive at any moment of the history of the science, as the hoped-for handbook should do.

An approximation of the handbook would have been the slim volume of 'bibliographical indications' that Maffeo Pantaleoni had promised to produce 'almost immediately' after the volume he published in collaboration with Romolo Broglio D'Ajano, *Temi, tesi, problemi e quesiti di economia politica teorica e applicata* (Bari: Laterza, 1923). It would have been a selection, the authors having declared that they did not intend 'to include bibliographical references to authors who only repeat things already said better by others' (p.XXIII). The themes numbered 1,018, but since a good many of them were descriptive or historical or at any rate did not address a problem that had already been treated or was important for the history of the doctrine, the authors having culled records of debates held at economic societies, topics of books and articles in scientific journals spanning perhaps a century, I think that the problems of real interest for the history of economics could probably be reduced to a few hundred. The only economist who grasped the importance of a bibliography organized according to historically important themes was the very diligent J.R. McCulloch, whose *Literature of Political Economy, a classified catalogue of select publications in the different departments of that science, with historical, critical and bibliographical notices* (London: Longman, 1845) to this day is still *the* only catalogue of its kind, has in turn become a bibliographical rarity and is consulted by all those who want to approach the original sources of knowledge. Does one wish to know, for example, the origins of the theory of rent? McCulloch gives the title of A. Anderson's famous pamphlet of 1777 ('Inquiry into the nature of the corn laws, with a view to the new corn bill proposed for Scotland,' Edinburgh, 1777) in which that theory was set forth for the first time. And since that pamphlet was impossible to find even then, in two pages he reproduces verbatim the passage essential for the history of the theory, and also, in their place, the titles of the other, equally famous pamphlets by Malthus and West, who simultaneously, in 1815, revised the theory before Ricardo put his stamp on it. However, McCulloch's book is also organized by systematic chapters rather than by individual problems, so that one has to dip into quite a few chapters, albeit with the aid of the references that the author provides, in order to know who has discussed a given problem. Above all, it dates back to 1845. Although consulting it teaches one to be modest, so numerous are the supposedly new problems that had already been illuminated by classical economics as its era was drawing to a close, often so well that it is sufficient to change the terminology and the mode of expression to obtain the same truth formulated in very modern terms, nevertheless 84 years have not passed in vain for economics. An updated catalogue *à la* McCulloch, logically organized by problems, with exact bibliographical references for the authors who truly made a contribution to their solution and verbatim quotations of the essential passages that are not easy to find in accessible copies: now that is a book that would be enormously valuable for even the most experienced scholars! It would be especially prized by those who know how hard it is to obtain the authentic texts of famous writings quoted by all. Paul Gemähling, in the preface to his very useful anthology entitled *Les grands économistes* (Paris: Sirey, 1925), which produces, with learned commentary, selected key passages of seventeen great economists, from Aristotle to Walras (no Italians, however, except for Saint Thomas Aquinas; in this, a contrast can be made in favour of A.E. Monroe's *Early Economic Thought* (Cambridge: Harvard University Press, 1927, which reproduces, without commentary, sixteen excerpts from sixteen economists before Adam Smith, of whom three Italians: Saint Thomas, Serra and Galiani) complains sorely about the deplorable condition of French libraries in terms of their scientific resources. The library of the faculty of Law of Paris apparently does not possess a copy of the English text of Malthus's *Essay* or Ricardo's *Principles* or Hume's *Discourses*, and neither does it have Cannan's critical edition of Smith or the German text of Menger's *Grundsätze*! Some specialized libraries in Italy are better endowed. In addition, we possess the major collections published by Custodi and the *Biblioteca dell'Economista*, research tools that do not exist in any other country of the world. Still, where is one to find the original texts of many writings not translated by the *Biblioteca dell'Economista* but nonetheless indispensable for research? Until the recent reprinting, I believe there wasn't a single copy in Italy of the first edition of Malthus's essay. Even today, the original texts of Godwin, which Malthus used as a springboard, and the above-mentioned essays by Anderson and West and a thousand others, are still unavailable. The main difficulty for the compilation of a handbook like the one proposed is the following: will an examination committee willing to award the editor a university chair ever be found? It should be evident that he would deserve one, for it takes more learning, experience and ingenuity to compile such a catalogue than to write most of the works that suffice to win university chairs. 'Come, now, a chair for a catalogue hound!' they would say.

13 The competition among different types of tax is one aspect of the competition between tax justice and tax injustice. On this point, see '*La cooperation internationale en matière fiscale*', in Académie de droit international de La Haye, *Recueil des cours*, xxv 1928, Paris, Librairie Hachette, 1929, pp. 5–119, § 86. On the characteristics of the three types of tax, see below, §§ 84 et seq.

14 This is the description of the working of a tax on 'produced' income. The tax on consumed income would exempt the L5,000 saved in period I and would tax the annual return of L250 at 10 per cent. The effects are identical, so that for the sake of clarity it is sufficient to consider only one.

15 In reality the net annual returns are neither L202.50 nor L225, as will be shown below (§§ 129 and 131), but as a first approximation it is legitimate not to confuse the reasoning with references to later stages of the process of re-equilibration subsequent to the tax.

16 On the importance of the expression *ceteris paribus* in economic reasoning see, *passim*, Umberto Ricci's recent paper 'Il metodo' in Economia Politica (Milan: Vallardi, 1928).

17 I have taken over the exposition by Fasiani, 'Sulla teoria dell'esenzione del risparmio dall'imposta', *Memorie della Reale Accademia delle scienze di Torino, series II, vol. LXVI, meeting of 28 May 1926*, p.2, footnote, of what appeared to him to be the essential content of my first study. This, as was obvious and as some critics, deceived by the form of the analysis, failed to see, did not set out to advocate any principle of justice, to propose any tax prescription, to condemn the method of taxing earned income as such, or to extol the opposite method of taxing consumed income, but simply to highlight the consequences of each method and to provide some proofs of the obvious tendency of lawmakers to accept the second principle in practice, while protesting that they wished to follow the first.

18 On the derivation of the postulate from a historical inquiry, see above, § 6.

19 Umberto Ricci, *Reddito e imposta* (Rome: Atheneaum, 1914), p.63, reproducing two articles which appeared in the *Giornale degli economisti e rivista di statistica,* August 1913, pp.93–126 and October 1913, pp.293–326.

20 In order to avoid misunderstandings, since it is difficult to know what these blessed 'facts' are, I will say that in this work I use the word as shorthand for the individual tax rules and laws and systems in force at present or in the past for the allocation of the tax burden. These 'facts' are therefore, roughly speaking, ideas of men that have crystallized in mandatory legal rules or in doctrinal systems of interpretation and application of such rules. They also include the economic quantities – capital, incomes produced, consumed and earned, prices, wages, rents, interest, and profit, etc. – that exist at any time and in which the tax law in force can produce a change.

21 It is curious to see how many critics adduced the argument of the possibility of fraud that would follow the explicit recognition of the principle of excluding savings from the tax base as a peremptory argument against Mill's demonstration of the principle itself. In other words they showed they had not understood that Mill had addressed the problem scientifically: by first examining the question on its own, through pure logical reasoning, without worrying about the practical consequences deriving from the application of the principle, and then looking, as a second approximation, at those consequences and, as the statesman he was, going back to the theoretical thesis in order to adapt its application to the need for prudence dictated by observation of taxpayers' incorrigible propensity to conceal. This is the procedure that must be followed in scientific investigation, not that of intermingling pure theory with contingent or secondary considerations, which is the main cause of the very little progress made by

the so-called science of finance compared with its elder sister, economics. The prudent warnings provided by history and observation of the inclination of taxpayers, and technicians' views on assessing the tax base must be given great consideration, but at the moment of applying the principles and not to negate or deform them and replace the logical chain of postulates, theorems and corollaries with a heterogeneous miscellany of precepts based on the variable and sentimental waves of so-called tax justice.

22 Perhaps, in providing the demonstration, it would have been advantageous to make use of instruments more refined than those of simple logic adopted by me. I hope to be pardoned for this, given that in substance what is important is first to put forward an argument and then to verify if it is right or wrong. If right, the possibly less elegant method adopted in formulating it was damaging for he who had to use it and not for the readers in the field of finance, who for the most part want demonstrations provided with the simple support of common logic.

23 The title of the paragraph is 'Proportionality of tax to costs or to income?' but it is not included in this volume.

24 The title of the paragraph is 'Mistake of taxing interests in order to tax savings income and impossibility to tax these', but it is not included in this volume.

25 Not in this volume.

26 Ricci, *Reddito e imposta*, § 62.

27 See the essay on 'The Optimum Theory of Population' by L. Robbins, T. E. Gregory and Hugh Dalton (eds), in *London Essays in Economics in Honour of Edwin Cannan* (London: Routledge, 1927), p.103ff, the history of the 'optimum' theory of population, a theory largely accepted in scientific debate.

28 For this reason it was said earlier (see above, § 11) that subsequently the effect on 'optimum' income of the 'use' of taxation in general would be disregarded, owing to its being common to all taxes. But it must be added that the disregarding of this effect is only temporary. In reality, if its aim is to facilitate the choice, among the various types of tax, of the optimum tax, then, in turn, only the optimum tax, so chosen, allows the optimum use of the revenue it generates. This is so since the choice of an inferior type of tax is necessarily connected to the existence of an 'imperfect' type of state, in which the use of the tax cannot be 'the most perfect'. The theory of the equilibrium or of the independence of all the factors determining a given economic, political, social tax situation allows us to deal with the problem in slices, in sections, on condition that the solution so reached, and it would otherwise be impossible to reach any conclusion at all, be temporary and be immediately tested in its ability to take its place, without friction and without breaks, within the general conception of the problem.

29 See the definition of 'hail' tax, 'ransom' tax and 'economic' tax in Einaudi, *Osservazioni critiche*, §§ 5 and 6. 'Hail' tax is something which takes away a fraction of income through an external force, increases the effort needed to achieve a given income and raises the interest rate. A 'ransom' tax is levied by a foreign or a tyrannical government and it is wasted without any advantage for the common good. It raises the interest rate even further than the 'hail' tax because of the erratic and dangerous nature of oppressive government. The 'economic' tax is levied by a democratic and representative government according to the calculation of the relative advantage of public services and private use of resources. It leads to the optimal distribution of resources between individuals and between public and private.

30 In *I primi principi dell'economia finanziaria*. De Viti develops a comment that was already present in his *Lezioni* of 1923, where he did not go beyond the statement that it was a 'frequent error' to 'consider taxation as a definitive subtraction and distribution of wealth' (p.65). In the new edition, the author starts from the

premise 'that public goods are, in the same measure for all, instrumental to the production of incomes', and draws a

> conclusion totally opposed to that affirmed by the followers of current theory: a tax increase for the production of new or improved public services, rather than increase the production cost of private goods, should decrease it. To fully understand this, all that is necessary is to leave aside the error that a tax is income destroyed, as soon as it is withdrawn from the accounts of the taxpayer, and to take account of the use that the state will make of it. Consider, for example, a consortium of landowners who maintain at their own expense a local road for the transportation of their crops. The transportation is part of their production cost. Now suppose that they agree among themselves to pay the state, as a tax, more or less the amount that they spend for their local road, and that the state builds and maintains a better road, on which the transport is easier and faster. It cannot be said that the tax has increased the previous cost of transport. It must be said that it has decreased it. From the particular example we move to the general case that the introduction of public services and their growth and improvement have reduced the costs of all of the country's productive activities. Therefore, the question needs to be examined under the most general hypothesis that the replacement of private enterprise with public enterprise brings an advantage for taxpayers. But even if one makes the contrary hypothesis, it will still have to be admitted that it is not the tax paid by the producer that decides but the nature of the public services produced and the level of utilization which in fact each individual producer can make of them. In conclusion, the previous production cost can be increased, left as it was, or reduced by a tax increase. In pure theory it must be said that it is reduced. (pp.139–40)

From the theory of cost reduction De Viti then draws some very important inferences for the theory of the displacement of taxes.

I am delighted that, by a different route and in a completely independent manner, De Viti has reached conclusions analogous to those which, arguing from the premise of the 'optimum distribution of wealth possessed' and from the economic theory of taxation, I too had reached in 1919. I was talking about an increase in the flow of income and he about a reduction in the cost of production. Despite its broader form, my formulation is equivalent to De Viti's. The conformity of our conclusions demonstrates how strong the need is to give a unified structure to the theory of finance, up to now studied too much in its individual parts and detached from economic theory as well as legal and political theory. The hypothesis of the optimum tax proposed in the text appears to be a useful logical key for achieving the objective. The optimum tax cannot in fact be conceived outside the contemporary hypothesis of an optimum use of the revenues deriving from it, of a perfect system of assessment and of tax justice and therefore outside the hypothesis of a perfect state. It all falls within the financial, economic and political order and each individual study cannot but be an initial provisional approximation, which must be filled out in successive ever-wider and more comprehensive approximations.

The thesis of *Osservazioni critiche* and that of De Viti are not in contradiction with the methodological point of view accepted above (see §§ 10 and 11), according to which, in studying the effects of a given kind of tax compared with that of other kinds, one must disregard the 'generic' effects of taxation. Indeed, Graziani (in *Istituzioni di scienza della finanza,* 3rd edn (Turin: UTET, 1929), p.457, in a footnote) asserts that:

> on the question of displacement one must never consider the effects of the employment of the sums obtained through the tax, which could be identical even if the tax had been levied, instead of on interest, on some other asset. And consequently the possible variation in the interest rate would not be connected to that tax.

Graziani's observation is a correct application of the *ceteris paribus* clause. It would be impossible to judge the specific effect of a type of tax if it were continually mixed with the study of the generic effects of taxation. Accordingly, in these pages the use of tax revenue is disregarded by supposing provisionally that it is equally optimum, or good or bad in all cases. In this way, an attempt is made to define the characteristics of that tax which, in and of itself, owing to the way it is devised, is incapable of producing undesirable effects of perturbation in the distribution of income between present and future uses and in the future flow of income and of the tax.

But it must not be forgotten that this study, though it is legitimately circumscribed so as to be able to arrive at a conclusion, is nonetheless incomplete. It is logical, when one wishes to study some other aspect of the problem, to disregard things that may be important from another point of view; but it is not logical to deny the existence of the problem. It is logical to disregard the use made of a tax when one wishes to choose among different types of taxes, but it cannot be denied that a tax and the use of a tax are two inseparable terms. When it institutes taxes, the state is not making art for art's sake, but is creating taxes in order to spend the revenue. It is possible to study the various ways to pay wages. But everyone can see that though the study of the comparative characteristics of paying wages by time, by piece work, by task etc. is legitimate, it is only one piece of reality and it must be completed by studying at another time the reasons for paying the wages and whether paying wages in one way or another has some impact on the productivity of labour. A complete theory of wages can only come from an overall synthesis of these partial studies. So it is with taxes. The study of the effects of a tax, by excluding the use of its revenue from the study, is legitimate and the arguments made for such purposes are correct. But the conclusions reached are provisional and must be completed by a study (attempted in fact in *Osservazioni critiche*) of the effects of a tax on the basis of the various possible uses of its revenue. Such a study is all the more important in that, owing to the reciprocal relationship in which all of the data of the economic problem are held, it is not possible to separate:

(a) the choice that is made, for example, of a type of tax likely in itself to increase the rate of interest from a use of its revenue such as to produce analogous consequences, so that the one effect adds to the other to produce a state of things commonly considered contrary to the elevation of the collectivity. The cost of an expensive method of collecting taxes is an index of the prevalence of ideas conducive to a non-economical use of the revenue generated by such taxes; so that the identical effect is produced in two different ways;

(b) or the choice that in another example may be made of a type of tax in itself having no influence on the rate from the 'optimal' use of its revenue and such as to produce a lowering of the interest rate, an increase in the flow of future incomes, so that the one effect by combining with the other leads to the maximum elevation of the collectivity;

I don't know why one should reserve the designation of 'problems of displacement, repercussion, amortization, diffusion etc. etc. of taxes' to the first slice of the real problem, which is the unified problem. I see no disadvantage in doing this from a purely terminological point of view, if one uses a different designation for the other slice or the other slices of the problem and one states clearly that they are only slices and that the real problem is the whole problem. I know, however, that if one seriously imagines that the problem of the effect produced by the tax, disregarding the use made of its revenue, is the problem of the displacement of the tax, one is in error; having been so invincibly pulled into supposing the absurdity that the tax is something 'taken away' from the taxpayer, that it strikes him and marks him, or it harms him and impoverishes him. All of this terminology of 'striking' and 'falling upon' is harmless as long as those who use it know that it has a meaning that is conventional, partial, provisional, and that in reality the substantial meaning corresponds to the one apparent in the sound of the words only when the tax is not well-designed, is poorly distributed, and its revenue is poorly used, or in other words when the tax is not in conformity with its proper nature. When a tax is in fact what it is in theory, it inevitably increases and does not diminish the flow of social income, it promotes saving, increases the value of capital. Or rather, when a tax is truly such, all the talk of 'incidences' and 'losses' is figurative talk, which creates confusion because it applies to the things of perfect states, words that people used to reason in times in which their governors were or are enemies, oppressors, looters and pillagers of the people.

31 Joseph de Maistre, *Considérations sur la France* (Lyon, 1822), p.51:

> There is only violence in the universe; but we are spoilt by modern philosophy, which has said that *all is good*; whereas evil has sullied everything and in a sense that is very true, all is evil, since nothing is in its place. *The whole creation groaneth* (St. Paul, Romans, VIII, 22) and tends, with exertion and pain, towards another order of things.

15 On the Source of Saving and the Taxation of Normal Income as an Approximation of the Exclusion of Income from the Tax Base

1 Louis Hémon, *Maria Chapdelaine, récit du Canada Français*. (Paris: Delagrave, 1916). Hémon appears to have left only notes unpublished.

2 As explained earlier (Section 64 et seq.), if on 1 January X possesses 100 units of capital goods and these are reduced, by wear and tear, to 90 and are not restored, the taxable income under the law in force is not equal to the 20 direct goods produced during the year but to this quantity *less* the impoverishment of 10 caused by the depreciation, not made good, of the capital goods. Instead the depreciation not made good must be taxed, not directly, of course, but by not deducting it from the quantity of direct goods to which the tax applies.

3 In the words of Carlo Cattaneo, cited in Luigi Einaudi, *La terra e l'imposta* (Turin: Giulio Einaudi Editore, new edition of 1942), p.137.

4 In my book *La terra e l'imposta*, in *Lezioni*, (1926), p.203 ff., and again in 'Ancora le sperequazioni e le evasioni nell'imposta di ricchezza mobile', *La Riforma Sociale*, January–February 1929, pp.13–21 I addressed the theoretical and practical phenomenon of the taxation of normal or cadastral income and the moves to extend it to non-agrarian incomes.

5 In the pages that follow, and in conformity with the description given below in the text, the adjectives normal and marginal, sub-normal and sub-marginal. super-normal and super-marginal are considered synonyms and used without distinction.

6 Those who are sub-marginal entrepreneurs would often be excellent clerks. But the blindness that has led them to believe they possess higher or different qualities from those they really have also leads them to maintain a standard of living higher than that of clerks and belonging to the entrepreneurial class and ruins them.
7 In *La terra e l'imposta*, pp.134–7, I have reproduced the classic passages by Gian Rinaldo Carli and Carlo Cattaneo from which the rule in the text is derived.
8 In this way one overcomes the objection that Ricci (in *Reddito e imposta*, (Rome: Atheneaum, 1914), p.66) draws from the example of the poor millionaire Hetty Green. If taxation exempted saving until the moment of consumption and 'Hetty Green put everything she had into bad investments, the state would lose millions. Whereas, if year by year Hetty Green had paid taxes on the new saving, the state would have received several sums with which it could have paid magistrates, soldiers and the like.' In reality the objection is not against the particular case of taxation that exempts saving but against the general case of taxation that falls on taxpayers' 'actual' income, if and insofar as they obtain it. Why, as noted in the text, must the state be paid for services it always provides, both to those who gain and to those who lose, only if taxpayers gain? This is the gist, entirely valid, of the objection, not the chance event that the loser is a fervent saver. This is a very rare case, whereas it is common for the losers to be those who are unable to conserve the saving accumulated by others. Why worry so much about an imaginary loss for the state when the much more frequent and serious one is overlooked?

The other objection based on the story of Hetty Green refers to the extreme case in which savers always save and never consume. The state would remain without resources. Ricci goes on to give a brilliant picture of the extreme case of a society made up of accumulators of wealth, all intent on saving, living a miserable life, without spiritual pleasures, without luxury. 'Is a community of sordid people, devoted exclusively to the multiplication of the species and to the accumulation of capital, therefore to be pointed to as the ideal society?' (ibid., p.71).

Since the aim of the whole of this work and of those that preceded it is to prove that the so-called exemption of saving is not exemption but exclusion from double taxation, and that the taxation of income produced or consumed leads to a situation of equilibrium, because taxpayers do not feel themselves induced *by taxation* to prefer consumption to saving and vice versa, the objection of the unhappy extreme case towards which society would be driven by an inexistent cause is overcome.

If it is true, as I flatter myself that I have made clear with at least the beginning of a proof, that the taxation of income earned leads to a situation of disequilibrium and really does cause consumption to be preferred to saving, let me in turn depict the extreme case towards which society would tend if that tax were to act with all its force and were not curbed by the taxes that apparently run counter to the principle of the tax on income earned (taxes on consumption, exemption of new incomes, of new houses, of afforestation, etc., etc.) that lawmakers are dragged into introducing by the evidence of common sense and the perception of the flaws in their theory? If the incorrect tax succeeded, through differential taxation, in curbing the accumulation of saving, the standard of living would rise for a time, the refinements of existence and spiritual pleasures would intensify for as long as humanity could exploit the stock of capital and durable goods accumulated earlier. But the fall would be harder, the decadence more painful at a later time, when, owing to the failure to replace the existing capital and to increase it, the flow of direct goods diminished. And it would be irremediable decadence because it appears much more difficult for a people that has fallen to raise itself up again than for a miser to recognize the uselessness of accumulating without cease, without ever tasting the delicious fruits of the wealth possessed. Examples of societies of this second type are very rare, almost unknown, whereas, unfortunately, examples of societies that have fallen as a consequence of excessive consumption and scanty spirit of renunciation are frequent. In which of the two types is the state stronger?

9 Or each of the equivalent rules into which it can be converted in accordance with the various requirements of the reality to which it is to be applied.

16 The Optimal Tax as a Neutral Tax, in the Physiocrats, in Smith and the Italian *Catastiti* of the Eighteenth Century

1 Not in this volume; it is a reference to a section of the original publication which is not translated here.

2 In 'Osservazioni critiche intorno alla teoria dell'ammortamento dell'imposta e teoria delle variazioni nei redditi e nei valori capitali susseguenti all'imposta', in *Atti della Reale Accademia delle scienze di Torino*, Vol. 54, 1918–19, ch. II, § 6; now in *Opere*, Series I, Vol. I, second of the essays on saving and taxation.

3 Not in this volume.

4 Tocqueville, *L'ancien régime et la révolution*, p.192ff.

5 Ibid., p.464ff.

6 Pierre Le Pesant de Boisguilbert, *Le Détail de la France, ou la France ruinée sous le règne de Louis XIV, par qui et comment. Avec les moyens de la rétablir en peu de temps* (Cologne: P. Marteau, 1696).

Chronology of the Life and Works of Luigi Einaudi in the Context of his Time

Publications indicated in italics are independent volumes, those indicated in normal characters are articles. **Bold characters** indicate that the text is included in the current collection.

	Luigi Einaudi's life	Einaudi's publications	Political events	Economic and financial events
1874	24 March: birth of Luigi Einaudi in Carrù, Piedmont.		Fall of Gladstone's first government in the UK.	The Latin Monetary Union limits silver coinage, beginning in fact the age of the international gold standard in France and Italy.
1893		First article: 'The distribution of land property in Dogliani'	First Giolitti government lasts only one year. Formation of Crispi government, birth of the Italian Socialist Party and social revolts in Sicily.	Collapse of the Banca Romana and of the Credito Mobiliare leads to the birth of the Bank of Italy and of the Banca Commerciale Italiana.
1895	Completes his university degree in law.	'The agrarian crisis in England', extracted from his thesis		
1896	Works for the Turin newspaper *La Stampa.*		Fall of the Italian Prime Minister Crispi after military defeat in Ethiopia.	Creation of a new commercial bank with German capital, the Credito Italiano. Beginning of the industrial revolution in Italy.
1898	Teaches political economy in a technical institute and participates in the organization of the General Exposition of Turin.	Articles on the Genoa strikes	Popular protests against high prices in Italy repressed by the army and through illiberal laws, followed by the collapse of the right-wing government.	

	Luigi Einaudi's life	Einaudi's publications	Political events	Economic and financial events
1900	Member of the board of editors of the review *La Riforma Sociale*.	*A Merchant Prince, Study on Italian Colonial Expansion*	Assassination by an anarchist of the King of Italy, Umberto I. Beginning of a period of left-leaning liberal governments in Italy.	Mass emigration from Italy reaches its apex until the First World War.
1902	Full Professor of Financial Sciences at the University of Turin.	*Studies on the Effects of Taxation*		Introduction of a progressive taxation of inheritance and social legislation.
1903	Becomes financial commentator for the largest Italian daily paper, *Il Corriere della Sera*, until 1925 and again in 1943–8 and 1953–61. Marries Ida Pellegrini.		Giolitti's government.	
1907		*Governmental Income in the Savoy State through the Budget and Treasury Accounts during the Spanish Succession War*		Financial crisis in the USA spreads to the UK and the rest of Europe. Collapse of the Italian Banking Society.
1908	Editor of *La Riforma Sociale*. Begins to write for *The Economist*.	*Lectures on Financial Sciences and Financial Law.*		Foundation of Olivetti and of Lancia.

	Luigi Einaudi's life	Einaudi's publications	Political events	Economic and financial events
1911		Articles against budget busters *(Trivellatori di Stato)*	Italy invades Libya.	
1914		*The Financing of War and Public Works*	Beginning of First World War, end of Giolitti's decade.	End of the Classical Gold Standard.
1918		'The dogma of sovereignty and the idea of the League of Nations'	First World War ends, planning of the League of Nations begins.	
1919	Appointed Senator of the Kingdom of Italy	Critical observations on the theory of amortization of tax and theory of income and capital value variation following taxation. Articles against inflation fuelled by excess monetary supply and in favour of financial stabilization.	Treaty of Versailles, birth of the Republic of Weimar. Beginning of a two-year period of social unrest in Italy led by the left, known as *biennio rosso*. Election victory of the Socialist and of the Catholic Party. Birth of Mussolini's fascist movement. Birth of the League of Nations.	End of wartime support for exchange rates, followed by currency depreciation and inflation in continental Europe.
1920	Appointed Director of the Institute 'Ettore Bocconi' of Milan, until 1926.	*Political Letters by Junius; The Problem of Housing*	In Italy Giolitti briefly returns to power, defeat of the leftist movements, fascist violence spreads.	Birth of the Italian confederation of industrialists.

	Luigi Einaudi's life	Einaudi's publications	Political events	Economic and financial events
1921		*The Ideals of an Economist*	The Communist Party is formed after a socialist split.	Collapse of the Banca Italiana di Sconto.
1922	Becomes Italian correspondent for *The Economist.*		Mussolini becomes Prime Minister after the March on Rome in October 1922.	Conference of Genoa on monetary stabilization.
1923		**The beauty of the struggle**	Stresemann becomes Chancellor in Germany. Fascism consolidates.	Hyperinflation in Germany; the Mark is replaced by the Rentenmark.
1924	Einaudi's declares against fascism with an article criticizing the Industrialists' silence about the murder of the socialist leader Matteotti.	*Labour's Struggle; Land and taxation;* **Banks with adjectives**	The Italian Socialist reformist leader Matteotti is murdered by the fascists. Churchill becomes Chancellor of the Exchequer.	Dawes plan on German war reparations, Sweden restores gold convertibility, Hungary and Poland form central banks.
1925	Resigns from *Il Corriere della Sera* in protest against the forced resignation of its editor-publisher. Driven out of teaching at the Bocconi and the Turin Polytechnic.		Mussolini claims responsibility for the Matteotti murder and transforms parliamentary government into a dictatorship.	Churchill resumes the gold standard in the UK, followed by Switzerland, the Netherlands, Hungary, Danzig, Australia and New Zealand. Final evacuation of the Ruhr by the French.
1926		**The end of laissez-faire**	Opposition political parties are prohibited in Italy. Poincaré becomes Prime Minister in France.	Canada and Belgium return to the gold Standard. The Latin Monetary Union is formally dissolved. The Bank of Italy acquires monopoly of issue.

	Luigi Einaudi's life	Einaudi's publications	Political events	Economic and financial events
1927		*War and the Fiscal System*	Construction of the repressive tools of the Italian totalitarian state.	Stabilization of the Lira at L90 per pound.
1928	Votes in the Senate for the Ruffini motion against fascist governmental policies.			Stabilization of the Franc by Poincaré. The International Gold Standard is again fully operational.
1929		*International Cooperation on Fiscal Matters;* **Contribution to the quest for an 'optimal tax'**	The Lateran Pacts normalize relationships between Italy and the Pope.	Beginning of the Great Depression. Young Committee to settle German war reparations established.
1930		**Are there too many banks in Italy?**	Briand's project for the United States of Europe presented to the League of Nations.	The Bank for International Settlements is formed. Smoot–Haley Act increases US tariff duties.
1931		**On the various meanings of the concept of economic liberalism and of its relation with that of political liberalism**	Formation of National Government in the UK under MacDonald but without the Labour Party.	UK abandons the Gold Standard. Bankruptcy of the Credit Anstalt of Vienna. Worldwide restrictions on trade of goods, movements of capital and currency convertibility.
1932		*Principles of Financial Sciences*	Victory of the National Socialists in German Parliamentary elections.	Glass–Steagall Act in the USA, protectionist duties in the UK. Roosevelt elected President of the United States.

	Luigi Einaudi's life	Einaudi's publications	Political events	Economic and financial events
1933	Luigi's son, Giulio, creates the publishing house *Giulio Einaudi Editore*, initially under the influence of his father. Luigi's first son, Mario, emigrates to the USA in order not to pledge loyalty to the fascist regime as required for university professors.	**My plan is not Keynes's**; *The Economic Conduct and the Social Effects of the Italian War*	Hitler becomes Chancellor. Germany leaves the League of Nations.	Roosevelt abandons the Gold Standard. Gold Block in part of continental Europe. Birth of the Istituto per la Ricostruzione Industriale in Italy (IRI) to save and nationalize ailing banking and industrial system.
1934		**Debts**	Murder of the Austrian Chancellor Dollfuss. Italy opposes *Anschluss*.	The US dollar is devalued; further economic restrictions are introduced.
1935	Two of Einaudi's sons, Giulio and Roberto, are arrested for antifascist activities. *La Riforma Sociale* closed by the fascist regime.	**On other Pseudo-commercial and Pseudo-bank containers.**	Italy invades Ethiopia. The League of Nations responds by imposing international sanctions against Italy.	Devaluation of the Belgian franc.
1936	Creates the *Rivista di Storia Economica*.	**The theory of imaginary money from Charlemagne to the French Revolution**	Victory of the Front Populaire in France, Léon Blum Prime Minister. Beginning of the Spanish Civil War. End of sanctions against Italy, which leaves the League of Nations.	Publication of *The General Theory* by J.M. Keynes. Gold Block collapses, franc and lira leave the Gold Standard. New banking law in Italy.

	Luigi Einaudi's life	Einaudi's publications	Political events	Economic and financial events
1937		*New Essays*	Neville Chamberlain becomes Prime Minister in the UK.	
1938	Votes in the Senate against the introduction of the racial laws.	***Myths and paradoxes on justice in taxation***	Germany invades Austria and operates the *Anschluss*. Racial laws introduced in Italy.	European states rearm in the expectation of war.
1939		'On money as a reserve of value and on other monetary problems'	Beginning of Second World War.	
1940			Churchill becomes British Prime Minister. Italy enters the war.	
1941		***Essays on savings and taxation***	The US enter the war after Pearl Harbor.	
1942		On the methods of writing about economic facts	Beginning of the battle of Stalingrad.	Adoption of the US policy of lend-lease to its Allies.
1943	Appointed Rector of the University of Turin after the fall of Fascism. Exile in Switzerland after 8 September 1943. Compelled to interrupt the *Rivista di storia Economica*.	**For a European Economic Federation**	Landing of the Allies in Italy, fall of Mussolini and Fascism, beginning of the fascist Republic of Salò in Northern Italy under German occupation.	

	Luigi Einaudi's life	Einaudi's publications	Political events	Economic and financial events
1944	Lives in Switzerland till December 1944.	**The economic tasks of the European federation; Lectures on the market**	Landing of the Allies in France. Government of the parties of the National Liberation Committee in Italy.	Bretton Woods agreements forming the IMF and the World Bank.
1945	Appointed Governor of the Bank of Italy. Member of the National Consultative Assembly (*Consulta*).	'Sketch of a liberal economic policy'	End of the Second World War. The Christian Democrat De Gasperi becomes Italian Prime Minister in a coalition with the left.	
1946	Elected at the Constituent Assembly for the Liberal Party.	*Wealth Tax;* 'Inheritance tax'; 'Against proportional representation'.	Italy becomes a Republic after a referendum.	
1947	Appointed Deputy Prime Minister and Budget Minister in the De Gasperi Government.	**The Concluding Remarks of the Governor of the Bank of Italy for the year 1946;** *Federated Europe.*	De Gasperi excludes Socialists and Communists from the Italian coalition government. Constitution approved.	'Einaudi Plan' for the stabilization of the lira and against inflation. The pound becomes convertible only for six weeks.
1948	Elected President of the Italian Republic.	*War and European Unity.*	Landslide victory of the Christian Democrats at the general election.	European Recovery Plan (Marshall Plan) begins.
1949		*Lectures on Social Policy*	Italy becomes a member of NATO.	British pound devalued.
1950		'Economic science and economists at the present day'	Schuman declaration on the need for a united Europe.	European Payment Union established.

	Luigi Einaudi's life	Einaudi's publications	Political events	Economic and financial events
1951				Birth of the European Community of Iron and Coal.
1953		*Biographical and Historical Essays on Economic Doctrines*	Failure of the project of European Defence Community. De Gasperi's last government. Russian intervention in eastern Germany. Stalin's death.	
1955	End of term of office as President. Becomes lifetime Senator and Professor.	*Il Buongoverno*; 'Fifty years of Italian economic thought (1896–1946)'		
1956		*The President's Desk; Useless Preaching*	Warsaw Pact invades Hungary.	
1957		***Political and Economic Liberalism***	The Treaty of Rome creates the European Economic Community.	European Investment Bank established.
1960		**Noise [on central bankers' intervention]**	Kennedy elected President of the USA.	The lira is voted best currency of the year by an international jury. Creation of the General Agreement to Borrow at the IMF.
1961	30 October: death of Luigi Einaudi.	Einaudi's last article for ***Il Corriere della Sera***: 'The Sunday preaching'	Failed landing at the Bay of Pigs in Cuba. Construction of the Berlin Wall.	

Index of Names

Notes: n = note; t = table; **bold** = extended discussion or heading emphasized in main text.

Index of Subjects